# Budgeting and Public Expenditures in OECD Countries 2019

OECD
BETTER POLICIES FOR BETTER LIVES

**Please cite this publication as:**
OECD (2019), *Budgeting and Public Expenditures in OECD Countries 2019*, OECD Publishing, Paris.
*https://doi.org/10.1787/9789264307957-en*

ISBN 978-92-64-30794-0 (print)
ISBN 978-92-64-30795-7 (pdf)



**Photo credits:** Cover © Stock_VectorSale/Shutterstock.com

Corrigenda to OECD publications may be found on line at: *www.oecd.org/about/publishing/corrigenda.htm*.

# *Foreword*

This inaugural edition of the report on Budgeting and Public Expenditures in OECD Countries comes at an important time for international budgeting practices.

The Global Financial Crisis occurred over 10 years ago and for most countries, the period of crisis and consolidation has given way to one of economic recovery. One needs to ask however, whether public financial management frameworks have sufficiently adapted to avoid repeating the pro-cyclical dynamic that was often a feature of the crisis; and whether these frameworks can provide assurances that the public will see value-for-money in how public resources are deployed.

This report looks at such questions and presents an overview of budgeting practices across OECD countries. Chapters 1 to 8 discuss thematic and OECD-wide perspectives on budget frameworks, parliamentary oversight and managerial controls, transparency and impact, the quality of public expenditure, and capital expenditure, including public-private partnerships. The Country Profiles in Chapter 9 provide a factual summary of how public financial management tools are applied in individual countries.

*Budgeting and Public Expenditures in OECD countries 2019* presents the findings of a Budget Practices and Procedures Survey together with those from a series of other parallel surveys carried out under the auspices of the OECD Working Party of Senior Budgeting Officials: the OECD Fiscal Plans and Budgeting Framework Survey; the OECD Performance Budgeting Survey; the OECD Survey of Capital Budgeting and Infrastructure Governance; and the new OECD PBO Network Survey on Parliamentary Budgeting Practices.

This report provides foundational material for a review of the 2015 *Recommendation of the Council on Budgetary Governance*, which codified the ten principles of modern budgeting adopted by the OECD Working Party of Senior Budgeting Officials (SBO) in 2014, the 2012 *Recommendation of the Council on Principles for Public Governance of Public-Private Partnerships* and the 2014 *Recommendation of the Council on Principles for Independent Fiscal Institutions*.

This report is co-authored by the team of people in the OECD's Budgeting & Public Expenditures Division, within the Public Governance Directorate – Bonifacio Agapin, Ivor Beazley, Andrew Blazey, Jon Blondal, Jaehyuk Choi, Ronnie Downes, Juliane Jansen, Anne Keller, Edwin Lau, Yvette Melo, Delphine Moretti, Scherie Nicol, Andrew Park, Ana Maria Ruiz Rivadeneira and Lisa von Trapp. The guest introduction is by Professor Allen Schick, and Sami Ylaoutinen, an OECD expert, contributed to the section on fiscal risks.

# *Table of contents*

## Tables



## Figures

## Boxes

# *Acronyms*

| | |
|---|---|
| SBO | Senior Budget Officials |
| PPP | Private Public Partnerships |
| CBA | Central Budget Authority |
| MTEF | Meddium-Term Expenditure Frameworks |
| PFM | Public Finance Management |
| SNA | System of National Accounts |
| ISO | International Standardization Organization |
| PPBS | Planning-Programming Budgeting Systems |
| PB | Performance Budgeting |
| SAI | Supreme Audit Institution |
| OMG | Office of Management and Budget |
| TSGC | Treaty on Stability, Coordination and Governance in the Economic and Monetary Union |
| TSA | Treasury Single Account |
| NTF | National Training Fund |
| SNDO | Swedish National Debt Office |
| MTBF | Medium-Term Budgetary Framework |
| PBO | Parliamentary Budget Office |
| IFI | Independent Fiscal Institution |
| NABO | National Assembly Budget Office |
| CEFP | Center for Public Finance Studies |
| CBO | Congressional Budget Office |
| LOLF | *Loi organique relative aux lois de finances* |
| ANAO | Australian National Audit Office |
| CAP | Cross-Agency Priority |
| PIP | Public Investment Programme |
| DPP | Development Programmes Plan |
| MRV | Monitoring, Reporting and Verification |
| PGPA | Public Governance, Performance and Accountability |
| GST | Goods and Services Tax |
| VFM | Value for Money |
| BFRG | *Bundesfinanzrahmengesetz* |
| FPS | Federal Public Service Budget and Management Control |
| MOF | Ministry of Finance |
| SPU | Stability Programme Update |
| PDCA | Plan-Do-Check-Action |
| PSBR | Public Sector Borrowing Requirement |
| CPB | Bureau for Economic Policy Analysis |
| IFRS | International Financial Reporting Standards |
| PPB | Portugal Participatory Budget |
| MTO | Medium-Term Objective |
| IMAD | Institute of Macroeconomic Analysis and Development |
| PFMC | Public Financial Management and Control |
| NAO | National Audit Office |

# *Executive Summary*

Effective budgeting underpins economic well-being and inclusive growth and supports trust in government. The OECD undertakes a series of surveys and analysis approximately every three years to understand the latest policies, frameworks and practices in budgeting and public expenditures across its member countries. This report presents these findings.

Most OECD countries have experienced robust fiscal performance relative to the fiscal cuts that were needed following the global financial and economic crisis. The turn around has not been automatic and countries have had to take difficult decisions to address complex economic and social issues. While fiscal health has broadly returned to pre-crisis levels across the OECD, increases in public debt have reduced the capacity of many governments to respond to the next economic downturn.

Developments in budgeting have assisted governments with their decisions through such things as fiscal rules which have been widely adopted, along with the complementary practices of medium-term expenditure frameworks and top-down budgeting. However, in many cases further refinement of how the fiscal frameworks perform is needed relative to the aspirations held at the time they were designed.

All OECD countries have some flexibility in the way they execute budgets in order to manage unexpected events. Mechanisms include reallocating budget expenditure across spending areas within a single budget period and carrying-over expenditure from one year to the next. When such flexibility is provided, supplementary budgets, in-year and year-end reports have become a core means through which parliaments can hold governments accountable for decisions. Over recent years, there has been a trend across OECD countries towards stronger engagement of parliaments across the budgetary cycle, with parliaments performing a crucial role before a budget is delivered. There is also increased parliamentary involvement in medium-term budgetary frameworks, driven in part by the evolving fiscal framework within the European Union. Around one-third of OECD countries have a specialist research unit in their legislatures with responsibilities to analyse the government's budget, and independent Parliamentary Budget Offices have become much more prevalent across the OECD.

This report includes a special focus on how governments manage and report fiscal risks. Based on the OECD survey data there are a variety of approaches in place across areas such as institutional responsibilities to the criteria for deciding which risks to report. The countries with the most advanced management of fiscal risks identified three channels to improve risk management practices. First, the comprehensive reporting of fiscal risks can increase awareness of the risks, which can then lead to more effective risk mitigation and management. Second, fiscal risk scenarios or stress tests can help to identify the channels through which public finances are most likely to be impacted during a crisis. Third, fiscal risk assessments can inform policymakers when setting fiscal targets or objectives.

As one of the most important and overarching policy documents, the budget should follow open and transparent processes, so that it -- and the policy decisions that it embodies -- is seen as the legitimate result of efforts to balance many competing interests and demands. Governments have made efforts to help citizens understand and engage in budget processes. Twenty three OECD countries now produce a citizen's guide to the budget and over 80% of OECD countries make available budget data in an open, reusable format. However, only a minority of OECD countries produce impact assessments showing how the budget as a whole affects issues such as income distribution, environmental impacts, gender equality and effects on minority groups. Gender budgeting is a tool of public financial management that is becoming relevant in OECD countries that seek information about how gender inequalities can become embedded in public policies and the allocation of resources. The number of OECD countries reporting the use of gender budgeting has increased from 12 to 17 since 2016.

OECD countries use a range of processes to inform the quality of public expenditures. These processes include spending reviews, performance budgeting and programme evaluation.

- Spending reviews are now in place in the majority of OECD countries and assist in identifying areas for potential savings, and re- the improving alignment of public expenditure withto strategic and political priorities. The approaches adopted in Canada and the United Kingdom emphasise the benefit of aligning reviews to thematic priorities and a framework of public value.
- Performance budgeting is increasingly prevalent but countries still struggle to make effective use of performance information in budgetary decision making. The use of performance "dashboards by countries such as Canada, France and the USA seems well aligned to the aspirations of the tool, similarly Australia's focus on indicators supports the communication of performance results.
- Programme evaluation has yet to demonstrate a close relationship to making budget decisions, although structured approaches that apply in Chile, Canada and Korea, appear to point to a way forward.

Having a sound framework to budget for capital expenditure is essential to ensure it meets a nation's development needs in a cost-effective and coherent manner. More than half of OECD countries report having a strategic infrastructure plan covering all sectors. A similar proportion now adopt a short-listing approach based upon cost-benefit analysis aligned to a government's strategic agenda. Further, a range of evaluative mechanisms are used to assess value-for-money, however it is notable that the evaluations are not yet routinely made fully available to the public. The number of public-private partnerships has increased over the past 10 years; however, the number remains low relative to the range of investment activities governments undertake. One institutional aspect related to these developments is an increase in the number of infrastructure and PPP agencies across OECD countries.

The final Chapter of this report provides short Country Profiles, summarising how OECD countries apply public financial management practices in their national context. While approaches are varying and distinctive, the OECD Recommendation of the Council on Budgetary Governance provides a frame of reference for considering how budgeting systems can better support fiscal and policy objectives and contribute to the legitimacy of expenditure decisions . Towards this end, it demonstrates that the various themes of Public Financial Management (PFM) are inter-connected and mutually supportive. In addition, the Country Profiles highlight that most OECD countries have one or more areas of national practice that are notable in international terms, and can provide useful points of reference and inspiration for other country practitioners.

# *Methodological Note*

Most data presented in *Budgeting and Public Expenditures in OECD Countries 2019* were generated by government officials' responses to a set of surveys distributed to all OECD countries. The Budget Practices and Procedures Survey was the central survey; and further surveys addressed the various sub-groups of the Working Party of Senior Budget Officials (SBO) and their respective areas of expertise (namely Infrastructure/Public Private Partnerships; Performance, Evaluation and Review; and Parliamentary Budget Oversight).

As such, the report and Country Profiles draw heavily upon self-reporting from governments representing the country's own assessment of current practices and procedures. Respondents were predominantly senior budget officials. Data refer mostly to central/federal governments and exclude the subnational level.

Data collection began in December 2017 and ended in July 2018. A preliminary version of the report was presented and shared at the 39th Annual Meeting of OECD Senior Budget Officials in June 2018 and provided an opportunity for the OECD SBO delegates to comment and validate the results. During the subsequent quality control process, the countries were invited to verify and clarify any substantial changes from the earlier data, potential inconsistencies and outliers. Furthermore, the pre-publication version was shared with OECD Senior Budget Officials in February 2019 allowing for a final check of the content.

Fiscal data and economic data relating to OECD countries are mostly based on the System of National Accounts (SNA), and were extracted from the Government at a Glance online database representing the last available update of the OECD National Accounts Statistics (database) and the Eurostat Government finance statistics (database) at the time of analysis: 28 June 2018 (financial government accounts: 3 July 2018).

In the figures and throughout the text of this report, the OECD average is presented either as the un-weighted, arithmetic mean or weighted average of the OECD countries for which data are available. OECD totals represent the sum of data for the OECD countries for which data are available.

The report also includes a new composite indicator on Gender Budgeting (for further details please refer to Chapter 6.3 and Annex B) and a General Government country data overview (Annex A) which provides baseline fiscal and economic data for the Country Profiles in Chapter 9.

## Country coverage

The report includes data for all 35 OECD countries[1] based on available information (July 2018).

**Overview of all surveys to which OECD countries responded**

| | 2018 OECD Budget Practices and Procedures Survey | 2018 OECD Fiscal Plans and Budgeting Framework Survey | 2018 OECD Performance Budgeting Survey | 2018 OECD Survey of Capital Budgeting and Infrastructure Governance | 2018 OECD PBO Network Survey on Parliamentary Budgeting Practices |
|---|---|---|---|---|---|
| Australia | x | x | x | x | x |
| Austria | x | x | x | x | x |
| Belgium | x | x | x | | x |
| Canada | x | x | x | | x |
| Chile | x | x * | x | x | x |
| Czech Republic | x | x | x | x | x |
| Denmark | x | x | x | x | x |
| Estonia | x | x | x | x | x |
| Finland | x | x | x | | x |
| France | x | x | x | x | x |
| Germany | x | x | x | x | x |
| Greece | x | x | x | x | x |
| Hungary | x | x | x | x | x |
| Iceland | x | | x | | x |
| Ireland | x | x | x | x | x |
| Israel | x | x | | x | x |
| Italy | x | x * | x | x | x |
| Japan | x | x * | x | x | x |
| Korea | x | x | x | | x |
| Latvia | x | x | x | | x |
| Luxembourg | x | x * | x | x | x |
| Mexico | x | x | x | x | |
| Netherlands | x | x | x | x | x |
| New Zealand | x | x | x | x | x |
| Norway | x | x * | x | x | x |
| Poland | x | x | x | | x |
| Portugal | x | x | x | x | x |
| Slovak Republic | x | x | x | x | x |
| Slovenia | x | x * | x | x | x |
| Spain | x | x | x | x | x |
| Sweden | x | x | x | x | x |
| Switzerland | x | | x | x | x |
| Turkey | x | x | x | x | x |

[1] On 3 May 2018, the OECD Council invited Lithuania to become a Member. This country entered officially as an OECD member on the 5 of July 2018. At the time of data collection, the deposit of Lithuania's instrument of accession to the OECD Convention was pending and therefore Lithuania does not appear in the list of OECD members and is not included in the calculation of the OECD average.

| | | | | | |
|---|---|---|---|---|---|
| United Kingdom | x | x * | x | x | x |
| United States | | | | | x |
| Total | 34 | 32 | 33 | 27 | 34 |

*Note:** Chile, Italy, Japan, Luxembourg, Norway, Slovenia and the United Kingdom did not provide the figures on government's Fiscal Policy Plans and Composition (separate section of the survey).

## Country codes (ISO codes)

The International Organization for Standardization (ISO) defines three-letter codes for the names of countries, dependent territories and special areas of geographical interest. For the geographical display of some figures, the following ISO codes are used.

| OECD countries | ISO | OECD countries | ISO |
|---|---|---|---|
| Australia | AUS | Korea | KOR |
| Austria | AUT | Latvia | LVA |
| Belgium | BEL | Luxembourg | LUX |
| Canada | CAN | Mexico | MEX |
| Chile | CHL | Netherlands | NLD |
| Czech Republic | CZE | New Zealand | NZL |
| Denmark | DNK | Norway | NOR |
| Estonia | EST | Poland | POL |
| Finland | FIN | Portugal | PRT |
| France | FRA | Slovak Republic | SVK |
| Germany | DEU | Slovenia | SVN |
| Greece | GRC | Spain | ESP |
| Hungary | HUN | Sweden | SWE |
| Iceland | ISL | Switzerland | CHE |
| Ireland | IRL | Turkey | TUR |
| Israel | ISR | United Kingdom | GBR |
| Italy | ITA | United States | USA |
| Japan | JPN | | |

## Survey approaches and use of data

The 2018 OECD Budget Practices and Procedure Survey was directed to delegates of the SBO and covers the entire budgeting process - from formulation, to approval, execution and reporting and also addresses cross-cutting and topical issues such as fiscal sustainability and budget transparency. Compared to the previous versions, the questionnaire has been extensively streamlined and restructured in line with the OECD's ten principles of budgetary governance. Newer areas of focus, including fiscal risk, comprehensive budget accounting and gender-related dimensions of budgeting, have also been addressed. This survey forms the core of the material in Chapter 3: Budgeting institutions, rules and frameworks, Chapter 4: Budgetary Management and Control and Chapter 6: Open, Transparent and Inclusive Budgeting.

The 2018 OECD Fiscal Plans and Budgeting Framework Survey outlines the fiscal consolidation plans in place across OECD countries and/or officially announced as of November 2017, along with institutional and process reforms to support the fiscal effort. The results of this survey are mainly used in Chapter 2: Fiscal Policy Management and the Country Profiles in Chapter 9. The position as set out in each Country Profile generally reflects the positions as of June 2018, and, if not indicated otherwise, has not been updated to reflect political, economic and budgetary developments since that time.

The 2018 OECD Performance Budgeting Survey collected data on performance budgeting, spending reviews and programme evaluation and is based on self-reporting by members of the OECD Senior Budget Officials Network on Performance and Results. Relevant data is presented in Chapter 7 of the report.

The 2018 Parliamentary Budget Officials (PBO) Network Survey on Parliamentary Budgeting Practices focuses on Parliament's role in budgeting (Chapter 5).

The 2018 OECD Survey of Capital Budgeting and Infrastructure Governance was sent to the SBO Network of Senior PPP and Infrastructure Officials and collected data on capital budgeting, PPPs, as well as on a set of governance dimensions, including strategic planning, sustainable infrastructure management, affordability and value for money (Chapter 8).

Thanks are due to the staff of member countries for their time and care in supplying survey material and in responding to follow-up queries.

# 1. An introduction to budgeting: Everywhere, budgeting is the same and different

By

Allen Schick

*This chapter takes a look at how modern budgeting has evolved in recent years, highlighting where budgeting remains specific to national traditions as well as areas where there are converging international practices. It goes on to identify four pervasive themes of contemporary reforms: (1) enablers that bolster capacity of central budget authorities to manage public finance and achieve government objectives; (2) constraints that limit the procedural or substantive discretion of budget makers (3) perennials that persist on reform agendas for an extended period, despite shifts in political and economic circumstances; and (4) demands that are rooted in political aspirations and the mobilisation of interests. Finally, it considers what the next generation of innovations might be, particularly in the context of modern information technology, and how this could impact the task of budgeting.*

Dr. Allen Schick is Research Professor at the Maryland School of Public Policy, University of Maryland, and a Governance Fellow of the Brookings Institution.

## 1.1. Introduction

Looking back at more than a century of evolution in budget policies and outcomes, one is inevitably struck by similar trends among advanced economies. All now allocate a much greater share of national output to government programmes and activities and all have reconfigured their budgets to spend a greater portion of national expenditure on income transfers. Most also have higher peacetime debt burdens than they had in the past and face the prospect of lower economic growth and greater fiscal stress in the decades ahead than they had in the boom decades after World War II. Their fiscal space has been constricted by demographic pressures on the one hand and by less buoyant growth trajectories on the other. These trends have made the practice of budgeting more urgent and more difficult, more urgent because the national budget has become the main or prominent source of income for many families and households, and more difficult because most incremental resources are claimed by statutory requirements before expenditure decisions are made.

These macro trends mask large differences among OECD countries, which have significant variation in public revenues and expenditure as a share of GDP, as well as in deficit and debt levels and the proportion of the budget spent on income transfers. Evidently, countries that have moved in the same direction have not moved in lockstep. The similarities are important because they speak to the enlarged role of the nation-state and to burgeoning financial strains on national governments; the differences are important because they reflect country-specific political cultures and institutions.

Differences within an overall pattern of similarities also have emerged in the core processes of budgeting that are surveyed in this report. In all advanced countries, macroeconomic forecasts inform the government at various stages of the budget cycle of key economic variables that impact the country's fiscal posture. All member countries provide for spending units to bid for financial resources, and for one or more central agencies to review these bids in the course of preparing the budget and submitting it to the national legislature. All have procedures for implementing the budget and auditing financial results and all have formal and/or informal means for negotiations between sectoral ministries and central authorities and for final Cabinet or executive decisions. But there are enormous differences among countries in the scope of parliamentary activity, ranging from Westminster-type arrangements which preclude or restrict independent legislative actions to separate governments that give parliament broad discretion to enact its revenue and spending preferences. Differences also emerge in the form of appropriation, and in procedures for amending the approved budget or varying from authorised spending levels.

Procedural similarities reflect norms of good budgeting that have been fashioned into established practice throughout the global budget community. Key differences are concentrated in budgetary innovations, which were introduced during the last decades of the previous century and early in the current century. Budgetary innovation has been a recurring focus of SBO meetings and networks, as budget officials have been eager to learn from the successes and disappointments experienced by counterparts in other countries. Through this learning process some procedural reforms became the next generation's accepted practice.

This OECD report casts a broader and more finely tuned net than previous surveys, and it thereby provides a valuable data base for member countries to decide whether and how to adjust their budget systems to contemporary political and fiscal conditions, as well as to the opportunities made possible by modern information technologies and evolving standards and norms. The findings reported in this inaugural edition enlighten practitioners and scholars about convergences and divergences in budgeting. This survey is, however, much more than a snapshot of budgeting drawn from country responses to a carefully crafted questionnaire. It will spur future learning and innovation in budgeting; when the next round of surveys is undertaken, some differences among OECD countries will have vanished or narrowed, and new ones will have emerged.

### *1.1.1. Continuity and Change in Budgeting*

Why do some budget practices converge across the OECD community while others diverge? An important part of the answer is that continuity and change have been enduring features of modern budgeting since it emerged as a vital responsibility of government in the 19th century. It is a distinctive characteristic of budgeting that the timing of critical actions normally is driven by a fixed calendar, not by the wills and preferences of government leaders. No matter how difficult or unpleasant the choices, the government must compile and publish revenue and spending plans for the upcoming fiscal period. Fixed routines, including milestones and deadlines standardise forms and procedures, delineation of the formal roles and responsibilities of participants in the process, ease preparation of the budget. Political leaders and officials do not have to reconsider procedures or prescribe new information requirements at the start of every cycle. During stable periods, the routinisation of budgeting produces both continuity within countries and similarities among countries. Through imitation and adaptation, one country's established procedures become another's reform, usually not right away, but once reforms have proven their worth and staying power in the country of origin. At the dawn of budgeting more than a century ago, accounting and controlling for specific items of expenditure was a novel practice in pioneering countries, but over time became accepted practice in most developed countries, and was long maintained without significant change. Economic and functional classifications also migrated across national boundaries, as did cash-based budgeting and the audit of expenditures. Perhaps the most important standardised practice has been annual budgeting; while preparing the budget and appropriating funds each year is standard operating procedure in almost all countries, the history of budgeting and processes certainly would have been different if the budget were prepared for the full term of government or on a multiyear planning schedule. The grip of annual budgeting is so powerful, that countries seeking a longer-term budget horizon have coupled new procedure such as medium-term frameworks and long-term projections to the single-year budget cycle.

However, some practices never become "internationalised" because they are embedded in critical political institutions. For example, the manner in which national legislatures respond to the government's budget has always varied significantly among OECD countries, though a pervasive theme of contemporary reforms has been to bolster parliaments' capacity to review the government's budget. The widespread adoption of line item budgeting and other core procedures demonstrated both continuity and convergence; variations in the power of the legislature to amend the budget demonstrated continuity without convergence. Perpetuation of established routines is not the whole story, however, for budgeting is a restless process that is in search of new methods. Based on more than half a century of observation, this writer has found that budget makers generally are both calmed and frustrated by inherited routines. Doing it approximately the same way every year facilitates timely production of the next budget but may not provide good enough information for optimal revenue and expenditure decisions. Often, governments disregard perceived shortcomings and make it through from one budget season to the next with little or no procedural adjustment. At times, however, governments or their central budget agencies venture in new directions, and supplement, or sometimes displace, the ordered routines with novel information requirements, revised classifications, new standards for allocating resources, time frames that spill beyond the next fiscal year, and other innovations. Disruption may be due to changing political or economic conditions, advances in information technology, demands by previously excluded or marginalised stakeholders, and other developments. Budgeting is an open system that has multiple sources of influence. It is a political process, but political institutions and culture do not fully explain the direction or fate of innovation. It is also an economic process, but a country's economic condition does not suffice to explain its impulse to innovate. History makes a difference, management style has an impact and the interests of leaders weighs heavily on the conduct of budgeting.

Once *de rigueur,* line item budgeting is now regarded by almost all member countries as an inadequate basis for allocating resources and controlling expenditures. But countries have taken different paths to displace line items. Many countries long ago consolidated the items into broad categories such as personnel and other operating expenditures, other supplemented the line items with programme or output classifications, a few purged central budget documents of input data. Having taken different routes, country budgets that converged on diminishing the place of line items, nevertheless diverge on how the budget should be structured.

Budgetary innovation also spawns differences among countries because there typically is a lag between first adopters and followers. When a few reform-driven countries moved from cash to the accrual basis or extended the time frame of budgeting from one year to the medium term, other countries generally waited before deciding whether to reengineer their own budget processes. Due diligence in reform has led to wider differences among governments on accruals than on cash, and on medium-term frameworks than on annual budget procedures.

The survey instrument that forms the basis of this publication reflects the winds of change that have buffeted the practice of budgeting in recent decades. A key question that frames the survey identifies two dozen areas of budgeting and financial management, and requests member countries to identify recent innovations, if any, in each area. Some of the listed innovations, such as performance budgeting and financial reporting, have been on reform agendas for decades and predate establishment of the SBO network almost 40 years ago. Quite a few contemporary innovations, such as fiscal rules and medium-term frameworks, have roots in the less buoyant economic growth and tighter fiscal conditions many member countries now experience. Budgeting continually adapts to changing political priorities; gender and green budgeting are manifestations of this process.

Over the course of the history of modern budgeting, it is possible to discern four themes of innovation, each with its own aims and techniques: (1) *enablers* that bolster capacity of central budget authorities to manage public finance and achieve government objectives; (2) *constraints* that limit the procedural or substantive discretion of budget makers (3) *perennials* that persist on reform agendas for an extended period, despite shifts in political and economic circumstances; and (4) *demands* that are rooted in political aspirations and the mobilisation of interests.

In specifying four distinct types of innovation, this writer recognises that others may disagree with the labels or with the reforms situated in each category. This writer's purpose is not to attach labels to innovations, but to make the point that budget reforms have multiple, sometimes conflicting, objectives. Furthermore, the way in which reforms are implemented may pull them away from their original purposes. An innovation that was designed to limit the budgetary discretion of government may turn into an innovation that enlarges discretion. Medium-term expenditure frameworks (MTEFs) that were first introduced to limit discretion by assuring alignment of the annual budget and future expenditure commitments has been refashioned into an empowering innovation that extends the reach of the annual budget to the medium term. The section below dealing with constraints will return to this issue.

Budgeting, like other human endeavours, is open to multiple perspectives and typologies. More than half a century ago, this writer adapted management concepts to identify and control management, and planning stages of budget reform. About 30 years later, he adapted economic concepts to identify aggregate fiscal discipline, strategic allocation, and operational efficiency as the three core functions of public financial management. The concepts introduced here from the previous classifications in that they focus on the types of innovation, rather than on the functions of budgeting. With more than a dozen prominent innovations currently in play, it is useful to distinguish those that constrict from those that empower, and to separately discuss those that persist for extended periods of a reform agenda, and that seek to enlarge the scope of interests that influence budget actions.

### *(1) Enabling*

*Enabling* reforms were critical during the formative period of budgeting in developed countries in the late 19th and early 20th centuries and remain important for those developing countries that still have incomplete budget institutions. These reforms include a single treasury account, establishment of the central budget office and basic steps in the annual budget cycle, and procedures for implementing the budget and controlling public expenditures. Because they pertain to the basic machinery of budgeting, enabling reforms exhibit a high degree of convergence among developed countries and continuity from one year to the next. The routines that are widely embedded in budget practices of Member countries are deeply rooted in formative reforms that enable governments to complete basic budget responsibilities.

Enabling reforms also reshaped budgeting during the apogee of Keynesian economics, when many national governments used the budget and other fiscal tools to maintain growth and counter economic weakness. Macroeconomic forecasting became a ubiquitous element of budget making, and most OECD countries consolidated their investment and operating budgets in a single process, and subsumed national planning within their budget. Although some countries now lack confidence in, or sufficient financial resources to mount full-fledged countercyclical fiscal interventions, OECD surveys give due recognition to these enduring features of budgeting by incorporating information on fiscal policy. The time when economic policy moved on one track and budget policy on a separate track is long over, but some fiscal tools now serve more as constraints than as enablers.

Enabling reforms are in vogue during periods of economic expansion and political optimism, when governments have confidence that they possess financial resources and managerial capacity to forge a better future for their people. During the buoyant decades after World War II, programme budgeting, early versions of performance budgeting, and various types of planning-programming budgeting systems (PPBS) were based on confidence that government has the material and analytic means to establish and finance bold policy initiatives. These enabling innovations were designed to free budgeting from incremental routines that build next year's expenditures on the previous year's, and to allocate the bounty of economic growth (and, in some countries, tax increases) to plan and finance new programmes across a broad swath of public objectives. Rather than looking back to previous budgets to decide how much to spend on public programmes and activities, budget makers would look forward to a prosperous future, articulate multiyear objectives for all major government responsibilities, and thereby build a society made better by cost-effective public expenditures. However, when (in the last decades of the 20th century) economic and political conditions became less hospitable to programme expansion, these enabling reforms were discarded or redefined to serve other budgetary purposes. Most PPBS systems withered away, programme budgeting became more a means of classifying expenditures than establishing objectives, and performance budgeting was transformed into a tool for informing rather than deciding the budget.

Spending reviews are distinctive enabling innovations that have gained traction during periods of fiscal stress, especially since the Great Recession that destabilised national budgets a decade ago. Their twin aims are to free government leaders from the iron grip of past budgets by closely scrutinising the purposes and value of existing programmes and expenditures and (in some countries) to expand fiscal space for policy initiatives. To be effective, spending reviews must have sufficient support to reduce or reallocate expenditures, and to override opposition from sectoral ministries and organised interests. Inevitably therefore, the structure and conduct of these reviews differ among countries and may also differ from year-to-year. Few countries have established systematic, recurring review processes; those that have include the Netherlands Policy Review, and Australia's comprehensive spending reviews. These countries have potent tools for reviewing public programmes and expenditures that are accepted by the major politcal parties. However, when reviews are conducted on an *ad hoc* basis, they tend to reflect policy differences among political parties.

### *(2) Constraints*

*Constraints* are innovations that limit the discretion of budget makers by proscribing or prescribing certain procedures, actions, or outcomes. Rules that limit deficits, debt, or other fiscal aggregates are the most common contemporary budget proscription; MTEFs that require government to set expenditure ceilings for each of the next several years are the most popular contemporary prescription. Other innovations that have potential to restrict budget actions include: an inter-temporal budget constraint that bars revenue or spending policies that would increase the present value of projected long-term fiscal gaps; the accrual basis which requires recognition in the budget of current liabilities that will be paid out in future years; fiscal risk estimates that require reporting of government exposure to various contingencies; and pre-budget review processes, such as the EU's review of country budget plans.

In contrast to the formative and expansionary periods of budgeting when enabling innovations predominated, during recent decades the most popular innovations aim to constrict budget policies. Weaker growth, persistent deficits, elevated debt level, and demographic pressures have impelled innovators to adapt the machinery of budgeting to current fiscal pressures, and (in some countries) to unfavourable long-term projections.

In design, constraint is the obverse of enablement. However, a country's political culture and party orientation strongly influence its response to budgetary constraints. Some countries welcome constraints that safeguard them against pressure to spend more or to tax less. In some countries, constraints on budgetary freedom of action are viewed by government leaders as impediments to their ability to satisfy poltical demands, and they therefore strive to undermine budget innovations that tie their hands. Sometimes, they go so far as to remake rules intended to constrain into enablers. Arguably, some EU countries appear to have treated the Stability and Growth Pact's 3% of GDP limit on deficits more as a green light to debt-finance expenditures up to the limit during good economic times, and some used aggressive accounting methods to permit higher spending while nominally keeping within the limit. The EU's post-crisis fiscal compact has sought to restore constraint by, among other features, strengthening its review of country budgets.

MTEF is an example of a highly popular innovation that started as a constraint, but now is deployed in quite a few countries to enable the government to make multiyear expenditure decisions through the annual budget process. When MTEF was first introduced, its architects emphasised that it imposed a "hard constraint" on future spending, but over time what was once regarded as a ceiling has come to be regarded in many countries as a floor. In these countries, when government rolls the MTEF forward each year, it starts building the next budget by considering whether previously authorised spending levels should be raised. Although it deviates from MTEF's original intent and weakens or disables outyear constraints, this behaviour is understandable, for raising the spending bar enables government to respond to fresh demands. Adhering to previously set spending levels for the full term of the MTEF would shackle the government to past spending decisions.

Moreover, an enabling MTEF may equip advanced countries with policy planning capacity that they would otherwise lack. No OECD countries have distinct planning ministries or processes; instead, they rely on budgeting (and often on sectoral ministries) to develop policies for the medium term and beyond. But annual budgeting may be an inadequate planning tool because of its short time horizon and the tendency to define issues principally in financial terms. Deploying MTEF as a planning tool that sets programme objectives and spending levels 3-5 years ahead is a sensible enhancement in government capacity.

The problem with constraints is not that governments are indifferent to fiscal limits, but that they face political and economic pressures that make compliance difficult and unpleasant. The financial burden of past commitments, often embedded in statutory entitlements and political expectations, is not eased by *ex ante* spending limits, nor are political demands to finance programme initiatives.

There is at least one circumstance in which MTEF may effectively constrain medium-term expenditures: When the government is formed through a detailed coalition agreement that sets forth national policies, including key budget policies, for the full term of the government. In this situation, MTEF can both enable programme planning and constrain expenditures by means of annual or multiyear budget decisions.

Fiscal rules provide another case study of innovative constraints that often fall short of promised constraint. In many countries, both within and outside the OECD community, quantitative limits have been a popular reform, but breaches have been commonplace, especially in countries which have fractured political systems and easy access to capital markets. Compliance has also been impaired by defects in first-generation fiscal rules, which failed to distinguish between periods of economic vigour and stagnation, imposed limits on a one-year-at-a time basis, did not provide workable pathways for correcting political imbalances, and lacked sturdy enforcement mechanisms. In the wake of the fiscal crisis early in this millennium, the EU adopted a fiscal compact which, in addition to remedying some defects, also transferred some enforcement authority from member countries to the European Commission. The lesson that may be derived from EU's experience is that supra-national action may be appropriate to bolster political will in individual countries.

But this is far from the whole fiscal story. Many countries have both breached and abided by fiscal limits. Although deficits, debt or expenditures have exceeded the limits, they probably have been below the levels that would have been reached in the absence of fiscal rules. Countries that have insufficient fiscal space to accommodate expenditure pressures within the rules sometimes buy wiggle room by spending a bit above the allowed levels. They pay attention to the rules but do not fully comply with them, and they thereby reconcile or muddle through the clash between fixed constraints and political or financial demands. MTEF has generated a similar response, with governments giving due regard to the levels set in the previous year's budget, but raising the ceiling to finance policy initiatives.

Every budget system has elements of enablement and constraint. Budgeting is inherently both an exercise of power and an exercise of discipline. It is the mobilisation of governmental power to plan public activities and expenditures, as well as to limit expenditures to authorised levels. The balance between enablement and constraint is impacted by the distribution of roles and authority within a country, and influences budget decisions and outcomes. This balance is not static; it shifts in response to changing political and economic conditions and to innovations that alter budget procedures and policies.

### *(3) Perennials*

*Perennials* are practices that are subject to recurring waves of innovation, either to upgrade standards or to remedy perceived shortcomings in previous reform efforts. Some are perennial, enablers, others are constraints; they are separately identified here because the impulse to innovate is continuous. Financial reporting is revisited on an ongoing basis to clarify existing standards or to deal with new situations. The work of perfecting financial reports never ends in countries where the supreme audit institution or the accounting standards board has authority to promulgate new rules and standards. The migration of reporting standards across countries is propelled by international accounting groups, as well as by country-based rule-making bodies. Recent enhancements to financial reporting include accrual-based accounting, estimates on government's exposure to contingent liabilities and other fiscal risks, comparisons of expected and actual performance, long-term fiscal projections, and pre-budget statements that signal the government's fiscal plans.

Performance budgeting (PB) is another perennial reform, but for a different reason. PB is a recurring focus of innovation because efforts to base allocations on results often fall short of the mark. Instead of abandoning the pursuit of performance, various countries have retained the PB label and reoriented it from performance-based to performance-informed budgeting, or from central budget decisions to performance management in line ministries. Many countries have repeatedly tinkered with the definition and classification of key concepts, such as outcomes and results, and with their use in the submission and review of budget requests. Others have shifted from PB's original focus as an instrument for deciding the budget to a means of classifying or displaying decisions taken during constructing the budget.

Some Member countries have had considerable success with PB-type arrangements by recognising that performance has to be embedded in the culture and systems of public management, especially the strategic processes and goals of government, and has a robust infrastructure across government to support the production and use of performance information. These critical linkages are recognised and defined in the OECD *Good Practices for Performance Budgeting.* To this writer, several key insights emerge from the *Good Practices* and if properly adopted, will open the door to more effective application of performance budgeting. First, PB cannot be a stand-alone innovation; it must be closely aligned to national performance and medium-term expenditure frameworks and evidence-based assessments of policies and resources. Second, PB should be adapted to country circumstances, with due regard to the role and interests of important stakeholders. Third, there should be systematic use of performance information, guided by the central budget authority, but also involving line ministries, the legislature and the supreme audit institution. Centres of Government (CoGs) have a critical stake in orienting programmes and line ministries to performance and results, but their role usually is limited. COGs can inspire and prod, they can demand performance information, and occasisionally review budget options in the light of evidence on results. Overall, however, COGs have many other things on their mind that crowd out sustained attention to performance. Moreover, they may regard it prudent or necessary to leave sensitive questions - for example, how to improve the performance of teachers and schools - to others.

PB is perennial because countries are unwilling to give up on the alluring idea that public money should be allocated based on achieved or expected results. Measured against this ideal, actual allocations persistently fall far short of the mark, sometimes because government lacks the capacity to reallocate money from less to more effective activities, sometimes because it lacks sufficient information to transfer resources, and most often because the deadline-driven, political-sensitive machinery of budgeting is more beholden to past commitments than to new possibilities.

Perennials have been significant drivers in the expansion of the overall SBO network that now spans more than half a dozen theme-based networks and annual meetings, in addition to regional networks and meetings. The SBO has sponsored active, long- running networks on financial reporting and performance budgeting, the two perennials discussed above, and newer networks on fiscal relations between levels of government, public-private partnerships, and on health financing, three issues that will definitely be of recurring interests to budget officials for many years. Networks have also been established in response to political demands on budgeting, including meetings on parliamentary budgeting and gender budgeting; these developments will be discussed in the next sections.

The SBO networks are situated at the frontier of budgeting, in areas where innovation is highly active and practice has not been standardised. It is in these areas where expermentation and variety are essential and adjustments are frequently in response to country findings and experiences. In fact, the impulse to learn and adjust is the greatest value provided by OECD's comprehensive survey of budget practices, especially in those areas where there is significant variation among countries.

### *(4) Political Demands*

*Political demands* have always been important features of budget reform; their principal aim is to give certain participants or interests greater influence in making budget decisions. Inherently, therefore, demand-driven innovations are redistributive, in that they seek to give some a greater voice in budget actions. There are two main pathways for redistributing budget power: one is to strengthen the capacity of some interests to participate; the other is to assure that certain issues or policies are given due attention when budget resources are allocated. The first approach focuses on changing the process, the second on changing expenditure and programme policies.

Process innovations include independent fiscal institutions that review and comment on the government's economic and budget assumptions, enlarged legislative staffs that assist parliamentarians in their budget work, expansion of the legislature's authority to amend the government's budget, and participatory budgeting arrangements, usually at subnational levels, that give citizens a voice on certain budget matters. Due to these and other innovations, there is now greater diversity on budget making within countries, with the process somewhat more open to different points of view. The impact of these innovations is greatest in countries that give the legislature free rein to amend the budget, but even in Westminster systems where parliament's vote on the budget is a matter of confidence, independent sources of information and analysis, such as Canada's Parliamentary Budget Office and the U.K's Office for Budget Responsibility, have given rise to more vigorous questioning of the government's budget and, arguably, to informal channels through which legislators persuade the government to revise some budget policies.

Although it also seeks to open budgeting to diverse views and interests, participatory budgeting warrants separate mention. It has had little application at the national level, and mixed results at municipal levels. Proponents of participatory schemes that empower citizens to vote on local public works projects and other activities laud its potential to democratise budgeting, but others point to the ease with which organised groups sometimes capture the process to serve their own interests.

Gender and green budgeting are the most prominent policy-oriented reforms; their principal objective is to promote gender parity and environmental sustainability in the allocation of public resources. Both movements have mobilised significant political support within the OECD community, especially in multiparty countries and countries with strong social democratic traditions. Gender and environmental impact statements are one possible instrument for operationalising these demands and incorporating them into ongoing budget routines.

Because political systems and cultures differ among advanced countries, there is much less convergence on innovations arising from political demands than on those focused on the machinery of budgeting. The pace of innovation will depend in part on the extent to which these demands are internationalised. It also remains to be seen whether other political demands, such as explicit allocating public funds among income or age classes or geographic entities, will make their way into the budgeting arena. If they do, budgeting may become more open and more contentious. The more likely path is for non-governmental actors -think tanks and advocacy groups- to develop their own metrics that highlight the distributional issues they are interested in.

### *1.1.2. Process and Policy*

The interaction between the process and policy paths gives rise to a fundamental question that affects most contemporary budget innovations. What is the connection between process and policy in budget innovation? Is it the case that modifying procedures regularly produces expected changes in substantive outcomes? For example, does lengthening the time horizon of budgeting to the medium-term or longer generate lower deficits or debt levels in future budgets? Are expenditure patterns significantly changed when the legislature has more information and more power? Will publication of fiscal risks held by government induce it to take less risks? Similar questions can be asked about many of the innovations surveyed in this OECD publication.

More than a decade ago, this writer suggested that the relationship between process and policy changes depends on whether an innovation is formulated as an analytical tool or as a decision rule. Obviously, decision rules have a more direct impact on policy, but even here, the relationship is not assured. To repeat a point made early in this essay, budgeting is an open system that takes it clues and cues from many sources. Process affects policy, but the two do not move in lockstep.

Because it is an open system, budgeting is impacted by developments outside its orbit. A strong case can be made that modern information technology is altering the fundamental relationship between government and the governed. The rise of social media already affects political institutions and policies in many countries, for it enables citizens to a far greater degree than in the past to produce and disseminate both information and misinformation on government policies and actions. Some countries have moved to constrain social media, but the course of liberal democracy leaves it largely beyond the reach of government. Thus far, IT-driven social interactions have paid less attention to budgeting than to elections, political personalities, and high profile issues. However, expenditure and tax matters certainly will be grist for social media in the near future, possibly driven by big data mining entities that have the capacity to instantly communicate with millions of people. It will be a brave new world in which most households get personalised messages on budget day telling them they are adversely affected by the just-announced tax and expenditure policies. If social media become instruments of agitation and mobilisation on budget matters, the task of budget making will become more urgent and more difficult.

# 2. Fiscal Policy Management

*The global expansion that has ensued since the financial and economic crisis of 2008 has peaked and global economic growth is projected to ease gradually over the next 24 months. OECD countries experienced sharp impacts on economic growth and on public finances following the crisis and have undertaken reforms to sure-up their economies. The recovery has been uneven over a period of years and the marks of the crisis are still evident: debt levels remain elevated, public investment has not fully recovered. In recent years, certain areas of public expenditure that were squeezed during the crisis, notably education and social protection, have been prioritised. A broad range of budgetary governance reforms have been progressed in the past three years, including fiscal rules, spending review and enhanced budget transparency as coutnries work to strengthen their management of fiscal policy.*

## 2.1. State of Public Finances

### *2.1.1. The economic context for public financial management*

The global financial crisis that was precipitated in 2008 had a profound effect on the levels of economic growth and the health of public finances of most OECD countries. On average, global growth of 5.5% p.a. in 2007 fell sharply to -0.6% in 2009. In OECD countries, the swing was from 2.6% p.a. GDP growth in 2007 to -3.5% in 2009. Since then, the global economy has been on a steady upward trajectory with GDP growth of 1.8% in 2016 and 2.6% in 2017 across OECD countries. However, the OECD's 2018 assessment of the macroeconomic situation suggests that the global expansion has peaked and is projected to ease gradually over the next two years as downside risks pose considerable challenges for policy makers. Further, strong self-sustained growth has yet to be achieved following accommodative monetary and fiscal policy settings[1].

**Figure 2.1. GDP growth (annual)**

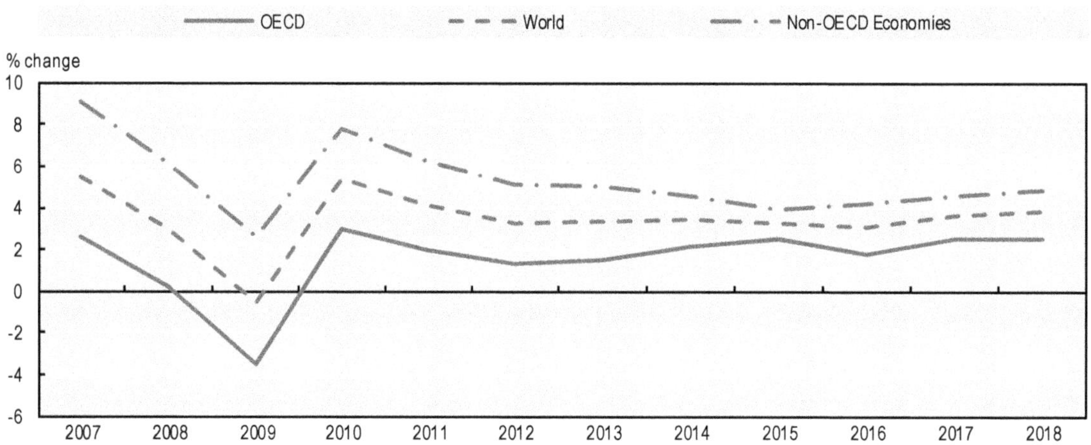


*Note*: Variable used: Annual GDP growth
*Source*: OECD (2018) Economic Outlook No. 103.

StatLink http://dx.doi.org/10.1787/888933946305

### *2.1.2. Fiscal balance and public debt*

Overall general government fiscal balances among OECD countries have continued to stabilise in recent years. Fiscal balances have improved among OECD countries, the average balance in 2016 reaching -2.8% of GDP, a more manageable deficit position than the low of -8.5% in 2009 and a modest improvement from -3.5% in 2014.

Even though general government structural fiscal balances[2] deteriorated in the wake of the financial crisis, the magnitude of structural deficits decreased across OECD countries: on average, OECD countries experienced a structural balance of -2.2% of potential GDP in 2016, improving from -6.3% in 2009 and -6.6% in 2010, and stabilising from -2.5% in 2014.

The average level of general government gross public debt reached 112% of GDP in 2016. The rate at which govenrments accumulate debt has slowed from 2013 as illustrated in Figure 2.3 below, but has not yet started to fall despite the increased stability of government finances.

**Figure 2.2. General government fiscal balance**

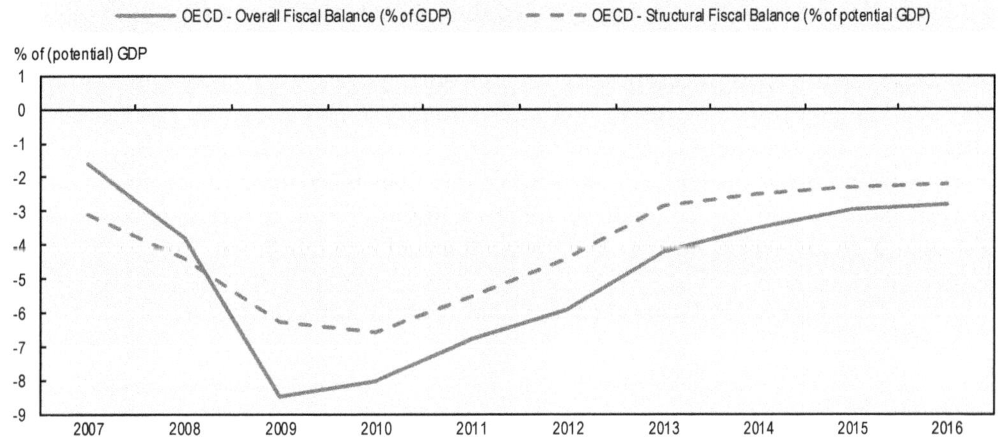


*Source*: For Overall Fiscal Balance: OECD National Accounts Statistics (database); for Structural Fiscal Balance: OECD (2018) Economic Outlook, No 103.

StatLink http://dx.doi.org/10.1787/888933946324

**Figure 2.3. General government public debt**

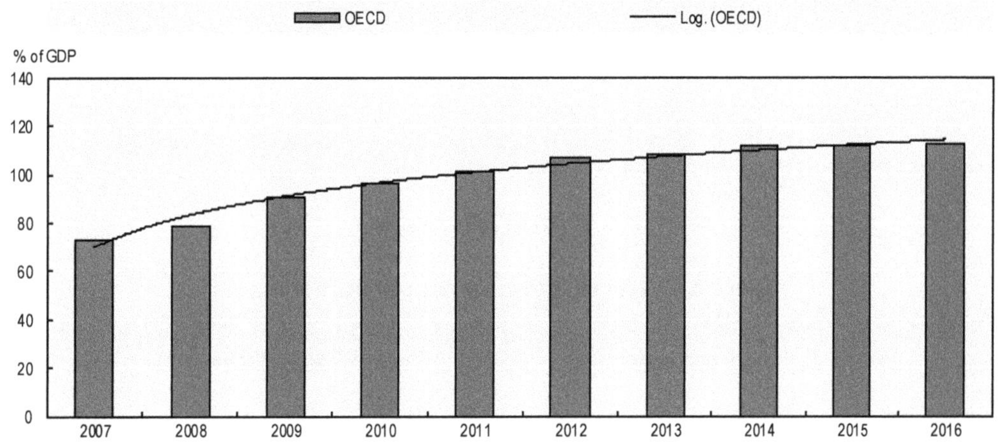


*Source*: OECD National Accounts Statistics (database).

StatLink http://dx.doi.org/10.1787/888933946343

### *2.1.3. Revenue, expenditure and public investment*

Across OECD countries, general government revenues[3] as a share of GDP have returned to pre-crisis levels. On average, revenues were 37.3% of GDP in 2007, decreased to 35.8% in 2009 and recovered back to 37.8% in 2013 and have since stabilised at this level.

Government expenditures in 2016 represented 40,6% of GDP on average across OECD countries. While this level is lower that the cyclical peak of 44.3% in 2009, as the recovery of GDP growth has outpaced the rate of growth of government expenditures, it remains elevated from the pre-crisis level of 38.9% in 2007.

Average government investment spending across OECD countries amounted to 3% of GDP in 2016, decreasing from 4.1% in 2009. As a proportion of the government's total expenditure, the decrease is more pronounced than the decrease as a proportion of GDP, as shown in Figure 2.5. The decreases reflect the fact that public investment was one of the earliest areas identified for discretionary savings during the crisis period, and has remained a relatively low priority for additional discretionary expenditure as the recovery has continued. It remains to be seen whether the level of public investment will return to their pre-crisis levels. One of the enduring lessons of the crisis is the need for capital investments to be well-targeted and to demonstrate value-for-money. The governance framework for infrastructure investment is discussed in more detail in Chapter 8.

**Figure 2.4. General government revenue and expenditure**

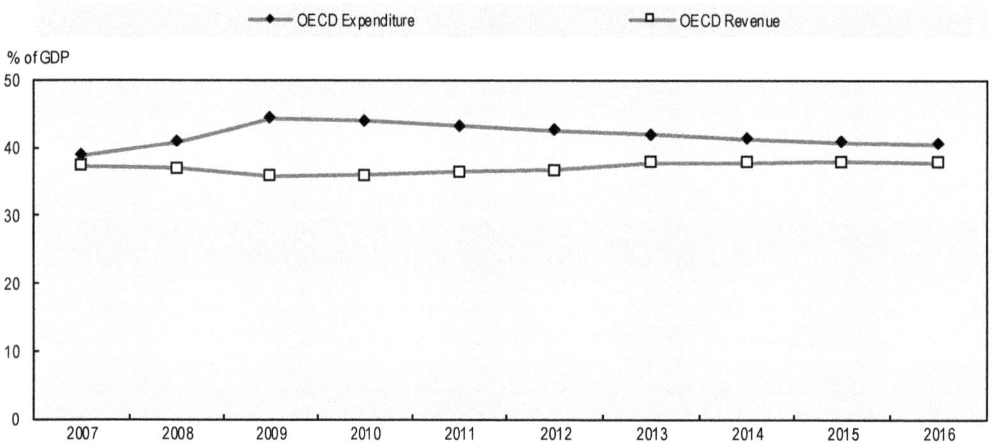


*Source*: OECD National Accounts Statistics (database).

StatLink http://dx.doi.org/10.1787/888933946362

**Figure 2.5. General government public investment**

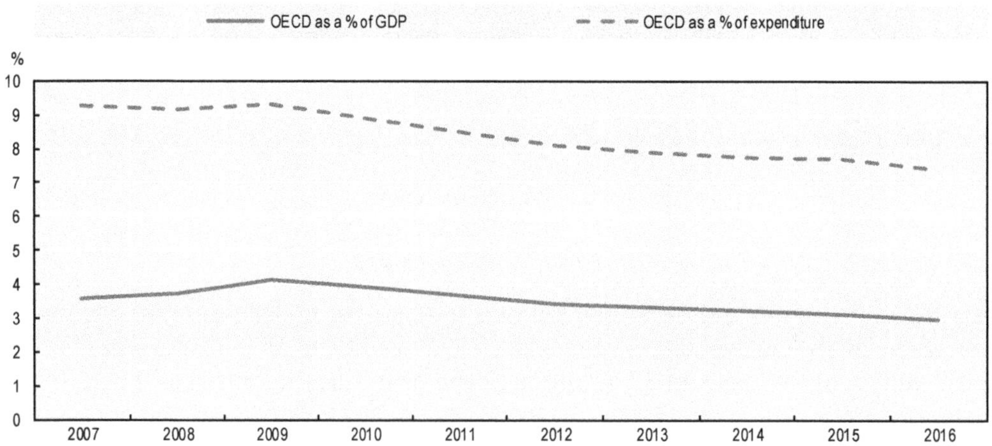


*Source*: OECD National Accounts Statistics (database).

StatLink http://dx.doi.org/10.1787/888933946381

### *2.1.4. Public expenditure: structure, composition and dynamics*

Governments' expenditures by function show how much governments allocate towards key areas, such as education, health, defence, social protection, public order and safety. In 2016, social protection represented the largest share of government expenditures across OECD countries, averaging 32.8%. Healthcare represented the second highest share reaching 18.9% of government expenditures on average. General public services – which include debt servicing – accounted for 13.2% of government expenditure in 2016, while education represented 12.5%. Defence, together with public order and safety, represented an average 9.4% of government expenditure among OECD countries for 2016; economic affairs reached 9.1% of public spending on average across OECD countries. The share of government expenditures is relatively low on other functions such as environmental protection, housing and community amenities and recreation, culture and religion.

Medium- or longer-term comparisons of government expenditures by function show some changes in the composition of expenditures across OECD countries. Between 2007 and 2016, the shares of spending in general public services, defence, public order and safety, economic affairs, education, and housing and community amenities have decreased, while the shares of health and social protection have increased. This suggests a "crowding out" of important areas of spending such as public security, as a result of increased pressures in the key demand-led areas of social protection and healthcare.

**Figure 2.6. Structure of general government expenditure by function (2016)**

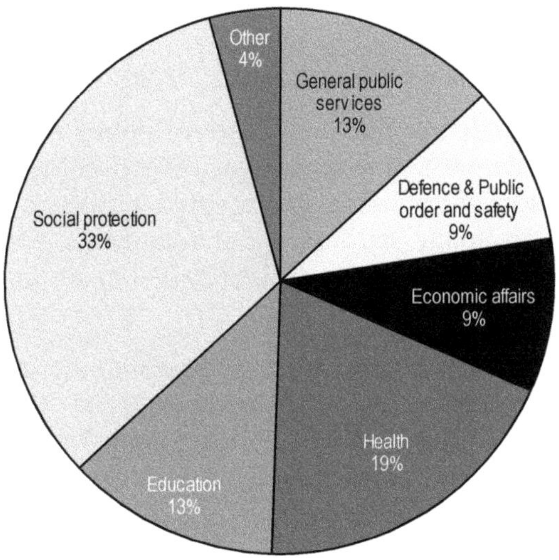


*Notes*: "Other" includes environment protection, recreation, culture and religion and housing and community amenities; Data are not available for Canada, Mexico, New Zealand and Turkey; Missing OECD member countries are not included in the OECD average.
*Sources*: OECD National Accounts Statistics (database); Eurostat Government finance statistics (database).

StatLink http://dx.doi.org/10.1787/888933946400

**Figure 2.7. Change in the structure of general government expenditure (2007-2016)**

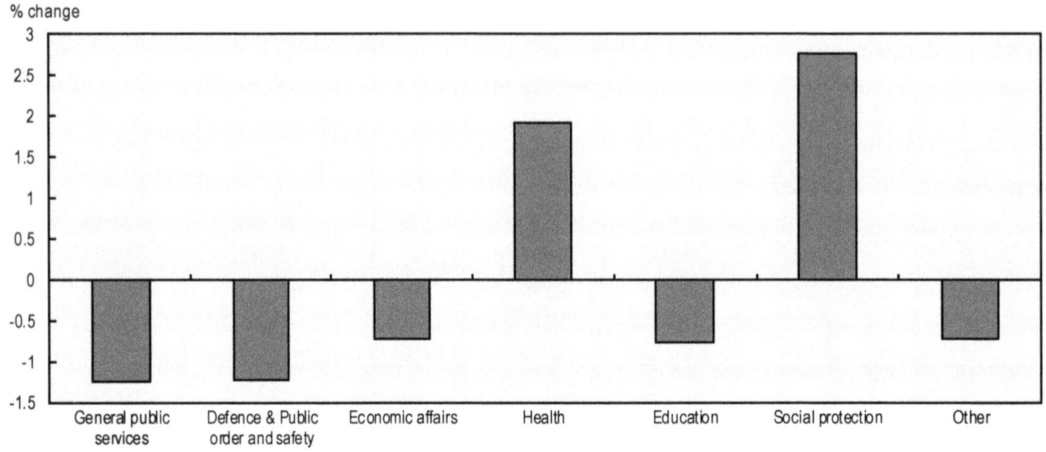


*Notes*: "Other" includes environment protection, recreation, culture and religion and housing and community amenities; Data are not available for Canada, Chile, Iceland, Mexico, New Zealand and Turkey. Missing OECD member countries are not included in the OECD average.
*Sources*: OECD National Accounts Statistics (database); Eurostat Government finance statistics (database);

StatLink http://dx.doi.org/10.1787/888933946419

## 2.2. Recent Fiscal Policy Developments

### *2.2.1. Continuity of fiscal policy and changed areas*

After the global financial crisis, distinctive phases of policy response are evident. In the wake of the financial crisis, an active/accommodative fiscal policy phase (2007-2009), during which fiscal balances significantly deteriorated, reflects a marked counter-cyclical response. With signs of economic stabilisation and concerns of rapid build-up of public debt, OECD countries entered a correction phase (2010-14) during which fiscal policy was geared towards gradual consolidation.

Sustained fiscal consolidation in a context of weak economic growth carries the risk of exacerbating pro-cyclical tendencies. To reconcile fiscal sustainability and growth objectives, OECD countries have pursued diverse and complex strategies by modifying the timing, speed and degree of fiscal correction and coordinating this approach with more carefully focused savings and efficiency exercises, and with targeted initiatives and structural reforms to spur growth.

From 2014, about a half (16) of OECD countries adopted a new fiscal policy plan, mostly in the context of changes of government or different political coalitions, or in some cases (Japan and Chile) in the same government. Of those other countries who reported that their fiscal policies were continuous, a significant minority (6 countries) reported that their fiscal policy plan had been significantly modified. Austria retained the same fiscal policy plan, although the government had changed. Sweden's plan was to turn large deficits to surplus. As this goal is achieved, the new fiscal plan is to maintain compliance with the targets of the fiscal policy framework (see Figure 2.8).

The changed areas of focus in cases of new or significantly modified fiscal policy plans are diverse. 7 countries (Chile, Finland, France, Japan, Mexico, Norway and Slovenia) pursued more rigorous fiscal consolidation, while 6 countries (Canada, Estonia, Hungary, Korea,

Netherlands and Slovak Republic) changed their course more towards fiscal expansion relative to the plans that were in place at the end of 2014.

In many cases, whether fiscal consolidation or expansion was at the fore, revised fiscal plans involved a changed composition of national revenues or expenditures compared to 2014 fiscal plans (see Figure 2.9).

**Figure 2.8. Continuity of fiscal policy**

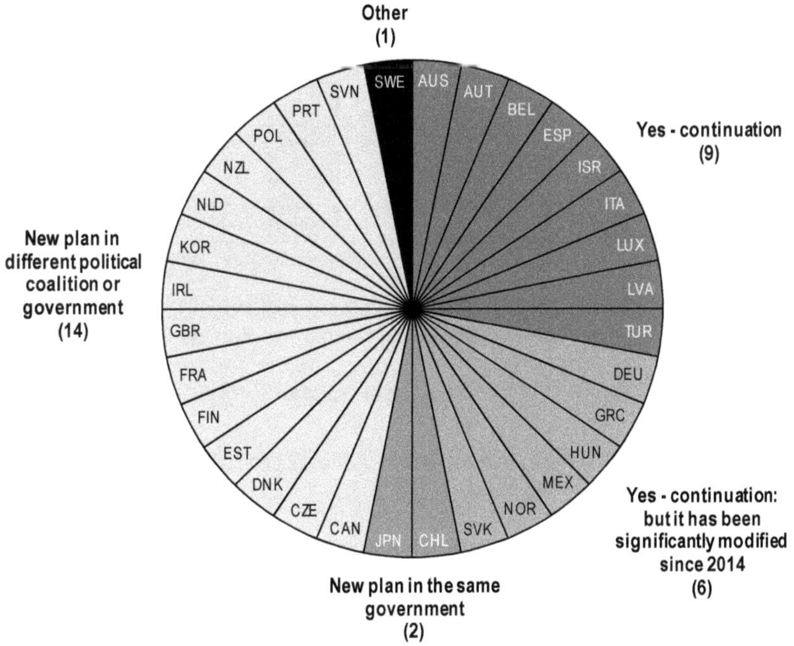


*Notes:* Austria has a same plan under new government. Sweden's plan was to turn large deficits to surplus. As this goal is achieved, the new plan is to continue to fulfil the targets of the fiscal policy framework; Data for Iceland, Switzerland and the United States are not available; Information on data for Israel: http://dx.doi.org/10.1787/888932315602.

*Source:* OECD (2018), OECD Fiscal Plans and Budgeting Framework Survey, Question 2, OECD, Paris.

StatLink http://dx.doi.org/10.1787/888933946438

**Figure 2.9. Changed areas in fiscal policy plans**

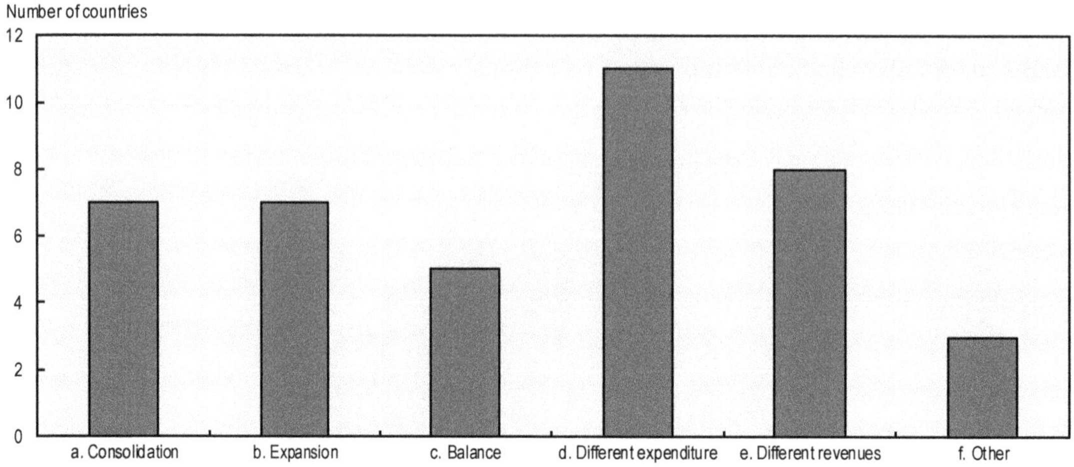


*Notes:* Data for Iceland, Switzerland and the United States are not available.
*Source:* OECD (2018), OECD Fiscal Plans and Budgeting Framework Survey, Question 3, OECD, Paris.

StatLink http://dx.doi.org/10.1787/888933946457

### *2.2.2. Priority areas that receive additional resources compared with the previous plan*

Priority areas of expenditure that receive additional resources show different features compared to the overall trends of changes in the structure of government expenditure since the financial crisis. While social protection and health remain high priority areas, defence and public order and safety received additional resources as security became a more pressing concern of European countries in the wake of terror attacks of recent years. In addition, many countries identified education as a priority area to support a high-skilled and dynamic economy. On the other hand, general public services, economic affairs, housing and community amenities and recreation, culture and religion received a lower priority.

**Figure 2.10. Priority areas that receive additional resources**

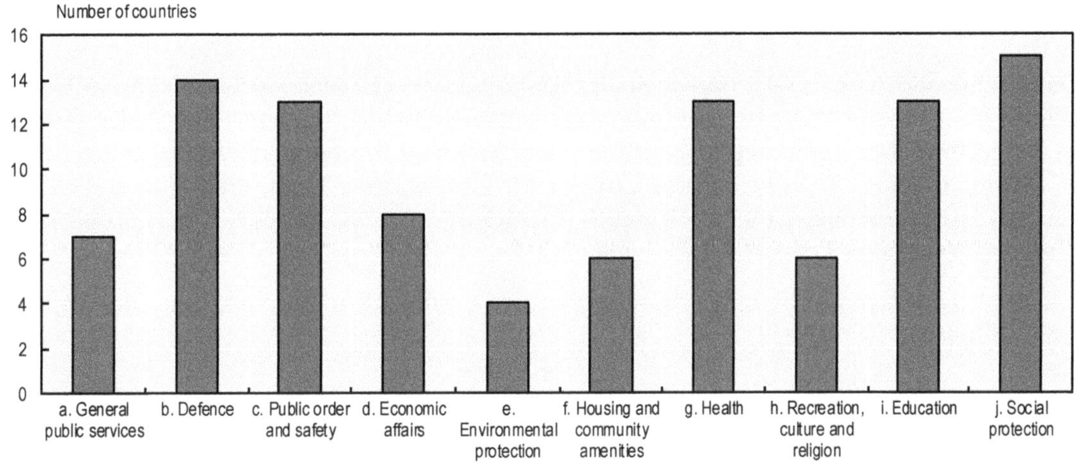


*Notes*: Data for Iceland, Switzerland and the United States are not available.
*Source:* OECD (2018), OECD Fiscal Plans and Budgeting Framework Survey, Question 4a, OECD, Paris.

StatLink http://dx.doi.org/10.1787/888933946476

## *2.2.3. Reform of budgetary governance*

Sound budgetary governance[4] is an important pillar of the overall framework of effective public governance, whereby the government and its agencies can identify and respond to the concerns of the public, resource and deliver public services in a sustainable manner, promote the wellbeing of citizens and command their trust. Developing a well-designed budgetary framework that is suitable to country-specific circumstances, while responding to international good practices, is a key to good budgetary governance.

Accordingly, since the end of 2014, countries have continued to place a priority on pursuing incremental reforms to the budgetary governance frameworks (see Table 2.1). Among the diverse budget reform approaches in the past three years, the most popular areas of attention have been fiscal rules (20 countries), spending reviews (18 countries), enhancements to the medium-term expenditure framework (13 countries) and improvements to budget transparency (13 countries).

Fiscal rules and fiscal objectives are helpful in managing budgets within clear, credible and predictable limits for fiscal policy and diverse efforts have been made in that regards. Some countries have set new fiscal rules (e.g. Italy, Slovenia); existing rules have been modified (Finland, the Netherlands and Portugal), replaced (Estonia) or repealed (Canada); or the fiscal target has been adjusted (Australia and Sweden).

A spending review[5] is an increasingly prevalent tool to improve the efficiency and effectiveness of public expenditure, as described in more detail in Section 7.2. Spending reviews have been newly implemented (Austria, Estonia, Hungary and Norway), modified in scope and approach (Canada and Ireland), linked to the annual budget (Israel), or supported through an independent authority (Spain).

In addition, various measures have been pursued to enhance budget transparency, openness and accessibility; review the process for economic projections; enhance the visualisation of data (Finland and Latvia) and provision of online date (Canada and Chile); and broaden national dialogue and civic participation (Ireland and Portugal). Chapter 6 provides further details of this topic.

Medium-term expenditure frameworks can be useful to align budgets with the medium-term strategic priorities. Reform efforts include introducing a legal framework (Israel and Italy) and clarifying the definitions and procedures in law (Czech Republic and Slovenia). Other areas of focus have been to improve financial reporting (9 countries; see also section 4.2), performance budgeting (9 countries; see Section 7.3) and to introduce independent fiscal institutions (8 countries; see Chapter 5). On the other hand, emerging and as-yet uncommon practices include green budgeting (2 countries) and fiscal risk analysis/reporting (5 countries; see Chapter 4.4.)

Each of these areas of budgetary governance are examined in more detail in the chapters that follow

**Table 2.1. Budget institutional framework reform (since the end of 2014)**

| | Fiscal Rules | MTEF | Budget transparency | Financial reporting | Performance budgeting | Green budgeting | Gender budgeting | Spending review | Fiscal risk analysis / reporting | Independent fiscal institutions |
|---|---|---|---|---|---|---|---|---|---|---|
| Australia | X | X | | X | | | | | | |
| Austria | | | | | | | | X | | |
| Belgium | | | | | | | | | | |
| Canada | X | X | X | X | X | | X | X | X | X |
| Chile | | | X | | | | | | | |
| Czech Republic | X | X | | | | | | | | X |
| Denmark | | | | | | | | | | |
| Estonia | X | | | | X | | | X | | |
| Finland | X | X | X | X | | X | | X | X | X |
| France | X | X | | | | | | X | | |
| Germany | | | | | | | | | | |
| Greece | | | | X | | | | | | |
| Hungary | X | | X | X | | | | | | |
| Ireland | | | X | | X | X | X | X | X | |
| Israel | X | X | X | | | | X | X | | |
| Italy | X | X | | | | | X | X | | X |
| Japan | X | X | | | | | | | | |
| Korea | X | X | X | | | | | | | |
| Latvia | | | X | | X | | | X | | |
| Luxembourg | | | | X | | | | X | | |
| Mexico | X | | | | | | | | | |
| Netherlands | X | X | X | | | | | | | X |
| New Zealand | | | | | | | | | | |
| Norway | X | | | | | | | X | | |
| Poland | X | X | | | X | | | X | | X |
| Portugal | X | X | X | X | X | | X | X | X | |
| Slovak Republic | | | | | X | | | X | | |
| Slovenia | X | X | X | | | | | X | | X |
| Spain | X | | X | | | | | X | | |
| Sweden | X | | | X | X | | | X | | X |

| | | | | | | | | | | |
|---|---|---|---|---|---|---|---|---|---|---|
| Turkey | | | X | X | X | | | X | | |
| United Kingdom | X | | | | | | | | X | |
| United States | | | | | | | | | | |
| Total | 20 | 13 | 13 | 9 | 9 | 2 | 5 | 18 | 5 | 8 |

*Notes*: Chile: Draft bill under approval by Congress which will create the Autonomous Fiscal Council (June 2018). If this project is approved, Chile would also appear in the table with "Independent fiscal institutions"; Data for Iceland, Switzerland and the United States are not available; Information on data for Israel: http://dx.doi.org/10.1787/888932315602.
*Source*: OECD (2018), OECD Fiscal Plans and Budgeting Framework Survey, Question 7, OECD, Paris.

## Notes

[1] General Assessment of the Macroeconomic Situation 2018 (OECD)

[2] The structural fiscal balance subtracts the cyclical effects and one-off events from both government expenditures and revenues. Separating the structural from the cyclical components of the fiscal balance provides a clearer picture of the underlying soundness and sustainability of fiscal policy.

[3] Government revenues include both taxes and social contributions.

[4] Budgetary governance refers to the processes, laws, structures and institutions in place for ensuring that the budgeting system meets its objectives in an effective, sustainable and enduring manner.

[5] Spending review is the process of identifying and weighting adopting savings options, based on the systematic scrutiny of baseline expenditure, which may take the form of efficiency reviews and/or strategic reviews, and may be either comprehensive in nature or more selective-focused.

# 3. Budgeting institutions, rules and frameworks

*In most OECD countries, the legislature has a constitutional authority over expenditure and revenue raising, while the various agencies of the executive branch, including the Central Budget Authority (CBA), more commonly have a legislative grounding. Over recent years, legally-based fiscal rules have become more prevalent in OECD countries, along with complementary practices such as medium-term expenditure frameworks (MTEFs) and top-down budgeting. In most cases, however, there appear to be gaps between the normative aspirations of these budgeting tools, and their binding character in practice: enforcement mechanisms for fiscal rules, MTEFs and top-down approaches are either weak or unclear. Some countries, however, appear to have been relatively successful at introducing consistent national frameworks which help the government to manage their public finances effectively and sustainably over the medium term.*

## 3.1. Institutional Frameworks

### *3.1.1. Legal basis for budgeting*

As a central process of public governance in all OECD countries, budgeting is based upon a range of different legal and constitutional frameworks in different countries. In many OECD countries, the budgetary role of the legislature (particularly with regard to authorisation of spending and revenue-raising) and of the Supreme Audit Institution (SAI) is grounded in the national constitution, while the roles and responsibilities of the different parts of the executive branch of government are mostly defined by law – see Table 3.1 below.

**Table 3.1. Legal and constitutional basis for budgeting**

| | Form and Structure of Budget | Roles and responsibilities of Executive | Roles and responsibilities of Legislature | Legislative authorisation of Spending | Legislative authorisation of revenue raising | Medium-term exepnditure framew ork | Supreme Audit Instiution |
|---|---|---|---|---|---|---|---|
| Australia | ⊗ | ⊟ | ⊗ | ◉ | ◉ | ⊗ | ⊗ |
| Austria | ◉ | ⊗ | ⊗ | ⊗ | ⊗ | ◉ | ⊗ |
| Belgium | ⊗ | ⊖ | ◉ | ⊗ | ◉ | ⊗ | ◉ |
| Canada | ⊟ | ⊗ | ◉ | ◉ | ◉ | ⊟ | ⊗ |
| Chile | ⊗ | ⊗ | ◉ | ◉ | ◉ | ⊗ | ◉ |
| Czech Republic | ⊗ | ⊗ | ⊗ | ⊗ | ⊗ | ⊗ | ◉ |
| Denmark | ⊞ | ⊟ | ⊞ | ◉ | ◉ | ⊗ | ◉ |
| Estonia | ⊗ | ⊖ | ⊗ | ⊖ | ⊗ | ⊗ | ⊖ |
| Finland | ◉ | ◉ | ◉ | ◉ | ◉ | ⊗ | ◉ |
| France | ◉ | ◉ | ◉ | ◉ | ◉ | ◉ | ◉ |
| Germany | ◉ | ⊗ | ◉ | ◉ | ◉ | ◉ | ◉ |
| Greece | ⊗ | ⊗ | ◉ | ⊗ | ◉ | ⊗ | ◉ |
| Hungary | ⊗ | ⊗ | ◉ | ⊗ | ⊗ | ⊗ | ◉ |
| Iceland | ⊗ | ⊟ | ⊞ | ⊗ | ⊟ | ⊗ | ⊗ |
| Ireland | ⊟ | ⊗ | ⊗ | ⊗ | ⊗ | ⊗ | ⊗ |
| Israel | ◉ | ⊗ | ⊗ | ⊗ | ⊗ | ⊗ | ⊖ |
| Italy | ⊗ | ⊗ | ◉ | ◉ | ◉ | ⊗ | ⊗ |
| Japan | ◉ | ◉ | ◉ | ◉ | ◉ | ⊞ | ◉ |
| Korea | ⊗ | ⊗ | ◉ | ◉ | ◉ | ⊗ | ◉ |
| Latvia | ⊗ | ⊗ | ◉ | ⊖ | ⊗ | ⊗ | ⊗ |
| Luxembourg | ◉ | ⊗ | ⊗ | ◉ | ◉ | ⊗ | ◉ |
| Mexico | ◉ | ⊗ | ◉ | ⊗ | ⊗ | ⊗ | ⊗ |
| Netherlands | ⊗ | ⊗ | ⊗ | ⊗ | ⊗ | ⊗ | ◉ |
| New Zealand | ⊗ | ⊗ | ⊗ | ◉ | ◉ | ⊗ | ⊖ |
| Norw ay | ⊗ | ⊖ | ◉ | ◉ | ◉ | ⊠ | ◉ |
| Poland | ⊗ | ◉ | ◉ | ◉ | ◉ | ⊗ | ◉ |
| Portugal | ◉ | ⊞ | ◉ | ⊗ | ◉ | ⊗ | ◉ |
| Slovak Republic | ⊗ | ⊗ | ⊗ | ⊗ | ⊗ | ⊗ | ⊗ |
| Slovenia | ◉ | ⊗ | ⊗ | ⊗ | ⊗ | ⊗ | ⊗ |
| Spain | ◉ | ⊗ | ◉ | ◉ | ◉ | ⊗ | ◉ |
| Sw eden | ◉ | ⊗ | ◉ | ◉ | ◉ | ⊗ | ◉ |
| Sw itzerland | ⊗ | ⊗ | ⊗ | ⊗ | ⊠ | ⊗ | ⊗ |
| Turkey | ◉ | ⊗ | ◉ | ◉ | ◉ | ⊗ | ◉ |
| United Kingdom | ⊞ | ⊞ | ⊞ | ⊞ | ⊞ | ⊗ | ⊗ |
| **Key** | **Total** | | | | | | |
| ◉ Constitution | 13 | 4 | 19 | 17 | 20 | 3 | 19 |
| ⊗ Law | 17 | 22 | 12 | 14 | 11 | 28 | 12 |
| ⊖ Regulation | 0 | 3 | 0 | 2 | 0 | 0 | 3 |
| ⊞ Organisational or internal rules | 2 | 2 | 3 | 1 | 1 | 1 | 0 |
| ⊟ No formal basis | 2 | 3 | 0 | 0 | 1 | 1 | 0 |
| ⊠ Not applicable | 0 | 0 | 0 | 0 | 1 | 1 | 0 |

*Notes*: Data for the United States are not available; Information on data for Israel: http://dx.doi.org/10.1787/888932315602.
*Source*: OECD (2018), OECD Budget Practices and Procedures Survey, Question 6, OECD, Paris.

StatLink http://dx.doi.org/10.1787/888933947483

The CBA[1] is in charge of leading the budget process and therefore has the capacity to influence institutional arrangements for budgeting. By steering the budget process, the CBA can contribute to achieve a well-structured budget that, in turn, can give a strategic direction of the government. The Ministry of Finance and/or Economics represents the most common choice of location across OECD countries. While the handling of the expenditure and revenue sides of the budget is managed separately in most countries, in three cases (Australia, Canada and Ireland) the CBA is formally split between two ministries. In the case of the United States, the expenditure and revenue policy is divided between the Office of Management and Budget (OMB) and the Department of the Treasury.

The head of the CBA is often the main person responsible for logistical planning and preparation of the government's budget. In this capacity, he or she is also responsible for liaising with other stakeholders (including other spending units) in order to facilitate the co-ordination of the budget process of and ensuring good relations. In over half of OECD countries (21 countries), the head of the CBA is a senior civil servant i.e. a government official who ordinarily remains in the position when there is a change in government; while in 11 countries the head of the CBA is a political appointee i.e. a person who generally does not remain in the position when there is a change in Government.

**Figure 3.1. Location of CBA**

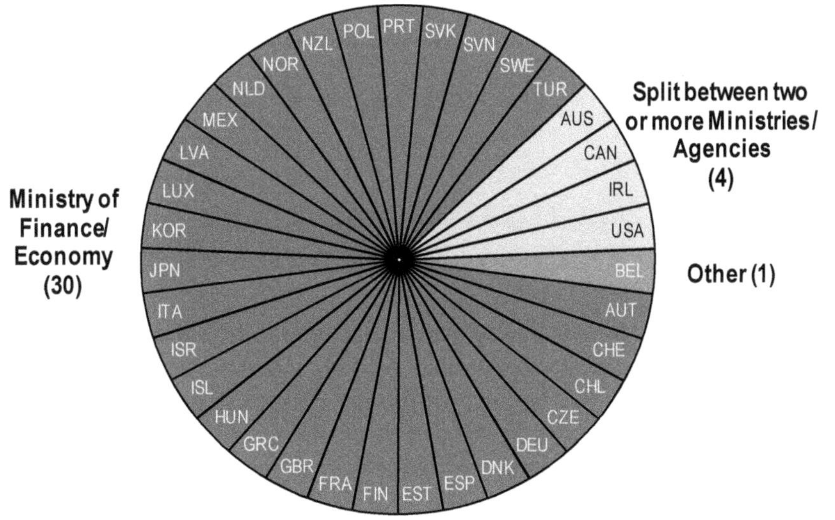


*Notes*: Information for the United States is not available through the survey but collected through publicly available data; Information on data for Israel: http://dx.doi.org/10.1787/888932315602.
*Source*: OECD (2018), OECD Budget Practices and Procedures Survey, Question 1a, OECD, Paris.

StatLink http://dx.doi.org/10.1787/888933946495

**Figure 3.2. Head of CBA**

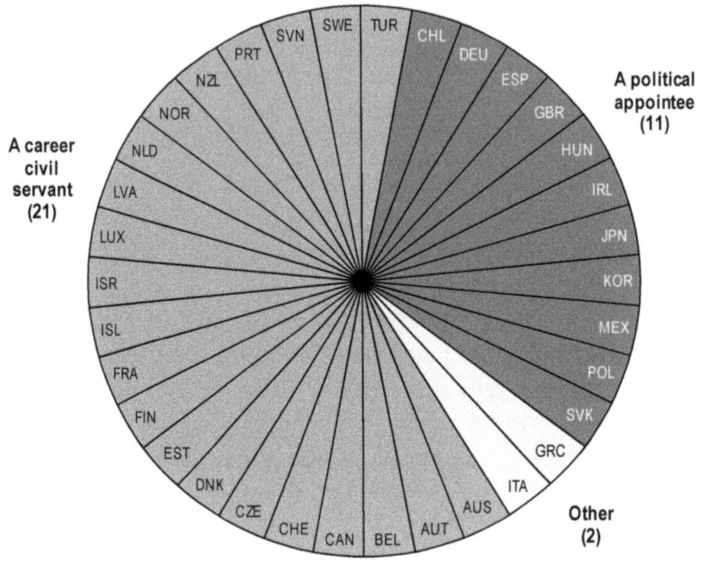


*Notes*: Data for the United States are not available; Information on data for Israel: http://dx.doi.org/10.1787/888932315602.
*Source*: OECD (2018), OECD Budget Practices and Procedures Survey, Question 2, OECD, Paris.

StatLink http://dx.doi.org/10.1787/888933946514

## *3.1.2. Responsibilities of the CBA*

The CBA takes care of a variety of tasks concerning the budget process. The extent and the nature of the CBA's involvement and its functions vary across countries (see Table 3.2 below).

In most OECD countries, the CBA exercises the responsibility of drafting budget circulars, determining ceilings for overall expenditure by line ministries, negotiating with the line ministries, developing executive budget proposals, and testifying before the legislature in regard to the exercise of these functions. For the majority of OECD countries, other tasks such as the methodology for fiscal projections and monitoring performance of line ministries are split with other institutions or agencies. In about half of OECD countries, the methodology for preparing macroeconomic forecasts is not among the responsibilities of the CBA.

**Table 3.2. Responsibilities of the CBA**

| Country | Drafting budget circular | Methodology for macroeconomic projections | Methodology for fiscal projections | Determining ceilings for aggregate/ overall expenditure | Determining ceilings for line ministries | Developing executive budget proposal | Testifying before legislature | Authorisation of line ministries outlays | Monitoring performance of line ministries/ agencies | Controlling public/ civil service employment |
|---|---|---|---|---|---|---|---|---|---|---|
| Australia | ◉ | ◉ | ⊗ | ◉ | ⊠ | ⊠ | ⊗ | ⊗ | ⊗ | ⊗ |
| Austria | ◉ | ⊖ | ⊗ | ◉ | ◉ | ◉ | ◉ | ◉ | ◉ | ⊖ |
| Belgium | ◉ | ⊖ | ⊗ | ◉ | ◉ | ◉ | ⊠ | ◉ | ◉ | ◉ |
| Canada | ◉ | ⊗ | ◉ | ◉ | ◉ | ◉ | ⊗ | ⊗ | ⊗ | ◉ |
| Chile | ◉ | ⊖ | ⊗ | ⊗ | ◉ | ◉ | ◉ | ◉ | ◉ | ◉ |
| Czech Republic | ◉ | ⊖ | ⊗ | ⊖ | ◉ | ◉ | ◉ | ◉ | ⊖ | ⊗ |
| Denmark | ◉ | ⊗ | ⊗ | ◉ | ◉ | ◉ | ○ | ⊖ | ◉ | ◉ |
| Estonia | ◉ | ◉ | ◉ | ◉ | ◉ | ◉ | ⊖ | ⊖ | ⊗ | ⊖ |
| Finland | ◉ | ⊖ | ⊖ | ⊖ | ⊖ | ◉ | ⊠ | ⊖ | ⊗ | ⊖ |
| France | ◉ | ⊗ | ⊗ | ◉ | ◉ | ◉ | ⊠ | ◉ | ⊗ | ◉ |
| Germany | ◉ | ⊖ | ⊖ | ◉ | ◉ | ◉ | ◉ | ◉ | ◉ | ◉ |
| Greece | ◉ | ⊖ | ⊗ | ◉ | ◉ | ◉ | ◉ | ⊖ | ⊗ | ⊗ |
| Hungary | ◉ | ◉ | ◉ | ◉ | ⊗ | ◉ | ◉ | ⊗ | ⊗ | ⊗ |
| Iceland | ◉ | ⊗ | ⊗ | ◉ | ◉ | ◉ | ⊗ | ⊗ | ⊗ | ⊗ |
| Ireland | ◉ | ◉ | ⊗ | ◉ | ◉ | ◉ | ⊖ | ⊖ | ⊗ | ⊖ |
| Israel | ◉ | ⊖ | ⊗ | ◉ | ◉ | ◉ | ◉ | ◉ | ◉ | ◉ |
| Italy | ◉ | ⊖ | ⊗ | ⊗ | ⊗ | ⊗ | ⊖ | ◉ | ⊗ | ◉ |
| Japan | ◉ | ⊖ | ⊖ | ◉ | ◉ | ◉ | ◉ | ⊖ | ⊗ | ⊖ |
| Korea | ◉ | ⊗ | ⊗ | ◉ | ◉ | ◉ | ⊗ | ⊗ | ⊗ | ⊗ |
| Latvia | ⊗ | ⊗ | ◉ | ◉ | ◉ | ⊗ | ⊗ | ⊠ | ⊗ | ◉ |
| Luxembourg | ⊗ | ⊖ | ⊗ | ⊗ | ⊗ | ◉ | ⊖ | ⊖ | ⊗ | ⊗ |
| Mexico | ◉ | ⊖ | ⊗ | ◉ | ◉ | ◉ | ◉ | ◉ | ◉ | ◉ |
| Netherlands | ◉ | ⊖ | ⊗ | ◉ | ◉ | ⊗ | ⊗ | ◉ | ◉ | ⊗ |
| New Zealand | ◉ | ◉ | ◉ | ⊠ | ⊠ | ◉ | ◉ | ◉ | ◉ | ⊖ |
| Norway | ◉ | ⊗ | ⊗ | ⊗ | ⊖ | ⊠ | ⊠ | ⊖ | ⊖ | ⊠ |
| Poland | ◉ | ◉ | ◉ | ◉ | ◉ | ◉ | ⊗ | ⊠ | ◉ | ⊠ |
| Portugal | ◉ | ⊖ | ⊗ | ⊖ | ⊖ | ⊗ | ⊖ | ⊖ | ⊖ | ⊖ |
| Slovak Republic | ◉ | ◉ | ◉ | ◉ | ◉ | ◉ | ◉ | ⊗ | ⊗ | ◉ |
| Slovenia | ◉ | ⊖ | ◉ | ◉ | ◉ | ⊗ | ◉ | ◉ | ⊗ | ⊖ |
| Spain | ◉ | ⊗ | ⊗ | ◉ | ◉ | ◉ | ⊖ | ⊖ | ⊖ | ⊗ |
| Sweden | ◉ | ⊖ | ⊗ | ◉ | ⊠ | ⊗ | ⊖ | ◉ | ⊗ | ⊠ |
| Switzerland | ◉ | ⊗ | ◉ | ◉ | ⊗ | ◉ | ◉ | ◉ | ◉ | ⊗ |
| Turkey | ⊗ | ⊗ | ⊗ | ⊗ | ⊗ | ◉ | ◉ | ◉ | ⊗ | ⊗ |
| United Kingdom | ⊠ | ⊗ | ⊗ | ◉ | ◉ | ◉ | ⊗ | ◉ | ⊠ | ◉ |
| Total | | | | | | | | | | |
| ◉ | 30 | 7 | 9 | 25 | 23 | 26 | 14 | 16 | 11 | 12 |
| ⊗ | 3 | 11 | 22 | 5 | 5 | 6 | 8 | 6 | 18 | 11 |
| ⊖ | 0 | 16 | 3 | 3 | 3 | 0 | 8 | 10 | 4 | 8 |
| ⊠ | 1 | 0 | 0 | 1 | 3 | 2 | 4 | 2 | 1 | 3 |

Key

| | |
|---|---|
| ◉ | Sole responsibility of CBA |
| ⊗ | Shared responsibility between CBA and other institutions |
| ⊖ | Not a responsibility of CBA |
| ⊠ | Not applicable |

*Notes*: Data for the United States are not available; Information on data for Israel: http://dx.doi.org/10.1787/888932315602.

*Source:* OECD (2018), OECD Budget Practices and Procedures Survey, Question 3, OECD, Paris.

StatLink http://dx.doi.org/10.1787/888933947502

## 3.2. Fiscal objectives and fiscal rules

### *3.2.1. Framework for sound and sustainable fiscal policy*

Sound fiscal policy is one which avoids build-up of large, unsustainable debts, and which uses favourable economic times to build up resilience and buffers against more difficult times, so that the needs of citizens and stakeholders can be addressed in an effective and enduring manner.

Table 3.3 below illustrates that fiscal policy objectives or constraints which are grounded in legislation, the constitution or binding international agreement – in other words "fiscal rules" – are now in force in 28 OECD countries. At least in the case of countries who are members of the European Union, there has been a strong impetus over the past 6 years towards introduction of national and Treaty-based fiscal rules, intended to safeguard against pro-cyclical fiscal policy. However several OECD countries have a requirement, whether arising from political convention or from a legislative provision, to establish medium-term fiscal objectives which are not, in themselves, legally binding but which function instead as elements of political accountability.

**Table 3.3. Frameworks for fiscal policy**

| | Political convention for set-up of medium-term fiscal policy objectives | Legal and/or constitutional requirement for set-up of medium-term fiscal policy objectives | National constiution contains specific fiscal rules | National legislation contains specific fiscal rules | International agreements contain specific fiscal rules |
|---|---|---|---|---|---|
| Australia | | X | | | |
| Austria | | | X | X | X |
| Belgium | X | X | | | X |
| Canada | X | | | | |
| Chile | | X | | | |
| Czech Republic | | X | | X | X |
| Denmark | X | | | X | X |
| Estonia | | | | X | X |
| Finland | X | | | X | X |
| France | | | | X | X |
| Germany | | | X | X | X |
| Greece | | | | X | X |
| Hungary | | | X | X | X |
| Iceland | | | | X | |
| Ireland | X | X | | X | X |
| Israel | | | | X | |
| Italy | | | X | X | X |
| Japan | X | | | X | |
| Korea | | X | | X | |
| Latvia | | | | X | X |
| Luxembourg | X | | | X | X |
| Mexico | | X | X | X | |
| Netherlands | X | X | | X | X |
| New Zealand | | X | | | |
| Norway | | | | | |
| Poland | | | X | X | X |
| Portugal | | X | | X | X |
| Slovak Republic | | | | X | X |
| Slovenia | | | X | | X |
| Spain | | X | X | X | X |
| Sweden | | X | | X | X |
| Switzerland | | | X | X | |
| Turkey | X | | | | |

| | | | | | |
|---|---|---|---|---|---|
| United Kingdom | | X | | | X |
| Total | 9 | 13 | 9 | 25 | 22 |

*Note*: In Norway, the fiscal rule is a political agreement in Parliament; All 19 Member States of the Eurozone (plus Denmark who has chosen to opt-in) are part of the European Fiscal Compact, which is the fiscal chapter of the Treaty on Stability, Coordination and Governance in the Economic and Monetary Union (TSCG). This intergovernmental treaty is here reflected as an international agreement.
Data for the United States are not available; Information on data for Israel: http://dx.doi.org/10.1787/888932315602.
*Source:* OECD (2018), OECD Budget Practices and Procedures Survey, Question 8, OECD, Paris.

### *3.2.2. Types and legal foundation of fiscal objectives and fiscal rules*

The OECD refers to "fiscal objectives" as targets that may not be legally binding but mandated through political decision or established custom and practice; on the other hand, "fiscal rules" are a standing constraint on fiscal policy through numerical limits on the budgetary aggregates, usually based in legislation. A fiscal rule has two fundamental characteristics. First, it presents a constraint that binds political decisions made by the legislature and by the executive. And second, it serves as a concrete indicator of the executive's fiscal management. The intention behind both fiscal objectives and fiscal rules is to provide a counterweight to the "deficit bias" that is presumed to be a feature of budgeting in democratic economies and to strengthen incentives towards responsible and sustainable fiscal policies (Schick, 2003).

Economic, political and social factors at the national level, as well as the specificities of the institutional arrangements of the budget process, must be taken into account in the formulation of fiscal rules. Four broad distinctive categories of fiscal objectives and rules exist: budget balance, debt, expenditure and revenue as outlined in Box 3.1 below.

**Box 3.1. Type of fiscal rules**

1. **Budget balance (i.e. deficit or surplus) rules:** directly target the budget balance (i.e. the gap between government spending and revenues), e.g. a requirement to run a balanced position; not to exceed a defined deficit limit; or a requirement to attain a defined surplus at minimum. Such rules can be expressed in nominal or cyclically-adjusted terms, usually by reference to a percentage of GDP.
2. **Debt rules**: limit the amount of government debt that can be accumulated and can be expressed in nominal terms, as a debt-to-GDP ratio, or as an explicit reduction of the debt-to-GDP ratio.
3. **Expenditure rules**: limit the amount of government spending, or the rate of growth in government spending, and can be expressed in nominal or real terms or as an expenditure-to-GDP ratio.
4. **Revenue rules**: impose constraints on the tax-to-GDP ratio and place restrictions on government revenues raised in excess of projected amounts.

Budget balance, debt and expenditure objectives and rules are prevalently used, while revenue objectives and rules are relatively less used across OECD countries.

Fiscal objectives and rules can have different national legal foundations. Fiscal rules may be enshrined in constitutions, or primary or secondary legislation which usually will have long-lasting constraints, while they may be stipulated in public political commitments or in internal rules or policies.

Most of fiscal objectives and rules are based on national legislation and the political basis comes next. Internal rules and policies are used less often.

**Table 3.4. Fiscal objectives and fiscal rules**

| | Budget balance (deficit / surplus) | | | | Debt | | | Expenditure | | Revenue | |
|---|---|---|---|---|---|---|---|---|---|---|---|
| | Headline / nominal budget balance | Structural / cyclical budget balance | Primary budget balance | "Golden rule" | Debt ceiling in a level or as a percentage of GDP | Debt reduction target | Debt target in a level or as a percentage of GDP | Expenditure level/ceiling | Expenditure growth rate | Upper limits on revenue | Constraints on allocation of higher than expected revenues |
| Australia | ◉ | | | | | ◉ | | | | ◉ | ◉ |
| Austria | ⊗ | ⊗ | ⊗ | | ⊗ | ⊗ | ⊗ | ⊗ | ⊗ | | |
| Belgium | | ◉ | | | ⊗ | ⊗ | ⊗ | | ⊗ | | |
| Canada | ◉ | | | | | | ◉ | | | | |
| Chile | | ⊞ | | | | | | ⊗ | | | |
| Czech Republic | ⊗ | ⊗ | ⊗ | ◉ | ⊗ | ◉ | ◉ | ⊗ | | ⊗ | ⊗ |
| Denmark | ⊗ | ⊗ | ⊗ | | ⊗ | | | ⊗ | | | |
| Estonia | ⊗ | ⊗ | | | ⊗ | | | ◉ | ⊗ | | |
| Finland | ⊗◉ | ⊗ | | | | | ⊗◉ | ◉ | ⊗ | | |
| France | ⊗ | ⊗ | | | | ⊗ | ⊗ | ⊗ | ⊗ | | ⊗ |
| Germany | ⊗ | ⊗ | | | ⊗ | | ⊗ | ◉ | ◉ | | |
| Greece | | ⊗ | ◬ | | ⊗ | ⊗ | | | | | |
| Hungary | ⊗ | ⊗ | | | ⊗ | ⊗ | ⊗ | | ⊗ | | |
| Iceland | ⊗ | ⊗ | ⊗ | | ⊗ | ⊗ | | | | | |
| Ireland | ⊗ | ⊗ | | | ⊗ | ⊗ | ⊗ | ⊗ | ⊗ | | ⊗ |
| Israel | ⊗ | | ⊗ | | | ◬ | ◬ | | ⊗ | | ⊗ |
| Italy | | ⊗ | | | | ⊗ | ⊗ | | ⊗ | | ⊗ |
| Japan | ⊗ | | ⊞ | ⊗ | | | ⊞ | ⊞ | ⊞ | | ⊗ |
| Korea | ⊞ | | | | | | ⊞ | ⊞ | ⊞ | ⊞ | ⊗ |
| Latvia | ⊗ | ⊗ | | | ⊗ | | ⊗ | ⊗ | ⊗ | ⊗ | |
| Luxembourg | | ⊗ | | | ⊗ | | ◉ | | ⊗ | | |
| Mexico | ⊗ | ⊗ | ⊗ | | ⊗ | ⊗ | ⊗ | ⊗ | ⊗ | ⊗ | ⊗ |
| Netherlands | ⊗ | ⊗ | | | ⊗ | ⊗ | ⊗ | ⊗ | ⊗ | ⊗ | ⊗ |
| New Zealand | ◉ | | | | | ◉ | ◉ | | ◉ | ◉ | |
| Norway | ◉ | ◉ | | | | | | | | | |
| Poland | ⊗ | ◬ | | | ⊗ | | | | ⊗ | | |
| Portugal | | ⊗ | | | ⊗ | | | ⊗ | | | |
| Slovak Republic | ◉ | ⊗ | | | ⊗ | ⊗ | ⊗ | ⊗ | ⊗ | ⊗ | ⊗ |
| Slovenia | ⊗ | ⊗ | | | ⊗ | ⊗ | ⊗ | ⊗ | ⊗ | | |
| Spain | ⊗ | ⊗ | | | ⊗ | ⊗ | ⊗ | ⊗ | ⊗ | | ⊗ |
| Sweden | ⊗ | ◉ | | | | | ◉ | ⊗ | ⊗ | | |
| Switzerland | | ⊗ | | | | | | | | ⊗ | |
| Turkey | ⊞ | ⊞ | ⊞ | | ⊗ | | ⊞ | ⊗ | ⊞ | | |
| United Kingdom | ⊗ | ⊗ | | | | ⊗ | | ⊗ | | | |
| **Key** | **Total** | | | | | | | | | | |
| ◉ political basis | 6 | 3 | 0 | 1 | 0 | 3 | 6 | 3 | 2 | 2 | 1 |
| ⊗ legal basis | 20 | 22 | 6 | 1 | 20 | 14 | 14 | 16 | 18 | 6 | 11 |
| ⊞ internal rules / policies | 2 | 2 | 2 | 0 | 0 | 0 | 3 | 2 | 3 | 1 | 0 |
| ◬ other basis | 0 | 1 | 1 | 0 | 0 | 1 | 1 | 0 | 0 | 0 | 0 |
| Not applicable | 7 | 6 | 25 | 32 | 14 | 16 | 11 | 13 | 11 | 25 | 22 |

*Notes:* All 19 Member States of the Eurozone (plus Denmark who has chosen to opt-in) are part of the European Fiscal Compact, which is the fiscal chapter of the Treaty on Stability, Coordination and Governance in the Economic and Monetary Union (TSCG). The main provisions of this intergovernmental treaty are the requirement to have a balanced budget rule in domestic legal orders and defined debt rules, among the requirement for reporting and correction mechanisms.

Data for the United States are not available; Information on data for Israel: http://dx.doi.org/10.1787/888932315602.

*Source:* OECD (2018), OECD Budget Practices and Procedures Survey, Question 11, OECD, Paris.

StatLink http://dx.doi.org/10.1787/888933947540

### *3.2.3. Enforcement of fiscal rules*

A longstanding issue concerning fiscal rules has been how to implement enforcement mechanisms in cases of non-compliance. In order to guarantee compliance, many economies have enforcement mechanisms in place outlining the procedures in the event of a deviation from the rule. An emerging trend among OECD countries is to combine political commitment with monitoring by independent fiscal institutions.

**Table 3.5. Enforcement of fiscal rules**

| | None | Automatic correction mechanisms | Automatic sanctions | Entity must implement measures | Proposal with corrective measures presented to the legislature | Explanation with reasons for non-compliance presented to legislature |
|---|---|---|---|---|---|---|
| Australia | x | | | | | |
| Austria | | | x | | | |
| Belgium | | | | x | | x |
| Canada | x | | | | | |
| Chile | x | | | | | |
| Czech Republic | | x | | x | x | x |
| Denmark | | x | x | | | |
| Estonia | | | | | x | x |
| Finland | | x | | | x | x |
| France | | x | | | x | x |
| Germany | | | | x | x | |
| Greece | | | | x | x | |
| Hungary | | | | | x | |
| Iceland | x | | | | | |
| Ireland | | x | | | x | x |
| Israel | | | | x | | |
| Italy | | | | x | | x |
| Japan | x | | | | | |
| Korea | x | | | | | |
| Latvia | | x | | | x | x |
| Luxembourg | | | | | x | |
| Mexico | | | | | | x |
| Netherlands | | | | | x | |
| New Zealand | | | | | x | x |
| Norway | x | | | | | |
| Poland | | x | x | | x | |
| Portugal | | | | | x | |
| Slovak Republic | | x | x | x | | x |
| Slovenia | | x | | x | x | x |
| Spain | | x | x | x | x | |
| Sweden | | | | | x | x |
| Switzerland | | x | x | | x | |
| Turkey | x | | | | | |
| United Kingdom | | | | | | x |
| Total | 8 | 11 | 6 | 9 | 18 | 14 |

*Note*: Data for the United States are not available; Information on data for Israel: http://dx.doi.org/10.1787/888932315602.
*Source:* OECD (2018), OECD Budget Practices and Procedures Survey, Question 12a, OECD, Paris.

Eighteen OECD countries have a procedure whereby the executive must propose corrective measures in the event on non-compliance, and 14 countries require formal explanation for non-compliance (a so-called "comply-or-explain" rule). Automatic correction mechanism and entity implementation of measures are also used widely; eight countries reported that they do not have enforcement mechanisms.

### *3.2.4. Alignment with medium-term strategic planning*

Governments can closely align their budgets with medium-term strategic and political priorities by developing a stronger medium-term dimension in the budgeting processes beyond the annual cycle, and by organising and structuring the budget allocations in a manner that corresponds with national objectives. In addition, nurturing a close working relationship between the CBA and the other institutions at the centre of government is important, given the inter-dependencies between the budget process and the achievement of government-wide policies.

Institutions with a primary responsibility for national strategic planning are diverse and include the CBA itself (8 countries), coalition/political parties (11 countries), other institutions at centre of government (7 countries) and a Committee of government (4 countries).

In order to secure alignment between budgeting and strategic planning, most OECD countries recognise a leadership role for the CBA (28 countries) while others point to a leadership role of another institution at the centre of government (8 countries). Mechanisms to promote such an alignment include discussion at Cabinet/Council of minister (15 countries) or the use a a medium-term expenditure framework MTEF which explicitly aligns budgetary allocations with medium-term plans and priorities (14 countries) – see Figure 3.4.

**Figure 3.3. Responsible institution of strategic planning**

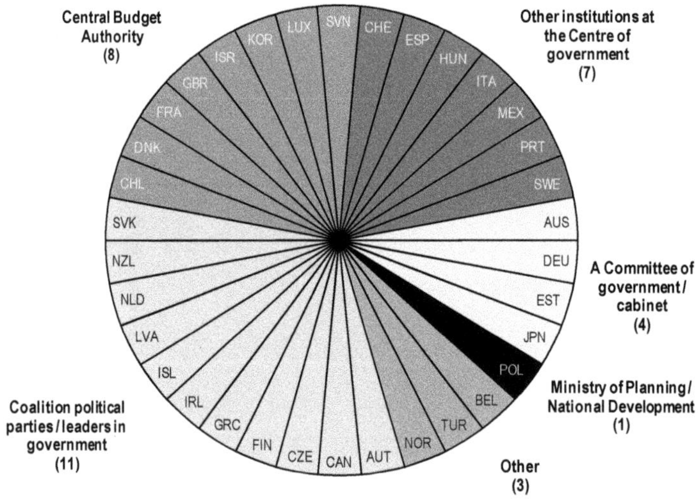


*Notes:* Data for the United States are not available. Information on data for Israel: http://dx.doi.org/10.1787/888932315602.
*Source:* OECD (2018), OECD Budget Practices and Procedures Survey, Question 18.

StatLink http://dx.doi.org/10.1787/888933946533

**Figure 3.4. Alignment mechanisms between budget and strategic planning**

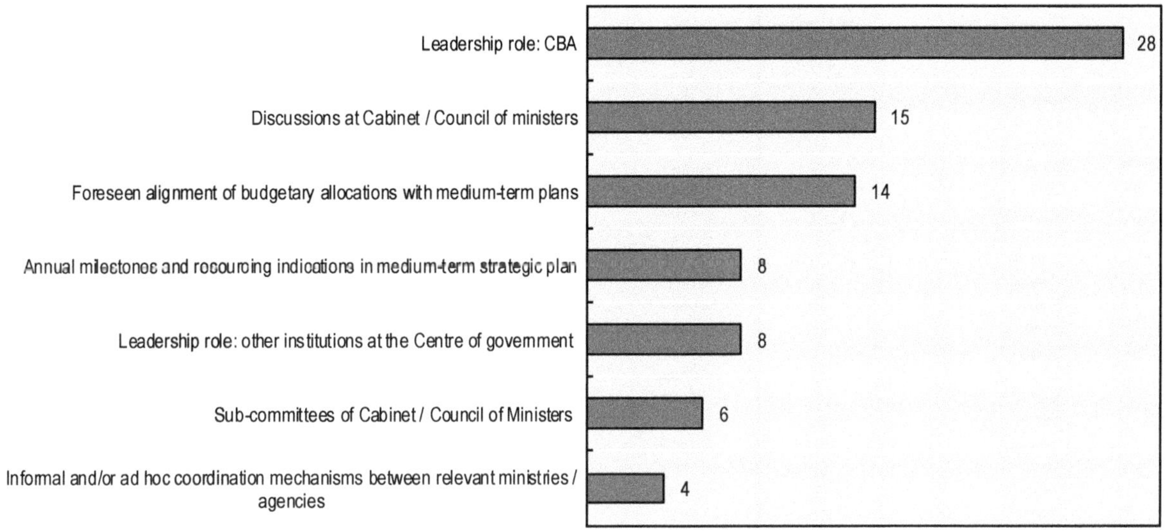


*Source:* 2017/2018 OECD Budget Practices and Procedures Survey. Question 20

StatLink http://dx.doi.org/10.1787/888933946552

## *3.2.5. Medium-term expenditure framework*

### *Main structure of MTEF*

A medium-term expenditure framework (MTEF) is a structured approach to integrating fiscal policy and budgeting over a multi-year horizon, and links fiscal forecasting, fiscal objectives or rules and forward planning of multi-year budget estimates. Forward estimates of expenditures become the basis of budget negotiations in the years following the budget and the forward estimates are reconciled with final outcomes in fiscal outcome reports. Successful implementation of MTEFs has many potential benefits. MTEFs can underpin fiscal discipline, to the extent that the forward ceilings are framed by reference to fiscal limits and available resources. MTEFs can improve the effectiveness of public spending by harmonising public expenditure with national priorities. Furthermore, from the point of view of line ministry and agency managers, the medium-term perspective signals the direction of policy and funding changes thereby giving them greater assurance about resource demands and availability over the multi-year horizon, and in turn promoting effective forward planning. Finally, MTEFs can facilitate the planning and resourcing of multi-year policies that may require an extended time horizon for implementation, such as large capital projects, new programmes, and organisational restructuring.

As Table 3.6 illustrates, most OECD countries use an MTEF, with only 3 countries reporting that they do not make use of this tool (Belgium, Mexico and Norway). MTEFs most commonly employ a 3-4 year time horizon and a rolling basis, which allows for annual revision and adjustment. Finland has a fixed 4-year timeframe and limits the adjustment to once within that period. Sweden has a rolling timeframe but refrains from adjusting the ceilings each year. Programme-based expenditure ceilings (10) and organisational ceilings (11) are used in about half of OECD countries; 9 countries rely only on an aggregate expenditure ceiling (whereas 14 countries use such an aggregate in conjunction with organisational or programme ceilings).

## Table 3.6. Main structure of MTEF

| | Existence and legal basis of MTEF | Main charecteristics | | | Target(s) of expenditure ceilings | | |
|---|---|---|---|---|---|---|---|
| | | Length of ceilings (including upcoming fiscal year) | Flexibility of framework | Frequency of annual ceilings revisions | Overall expenditures | Programme or sector expenditures | Organisational or other expenditures |
| Australia | ⚠ | 4 years | Rolling basis | More than once per year | | | |
| Austria | ⊗ | 4 years | Rolling basis | Annually | x | | x |
| Belgium | | | | | | | |
| Canada | ⊟ | 5 years | Rolling basis | Annually | | x | |
| Chile | ⊖ | 4 years | Rolling basis | More than once per year | | x | |
| Czech Republic | ⊗ | 3 years | Fixed period | Annually | x | | |
| Denmark | ⊗ | 4 years | Rolling basis | Other | | x | |
| Estonia | ⊖ | 4 years | Rolling basis | More than once per year | | | x |
| Finland | ⊗ | 4 years | Fixed period | Once per fixed period | x | | x |
| France | ⊗ | 3 years | Fixed period | Every 2 to 3 years | x | x | |
| Germany | ⊖ | 4 years | Rolling basis | Annually | | | x |
| Greece | ⊗ | 4 years | Rolling basis | Annually | | | x |
| Hungary | ◉ | 3 years | Rolling basis | Annually | x | | x |
| Iceland | ⊗ | 5 years | Rolling basis | Annually | x | x | |
| Ireland | ⊖ | 3 years | Rolling basis | Annually | x | | x |
| Israel | ⊗ | 3 years | Rolling basis | More than once per year | x | | |
| Italy | ⚠ | 3 years | Rolling basis | Other | | | |
| Japan | ⊟ | 3 years | Fixed period | Not revised | x | x | |
| Korea | ⊗ | 5 years | Rolling basis | Annually | x | x | |
| Latvia | ⊗ | 3 years | Rolling basis | Annually | x | | x |
| Luxembourg | ⊖ | 4 years | Rolling basis | Annually | x | | |
| Mexico | | | | | | | |
| Netherlands | ◉ | 4 years | Fixed period | Other | x | x | |
| New Zealand | ⚠ | 4 years | Rolling basis | Annually | x | | x |
| Norway | | | | | | | |
| Poland | ⊖ | 3 years | Rolling basis | Annually | x | | |
| Portugal | ⊖ | 4 years | Rolling basis | Annually | x | x | |
| Slovak Republic | ⊖ | 3 years | Rolling basis | Annually | x | | |
| Slovenia | ⊗ | 3 years | Rolling basis | Annually | x | | |
| Spain | ⊖ | 3 years | Rolling basis | Annually | x | | |
| Sweden | ⊗ | 3 years | Rolling basis | Not revised | x | | |
| Switzerland | ⚠ | 4 years | Rolling basis | Annually | x | | |
| Turkey | ⊖ | 3 years | Rolling basis | Annually | x | x | x |
| United Kingdom | ⊟ | 4 years | Fixed period | Every 2 to 3 years | x | | x |
| **Key** | **Total** | | | | **Total** | | |
| ◉ Yes: a law stipulating that aggregate / overall public spending should be managed in line with medium-term limits | 2 | | | | 23 | 10 | 11 |
| ⊖ Yes: a law stipulating the creation of a MTEF, whereby annual budgets are managed in line with indicative medium-term ceilings | 10 | | | | | | |
| ⊗ Yes: a law stipulating the creation of a MTEF, whereby annual budgets are determined on the basis of fixed medium-term ceilings | 12 | | | | | | |
| ⊟ A strategy/policy stipulating the MTEF and/or budget ceilings | 3 | | | | | | |
| ⚠ Other | 4 | | | | | | |
| No | 3 | | | | | | |

*Notes*: Belgium, Mexico and Norway do not apply a MTEF; In Poland MTEF overall expenditure ceilings, as adopted annually in Multiyear State Financial Plan (Update of Convergence Programme) in April 2018, may be revised while adopting the draft budget act, reflecting i.a. changes to parameters underpinning the Stabilising Expenditure Rule that occurred after adoption of the Multiyear State Financial Plan.
Data for the United States are not available; Information on data for Israel: http://dx.doi.org/10.1787/888932315602.
*Source:* OECD (2018), OECD Budget Practices and Procedures Survey, Questions 21, 22, 24, 23, OECD, Paris.

StatLink http://dx.doi.org/10.1787/888933947578

### *Approval, coverage and monitoring of MTEF*

An approval of the MTEF can be done by the Ministry of Finance, Cabinet, legislature or other independent institutions. A comprehensive coverage of expenditure in the MTEF (i.e.

the share of expenditures subject to the ceiling) lends itself to greater credibility. A broad-based MTEF allows for the relevant budget discussions to encompass the broad range of policy options and trade-offs, including the mandatory spending which might otherwise fall outside of consideration at the expense of so-called "discretionary" items. Table 3.7 below highlights the broad commonalities that exist across OECD countries in the coverage of MTEFs, although monitoring and reporting practices are more varied.

**Table 3.7. Approval, coverage and monitoring of MTEF**

| Country | Approval | Areas of public expenditure spending | Monitoring / Reporting |
|---|---|---|---|
| Australia | Cabinet / Council of Ministers | ◉⊗⊖⦶ | Internal monitoring |
| Austria | Legislature | ◉⊗⊖⦶ | Other |
| Belgium | | | |
| Canada | MoF / MoE | ◉⊗⊖⦶ | Government reports to parliament |
| Chile | MoF / MoE | ◉⊗⊖⦶ | Internal monitoring |
| Czech Republic | Cabinet / Council of Ministers | ◉⊗⊖⦶⚠ | Other |
| Denmark | Legislature | ◉⊗⊖ | Other |
| Estonia | Cabinet / Council of Ministers | ◉⊖⦶ | No |
| Finland | Cabinet / Council of Ministers | ◉⊗⊖⦶ | Other |
| France | Legislature | ◉⊗⊖⦶ | Government reports to parliament |
| Germany | Cabinet / Council of Ministers | ◉⊗⊖⦶ | Government reports to parliament |
| Greece | Legislature | ◉⊗⊖⦶ | Other |
| Hungary | Cabinet / Council of Ministers | ◉⊗⊖⦶ | Other |
| Iceland | Legislature | ◉⦶ | Government reports to parliament |
| Ireland | Cabinet / Council of Ministers | ⊗⊖⦶ | Other |
| Israel | Cabinet / Council of Ministers | ◉⊗⊖⦶ | Government reports to parliament |
| Italy | Other | ⚠ | Other |
| Japan | Cabinet / Council of Ministers | ◉⊗⊖⦶ | Internal monitoring |
| Korea | Cabinet / Council of Ministers | ◉⊗ | Government reports to parliament |
| Latvia | Legislature | ◉⊗⊖⦶ | Other |
| Luxembourg | Other | ◉⊗⊖⦶ | Other |
| Mexico | | | |
| Netherlands | Cabinet / Council of Ministers | ◉⊗⊖⦶ | Other |
| New Zealand | Other | ⚠ | Government reports to parliament |
| Norway | | | |
| Poland | Cabinet / Council of Ministers | ◉⊗⊖⦶ | Other |
| Portugal | Legislature | ◉⊗⊖⦶ | Government reports to parliament |
| Slovak Republic | Cabinet / Council of Ministers | ⚠ | No |
| Slovenia | MoF / MoE | ⚠ | No |
| Spain | Cabinet / Council of Ministers | ◉⊗⊖⦶ | Other |
| Sweden | Legislature | ◉⊗⊖⦶ | Government reports to parliament |
| Switzerland | Cabinet / Council of Ministers | ⚠ | Government reports to parliament |
| Turkey | Other | ◉⊗⊖⦶ | Government reports to parliament |
| United Kingdom | MoF / MoE | ⊗⊖⦶ | Internal monitoring |

| Key | | Total |
|---|---|---|
| ◉ | Mandatory spending | 24 |
| ⊗ | Discretionary spending | 24 |
| ⊖ | Operational spending | 24 |
| ⦶ | Investment spending | 24 |
| ⚠ | Other | 6 |

*Note*: Belgium, Mexico and Norway do not apply a MTEF.
Data for the United States are not available. Information on data for Israel: http://dx.doi.org/10.1787/888932315602.
*Source:* OECD (2018), OECD Budget Practices and Procedures Survey, Questions 25, 26, 27, OECD, Paris.

StatLink http://dx.doi.org/10.1787/888933947597

## 3.3. Top-down budgetary management

### *3.3.1. Approaches to top-down budgetary management*

'Top-down budgeting' refers to the practice whereby the fiscal targets are determined from the outset, with annual and multi-annual budgetary policies subsequently determined in conformity with these overall levels. Typically in top-down budgeting, the executive first determines aggregate public finance targets (spending and revenue levels) given medium-term fiscal objectives and prevailing economic conditions. Within this aggregate, sectoral ceilings may be set (and approved by cabinet) reflecting existing commitments, political priorities in general and key new policy initiatives. To be implemented effectively, it is helpful for top-down budgeting to be combined with complementary fiscal management practices such as fiscal rules and MTEFs.

Most OECD countries report the use of a top-down system, with only 4 countries reporting otherwise. The top-down approach mainly centres on the assignment of line ministry ceilings. However if the eventual spending request is higher than the ceilings, formal or routine penalties are not generally applied. Only 5 countries (Belgium, Greece, the Netherlands, Norway and Slovenia) report the use of a mechanism to apply a mandatory reduction in line with the original budget ceiling – see Table 3.8 below.

**Table 3.8. Structure of Top-down management**

| | No | Budget ceilings of line ministry | | | Characteristics of ceilings | If spending request are highter than ceilings |
|---|---|---|---|---|---|---|
| | | Overall/total | Programme/sector | Agency/organisation | | |
| Australia | x | | | | | |
| Austria | | x | | | relevant line ministry | no penalty |
| Belgium | | | x | | | mandatory reduction (in line with budget ceiling) |
| Canada | | | x | x | | no penalty |
| Chile | | x | | | relevant line ministry | no penalty |
| Czech Republic | | | | | made public | no penalty |
| Denmark | | x | x | | | no penalty |
| Estonia | | x | | | within the government | no penalty |
| Finland | | x | | | made public | no penalty |
| France | x | | | | | |
| Germany | | x | | | within the government | no penalty |
| Greece | | x | | | made public | mandatory reduction (in line with budget ceiling) |
| Hungary | x | | | | | |
| Iceland | | | x | | made public | no penalty |
| Ireland | | x | | | made public | no penalty |
| Israel | | x | | | made public | no penalty |
| Italy | | | | | made public | no penalty |
| Japan | | x | x | | made public | spending request can not exceed ceiling |
| Korea | | x | | | | penalties |
| Latvia | | x | | | made public | |
| Luxembourg | | | x | x | within the government | no penalty |
| Mexico | | x | | | within the government | |
| Netherlands | | x | | | made public | mandatory reduction (in line with budget ceiling) |

| | | | | | | |
|---|---|---|---|---|---|---|
| New Zealand | | | | | | |
| Norway | | x | | | within the government | mandatory reduction (in line with budget ceiling) |
| Poland | | x | | | relevant line ministry | no penalty |
| Portugal | | | x | | made public | no penalty |
| Slovak Republic | | x | | | relevant line ministry | |
| Slovenia | | x | x | | made public | mandatory reduction (in line with budget ceiling) |
| Spain | | x | | | relevant line ministry | no penalty |
| Sweden | x | | | | | |
| Switzerland | | x | | | | |
| Turkey | | | | x | made public | no penalty |
| United Kingdom | | x | | | within the government | |
| Total | 4 | 21 | 8 | 3 | | |

*Notes*: Data for New Zealand and the United States are not available; Information on data for Israel: http://dx.doi.org/10.1787/888932315602.

*Source:* OECD (2018), OECD Budget Practices and Procedures Survey, Questions 14, 15, 16, OECD, Paris.

StatLink http://dx.doi.org/10.1787/888933947616

### *3.3.2. Resolution of budgetary disputes*

In the course of the process to settle the budgetary ceilings, disagreements between the CBA and line ministries about resource allocation can often arise. Such disagreements require resolution by a party with the authority to decide on budgetary matters and the capacity to balance budgetary interests. In OECD countries, resolution of budgetary disputes takes place at various levels and through various mechanisms. As the significance of the disputed issue increases, resolution tends to move up through the ranks of the civil service hierarchy to reach the ministerial level and, finally, the office of the head of government. The preferences of high-level decision-makers can influence lower-level negotiations where, in practice, most disputes are resolved. The stronger the authority of the minister of finance, for example, the stronger the authority of his or her civil servants in interdepartmental negotiations will be. A strong institutional role may grant the finance minister the 'final say' in budget disputes; lacking this individual authority, however, collective mechanisms such as the cabinet or committees may be required to resolve disputes.

Ultimate authority for dispute resolution varies across OECD countries. Allocation disputes are resolved by the cabinet in a collective manner in less than half of countries (15 countries) and by ministerial committee in two cases (Australia and Luxembourg). In other cases disputes are settled on the authority of the CBA (9 countries), Prime minister (5 countries) or President (1 country, Chile).

**Figure 3.5. Resolution of budgetary disputes**

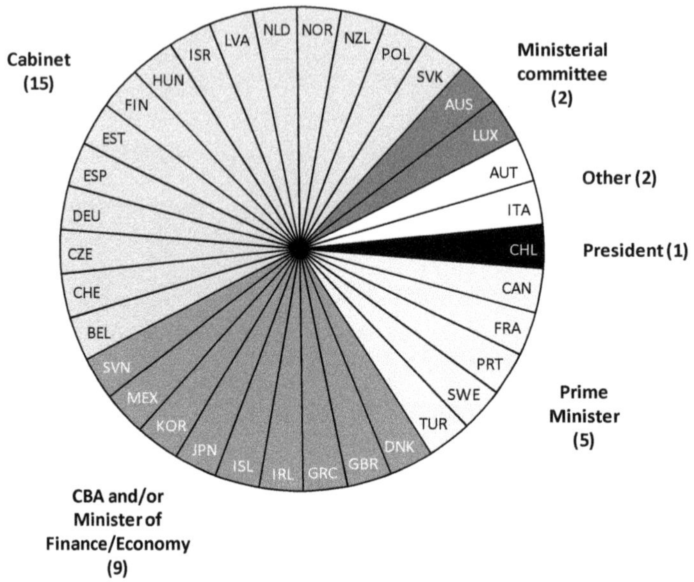


*Notes:* Data for the United States are not available; Information on data for Israel: http://dx.doi.org/10.1787/888932315602.

*Source:* OECD (2018), OECD Budget Practices and Procedures Survey, Question 17, OECD, Paris.

StatLink http://dx.doi.org/10.1787/888933946571\

## Note

[1] The Central Budget Authority (CBA) is the public entity, or several co-ordinated entities, located at the central/national/federal level of government, which is responsible for the custody and management of the national/federal budget and is the hub of the central government budget process.

## References

Schick, A. (2003), "The role of fiscal rules in budgeting", *OECD Journal on Budgeting, vol. 3/3*, https://doi.org/10.1787/budget-v3-art14-en.

# 4. Budgetary Management and Control

*In all OECD countries, central budgetary authorities (CBAs) have developed tools and approaches to make their budget execution robust and flexible – that is addressing the demands of legislative control while providing managerial authorities greater agency to address unanticipated developments.*

*Survey results show that OECD countries have a wide range of systems, instruments, and processes that allows for flexibility in budget execution, including authorisations for line ministries and agencies to realise re-allocation of funds and carry-overs. As greater flexibility is provided in budget execution, requirements for in-year and year-end reports have become sounder and constitute one of the core mechanisms through which parliaments can hold governments accountable for their decisions made during budget execution. In parallel, external audit, an important safeguard for of integrity in government reporting has been reinforced in most OECD countries.*

*This chapter takes a special focus on fiscal risks by taking stock of progress achieved by OECD countries in areas of identifying fiscal risks, their disclosure and analysis, and mitigation measures taken through risk management. Survey results show that public reporting on these risks is now common practice, although a great variety of approaches exists in other areas such as the definition of risks, the depth and breadth of the information published and mitigation approaches.*

## 4.1. Budget execution

### *4.1.1. Flexibility in budget execution*

During the course of budget execution, governments need to have available a range of instruments -often called flexibility measures- that allow them some room to accommodate new fiscal developments or opportunities as they arise. An increasing number of governments also wish to provide greater autonomy to public managers on how they use and allocate their resources. Therefore, in the bulk of OECD countries (30 countries), at least one flexibility measure is used in budget execution, which allows shifting funds among items of expenditure.

**Figure 4.1. Flexibility Measures**

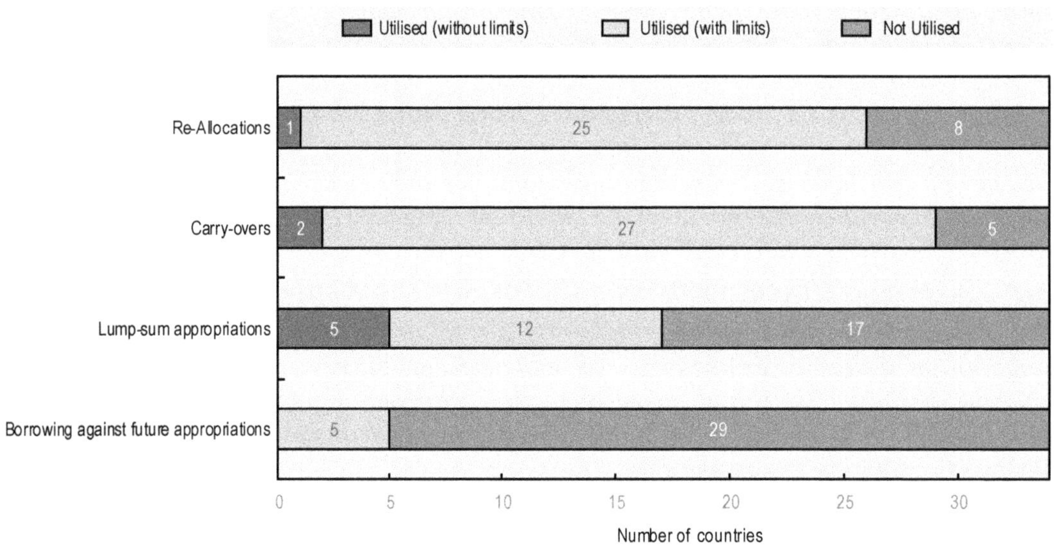


*Notes:* Formulation of 'Utilized (with limits)' was done by accounting survey responses which had at least one indication of either a 'threshold' or an authorising body requiring approval (e.g. CBA) on the usage of Flexibility Measures. Accordingly, 'Utilized (without limits)' denote responses that indicated no 'thresholds' nor an additional approving body (e.g. CBA) for the usage of these measures.
Data for the United States are not available; Information on data for Israel: http://dx.doi.org/10.1787/888932315602.
*Source:* OECD (2018), OECD Budget Practices and Procedures Survey, Questions 61a, 62, 63 and 66a, OECD, Paris.

StatLink http://dx.doi.org/10.1787/888933946590

*Two flexibility measures are widely used:*

- Firstly, carry-overs are used in a large majority of OECD countries (29 countries). This means that appropriations that could not be used in a given budget year may be carried over for use during the following year. Such a practice may be authorised for all expenditures (13 countries) or for specific ones. In most cases, it is allowed only under very strict conditions, i.e. a threshold is set in the law or regulations or pre-approval from the central budgetary authority is required. Only 5 countries (Belgium, Greece, Japan, Mexico and Slovenia) do not permit carry-overs at all.
- Secondly, re-allocation of funds is authorised in three-quarters of OECD countries (26 countries). This means that ministries or agencies can transfer funds across line items within their own budget envelope. Of these countries that allow re-

allocations, 15 countries require an authorisation by the central budgetary authority, with or without a threshold. A group of 6 countries note that there are specific conditions attached with re-allocations, such as not switching resources between stated performance outcomes (Australia) or having eligibility for re-allocation pre-approved by parliament (Germany).

*Other flexibility measures are used to varying degrees:*

- Lump-sum appropriations are a system under which responsible officers are granted full autonomy in deciding how to use their resources for implementing their stated policies. It is used by only 5 countries (Australia, Canada, Finland, Iceland, and Sweden). In an additional 12 countries, however, lump-sums appropriations are used with sub-limits for certain items, such as wages (7 countries), capital spending (6 countries), office expenses (4 countries) and travel expenses (2 countries). In addition, 2 countries (France and Portugal) specify that they use lump-sum appropriations for agencies, although they do not for ministries;
- Very few countries (Denmark, Norway and Sweden) authorise borrowing against future appropriations – that is, authorising line ministries or agencies to overspend in one year and compensate by underspending in the following year. Denmark and Norway use this system for investment expenditure and Sweden for both investment and operational expenditure.[1] In all cases, a pre-authorisation has to be granted by the central budget authority.

Lastly, legal provisions exist in virtually all countries allowing supplementation and cancellation of expenditure for unexpected requirements during the year. In 10 countries, increases in spending can be done only with approval of Parliament. Increases without approval of Parliament are permitted generally only for certain categories of expenditures (e.g. mandatory spending, such as healthcare), or under a certain criterion (e.g. threshold). Cancellation of appropriations without returning to the parliament is possible in most countries (exceptions being Finland, Iceland, Italy, Japan, Norway, and Mexico).

### *4.1.2. Control and Monitoring*

Control and monitoring of budget execution is a key concern in all countries, but one where sharp differences exist in the systems used. Indeed, in some countries, the central budgetary authority exercises centralised control, while in others, most or all controls are given to line ministries and agencies. In the former case, monitoring and control are often done through *ex ante* authorisation of spending commitments by the central budgetary authority, while in the latter, ministries and agencies may spend as they deem fit within their delegated budget, with the central budget authority often doing monitoring and control of actual spending through reconciliations and analyses between summary fiscal aggregates. In these countries, "pre-execution budget profiles" are often used for identification of budget overruns, underspends, and other risks. In the OECD, of the 21 countries that establish such pre-execution budget profiles, 13 do so monthly, 3 on a quarterly basis and 1 twice a year.

As underlined by OECD *Recommendations for Budgetary Governance,* a Treasury Single Account, or TSA, is an effective mechanism for exercising effective regulation and control during budget execution. A TSA systems, which consolidates government cash balances, facilitates indeed the ministry of finance and/or treasury's oversight of all government cash flows. Consistent with OECD recommendations, such TSA is used by over three-thirds of OECD countries (28 countries) as the standard means of collecting and disbursing central government funds. Primary objectives of maintaining a TSA are generally to ensure effective aggregate control over government cash balances, minimising transaction costs during budget execution, notably by controlling the delay in the remittance of central government revenues, and making payments of government expenses that are compliant with relevant laws and regulations.

However, design for TSA systems vary considerably. In theory, all cash flows related to government revenue, expenditure, debt issuance and amortisation should be fully integrated in the TSA system. However, in practice, OECD countries try to strike a balance between this "ideal" system and the claims of some categories of public entities to operational autonomy. Therefore, in 6 countries, the TSA excludes some major public-service funds (e.g. social security and health care). A group of 8 countries declares additional exceptions, for example, national security funds in the case of Chile and others noting a variety of other funds stipulated by law or regulations.

**Figure 4.2. Use of Treasury Single Account**

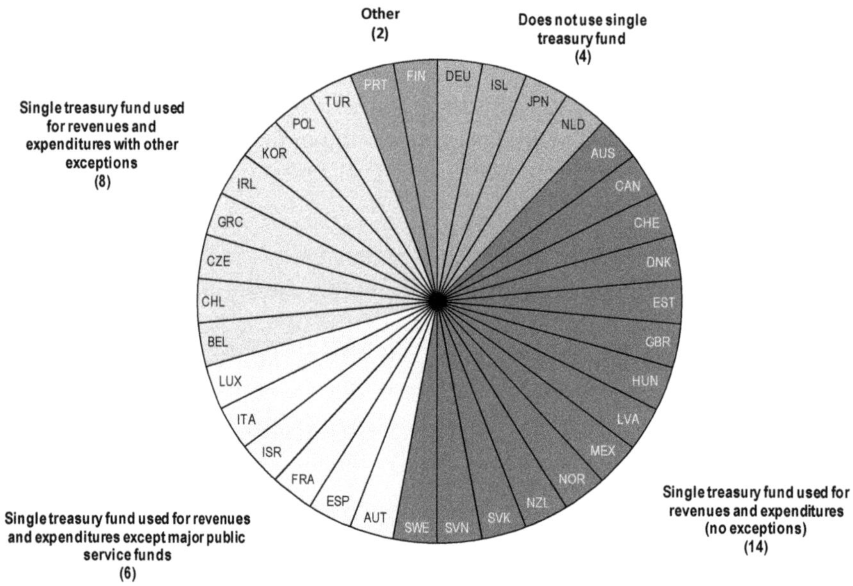


*Note:* Portugal does not use a single account but uses a central treasury account systems where all general revenues deposited are used as state budget funds. Finland uses a consolidated account (instead of a treasury fund) administered by the State Treasury.

Data for the United States are not available; Information on data for Israel: http://dx.doi.org/10.1787/888932315602.

*Source:* OECD (2018), OECD Budget Practices and Procedures Survey, Question 55, OECD, Paris.

StatLink http://dx.doi.org/10.1787/888933946609

### *4.1.3. Supplementary budgets*

Many countries' legal frameworks permit, but do not require, a supplementary budget to be presented to the legislature during the fiscal year, should the need arise. Such supplementary budgets are authorised by the legislature in a majority of OECD countries (29 countries). Within this group, in 7 countries, *ex ante* approval of supplementary budgets by parliament is necessary only when changes are done to meet certain criteria specified by law. For example, in the case of Israel, the criteria is a nominal amount of more than USD 0.7 million; in the case of Latvia, a transfer between ministries with no amount limit;

and in the case of Czech Republic, changes above a certain percentage of total spending. In other countries, such approval is not required although supplementary budgets may be presented to the legislature for discussion or information.

The law seldom restricts the number or timing of supplementary budgets. Survey results show that 11 countries did not present any supplementary budgets over the last four years.[2] In a majority of countries, one to two supplementary budgets were adopted by the legislature (22 countries presented one to two supplementary budgets to parliament; 2 countries presented more than two supplementary budgets to parliament).

**Figure 4.3. Parliamentary ex ante approval of supplementary budgets**

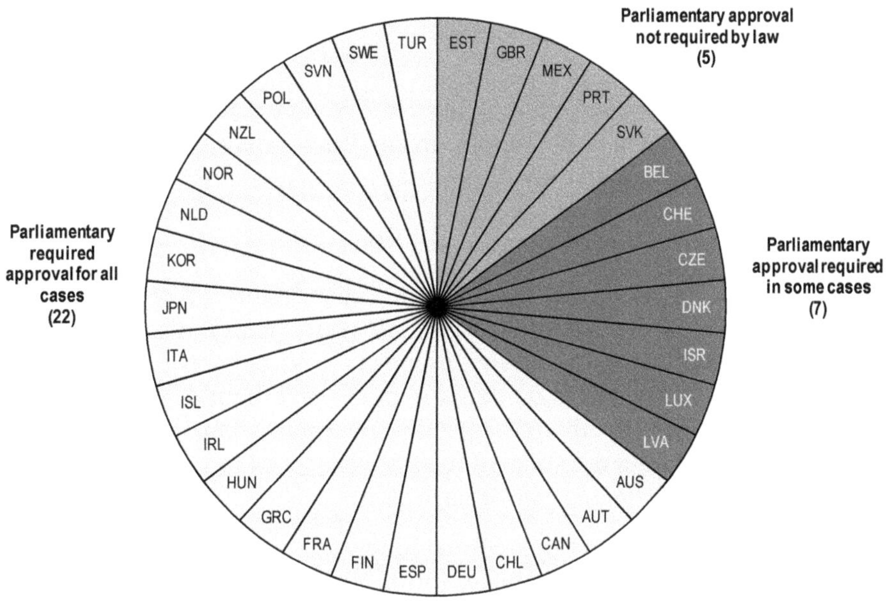


*Notes*: Data for the United States are not available; Information on data for Israel: http://dx.doi.org/10.1787/888932315602.
*Source:* OECD (2018), OECD Budget Practices and Procedures Survey, Question 57, OECD, Paris.

StatLink http://dx.doi.org/10.1787/888933946628

## 4.2. Budget Reporting

### *4.2.1. Comprehensiveness of budget documents and financial reports*

#### *Accounting basis*

Historically, government fiscal reports used to be prepared mainly on a cash basis under which revenues and expenditures were included in financial reports when the related cash was received or paid. In recent decades, however, governments have started adopting the accrual accounting basis under which revenues and expenses are reported when they are earned or incurred, regardless of the timing of the related cash receipts and payments. The accrual basis of accounting, because it reports assets and liabilities in addition to cash movements, is considered to be more comprehensive.

Survey answers, as well as those to the 2016 OECD Accruals Survey, highlight that the trend, in a majority of OECD countries, is now to combine the cash and accrual bases in the budget documents and financial reports. In a large majority of countries, year-end financial reports comprise both a cash basis (or commitment) outturn and accrual financial statements. The content of the accrual basis financial statements, however, vary widely. In particular, if 27 countries prepare an accrual basis income statement, only 22 countries prepare a balance sheet.

This confirms that cash and accrual accounting bases are not mutually exclusive and each have their own benefits and challenges, as noted in the OECD *Recommendations for Budgetary Governance*. In particular, "traditional" cash (or commitments) accounting is still favoured for setting spending limits while accrual accounting provides more comprehensive information for year-end accountability on the government's financial situation.[3]

### *Coverage of expenditures*

Comprehensive budget documentation should involve disclosing all government expenditures and revenues in a single document. In this area also, the survey shows encouraging results. In particular, only 9 countries have expenditures maintained in special accounts and information on these special accounts is systematically included in budget proposals, except for two countries (Greece and Slovenia).

In 27 countries, the central government incurs expenditures (in the form of transfers usually) relating to social security funds (e.g. pension funds). These expenditures are systematically accounted for in the budget proposal, with only two exceptions (Belgium and Slovenia). This development is particularly positive in light of the large size of these expenditures, ranging from less than 5% of GDP (Germany, Israel) to more than 20% of GDP (France), with most countries declaring expenditures of around 10% of GDP (Czech Republic, Hungary, Latvia, Poland, Slovenia, Spain).

In addition, in 29 countries, central government incurs expenditures relating to health care funds. These expenditures are accounted for in the budget documentation with four exceptions (Austria, Belgium, Poland, Slovenia). The size of these expenditures is around 5% in most countries (Hungary, Latvia, Poland, Portugal, Slovenia, Spain), but is less than 2% of GDP for three countries (Czech Republic, Germany, Israel) and around 10% for one country (France).

## *4.2.2. Institutional coverage of fiscal reports*

Survey results show that, in a majority of countries, the institutional coverage for the budget, year-end budget execution report and financial statements is aligned. However, some countries prepare year-end financial statements that provide information on the amount and composition of public spending and revenue and, sometimes, the related accumulation of government assets and liabilities beyond the institutional coverage of the budget outturn. For example, in Australia, the budget covers only the central government, but the year-end accounts cover the central public sector. Similarly, in Turkey, the budget covers only the budgetary central government, but the year-end accounts cover the general government.

However, very few countries have decided to provide a full overview of the public sector in their fiscal reports. As underlined in previous OECD reports (2017), this may be due to constitutional provisions on the independence of local governments, the technical and practical challenges of consolidation, and a lack of appreciation of the need to use the full view of public finances in financial statements.

**Table 4.1. Institutional coverage of the main reports on public finances**

| | Executive's budget proposal | Year-end budget execution reports | Year-end financial statements |
|---|---|---|---|
| Australia | ⊗ | ■ | ■ |
| Austria | ⦿ | ⦿ | ⦿ |
| Belgium | ⊗ | ⊗ | ⊗ |
| Canada | ⊗ | ⊗ | ⊗ |
| Chile | ⊗ | ⊖ | □ |
| Czech Republic | ⦿ | ⦿ | ⦿ |
| Denmark | ⦿ | ⦿ | ⦿ |
| Estonia | ⦿ | ⦿ | ⊖ |
| Finland | ⊗ | ⊗ | ⊗ |
| France | ⊖ | ⊗ | ⊖ |
| Germany | ⦿ | ⦿ | ⦿ |
| Greece | ⊖ | ⊖ | ⦿ |
| Hungary | ⊖ | □ | □ |
| Iceland | ⊗ | ⊗ | ⊗ |
| Ireland | ⊗ | ⊗ | ⊗ |
| Israel | ⦿ | ⦿ | ⊗ |
| Italy | ⦿ | ⦿ | ⦿ |
| Japan | ⊗ | ⊗ | ⊗ |
| Korea | ⦿ | ⦿ | ⦿ |
| Latvia | ⦿ | ⊖ | ⊖ |
| Luxembourg | ⦿ | ⦿ | ⦿ |
| Mexico | ■ | ■ | ■ |
| Netherlands | ⊗ | ■ | ⊗ |
| New Zealand | ⊗ | ⊗ | ⊗ |
| Norway | ⦿ | ⦿ | ⦿ |
| Poland | ⊖ | ⊖ | ☒ |
| Portugal | ⊖ | ⊖ | ☒ |
| Slovak Republic | ⊖ | ⊖ | ⊖ |
| Slovenia | ⊗ | ⊗ | ⊗ |
| Spain | ⊗ | ⊖ | ⊗ |
| Sweden | ⊗ | ⊗ | ⊗ |
| Switzerland | ⊗ | ⊗ | ⊗ |
| Turkey | ⦿ | ⊖ | ⊖ |
| United Kingdom | □ | ☒ | □ |
| **Key** | **Total** | | |
| ⦿ Budgetary central government | 12 | 10 | 9 |
| ⊗ Central government | 14 | 11 | 13 |
| ⊖ General government | 6 | 8 | 5 |
| ■ Central public sector | 1 | 3 | 2 |
| □ Public sector | 1 | 1 | 3 |
| ☒ Not applicable | 0 | 1 | 2 |

*Notes*: Data for the United States are not available; Information on data for Israel: http://dx.doi.org/10.1787/888932315602.
*Source*: OECD (2018), OECD Budget Practices and Procedures Survey, Question 45, OECD, Paris.

StatLink http://dx.doi.org/10.1787/888933947635

### *4.2.3. Frequency of budget execution reports*

In line with the OECD *Best Practices for Budget Transparency*, over 75% of OECD countries (27 countries) report producing monthly financial reports, giving a snapshot of budget implementation throughout the year. Exceptions are Belgium and Denmark, which prepare three in-year reports; and the Netherlands, which prepares a combination of monthly in-year reports (not published) and publicly available biannual budget execution reports. In Italy, monthly budget reports are prepared internally but not published.

Unsurprisingly, all OECD countries publish information on expenses and revenue incurred at the date of the publication, in the form of cash or commitment budget outturn, a cash flow statement, or an income statement. However, despite the adoption of accrual accounting by a large majority of OECD countries, very few countries (Australia, Canada, Finland, Hungary, Mexico and New Zealand) prepare or publish monthly balance sheets.

### *4.2.4. External Audit*

All OECD countries have an independent Supreme Audit Institution (SAI), which is a core actor in a country's accountability chain. Its independence is established by the constitution in 23 countries and in primary legislation in 7 countries.

Survey answers show that Supreme Audit Institution's functions are evolving. The traditional function of SAIs with regard to compliance controls on public expenditure is still carried out in a majority of countries[4], but in a large group of countries compliance controls have been replaced, or are complemented, with financial audits done in compliance with international auditing standards. In these countries, the SAI delivers an opinion on whether the financial statements present a true and fair view of the financial situation of the government.

A notable trend is that performance information published at year-end is also increasingly submitted to external scrutiny. A large group of 15 countries declares that this information is reviewed or audited by the SAI, even though the nature and extent of the controls realised vary, in the absence of any international standard or guidance in this area.

## 4.3. Conclusion

In all OECD countries, central budgetary authorities have developed tools and approaches to make their budget execution more flexible, to allow managerial autonomy to adjust to unexpected events. In other terms, most countries use mechanisms such as reallocations and carry-overs to give some level of autonomy to ministries, departments and agencies in how they spend. These mechanisms also allow them to deliver the level and quality of services requested in their mission letters or key performance indicators, and give them the autonomy to adapt to new circumstances, while also enabling the government to achieve its targets for aggregate spending.

As greater flexibility is provided to governments in budget execution, in-year and year-end reports have become a core mechanism through which parliaments can hold governments accountable for their decisions made during budget execution. Accordingly, investment in producing more comprehensive, regular and reliable reports is clear, as most OECD countries now produce comprehensive monthly budget reports and publish accrual basis financial statements at year-end. In parallel, external audit, which is one of the main safeguards of the integrity of government reports, has been significantly reinforced.

**Table 4.2. SAI's responsibilities with regard to the year-end financial reporting**

| | Compliance control on public spending against parliamentary authorisation | Audit of government financial report according to international auditing standards | Audit or quality control of performance information provided in year-end reports |
|---|---|---|---|
| Australia | | x | |
| Austria | x | x | x |
| Belgium | x | x | x |
| Canada | x | x | |
| Chile | x | | |
| Czech Republic | x | | |
| Denmark | x | x | |
| Estonia | x | x | x |
| Finland | x | | x |
| France | x | x | x |
| Germany | x | | |
| Greece | x | x | |
| Hungary | x | x | |
| Iceland | | x | |
| Ireland | | | x |
| Israel | | | |
| Italy | x | | |
| Japan | x | x | x |
| Korea | x | | x |
| Latvia | x | x | |
| Luxembourg | x | | |
| Mexico | x | x | x |
| Netherlands | x | x | x |
| New Zealand | x | x | x |
| Norway | x | x | x |
| Poland | x | | |
| Portugal | x | | |
| Slovak Republic | x | | |
| Slovenia | x | x | x |
| Spain | x | | |
| Sweden | | x | |
| Switzerland | | x | |
| Turkey | x | x | x |
| United Kingdom | x | x | x |
| Total | 28 | 21 | 15 |

*Note*: Italy indicated that the Corte dei Conti exercises prior control of legitimacy over the acts of the Government, and also ex-post on the management of the State budget. It also participates, in the cases and in the forms established by law, to the control of the financial management of certain entities. Poland indicated that the Supreme Audit Institution controls the legality, economic prudence, efficacy and diligence of the activities of relevant public entities. Portugal indicated that the Court of Auditors will assess the financial activity of the State during the year covered by the Accounts, in the areas of revenue, expenditure, treasury, use of public borrowing and national assets.

Data for the United States are not available; Information on data for Israel: http://dx.doi.org/10.1787/888932315602.

*Source*: OECD (2018), OECD Budget Practices and Procedures Survey, Question 83, OECD, Paris.

## 4.4. Special focus: Fiscal risks

### *4.4.1. Introduction*

In OECD countries, the government has the ultimate responsibility to ensure that society as a whole functions smoothly and therefore has to assume a number of different responsibilities. This, in turn, means that the risks affecting government finances can emanate from countless sources and government forecasts are constantly at risk of being proven wrong (see Box 4.1). Therefore, the OECD Best Practices for Budget Transparency (2002) have long advocated disclosing deviations from the forecast of the key economic assumptions underlying the budget as the government's "key fiscal risk".

Although fiscal risks may now be regarded as an old concept, their systematic identification, measurement and management is a relatively new practice. For example, it was only in 2015, in the *Recommendation of the Council on Budgetary Governance*, that the OECD formulated recommendations going beyond the identification of deviations from forecasts and advised governments to "identify, assess and manage prudently longer-term sustainability and other fiscal risks".

Recognition seems, however, to be growing in finance ministries that acknowledgement of the complexity of the economic system and responsibilities of the State, which has become *de facto* a last resort insurer for society. It is necessary to give an accurate picture of public finances which should allow the State, in turn, to make better decisions on mechanisms for mitigating risks and provide clear allowance for uncertainty. This special section of the *Budgeting and Public Expenditures* aims, therefore, at taking stock of progress done by OECD countries in this area, in terms of identification of fiscal risks, their disclosure and analysis, as well as risk management.

**Box 4.1. Deviations from forecasts OECD countries**

One way to estimate the impact of fiscal risks on governments' public finances is to compare forecast of central economic variables with actual outcomes. With the use of the OECD's recurrent flagship publication, the *OECD Economic Outlook*, deviations have been evaluated during the period 1997-2016 in a total of 23 member countries, for three variables: general government net lending, general government gross financial liabilities, and general government debt (all measured with the Maastricht definition and expressed in terms of GDP).

As evident in the table below, deviations from expected outcomes are substantial over all three variables and over both the one and two-year forecasts. Focusing on the t-1 forecast, the mean absolute deviation is 1.67% of GDP for net lending, 8.11% of GDP for gross financial liabilities, and 5.34% of GDP for the Maastricht debt. As expected, the deviations from the t-2 forecast are slightly larger. The deviations tend to be in the directions of higher deficits and bigger debt also when measured as gross financial liabilities.

| | Observations | | Mean Deviation | | Mean Abs. Deviation | | Standard Dev. (distribution) | |
|---|---|---|---|---|---|---|---|---|
| **Measure** | **t-1** | **t-2** | **t-1** | **t-2** | **t-1** | **t-2** | **t-1** | **t-2** |
| **Net Lending** | 439 | 417 | -0.50 | -0.81 | 1.67 | 2.19 | 2.57 | 3.19 |
| **Gross Fin. Liabilities** | 389 | 370 | 2.43 | 4.46 | 8.11 | 10.27 | 10.59 | 12.80 |
| **Maastricht Debt** | 257 | 244 | -0.84 | 0.47 | 5.34 | 7.47 | 7.64 | 10.81 |

The additional table below divides the sample into two groups (one for the years 1997-2006 and one for the 2007-15) and shows, in a crude way, that both the size of deviations and the direction have been impacted by the financial crisis starting in 2007. In general, the absolute deviations and standard deviations are larger in the later period – implying a more dispersed distribution with larger deviations compared to forecasts. As expected, the mean of the deviations in the later period also tells us a coherent story: the deviations are, set to sample as a whole, clearly in the direction of higher deficits and debt levels compared to forecast.

| | Observations | | Mean Deviation | | Mean Abs. Deviation | | Standard Dev. (distribution) | |
|---|---|---|---|---|---|---|---|---|
| **Measure, 1997-2006** | **t-1** | **t-2** | **t-1** | **t-2** | **t-1** | **t-2** | **t-1** | **t-2** |
| **Net Lending** | 220 | 198 | -0.33 | -0.52 | 1.48 | 1.88 | 1.98 | 2.46 |
| **Gross Fin. Liabilities** | 199 | 180 | 2.58 | 3.53 | 6.81 | 8.00 | 8.13 | 9.42 |
| **Maastricht Debt** | 130 | 117 | -2.89 | -2.31 | 4.76 | 5.53 | 5.16 | 6.43 |
| **Measure, 2007-2015** | | | | | | | | |
| **Net Lending** | 219 | 219 | -0.67 | -1.08 | 1.86 | 2.47 | 3.06 | 3.71 |
| **Gross Fin. Liabilities** | 190 | 190 | 2.25 | 5.33 | 9.48 | 12.43 | 12.68 | 15.31 |
| **Maastricht Debt** | 127 | 127 | 1.25 | 3.03 | 5.92 | 9.26 | 9.09 | 13.18 |

*Notes*: Forecasts have been collected from different vintages of the autumn/winter edition of the OECD Economic Outlook and both one- and two-year forecasts are included. In the period 1996-2012, the publication was published in December, whereas the period 2013-2015 was publicized in November. All figures have been collected from openly available databases, one for each edition of the Economic Outlook, published by the OECD. Only countries where forecasts are available for the entire 19-year period were included in the sample. The 1996 autumn edition is chosen as starting point due to data availability. Actuals for each year have been collected from the November 2017 Economic Outlook.

### *4.4.2. Institutional arrangements*

In over 75% of OECD countries, institutional arrangements exist that establish division of tasks for fiscal risk management (identification, monitoring, analysis and disclosure) and stakeholders' internal co-ordination.

**Figure 4.4. Government unit responsible for identification and management of overall fiscal risks in country**

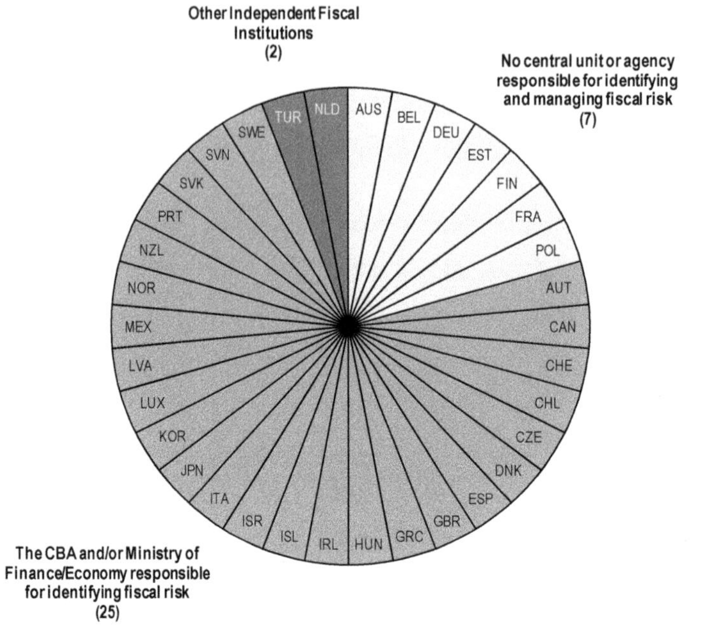


*Note*: In the Netherlands, the Bureau for Policy Analysis is reponsible. In Turkey, the Economic Coordination Board is responsible.

Data for the United States are not available; Information on data for Israel: http://dx.doi.org/10.1787/888932315602.

*Source*: OECD (2018), OECD Budget Practices and Procedures Survey, Question 72, OECD, Paris.

StatLink http://dx.doi.org/10.1787/888933946647

Generally, responsibility for measuring and disclosing fiscal risks is centralised and lies with the institution also in charge of establishing fiscal forecasts. In almost two-thirds of OECD countries (25 countries), this institution is the finance ministry, and within the finance ministry, the economics department or budgetary central authority is generally in charge of fiscal risks. Other arrangements may exist however. For an example, Chile has a Sub-Department of Contingent Liabilities and Concessions at the Public Finance Division of the Budget Office with the role of identifying and reporting specific risks.

Also, some examples have emerged of practices with the potential to enhance co-ordination of actors involved in fiscal risks management. Austria, for example, has a dedicated committee chaired by the minister of finance comprising of all directors-generals. In the United Kingdom, a Fiscal Risks Groups has been established within the Treasury, which operates under the supervision of the Treasury Executive Board and, ultimately, the Chancellor. This group supervises work done by other specialised groups within the Treasury (spending risks, tax risks, and balance sheet risks groups). In Mexico, several units within the ministry of finance contribute to the identification and monitoring of fiscal risks. In Germany, the Stability Council - a joint body comprising of finance ministers of the federal government and *Länder* – plays an important role in monitoring risk to compliance with the fiscal rule in connection with the upper limit of the structural general government budget.

As discussed in Chapter 5 , the growth of independent fiscal institutions (independent parliamentary budget offices and fiscal councils), has moved at a remarkably fast pace in the OECD. Accordingly, independent fiscal institutions are increasingly involved in fiscal risks monitoring, albeit with different roles depending on the country considered. In the Netherlands, the ministry of finance establishes a fiscal risks assessment, but the independent fiscal council also reports biannually, as well as at the start of the mandate of each new government, on the situation of public finances and fiscal risks. In Belgium, the Czech Republic and Luxembourg, the independent fiscal institution identifies and analyses fiscal risks as part of its oversight function of government's economic and/or fiscal forecasts. In the United Kingdom, the independent fiscal institution is tasked with producing a regular report on fiscal risks, aiming at identifying specific shocks or pressures that that could push public finances away from the forecasts, to which the government has committed to responding formally.

Although the monitoring and disclosure functions are often centralised, in virtually all cases, the responsibility for identifying fiscal risks lies in other institutions, which report to the finance ministry. In particular, several countries indicate that each line ministry and agency has the responsibility to monitor relevant fiscal risk. For example, in Ireland, risk identification is done by all line ministries and agencies. This identification is supported by the National Risk Assessment which presents a collaborative, higher level and thematic, view of the risks facing Ireland which runs in parallel to the work of line ministries and agencies. In New Zealand, any unit responsible for leading a policy change advises the Treasury of fiscal risks are associated with the proposed change. In Austria, each line ministry produces its own risk management reporting collected by the central risk management unit. In Greece, line ministries' chief financial officers are tasked with identifying near term fiscal risks and propose corrective measures, while the ministry of finance is more specifically in charge of identifying macro-economic risks.

Some countries also stress the role of various other actors. The Netherlands underlines that there are both *ad hoc* commissions and permanent, independent organisations outside line ministries tasked with identifying and managing fiscal risks. An example of the former is the commission on ageing, which brings together representatives from several stakeholders, including line ministries. An example of the latter is the Netherlands Environmental Assessment Agency, which reports on the risks related to natural disasters. In Sweden, monitoring of certain risks is part of the mandate of some agencies. Several countries, including Turkey, have established oversight bodies for the banking sector that are tasked with identifying associated fiscal risks.

Finally, a smaller group of countries fully decentralise fiscal risks monitoring. Australia, for example, adopted an approach in which all departments are responsible for monitoring and reporting on risks in their area of responsibility. To this aim, drafting guidance is provided to departments and agencies regarding the reporting of their fiscal risks. Risks emanating from the sensitivity of budget estimates to changes in the key assumptions underlying forecasts are also published, centrally, at each budget update. In Denmark, identification, analysis and disclosure of fiscal risks is a function of a number of specialised institutions, the Systemic Risks Council, the Danish Economic Council and the National Bank. Each stakeholder focuses on risks that are relevant to their area of competency, in cooperation with the Ministry of Finance.

### *4.4.3. Framework for fiscal risks management*

The trend is clear: most OECD countries have taken steps to improve their framework for fiscal risk identification, measurement and management. A majority of the countries in the survey (20 countries) have in place a framework or guidance – in the form of a supra-national directive or national law, regulation or policy document – for monitoring fiscal risk. Precision on the nature of the tasks to be performed with regards to fiscal risks management, which should ideally cover risks' identification, measurement, monitoring and mitigation, and institutional responsibilities for realising these tasks vary, however, very significantly.

For some countries, focus seems to be on being transparent on decisions made for preparing the forecasts, while others emphasise management issues. In practice, at one end of the spectrum, the framework consists of disclosure requirements alongside the fiscal forecasts without specifications on how the identification and measurement shall be done. At the other end of the spectrum, the framework comprises a law that defines stakeholders' responsibilities and tasks , as well as policy documents specifying underlying processes (e.g. the United Kingdom), or even general risks management guidelines (e.g. Latvia).

**Figure 4.5. Framework or guidance for fiscal risks management**

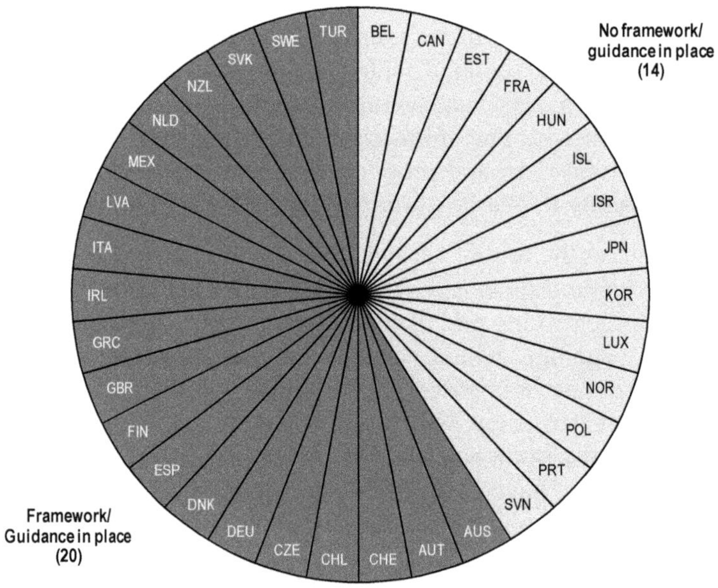


*Notes*: Data for the United States are not available; Information on data for Israel: http://dx.doi.org/10.1787/888932315602.
*Source*: OECD (2018), OECD Budget Practices and Procedures Survey, Question 75, OECD, Paris.

StatLink http://dx.doi.org/10.1787/888933946666

Only one country (Sweden) notes that legislation specifies risks the State is willing to carry and boundaries within which these risks are taken – in other words, that the framework for fiscal risks management clarifies what the "risk appetite" of the State is. In Sweden, the Budget Organic Law stipulates three particular principles for issuing guarantees and loans: recovering of costs, risk management, and transparency.[5]

Despite this progress, centrally defined criteria to decide which fiscal risks need to be monitored are lacking in most countries, leaving, in practice, their identification to the judgement of those who are in charge of their monitoring.

For these countries that define fiscal risks, the timeframe considered may be the near, medium or long term. For example, the United Kingdom considers factors that can impact the outlook over two-time horizons: the next five years and the fiscal sustainability over the next 50 years. The United Kingdom's Fiscal Risks Report shows that the time horizon has direct impact on the nature of fiscal risks, with, for example, revenue risk threatening public finances over the medium term but disappearing over the long term, and vice-versa for risks associated with ageing.

Around a third of countries use numerical criteria and threshold for identifying fiscal risks – that is for clarifying how decisions are made on which potential developments and events shall be included or not in the forecasts. In Australia, for example, fiscal risks are defined as general developments or specific events that may affect the fiscal outlook but are not included in the estimates "because the timing or magnitude is not known". In New Zealand, events identified as fiscal risk in the fiscal update shall be "over $10 million in any year of the medium-term forecasts" and be "reasonably possible i.e. between 20% and 50% probability". It should be noted that, somehow surprisingly, criteria for identification of fiscal risks do not include, in any country, an explicit reference to fiscal risks evidenced from past deviations from forecasts.

**Figure 4.6. Criteria for fiscal risks identification**

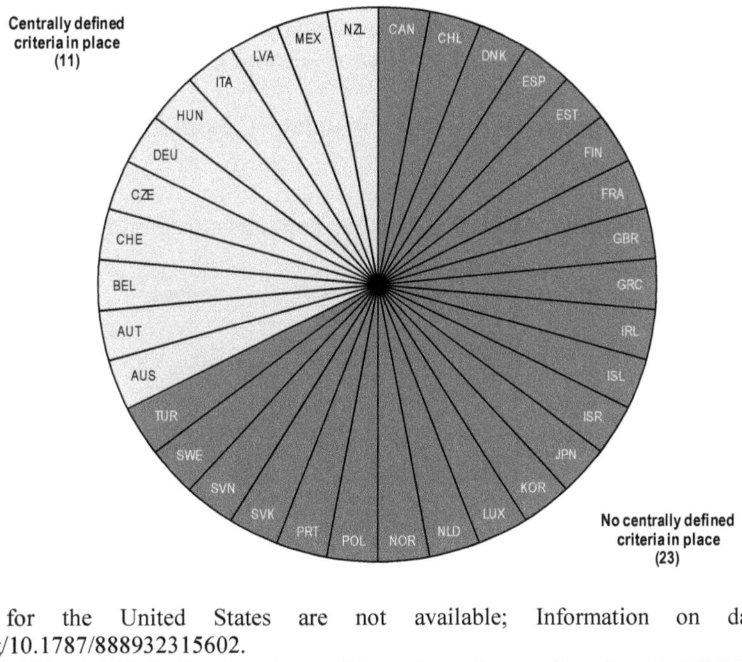


*Notes*: Data for the United States are not available; Information on data for Israel: http://dx.doi.org/10.1787/888932315602.
*Source*: OECD (2018), OECD Budget Practices and Procedures Survey, Question 76, OECD, Paris.

StatLink http://dx.doi.org/10.1787/888933946685

Some countries have developed classifications of fiscal risks. Finland, for example, classifies fiscal risks into risks associated with macro-economic developments, with government liabilities, which are further classified into sub-categories, and with government assets. The United Kingdom uses the most developed categorisation of fiscal risks, in addition to being the country that identifies these risks over the longer time period. Categories include macroeconomic risks, financial sector risks, debt interest risks revenue risks, spending risks and balance sheet risks. Each risk is further ranked in terms of their potential impact on the public sector net debt and probability of crystallisation.

### *4.4.4. Monitoring, measurement and disclosure of fiscal risks*

#### *Monitoring*

Notwithstanding a lack of a shared definition, countries declare monitoring similar fiscal risks. Based on the survey, the first type of risks identified by more than half of countries are macroeconomic variables – especially interest rates, growth, the demography, the stability of the financial sector – that underlie economic and fiscal forecasts. The second type of risks is potential claims on budgetary resources due to obligations that the Government has entered in to – generally guarantees, or liabilities stemming from litigations.

Within these broad categories, each country identifies specific fiscal risks, depending on its own circumstances. Risks related to government debt can include financing risks (liquidity and refinancing risks), market risks (interest and foreign exchange risks), credit risks, legal and operational risks, and model risks. Risks related to the macro-economy can include the fiscal impact of the unexpected fall in output, whereas risks related to the demography usually include the increase in the age-related expenditure, such as pensions and health care expenditure.

Litigations, guarantees associated with public-private partnerships (PPPs), recapitalisation of state-own enterprises (SOEs), bail-outs of sub-national governments (SNGs), or natural disasters (see Box 4.2) are identified as fiscal risks by fewer countries. Other fiscal risks mentioned include tax expenditures (France), mandatory spending (Italy), or pensions and healthcare spending (Mexico).

**Figure 4.7. Nature of fiscal risks identified, measured and disclosed**

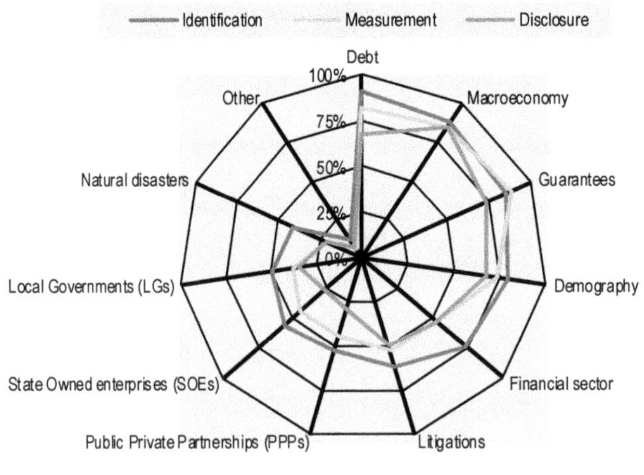


*Notes*: Data for the United States are not available; Information on data for Israel: http://dx.doi.org/10.1787/888932315602.
*Source*: OECD (2018), OECD Budget Practices and Procedures Survey, Question 77, OECD, Paris.

StatLink http://dx.doi.org/10.1787/888933946704

**Box 4.2. Selected countries: monitoring and mitigating natural disasters risks**

Large-scale catastrophic and smaller recurrent natural disasters generate considerable economic losses across OECD countries. Single shocks, such as recent earthquakes in New Zealand and Chile, have caused damages in excess of 20% of gross domestic product (GDP), affecting local economies and populations disproportionately.

Governments tend to shoulder a significant share of the costs of disasters, particularly in countries with modest insurance coverage rates. The nature of these costs range from payments made to compensate for private losses to public asset recovery and includes decline in tax and non-tax revenues as a consequence of economic disruptions. Government budgets can be also affected by possible deteriorations in the terms governments can refinance or raise new public debt.

In a recent report, the OECD identifies the costs disasters impose on governments is as a type of contingent liability (and contingent revenue losses) and finds that damage to public assets, such as public buildings and infrastructure are the largest disaster-related contingent liabilities for central and subnational governments, along with post-disaster assistance for individual households, after a review of 9 OECD countries and APEC Economies.

The liabilities most difficult to control are those that sem from damages to assets and infrastructure owned by subnational governments. These damages become a central government liability where rulezs about the responisibility for associated costs are unclear or where capacity constraints at subnational level lead central governments to assume responsibility for these costs. The study also finds that information is often stored in a scattered way through different parts of the government and are rarely brought together to inform financial planning, including fiscal risk monitoring and mitigation.

The report also shows natural disaster costs tend to be higher in countries that have made limited or only very general explicit commitments to provide assistance prior to a disaster. The OECD report therefore argues that *ex ante* identification and quantification of disaster-related risks and mitigation strategies in the form of clear government commitments for assistance is needed to increase countries' financial resilience to natural disasters. In particular, the report calls for designing clear framework rules for a government's post-disaster financial assistance; for establishing clear cost sharing mechanisms across levels of government; for including the assessment of disaster related contingent liabilities in fiscal risk management frameworks; for making risk reduction part of the framework conditions for financing post-disaster needs, and finally for making provisions for managing residual risks.

*Source*: OECD (2019). Boosting Fiscal resilience to disasters: Managing Disaster Related Contingent Liabilities in Public Finance Frameworks. OECD Publishing, Paris.

### *Measurement*

Debt, macroeconomic, and demography risks are virtually always measured. Debt interest rates, for example, are short and medium-term fiscal risks in most countries, and their measurement often involves examining the change in interest expenses if the general interest rate level were to rise permanently by one percentage point. In Ireland and France, for example, the budget documentation includes an estimate of the effect of a one percentage point increase in interest rates. Macroeconomic risks are often measured through sensitivity analyses or alternative macroeconomic scenarios. The effects of the changes in demography can be captured by so-called sustainability calculations, which demonstrate the impact of the development in age-related expenditure over time under current policies.

Regarding guarantees, and more generally government liabilities, the least complicated system used by many countries involve reporting the nominal value of liabilities, possibly as a ratio of a key figure, such as the state budget or nominal GDP. The nominal value of liabilities indicates the maximum loss if the government was required to settle all of the liabilities shown in full, assuming no provisions, such as a funding system, had been made (e.g. New Zealand, Australia, Finland and the Netherlands). A complementary, but more challenging method would involve calculating the market value (fair value) of liabilities, which would show the amount a state would need to pay for transferring its liabilities to a third party (e.g. US).

Measurement of fiscal risks associated with the financial sector is not an easy task, as highlighted by the fact that fewer countries measure them. Countries that discuss financial sector risks can use various indicators of its size, concentration, capital-adequacy ratios, among other, are discussed (e.g. Finland). Some countries may also include fan charts which shows expected losses from financial market turmoil under specific assumptions (e.g. New Zealand, the Netherlands).

**Figure 4.8. Disclosure of fiscal risks in a report**

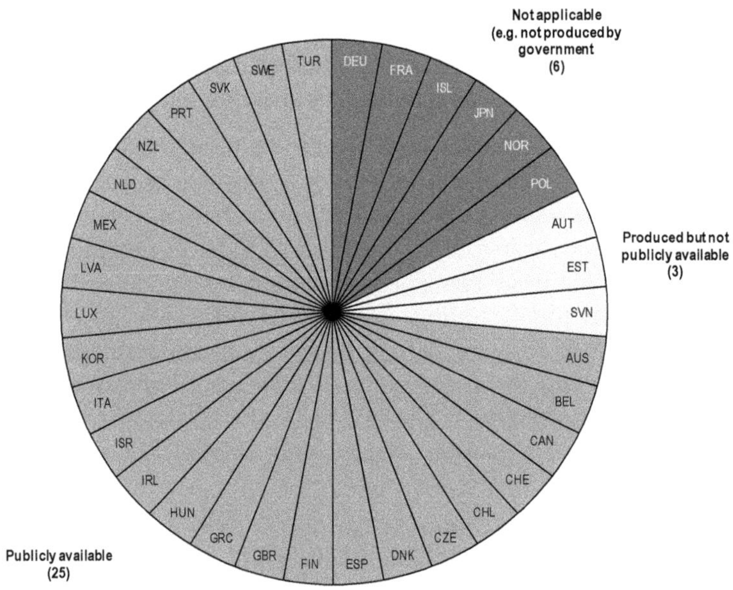


*Notes*: Data for the United States are not available; Information on data for Israel: http://dx.doi.org/10.1787/888932315602.
*Source*: OECD (2018), OECD Budget Practices and Procedures Survey, Question 5, OECD, Paris.Disclosure.

StatLink http://dx.doi.org/10.1787/888933946723

### *Disclosure*

Although three-quarter of OECD countries publicly disclose some information on their fiscal risks, the means for disclosing fiscal risks, as well as the breadth and depth of information published, is extremely variable.

Information on fiscal risks is often provided in the annual budget documentation, alongside economic and fiscal forecasts. For example, Canada includes a chapter on "Upside and Downside risks to the economic and fiscal outlook" in its budget plan. A few countries (Finland and the United Kingdom) have decided to establish stand-alone fiscal risks reports. There are also some countries, like Sweden, which disclose high-quality information on specific risks in a range of reports but do not provide a consolidated vision. In terms of the depth of the information published, at one end of the spectrum, disclosure of fiscal risks may be limited to a couple of pages on contingent liabilities and non-performing loans; at the other end of the spectrum, detailed fiscal risks reports may be published by governments (the United Kingdom).

It is notable, also, that two countries (New Zealand and the United Kingdom) realise stress tests of the government balance sheet. These stress tests apply shock scenarios, such as large macroeconomic shocks, to the balance sheet. They show impacts of the shock as well as highlight the correlation of various types of fiscal risks - for example, a fall in asset prices and realisation of implicit liabilities. Finland also produces a fiscal stress test in the context of its report on fiscal risks which captures the effects of a macro-economic shock to its public deficit and debt.

### *4.4.5. Mitigation of fiscal risks*

Examples of good practices and progress in mitigation of specific fiscal risks exist in virtually all OECD countries. Though mitigation of risks to overspend has traditionally been at the heart of ministries of finance activities, it can be said that more systematic fiscal risks identification and measurement expanded the scope of the ministries' monitoring and mitigation strategies.

In particular, recording provisions and contingent liabilities have made governments more conscious of risks associated with them and some countries are now trying to subject them to the same degree of scrutiny and control as ordinary spending. Interestingly, the Netherlands and the United Kingdom established guidance for approval of contingent liabilities. In the United Kingdom, for example, each new contingent liability must go through a checklist composed of five key elements: 1) rationale; 2) exposure; 3) risk and return; 4) risk management and mitigation; and 5) affordability.

A large majority of OECD countries (31 countries) set allowances for emergencies and future spending pressures. Specifically, 23 countries have contingency reserves and 15 countries have policy reserves. The purpose of the contingency reserve, generally, is to finance unanticipated events. In Australia, however, the contingency reserve is rather an allowance for anticipated events which cannot be assigned to individual programmes and, separately from the contingency reserve, another "provision" can be used to finance unanticipated events.[6]

Also, Sweden has a "safety margin" in its budget to use as a buffer in case some fiscal risks materialise.[7] Only one country, Latvia, sets a reserve that is explicitly linked to its fiscal risks assessment. Specifically, in Latvia, legal requirements oblige the government to set a Fiscal safety reserve, which is calculated based on quantifiable fiscal risks included in the Declaration of fiscal risks and shall be at least of 0.1% of GDP.

Seven countries have established funds to finance costs associated with the realisation of specific fiscal risks. For example, in Italy, there are several such funds, including the *Reserve fund for obligatory spending*, whose purpose is to guarantee mandatory spending (salaries, pensions, interest payments, etc.).

In addition, seven countries have established counter-cyclical stabilisation funds. For example, in Latvia, the Long-term Stabilisation Reserve is a fiscal policy instrument whose purpose is to reduce general economic risks; avoid socio-economic crises and ensure the availability of financial resources in the case of emergency situation. Funds are also used for funding natural disasters risks.

Funds do not aim only at funding future costs but can be used to send pricing signals in order to change behaviours of beneficiaries. For example, in Sweden, State guarantee and loans should be self-financed over the long-term. To that aim, a fee corresponding to the State's expected loss and costs is set by the responsible authorities, following public methodologies.[8] Several techniques can be used to estimate the expected loss of the guarantee or loan, including simulation models, rating analysis and option pricing. In principle, consequently, if beneficiaries adopt more risky behaviours, they will carry the associated costs. In addition, the fees collected are wired to the Swedish National Debt Office and reported against a notional reserve account. If a guarantee is called, the government also maintains a claim on the guaranteed company to recover costs.

**Figure 4.9. Contingency and reserve funds**

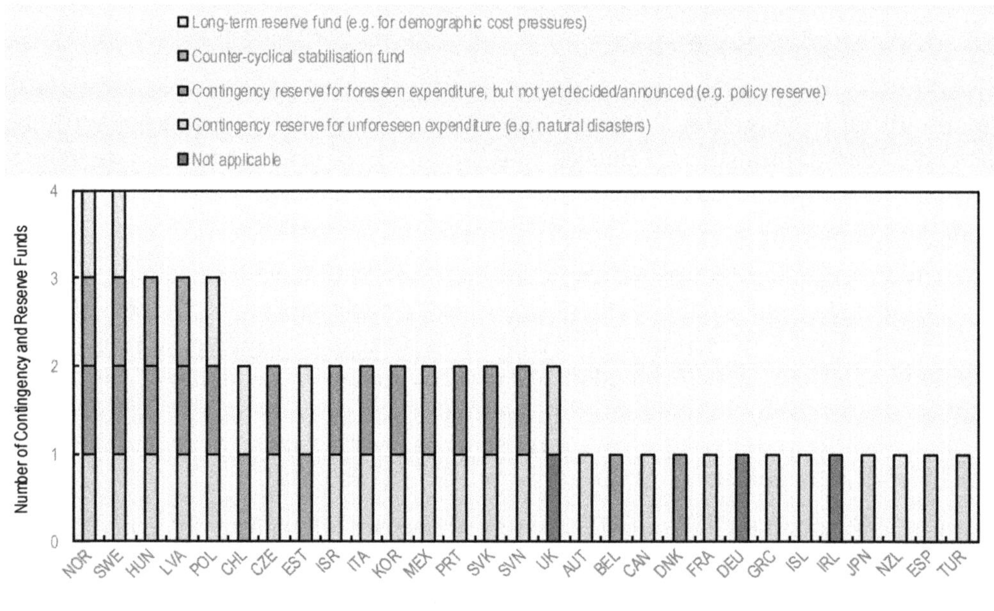


*Note*: Ireland is currently awaiting legislative approval for a "Rainy Day Fund" contingency reserve (as of 2018). However, Ireland's Strategic Investment Fund (SIF) and to an extent the National Training Fund (NTF), have an element of contingency/counter-cyclicality, i.e: receipts in times of high employment accumulate into a surplus. This can then be used in downturns funding unemployment expenditures.; Luxembourg has mandatory minimums for health care and pension schemes; Netherlands plans to finance unforeseen expenditures directly out of the regular budget. Australia, Finland and Switzerland did not report using any of the above instruments.

Data for the United States are not available; Information on data for Israel: http://dx.doi.org/10.1787/888932315602.

*Source:* OECD (2018), OECD Budget Practices and Procedures Survey, Question 79, OECD, Paris.

StatLink http://dx.doi.org/10.1787/888933946742

A group of countries, among which Sweden, New Zealand and Germany, places emphasis on adopting a prudent fiscal policy stance for mitigating very large fiscal risks. For these countries, because fiscal risks are, by definition, uncertain, the awareness and understanding of them will never be complete and fiscal policy should make allowance for dealing with this uncertainty. For example, Sweden considers that its net lending surplus target is crucial for maintaining long-term sustainability of public finances, having sufficient room for fiscal manoeuvre in severe economic downturns, as well as funding temporary and unexpected changes in demography. New Zealand underlines the importance of the government balance sheet in providing an assessment of the resilience of public finances, its capacity to absorb shocks and stresses, and capacity to adapt and rebound from them. Rather than just a single debt measure, the whole structure of the balance sheet is assessed, including the reserves and other financial instruments the government owns, in terms of the capacity and options it has to adapt in response to shocks.

### *4.4.6. Conclusion*

Public reporting on fiscal risks is increasingly common practice among OECD countries. However, the survey shows a great variety of approaches in almost all areas, from institutional responsibilities to formal criteria for fiscal risks' identification. In addition, although solid practises for fiscal risk identification, measurement and reporting are increasingly recognised as important, a missing piece of the puzzle in most countries seems to be on how reporting of fiscal risks can be used in policymaking.

Three possible channels are identified by these countries that are most advanced in fiscal risks management. First, a comprehensive and transparent reporting of fiscal risks can increase awareness of such risks among the public and policymakers and expose potential weak spots, which then can lead to steps in making fiscal risk mitigation or management more effective. Second, a consideration of interlinkages between various types of risks – in the form of fiscal risk scenarios or stress tests – can help to identify what are the channels that public finances are most likely to be affected by during a crisis. These are the areas where the attention probably should be focussed when enhancing fiscal risk management. Finally, fiscal risks assessments and fiscal stress tests can also help to inform policymakers when setting their fiscal targets or objectives. Such targets should ideally be set in a way that reflect actual risks faced by a country and create a buffer that can cater to the effects of fiscal crises to public finances.

## Notes

[1] In Denmark, when borrowing against future appropriations is used, the following year's appropriations are affected by depreciations and interest on the loan. Every agency has a 'borrowing limit' that they have to stay within and the limit can be changed in the budget process.

[2] For countries with the Westminster budget tradition, annual forecasts are included, together with a discussion of fiscal policy and government priorities, in a budget statement debated in Parliament which has the *de facto* status of a vote of confidence in the government. Annual authority to spend is granted through separate documents: the so called "estimates" or "supply" bills or other laws which permanently appropriate money for specific departments and programmes (so called "entitlements"). Some of these countries (Australia, New Zealand) specify that though they do not prepare supplementary budgets, they present to parliament supplementary estimates or "imprest supply" that seek to amend, where necessary, the ministries' and agencies' initial spending requirements as shown in estimates.

[3] Spending limits are presented on cash and/or commitment bases by 16 countries, on both cash (or commitment) and accrual bases by 10 countries and on accrual basis by only 6 countries.[3]

[4] Compliance controls consist of assessing the conformity of annual expenditures with the Parliamentary authorisation and all other applicable laws and regulations.

[5] These principles are implemented as follows: i) with regard to cost recovery, State guarantee and loans should also be self-financed over the long-term. To that aim, a fee corresponding to the State's expected loss and costs (e.g., administrative costs) is set by the responsible authorities, following public methodologies. The fees collected are wired to the Swedish National Debt Office ("*Riksgalden*", or SNDO) and reported against a notional reserve account; ii) with regard to risk mitigation, the main principle is that authority should perform due diligence to insure that beneficiaries are financially viable at the time of the issuance of the guarantee or loan. The commonly used methodology is credit rating, except for student loans; and iii) with regard to reporting, the Budget Act states that the stock of guarantee and on-lending should be reported in the Annual Report. Other information requested includes: The identification and assessment of essential risks factors (e.g., sector concentration), comments on the ability of the SDNO as the debt manager to handle potential cash payments if guarantees were being called, various information on the portfolio (such as the maturity structure) (OECD, 2016).

[6] There are often criteria associated with the reserve. It may include decisions taken but not yet announced by the Government, and decisions made too late for inclusion against individual entity estimates. The provision can be used only in case of an erroneous omission or understatement in the budget or due to unforeseen expenditures realised after the last day it was practicable to provide for it in the budget.

[7] The guideline for the minimum size of the budget margin, the so-called safety margin, is the government's assessment of the minimum size of the budget margin in the budgeting phase to deal with uncertainties, primarily because of cyclical development. According to the guideline, the safety margin should amount to at least 1% of the ceiling-based expenditure for the current year (t), at least 1.5% for the following year (t + 1), at least 2% for the second following year (t + 2) and at least 3% for the third following year (t + 3). The increasing size is motivated by the fact that uncertainty about expenditure development is greater in the longer term.

[8] Unless Parliament determines otherwise.

## References

Kopits, G. (2014), "Coping with fiscal risk: Analysis and practice", *OECD Journal on Budgeting*, vol. 14/1, https://doi.org/10.1787/budget-14-5jxrgssdqnlt.

Moretti, D. (2016), "Accrual practices and reform experiences in OECD countries Results of the 2016 OECD Accruals Survey", *OECD Journal on Budgeting*, Vol. 16/1, https://doi.org/10.1787/budget-16-5jlv2jx2mtzq.

Towe C. et al. (2016), *Analyzing and Managing Fiscal Risks - Best Practices*, International Monetary Fund, Washington.

Ulla, P. (2006), "Assessing Fiscal Risks through Long-term Budget Projections", *OECD Journal on Budgeting*, vol. 6/1, https://doi.org/10.1787/budget-v6-art5-en.

# 5. Parliament's role in budgeting

*In all OECD countries, the legislature has a traditional role in authorising public expenditures and revenue-raising. Over recent years, there has been a trend towards stronger engagement of the parliament across the full budget cycle, with more countries reporting an ex ante role. In many cases this is related to the division of the budgetary cycle into a fiscal policy semester, followed by a resource-allocation (budgeting) semester, which allows for a sequential engagement by parliament and its committees at various phases; in other cases, the ex ante engagement relates to signalling of policy choices and priorities. There is also a marked tendency towards parliamentary approval or discussion of medium-term budgetary frameworks, driven in part by the evolving fiscal framework within the European Union.*

*As to the powers of the legislature, more than half of OECD countries report wide-ranging powers to amend the budget; but such powers are not widely used in practice, in part because the government's authority over the budget is usually a 'confidence matter' which can precipitate a change of government. Two-thirds of OECD countries have a single budget committee in parliament; the sectoral committees, which are most closely linked to policy issues in their areas, generally have weak links to budget policy-making – even on issues such as performance budgeting where a stronger sector-specific role might be envisaged. About one-third of OECD legislatures have a specialist research unit for budget analysis, and Parliamentary Budget Offices have become much more prevalent across the OECD.*

## 5.1. Introduction

The OECD Recommendation on Budgetary Governance (2015) states that "parliament has a fundamental role in authorising budget decisions and holding government to account" and that governments should "provide for an inclusive, participative and realistic debate on budgetary choices, by offering opportunities for the parliament and its committees to engage with the budget process at all key stages of the budget cycle, both *ex ante* and *ex post…*".

OECD legislatures are subject to a range of different legal frameworks, procedures, customs, and traditions, but the vast majority can be termed "budget-influencing", with the authority and capacity to amend or reject the executive's budget proposal.

While the budget approval phase is still where most legislatures come to the fore in the budget process, there is a trend away from treating the budget as a set-piece event towards continuous financial scrutiny throughout the year.

The sections below examine several institutional design features and practices that can enhance legislative influence in the budget process while also promoting fiscal prudence. Of course, these are only part of the story. The budgetary oversight culture of the legislature also reflects factors such as the constitutional division of responsibilities, party and electoral systems, whether governments traditionally have large majorities or whether coalition governments are the norm, and constraints related to the level of mandatory spending and available fiscal space. Moreover, it is important to keep in mind that a parliament is not a monolithic institution but a collection of actors with diverse and changing strategies and incentives in the budgetary process.

## 5.2. Encouraging fiscal responsibility

A realistic debate on budgetary choices takes into account overall fiscal constraint, including in the medium and longer-term. A budgetary process that informs and consults the legislature on fiscal policy and medium-term budget policy, and that takes the views of the legislature into account during the budget formulation phase, promotes transparency and encourages fiscally responsible legislative decision-making. Such a process may ultimately lead to less need for amendments in the budget approval phase.

### *5.2.1. Pre-budget debate*

The survey results point to a growing trend for OECD parliaments to debate the broad direction of fiscal policy, as well as budgetary priorities and trade-offs before the annual budget is submitted for approval. Although a similar number of countries reported that the government submits a pre-budget report to the legislature in 2012 (19 countries) and in 2018 (22 countries)[1], there is a marked change in the number of countries that report that the legislature holds a pre-budget debate – up from only three countries in 2012 to 13, or just over a third of OECD legislatures, in 2018. Of these about half send the results of the pre-budget debate as a report to the government.

Among the most well-known examples, the Swedish Riksdag, has a two-step legislative process in which the Spring Fiscal Policy Bill (submitted in April) allows for a more general debate on fiscal policy and the debate on the Budget Bill (submitted in September) covers the government's detailed spending proposals for the next budget year.

Several legislatures also reported that while there is not a formal debate in the plenary, the Budget Committee may engage in the pre-budget phase. In the Czech Republic the Committee on the Budget holds a pre-budget debate and passes a resolution on the budget strategy and convergence programme. In Ireland the newly established[2] Committee on Budgetary Oversight holds pre-budget hearings on budgetary priorities and issues a report to the plenary. In Israel the Finance Committee has at times chosen to have pre-budget discussions in order to signal their preferences during budget formulation.

**Figure 5.1. Does the legislature hold a pre-budget debate?**

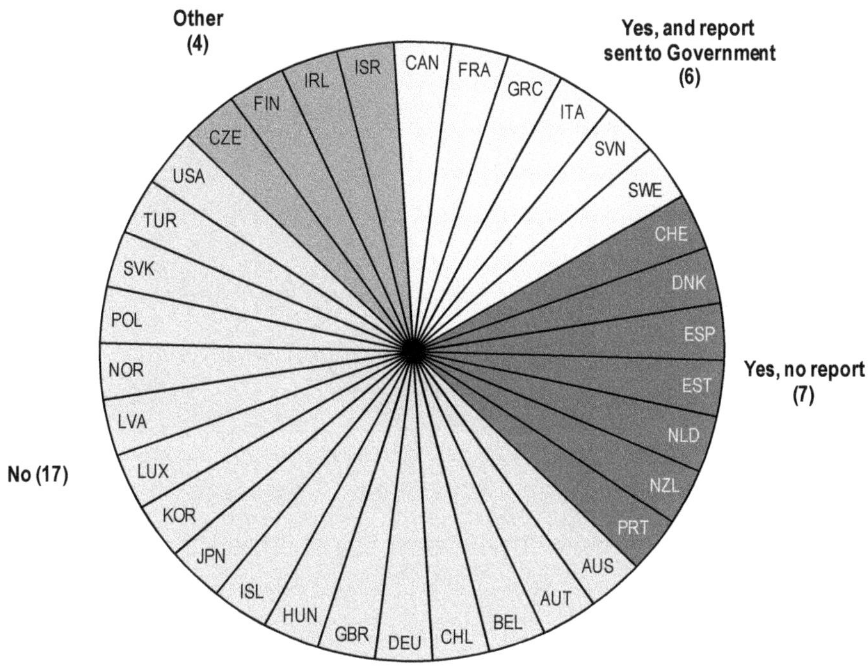


*Notes*: Data for Mexico are not available; Information on data for Israel: http://dx.doi.org/10.1787/888932315602.
*Source*: OECD (2018), OECD PBO Network Survey on Parliamantary Budgeting Practices, Question 1, OECD, Paris.

StatLink http://dx.doi.org/10.1787/888933946761

## *5.2.2. Legislative scrutiny of medium term budgetary frameworks*

Most fiscal measures have budgetary implications that go well beyond the annual budget. Legislative scrutiny of the medium term budgetary framework (MTBF) is now a common practice in OECD legislatures. Twenty-four OECD legislatures report that they debate the MTBF and 13[3] of these report that they formally approve the MTBF.

**Figure 5.2. Does the legislature debate or approve the medium-term budgetary framework?**

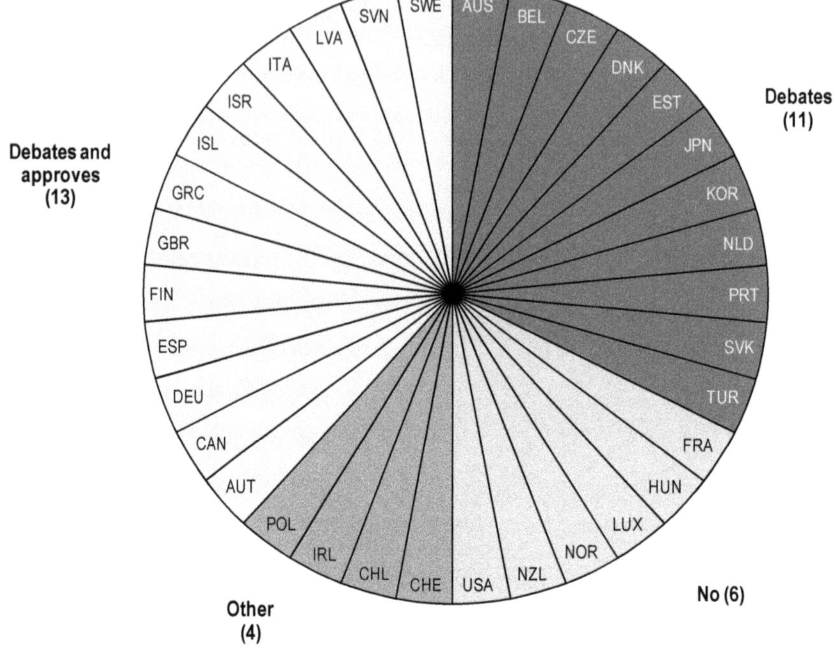


*Notes*: Data for Mexico are not available; Information on data for Israel: http://dx.doi.org/10.1787/888932315602.

*Source*: OECD (2018), OECD PBO Network Survey on Parliamantary Budgeting Practices, Question 3, OECD, Paris.

StatLink http://dx.doi.org/10.1787/888933946780

### *5.2.3. Legislative scrutiny of long-term sustainability*

Medium-term analysis provides the basis for long-term analysis, another important tool to help illustrate the risks and allocative trade-offs societies may be faced with when pursuing sustainable public finances. For most OECD countries the importance of long-term analysis has only grown as societies age and as the impact of programmes that involve intergenerational transfers expands.[4]

Independent fiscal institutions provide an important source of long-term analysis (typically 10-50 years) for many OECD legislatures. Since the *2012 OECD Budgeting Practices and Procedures Survey* the number of IFIs in the OECD has doubled and the majority of these new institutions produce long-term sustainability analysis, although this analysis may not always be taken up in a meaningful way by the legislature yet.

**Figure 5.3. Does the legislature receive and debate long-term sustainability analysis?**

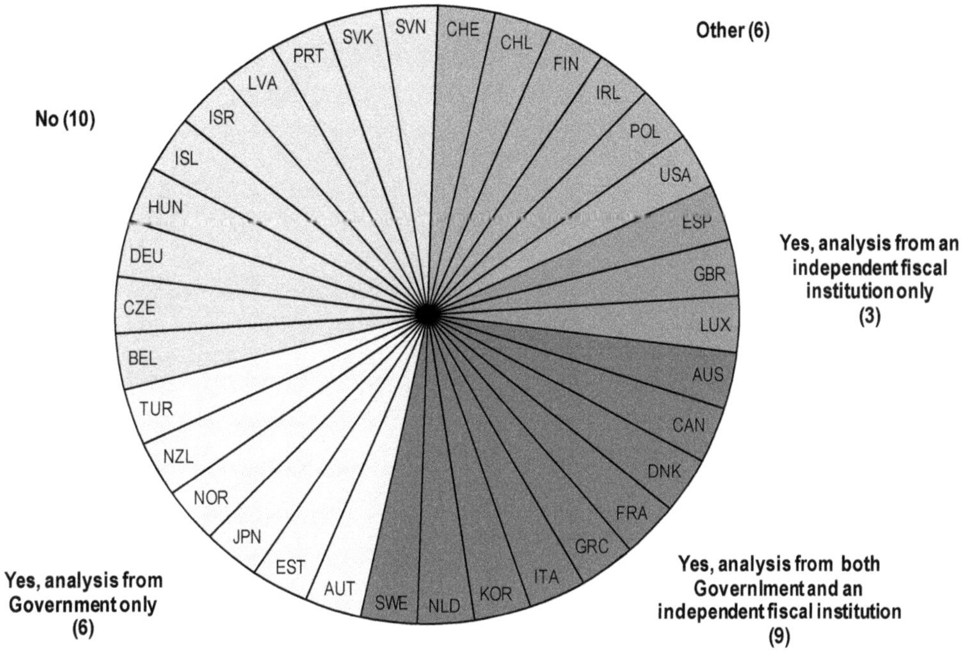


*Notes*: In Finland the parliament receives long-term sustainability analysis from government and can also ask the IFI for additional long-term analysis if it wishes. While the Latvian Fiscal Discipline Council is not required to produce long-term sustainability analysis, it is beginning to undertake this type of analysis at its own initiative.
Data for Mexico are not available; Information on data for Israel: http://dx.doi.org/10.1787/888932315602.
*Source*: OECD (2018), OECD PBO Network Survey on Parliamantary Budgeting Practices, Question 4, OECD, Paris

StatLink http://dx.doi.org/10.1787/888933946799

## 5.3. The budget approval process

### *5.3.1. Bicameralism – what role for upper houses?*

Half of OECD legislatures are bi-cameral, with upper chambers typically playing a much more limited role in budget approval, or no role at all. For the majority of bicameral legislatures there are different rules for the upper chamber regarding budgets and other financial proposals. For example, upper chambers tend to have a much shorter period to debate the budget, and they often do not have the right to amend or reject budget bills.

Only four OECD parliaments report that the upper and lower chambers have co-equal budgetary powers (Chile, Italy, Switzerland, and the United States). It is more common for the lower house to have the prerogative in the budget process. In the Netherlands, for example, only the lower chamber can amend the budget while the upper chamber can only agree or disagree.

**Figure 5.4. Role of each chamber in the budget process**

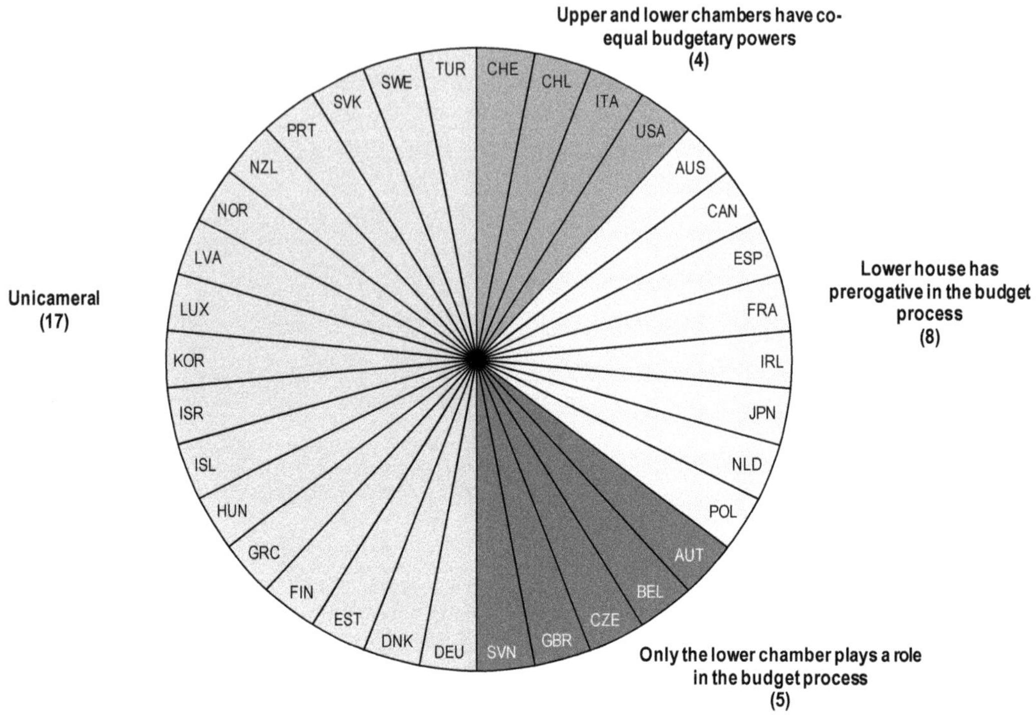


*Notes:* Data for Mexico are not available; Information on data for Israel: http://dx.doi.org/10.1787/888932315602.

*Source*: OECD (2018), OECD PBO Network Survey on Parliamantary Budgeting Practices, Questions 5 and 5a, OECD, Paris.

StatLink http://dx.doi.org/10.1787/888933946818

## *5.3.2. Time available for legislative debate*

Legislatures and their committees require an adequate amount of time to review and debate budget documents, and propose and debate amendments. The *OECD Best Practices for Budget Transparency* (2002) recommend that the executive should submit its budget proposal to the legislature at least three months prior to the start of the fiscal year and that the legislature should approve the annual budget law prior to the start of the new fiscal year.

Around 60% of OECD countries meet the former recommendation and the vast majority meet the latter. The exceptions tend to be in Westminster style parliaments where the estimates tend to be approved after the start of the fiscal year (including Canada, Ireland, New Zealand and the UK). Ireland stands out as the sole example where the formal legislative appropriation of moneys for the budget year (via the Appropriation Act) does not take place until the end of the budget year, after the money has been spent.

**Figure 5.5. Time available for legislative debate of the budget proposal**

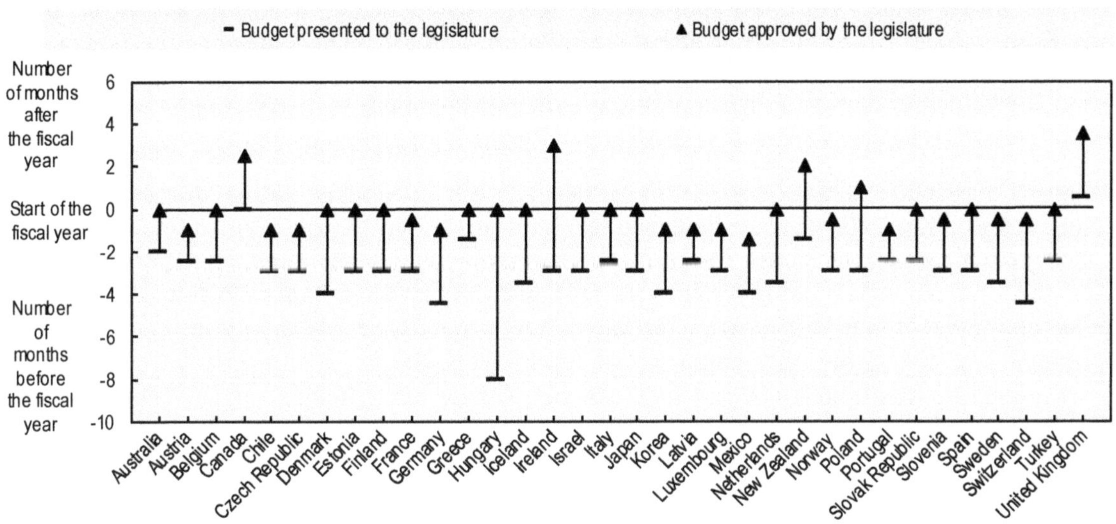


*Notes*: Where timelines differ for the approval of tax and expenditure policy measures, the timeline for the approval of expenditure measures is shown.

In Hungary since 2015 the budget is submitted to the parliament at the end of April. While the parliament legally has until end December to approve the budget, in practice it has been approving the budget in early July before the summer recess; In Ireland all of the Estimates that have been voted by the legislature for the budget year are not finally implemented in legislation until the annual Appropriation Act is passed. It is usually one of the last pieces of legislation to be enacted each year. Statutory confirmation of the appropriation of moneys, pursuant to Article 17.1.2 of the Constitution, therefore takes place after these moneys (or almost all of them) have been spent, almost 12 months after the start of the budget year.

Data for the United States are not available; Information on data for Israel: http://dx.doi.org/10.1787/888932315602.

*Source*: OECD (2018), OECD Budget Practices and Procedures Survey, Question 7a+f+h, OECD, Paris.

StatLink http://dx.doi.org/10.1787/888933946837

### *5.3.3. Voting on budget totals*

In addition to the practices described earlier in the chapter, a budget approval process where the legislature votes first on the budget totals, providing a strict frame for the subsequent debate on allocative choices and potential amendments, can further promote fiscal responsibility and focus attention on budget priorities. Some OECD legislatures do this by passing a separate piece of legislation to fix the aggregate totals before the annual appropriations and revenue measures are considered.

This practice may be complemented and strengthened by a committee process where the budget committee is responsible for setting the budget totals and the aggregate sectoral allocations and ensuring that they are respected, while sectoral committees allocate funding to individual appropriations in their expenditure areas within the agreed totals (see section on the role of committees below).

Just under two-thirds of OECD countries report that the legislature votes on the budget totals (aggregate and specific ceilings for expenditure areas). The response is essentially the same as that for the 2012 survey, with only Greece reporting that in the meantime they have introduced this practice.

### *5.3.4. Amendment powers*

Amendment powers are a key indicator for the potential of the legislature to impact the budget. At one end of the spectrum, the legislature in the United States has the power to rewrite the government's proposed budget and does so in practice. At the other end are legislatures such as Ireland that can only approve or reject the budget.

Over half of OECD countries report unrestricted amendment powers. The second most common practice is that the legislature can amend the budget within the executive's aggregates. Similarly in New Zealand, the legislature may propose amendments to the budget subject to an executive veto if the amendment would have more than a minor impact on the government's fiscal aggregates. In Turkey the Budget and Plan Committee can make any changes, but in plenary session the legislature cannot increase expenditures or decrease revenues. Chile is the only country that reports that the legislature can only decrease spending. In Australia the legislature can only make amendments on new policies. In Korea, the executive must approve the amendments proposed by the legislature.

**Figure 5.6. Formal powers of the legislature to amend the budget proposed by the executive**

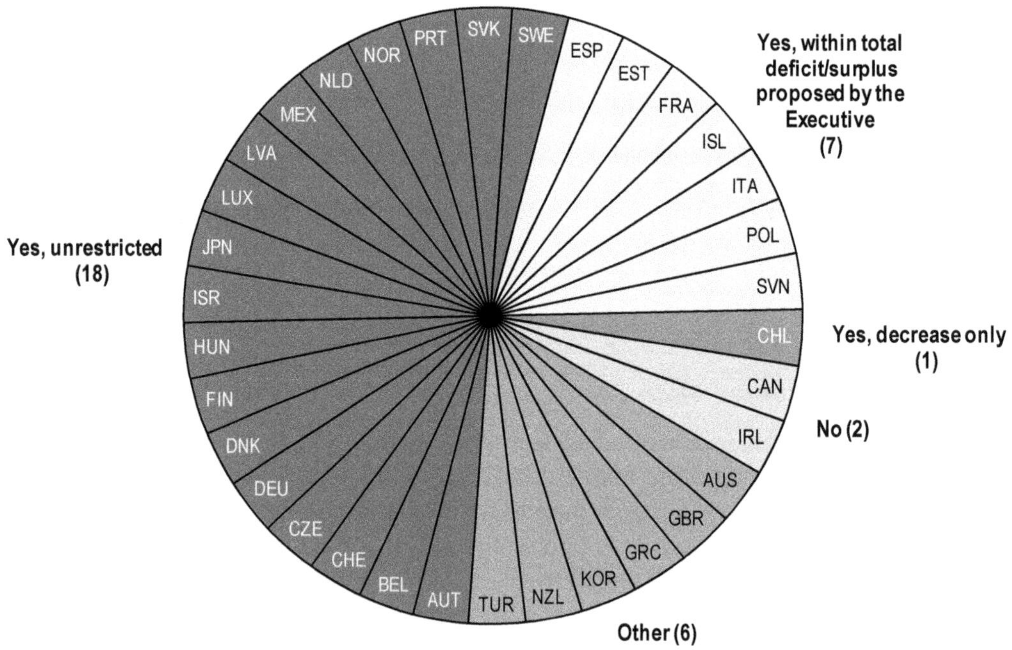


*Notes*: Data for the United States are not available; Information on data for Israel: http://dx.doi.org/10.1787/888932315602.
*Source*: OECD (2018), OECD Budget Practices and Procedures Survey, Question 39, OECD, Paris.

StatLink http://dx.doi.org/10.1787/888933946856

But formal amendment powers do not tell the whole story. In practice, most OECD legislatures only make minor adjustments to the executive's budget proposal. Where government has a large majority in parliament, it is unlikely that its budget will be significantly changed. Fiscal rules and mandatory spending may constrain the ability of the legislature to make any significant amendments. Consultation and bargaining during the budget formulation stage may also reduce the size of the legislature's actual amendments during the approval stage. And in many countries, the legislature may effectively be restrained from using amendment powers as votes on the budget are considered confidence votes.

Although changes tend to be minor, this does not mean that amendment powers are unimportant. Arguably, even a moderate level of amendment activity signals to the executive that it needs to take legislative scrutiny seriously.

**Figure 5.7. Notwithstanding the formal powers of the legislature to modify the budget, is a vote on the budget generally considered a vote of confidence in the government?**

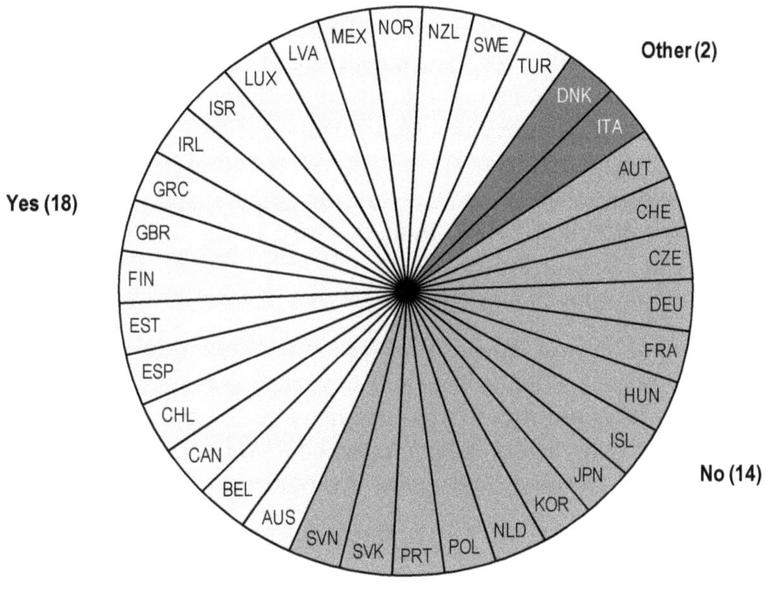


*Notes*: For Greece, it is a confidence vote in practice. Although Sweden answered yes, in 2014 when government failed to pass its budget, it reached a deal with the main opposition avoiding the need for snap elections.

Data for the United States are not available; Information on data for Israel: http://dx.doi.org/10.1787/888932315602.

*Source*: OECD (2018), OECD Budget Practices and Procedures Survey, Question 40, OECD, Paris.

StatLink http://dx.doi.org/10.1787/888933946875

## 5.4. The role of committees

Described as the "engine room" of the legislature, committees provide an opportunity for more in-depth, specialised scrutiny and can sustain an informed "accountability dialogue" with government ministries and agencies.

A strong budget committee can promote co-ordination and consistency in legislative budget action and facilitate fiscal discipline while involving sectoral committees allows the legislature to draw on their specific expertise when reviewing departmental spending plans (Posner and Park, 2007; Schick, 2002). In this way the parliamentary committee process can be viewed as mirroring that of the Finance Ministry vis-à-vis the line ministries.

In two-thirds of OECD legislatures a single budget committee is responsible for overall budget review and for co-ordinating varying levels of input from sectoral committees. A further eight countries have a committee review process in which the budget committee considers budget aggregates while sectoral committees consider sector specific appropriations. Only Australia and the UK do not have the equivalent of a budget committee. In Australia, committees in the lower house play little role and budget scrutiny is largely done through highly publicised estimates hearings in the Senate.

The vast majority of OECD countries use performance information in budgeting. Sectoral committees, which have developed significant subject expertise, may be best placed to review the performance information for their portfolios. However, in Germany the Budget Committee's rapporteur system ensures that even without the input of the sectoral committees, the budget committee develops significant expertise on departmental budgets. Currently 21 OECD legislatures report that it is the budget committee and/or a subcommittee of the budget committee that has the main responsibility for reviewing performance information attached to the budget. Only in 11 countries do the sectoral committees take the lead (among these Greece and Italy indicated that both the budget committee and sectoral committees take the lead).

Giving the chairmanship of on oversight committee to the opposition signals a commitment to operate the committee in a nonpartisan and consensual manner. This is a common practice for public accounts committees in Westminster style parliaments (see Section 5.5 below). A handful of OECD legislatures have adopted a similar tradition for their budget committees, such as France, Germany, Hungary, Portugal, and Spain.

## 5.5. In-year and *ex post* oversight

After the budget is approved, the legislature continues in its budgetary oversight role. Oversight of budget implementation is facilitated by information on in-year actual spending and timely, comprehensible audit reports. In line with the OECD *Best Practices for Budget Transparency* around 70% of OECD countries report producing monthly financial reports[5], giving a snapshot of budget implementation throughout the year. A further handful produce such reports on a quarterly basis only. Monthly reports support the information in the much more comprehensive mid-year review.

Any material changes to the approved budget should also be reviewed and authorised by the legislature. Over 75% of OECD countries need legislative approval for supplementary budgets. Legislatures may have little choice but to approve these requests but they can at least express policy concerns.

The year-end report is government's key accountability document. Legislative scrutiny of audit findings ensures that public funds have been used for the purposes intended, and that policies achieved their intended results. Many OECD legislatures have a specialised Audit or Public Accounts Committee to deal with the reports produced by the supreme audit institution. For others, this review takes place in the Budget Committee or a sub-committee of the Budget Committee. Despite this, two thirds report that there is no formal process for integrating the recommendations of the committee responsible for reviewing the year-end audited report into the following year's budget approval process.

**Figure 5.8. Supplementary budgets and reports submitted to the legislature**

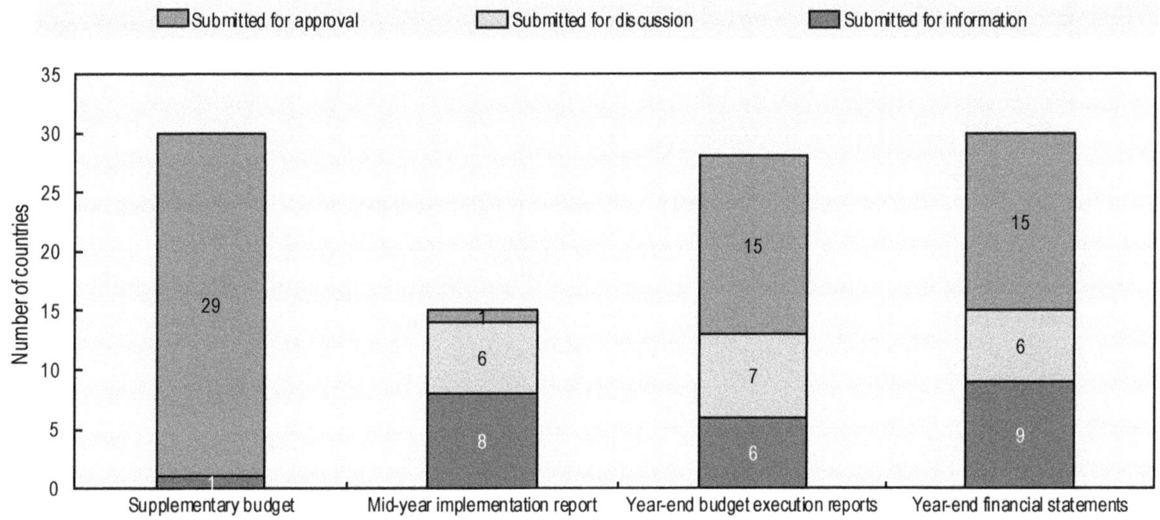


*Notes:* Data for the United States are not available; Information on data for Israel: http://dx.doi.org/10.1787/888932315602.

*Source*: OECD (2018), OECD Budget Practices and Procedures Survey, Question 37, OECD, Paris.

StatLink http://dx.doi.org/10.1787/888933946894

Nevertheless some examples have emerged of practices with the potential to strengthen the link between the audit phase and the subsequent budget approval phase. In Germany, representatives from the supreme audit institution attend and provide advice during the initial consultation meetings between the Budget Committee's rapporteurs and ministry officials, as well as the Budget Committee meetings where the reports and proposed amendments are presented. In Austria, the budget documentation shows the most recent and most relevant Court of Audit recommendations for different expenditure areas. In France specialised members of the Finance Committee are charged with ensuring that audit findings are taken into account in the subsequent budget debate.

## 5.6. Analytical support

Sufficient analytical capacity is a necessary prerequisite for a legislature to exercise its budgetary functions. Hiring adequate committee staff, allowing committees to consult or employ experts, and strengthening independent research capacity, all serve to enhance legislative effectiveness and redress the capacity imbalance between the legislature and the executive.

### *5.6.1. Committee staff*

The number of budget committee staff varies widely across OECD legislatures and staff may have a legal background versus a technical background in budgeting. Two to three staff members is most common but numbers on the higher end range from 10 in Japan, 21 in Korea, 25 for each house in France, 28 in Turkey and 35 for the US House of Representatives and 47 for the US Senate.

In addition to the above, committees may seek outside advice. All of the respondents reported that their budget committee has the right to consult outside experts.[6] Over a third also have the right to employ outside experts.

### *5.6.2. Specialised research services or staff*

Over a third of OECD legislatures report that there is a specialised unit for budget analysis in the research services. Typically these units have around 10 staff, although Spain reports 2 staff and Turkey reports 40 staff. The UK House of Commons Scrutiny Unit has 14 staff. It supports departmental select committees and undertakes systematic reviews of the main and supplementary estimates, departmental annual reports and accounts, spending review, settlements, Budget Statements and Autumn Statements, among other things.

Some legislatures do not have a specialised unit but do report having a small number of specialised staff within the research services (between 5 and 7 FTE). This is the case in Canada, Czech Republic, Estonia, Latvia, and Norway.

### *5.6.3. Independent fiscal institutions (IFIs)*

The growth of independent fiscal institutions (independent parliamentary budget offices and fiscal councils), has moved at a remarkably fast pace – they are now the norm, not the exception in OECD countries and some countries report multiple institutions.

Legislative budgetary discussions provide a unique opportunity to consider IFIs' analysis, Among the core functions common across IFI models, are a role in producing, assessing and/or endorsing macroeconomic or fiscal forecasting, monitoring compliance with fiscal rules, policy costing, long-term fiscal sustainability analysis, and supporting the legislature in budget analysis.

**Table 5.1. Budget and staffing in select PBOs in the OECD**

| Country | **Institution name** | **Year** | **Budget** (USD) | **Staffing** (FTE) |
|---|---|---|---|---|
| Australia | Parliamentary Budget Office (PBO) | 2017 | 5.1 million | 40 |
| Austria | Parliamentary Budget Office (PBO) | 2017 | 1.1 million | 8 |
| Canada | Parliamentary Budget Office (PBO) | 2018 | 3.9 million | 27 |
| Greece | Parliamentary Budget Office (PBO) | 2017 | 0.6 million | 16 |
| Ireland | Parliamentary Budget Office (PBO) | 2018 | 1.0 million | 12 |
| Italy | Parliamentary Budget Office (PBO) | 2017 | 7.1 million | 27 |
| Korea | National Assembly Budget Office (NABO) | 2017 | 13.1 million | 138 |
| Mexico | Center for Public Finance Studies (CEFP) | 2016 | 2.7 million | 60 |
| US | Congressional Budget Office (CBO) | 2016 | 46.5 million | 235 |

*Note*: National currency converted into US dollars as of September 2018.
*Source*: OECD IFI Database (2018).

## 5.7. Openness and public participation

Parliaments play a critical role in promoting transparency and accountability. At the same time, they too must work in a transparent manner and be accountable to the electorate on an ongoing basis. In recent years, parliaments, together with civil society, have increasingly engaged around the concept of parliamentary openness.

**Figure 5.9. Are meetings of the budget committee open to the public?**

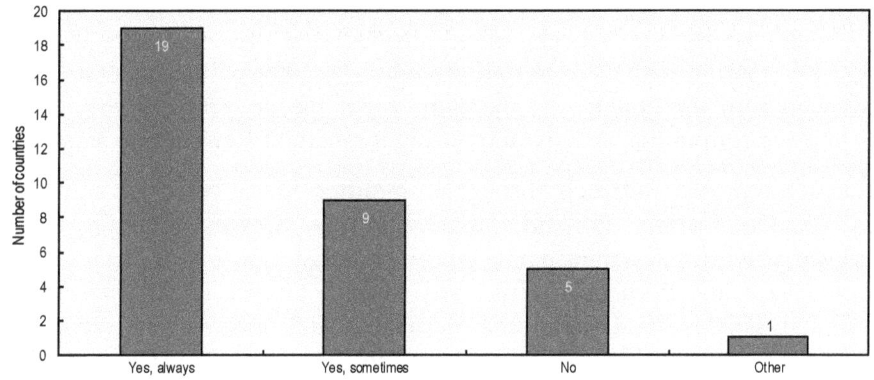


*Notes*: Data for Mexico are not available; Information on data for Israel: http://dx.doi.org/10.1787/888932315602.
*Source*: OECD (2018), OECD PBO Network Survey on Parliamantary Budgeting Practices, Question 9, OECD, Paris.

StatLink http://dx.doi.org/10.1787/888933946913

**Figure 5.10. Are committee reports published?**

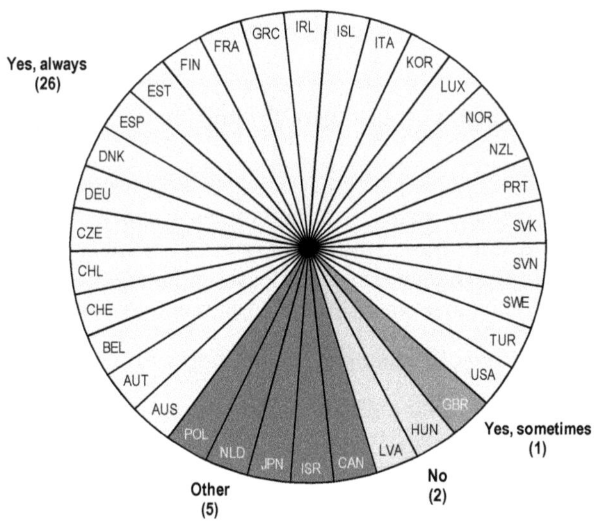


*Notes*: Data for Mexico are not available; Information on data for Israel: http://dx.doi.org/10.1787/888932315602.
*Source*: OECD (2018), OECD PBO Network Survey on Parliamantary Budgeting Practices, Question 12, OECD, Paris.

StatLink http://dx.doi.org/10.1787/888933946932

It is common practice for OECD legislatures to open committee meetings to the public or to broadcast committee meetings via television or the internet. The vast majority of OECD legislatures also publish committee reports.

The survey also asked about specific tools OECD legislatures are using to encourage public participation in the budget process. The results show that, at least where the budget is concerned, OECD legislatures continue to rely mainly on traditional participatory mechanisms such as public hearings of permanent committees (25 countries) but have been slow to adopt approaches that take advantage of digital tools with the potential to reach a wider group of stakeholders. This may be in part because parliaments have focused first on educational and transparency aspects when introducing a more participatory approach – e.g. sharing information with citizens and promoting greater public understanding of how parliament works on the budget. At the same time, the government may already have processes in place for public participation during the budget formulation stage.

Eight countries reported outreach through committee visits or town hall style events (Australia, Canada, Estonia, Finland, Japan, Portugal, Slovak Republic, and the US). Another seven countries reported using e-petitions (Estonia, Finland, Germany, Korea, Luxembourg, NZ[7], and Portugal); while only France, Greece and Switzerland reported holding "digital debates on social media platforms" and only Austria reported that it is preparing to do "crowdsourcing of ideas for scrutiny" in the future. The Netherlands gave an example of an innovative new practice introduced in 2017, the "V-100". Organised by the Dutch Parliament, the "V-100" brings together 100 participants from society who scrutinise the annual budget reports and make suggestions to committees on potential questions for the responsible minister.

It should be noted that this question does not capture some of the work parliaments have been doing to explain the budget to citizens. There is also the caveat that answers apply to the budget process to date, for example, the UK parliament has never had an e-petition or held a digital debate related to the budget but it has used both tools for other policy debates.

## Notes

[1] Sometimes combined with mid-term evaluation of the previous year.

[2] Established in July 2016.

[3] 10 of the 13 are also EU member states. EU requirements appear to have encouraged greater involvement of the legislature in medium term planning in EU member countries. According to the EU database on MTBFs, all EU member countries at least send medium term plans to the parliament and in the vast majority of EU member countries the parliament votes on the medium term plans.

[4] Anderson, B. The Changing Role of Parliament in the Budget Process (2009)

[5] In the case of New Zealand, there is no monthly report for the first two months of the year.

[6] Not applicable for Australia and the UK.

[7] The electronic petitions system was introduced in March 2018.

## References

OECD IFI Database (2018), www.oecd.org/gov/budgeting/OECD-Independent-Fiscal-Institutions-Database.xlsx

OECD (2015), *Recommendation on Budgetary Governance*, www.oecd.org/gov/budgeting/Recommendation-of-the-Council-on-Budgetary-Governance.pdf

OECD (2002), "OECD Best Practices for Budget Transparency", *OECD Journal on Budgeting*, vol. 1/3, https://doi.org/10.1787/budget-v1-art14-en.

Posner, P. and C. Park (2007), "Role of the Legislature in the Budget Process: Recent Trends and Innovations", *OECD Journal on Budgeting*, vol. 7/3, https://doi.org/10.1787/budget-v7-art15-en.

Schick, A. (2002), "Can National Legislatures Regain an Effective Voice in Budget Policy?", *OECD Journal on Budgeting*, vol. 1/3, https://doi.org/10.1787/budget-v1-art15-en.

# 6. Open, Transparent and Inclusive Budgeting

*This chapter focuses on openness, transparency and inclusiveness in budgeting; all of which are increasingly viewed as fundamental to promoting good governance and underpinning trust between citizens and governments. Key aspects of open, transparent and inclusive budgeting include the regular publication of key budget documents, reporting with simplicity and clarity, making budget information available and accessible to citizens - including through open data formats - and using consultative mechanisms to engage citizens.*

*This chapter also includes a special focus on gender budgeting. Gender budgeting is a tool of public financial management that is used to address the range of inequalities that have become embedded in public policies and the allocation of resources.*

## 6.1. Budget Transparency

The principle of budget transparency – including the clarity, comprehensiveness, reliability, timeliness and accessibility of reporting on public finances – is now well established in OECD countries. The *OECD Toolkit on Budget Transparency (2017)* summarises that "budget transparency means being fully open with people about how public money is raised and used".

### *6.1.1. Budget documents published*

It is important that comprehensive budget information is presented publicly to enable policy debate. In general terms, budget transparency has improved in participating OECD countries in recent years. The largest gains from 2012 to 2018 are seen in relation to the publication of independent review of economic/fiscal assumptions (increased from 47% to 85%) and long-term fiscal sustainability reports (increased from 41% to 74%).

**Figure 6.1. Changes to the publication of budget information over time**

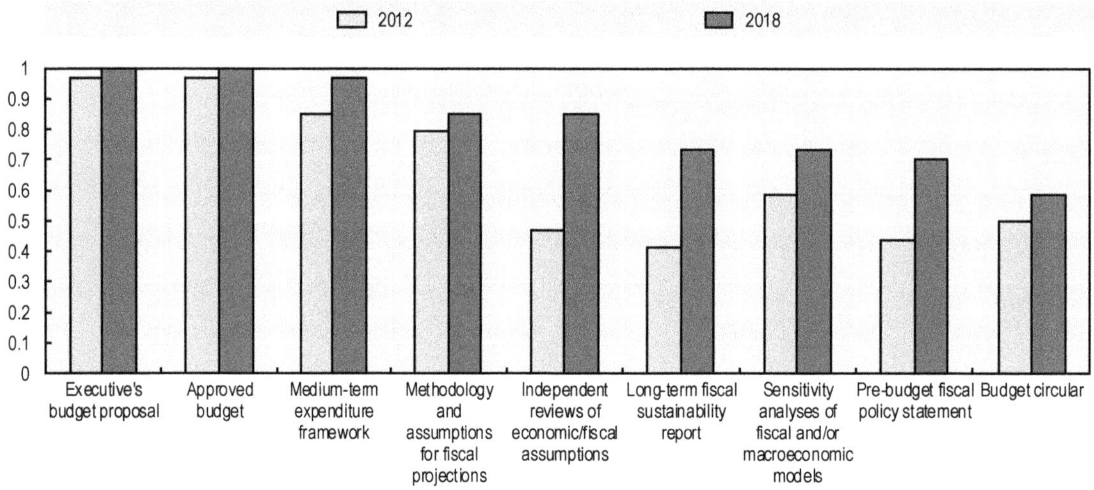


*Notes*: Percentage of participating OECD countries (34 in 2012 and 34 in 2018).
2018 data for the United States are not available; Information on data for Israel: http://dx.doi.org/10.1787/888932315602.
*Sources*: OECD (2018), OECD Budget Practices and Procedures Survey, Question 5, OECD, Paris; OECD (2012), OECD Budget Practices and Procedures Survey, Question 61, OECD, Paris.

StatLink http://dx.doi.org/10.1787/888933946951

Drawing on the established international standards and guidelines, the *OECD Toolkit on Budget Transparency (2017)* lists the principal budget reports that governments can produce to inform more open and transparent scrutiny and decision-making throughout the budget cycle. These are: the pre-budget statement, the executive's budget proposal (or draft budget), the approved budget, a supplementary budget, pre-execution budget profiles or cash flow forecasts, in-year budget execution reports, the mid-year implementation report, year-end reporting, the long-term report and reporting on fiscal risk.

All participating OECD countries now publish a draft budget and the approved budget. More than 90% of participating OECD countries also publish their year-end financial statements (32), year-end execution reports (32), and a supplementary budget (31).

However, just a fifth of participating OECD countries publish pre-execution budget profiles or cash flow forecasts (Belgium, Chile, France, Greece, Mexico, Poland and Sweden).

**Table 6.1. Publication of key budget documents**

| | Pre-budget statement | Budget proposal | Approved budget | Supplementary budget | Pre-execution budget profiles | In-year budget execution reports | M/Y implementation report | Y/E budget execution report | Y/E financial statement | LT fiscal sustainability report | Report on fiscal risks |
|---|---|---|---|---|---|---|---|---|---|---|---|
| Australia | | x | x | | | x | x | x | x | x | x |
| Austria | | x | x | x | | x | x | x | x | x | |
| Belgium | x | x | x | x | x | x | x | x | x | x | x |
| Canada | x | x | x | x | | x | x | x | x | x | x |
| Chile | | x | x | | x | x | x | x | x | x | x |
| Czech Republic | x | x | x | x | | x | x | x | x | x | x |
| Denmark | | x | x | x | | | | x | x | x | x |
| Estonia | x | x | x | x | | x | | x | x | | |
| Finland | x | x | x | x | | x | | x | x | x | x |
| France | x | x | x | x | x | x | x | x | x | | |
| Germany | | x | x | x | | x | | | x | x | |
| Greece | x | x | x | x | x | x | | x | x | | x |
| Hungary | x | x | x | x | | x | x | x | x | x | x |
| Iceland | x | x | x | x | | x | | x | x | | |
| Ireland | x | x | x | x | x | x | x | x | x | x | |
| Israel | x | x | x | x | | x | | x | x | | x |
| Italy | x | x | x | x | | | | x | x | x | x |
| Japan | x | x | x | x | | x | | x | x | | |
| Korea | | x | x | x | | | | x | x | x | x |
| Latvia | x | x | x | x | | x | | x | x | x | x |
| Luxembourg | | x | x | | | x | x | x | x | x | x |
| Mexico | x | x | x | x | x | x | x | x | x | x | x |
| Netherlands | | x | x | x | | x | x | x | x | x | x |
| New Zealand | x | x | x | x | | x | x | x | x | x | x |
| Norway | | x | x | x | | x | x | x | x | x | |
| Poland | x | x | x | x | x | x | | x | | | |
| Portugal | x | x | x | x | | x | | x | | | x |
| Slovak Republic | x | x | x | x | | | x | x | x | x | x |
| Slovenia | x | x | x | x | | x | x | x | x | x | |
| Spain | x | x | x | x | | x | x | x | x | x | x |
| Sweden | x | x | x | x | x | x | | x | x | x | x |
| Switzerland | | x | x | x | | x | x | x | x | x | x |
| Turkey | x | x | x | x | | x | x | x | x | x | x |
| United Kingdom | x | x | x | x | | x | x | | x | x | x |
| Total OECD | 24 | 34 | 34 | 31 | 8 | 30 | 20 | 32 | 32 | 26 | 24 |

*Notes*: Data for the United States are not available; Information on data for Israel: http://dx.doi.org/10.1787/888932315602.
*Source*: OECD (2018), OECD Budget Practices and Procedures Survey, Question 5, OECD, Paris.

## *6.1.2. Citizen's budget guides*

Budget documents are often technically complex and long documents. By reporting and explaining budget decisions and the state of public finances with simplicity and clarity, the government can help to demystify the budget. Publication of a citizen's guide allows a government to explain in plain language the objective and impacts of its budget.

In 2012, citizen's guides to the budget were produced in 14 OECD countries. Citizen's guides, of one form or another, are now produced in 23 OECD countries. In 2018, Citizen's guides are most often published for the approved budget and the executive budget proposal (both 14 OECD countries). They are less likely to be published for the wider range of budget-related documents, such as the medium-term expenditure framework (7), year-end financial statements (6), year-end budget execution reports (5) and supplementary budgets (4).

**Figure 6.2. Citizen's guides for budget-related documents**

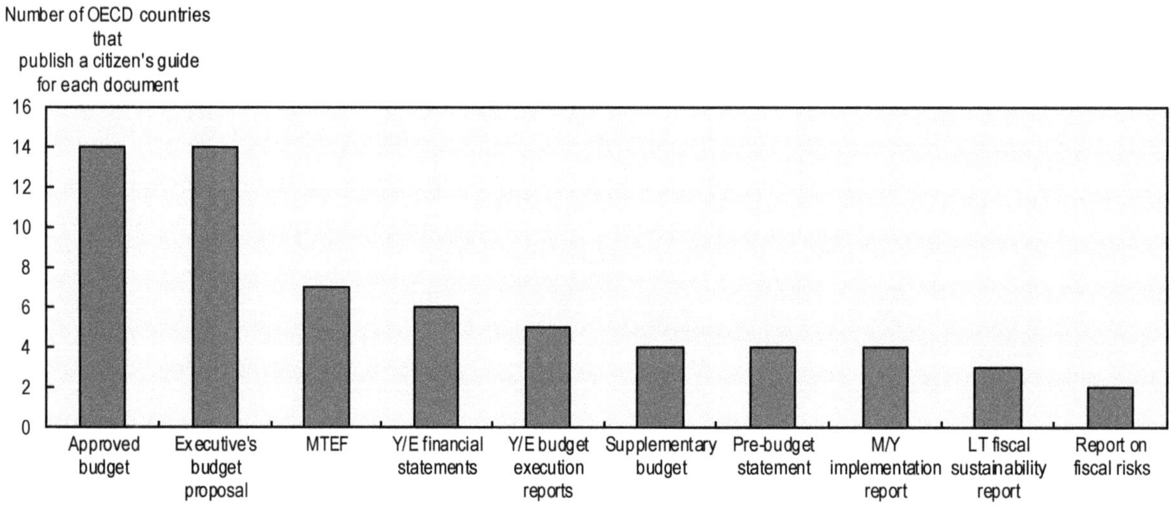


*Notes:* Data for the United States are not available; Information on data for Israel: http://dx.doi.org/10.1787/888932315602.

*Source*: OECD (2018), OECD Budget Practices and Procedures Survey, Question 30, OECD, Paris.

StatLink http://dx.doi.org/10.1787/888933946970

**Figure 6.3. The publication of citizen's guides across OECD countries**

Citizen's guide to budget proposal

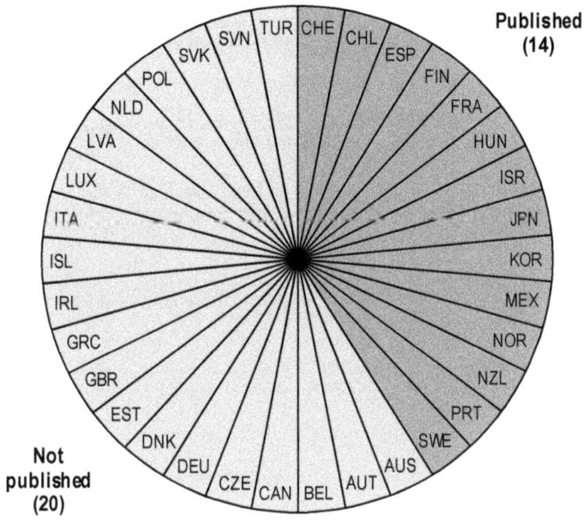


Citizen's guide to approved budget

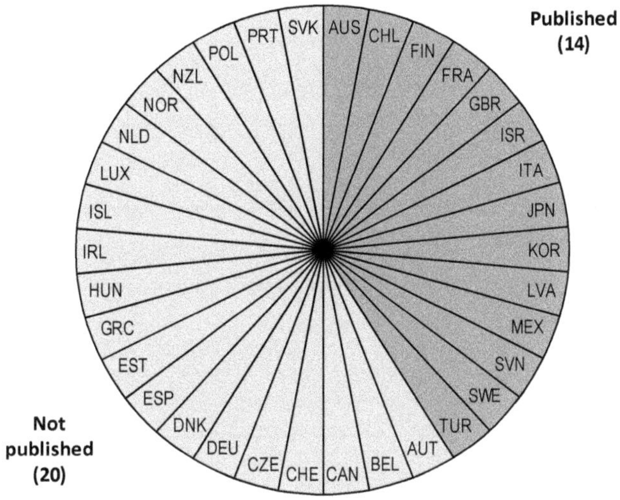


*Notes*: Data for the United States are not available; Information on data for Israel: http://dx.doi.org/10.1787/888932315602.
*Source*: OECD (2018), OECD Budget Practices and Procedures Survey, Question 30, OECD, Paris.

StatLink http://dx.doi.org/10.1787/888933946989

## *6.1.3. Open budget data*

Open data promotes transparency, accountability and value creation by making government data available to all. The majority of OECD countries provide the approved budget (28 OECD countries), the executive's budget proposal (24), year-end execution reports (23), supplementary budgets (22) and year-end financial statements (21) in open data format.

Over a third of OECD countries publish their medium-term expenditure framework (15) and long term fiscal sustainability report (13) in open data format.

**Table 6.2. Budget documents available in open data format**

| | Approved budget | Executive's budget proposal | Y/E budget execution reports | Supplementary budget | Y/E financial statements | MTEF | LT fiscal sustainability report | Mid-year implementation report | Report on fiscal risks | Pre-budget fiscal policy statement |
|---|---|---|---|---|---|---|---|---|---|---|
| Australia | x | | x | | x | x | x | x | x | |
| Austria | x | x | x | | x | | x | | | |
| Belgium | | | | | | | | | | |
| Canada | x | x | | x | | x | | | | |
| Chile | x | x | | | | | | x | | |
| Czech Republic | x | x | x | x | x | x | x | x | x | |
| Denmark | x | x | x | x | x | | | | | |
| Estonia | x | | x | x | x | | | | | |
| Finland | x | x | | x | x | | | | | |
| France | x | x | x | x | x | | | | | |
| Germany | x | x | | x | x | | | | | |
| Greece | | | x | | | | | | | |
| Hungary | x | x | x | x | x | x | x | x | x | x |
| Iceland | x | x | | | | x | | | | x |
| Ireland | x | | x | x | | | | | | x |
| Israel | x | x | x | x | x | x | | | | |
| Italy | x | x | x | x | x | | | | | |
| Japan | x | | x | x | x | | | | | |
| Korea | x | x | x | x | x | x | x | | x | x |
| Latvia | | | | | | | | | | |
| Luxembourg | | x | | | | | | | | |
| Mexico | x | x | x | x | | | | x | | |
| Netherlands | x | x | x | x | x | x | x | x | x | x |
| New Zealand | | | | | | | x | | | |
| Norway | x | x | x | x | x | | | x | | |
| Poland | x | x | x | x | | x | | | | x |
| Portugal | x | x | x | | | | | | | |
| Slovak Republic | x | x | x | x | x | x | x | x | x | |
| Slovenia | x | | x | x | x | x | x | x | x | x |
| Spain | x | x | x | x | x | x | x | x | x | x |
| Sweden | | x | | | | | | | | x |
| Switzerland | x | x | x | x | x | x | x | x | x | |
| Turkey | x | x | x | x | x | x | x | x | x | x |
| United Kingdom | x | | | | x | x | x | | x | |
| Total OECD | 28 | 24 | 23 | 22 | 21 | 15 | 13 | 12 | 11 | 10 |

*Note*: Data for the United States are not available; Information on data for Israel: http://dx.doi.org/10.1787/888932315602.

*Source*: OECD (2018), OECD Budget Practices and Procedures Survey, Question 30, OECD, Paris.

For the most part, open data is made available in downloadable form, e.g., spreadsheet (29 OECD countries), although some countries also provide data-visualisation tools (12) and some provide open data through an online portal (11).

### *6.1.4. Budget impact assessments*

Budget impact assessments are useful tools for highlighting the distributional impact of individual policies or a group of policies. They are a relatively specialised tool across the OECD. While almost half of OECD countries (16) report that they undertake impact analyses of some nature for individual measures, just ten countries publish impact analyses for the budget as a whole. It is most common for these to look at the budget's effects on households at different levels of income (5 OECD countries) or effects on overall income inequality (5).

**Table 6.3. Budget impact analyses published for budget as a whole**

OECD countries which publish each type of impact analyses for the budget as a whole

| | |
|---|---|
| a. Effects on households at different levels of income | Finland, Germany, Netherlands, Sweden, United Kingdom |
| b. Effects on overall income inequality (e.g. Gini coefficient) | Finland, Germany, Ireland, Netherlands, Sweden |
| c. Effects on poverty/social deprivation | Germany, Ireland, Netherlands, Sweden |
| d. Gender impacts | Germany, Italy, Spain, Sweden |
| e. Impacts on different age cohorts | Germany, Slovenia |
| f. Impacts on minority groups | Germany |
| g. Regional distribution of budget costs / benefits | Germany, Italy, Latvia, Spain |
| h. Environmental impacts / Climate change | Germany, Italy |
| i. Effects on range of societal wellbeing indicators | Germany, Italy, Netherlands |

*Source:* OECD (2018), OECD Budget Practices and Procedures Survey, Question 29, OECD, Paris.

## 6.2. Citizen consultation

Heightened engagement with societal stakeholders is a major trend in modern public governance. It is considered "critical to building citizen trust and is a key contributor to achieving different policy outcomes in diverse domains" (OECD Recommendation of the Council on Open Government 2017).

### *6.2.1. Consultative mechanisms used to engage citizens*

It is relatively common practice for OECD public institutions to undertake public consultation and engagement during the budget process. At the pre-budget stage it is most common for OECD governments to engage in meetings with stakeholders, whether they are private (15 OECD countries) or formal minuted meetings (11). Just eight OECD countries have a public call for proposals and six have public meetings. Public engagement and consultation is less frequent at the post-budget stage. However, OECD parliaments will often encourage public participation as part of their scrutiny of the draft budget proposal. Permanent committees hold public hearings on the budget in 25 OECD countries, and select committees hold hearings in 11 OECD countries.

**Table 6.4. Public consultation and engagement during the budget process**

| | Pre-budget | | | | | | Post-budget | | | |
|---|---|---|---|---|---|---|---|---|---|---|
| | Public call for proposals | Public meetings | Focus groups | Private meetings with key stakeholders | Formal (minuted) meetings with key stakeholders | Public roundtable with key stakeholders | Public meetings | Private meetings with key stakeholders | Formal (minuted) meetings with key stakeholders | Public roundtable with key stakeholders |
| Australia | x | | | x | | | | x | | x |
| Austria | | | | | | | | | x | |
| Belgium | | | | | | | | | | |
| Canada | x | x | x | x | x | x | | | | |
| Chile | | | | | x | | | | | |
| Czech Republic | | x | x | x | x | x | | x | x | x |
| Denmark | | | | | | | | | | |
| Estonia | | | | | | | | | | |
| Finland | | | | | | | | | | |
| France | | | | x | | | | x | x | |
| Germany | | | x | x | | | | x | | |
| Greece | | | | x | | | x | | | |
| Hungary | | | | | | | x | x | x | x |
| Iceland | x | | | x | x | | x | x | x | x |
| Ireland | | x | | | x | x | | | | |
| Israel | | | | x | x | | | | | |
| Italy | | | | x | | | | | x | |
| Japan | | | | | | | x | x | | |
| Korea | x | x | x | x | x | | x | | | |
| Latvia | | | | x | x | | | | | |
| Luxembourg | | | | | | | | x | | |
| Mexico | x | x | | x | x | | x | x | x | x |
| Netherlands | x | | | x | | | | | | |
| New Zealand | | | | | | | x | | | |
| Norway | | x | | x | | | | | | |
| Poland | | | | | | x | | | | |
| Portugal | | | | | | | x | | | |
| Slovak Republic | | | | | | | | | | |
| Slovenia | x | | | | x | | | | x | |
| Spain | | | | | | | x | x | x | x |
| Sweden | | | | | | | | | | |
| Switzerland | | | | | | | | | | |
| Turkey | | | | | | | | | | |
| United Kingdom | x | | | x | x | | x | x | | x |
| Total OECD | 8 | 6 | 4 | 15 | 11 | 4 | 10 | 11 | 9 | 7 |

*Notes*: Data for the United States are not available; Information on data for Israel: http://dx.doi.org/10.1787/888932315602.
*Source*: OECD (2018), OECD Budget Practices and Procedures Survey, Question 42, OECD, Paris.

### *6.2.2. Participative budgeting*

Participative budgeting is a technique for engaging the interests of citizens, and promoting 'budget literacy', that is practised to an increasing extent at municipal and local level in countries in the OECD and further afield. Typically, participative budgeting involves setting aside a limited proportion of the overall budget and inviting the public, or local neighbourhoods, to express their view about the best use of these resources. While the practice has now become well-established in some municipalities (the *budget participatif* of Paris is a leading international example), it is not yet prevalent at central/federal level in OECD countries. Only four OECD countries report the introduction of participative budgeting at the central/federal level (Canada, Korea, Mexico and Portugal).

## 6.3. Special Focus: Gender Budgeting

Gender budgeting means the systematic application of analytical tools and processes, as a routine part of the budget process, in order to highlight gender equality issues and to inform, prioritise and resource gender-responsive policies.

The *OECD Recommendation on Gender Equality in Public Life (2015)* and its implementation Toolkit identify gender budgeting as a key tool of a system-wide government approach to deliver gender equality outcomes.

### *6.3.1. Existence of gender budgeting*

The number of OECD countries that have introduced gender budgeting increased from 12 in 2016 to 17 in 2018 (Austria, Belgium, Canada, Chile, Finland, Germany, Iceland, Ireland, Israel, Italy, Japan, Korea, Mexico, Portugal, Spain and Sweden). In addition, two countries have plans to introduce it (France and Turkey).

**Figure 6.4. OECD countries that practise gender budgeting**

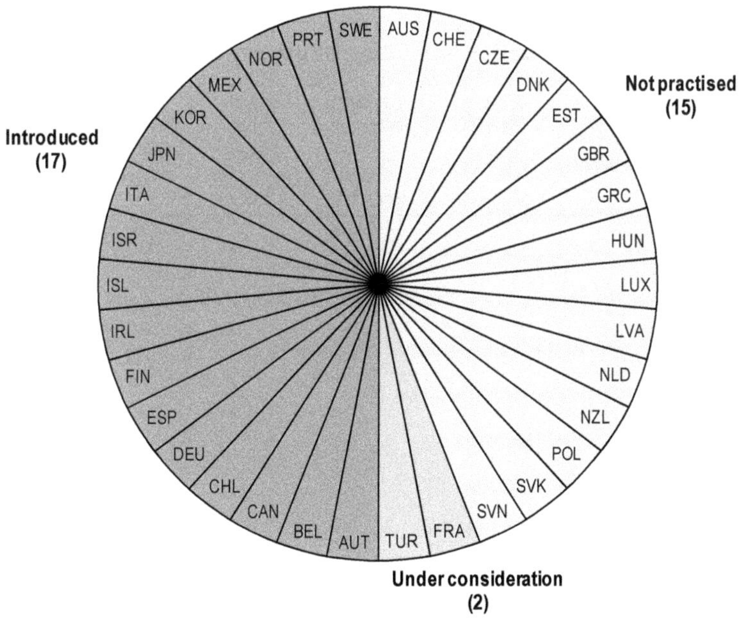


*Notes*: Data for the United States are not available; Information on data for Israel: http://dx.doi.org/10.1787/888932315602.
*Source*: OECD (2018), OECD Budget Practices and Procedures Survey, Questions 32 and 36, OECD, Paris.

StatLink http://dx.doi.org/10.1787/888933947008

### *Legal foundations for gender budgeting*

Implementing an effective and sustainable gender budgeting approach can be challenging. Some challenges derive from the differing levels of importance given to gender equality by successive governments, whereas others relate to fiscal constraints or more broadly to the challenges faced when implementing any new PFM practice or procedure in government. Legislation that is fully tested and debated in parliament can help embed gender budgeting as a valued and enduring feature of public policy making and insulate it, as far as possible, from fluctuations arising from the economic or political environment. Of the 17 OECD countries that have implemented gender budgeting, nine countries have legal provisions underpinning the practice (Austria, Belgium, Iceland, Italy, Korea, Mexico, Norway, Portugal, and Spain).

## *6.3.2. Tools of gender budgeting*

The OECD has identified a range of tools which can be used to systematically embed gender considerations throughout the budget cycle. In general, a broad range of gender budgeting tools are used by OECD countries. Over half of the OECD countries which have introduced gender budgeting use four or more tools (Austria, Canada, Germany, Iceland, Japan, Korea, Mexico, Norway, Spain and Sweden).

The most common tools of gender budgeting are *ex ante* gender impact assessment of policies (used by 76% of OECD countries that have introduced gender budgeting), *ex post* gender impact assessment of policies (59%), a gender dimension in performance setting (59%), a gender dimension to resource allocation (53%), and gender needs assessment (53%).

**Table 6.5. Tools of gender budgeting in use across OECD countries**

| | Needs assessment | Gender dimension in performance | Baseline analysis | *Ex ante* gender impact assessment of policies | Gender dimension in resource allocation | *Ex post* gender impact assessment of policies | Gender audit of budget | Gender dimension to performance audit | Audit of gender budgeting systems | Gender dimension to spending review |
|---|---|---|---|---|---|---|---|---|---|---|
| Austria | | x | | x | x | x | | x | x | |
| Belgium | | | | | x | | | | | |
| Canada | x | x | | x | | x | | x | | x |
| Chile | | x | | x | | x | | | | |
| Finland | | | | x | | | | | | |
| Germany | x | | x | x | | x | | | | |
| Iceland | x | x | x | x | x | x | x | x | x | |
| Ireland | | x | | | | | | | | |
| Israel | | | x | x | x | | | | | |
| Italy | | | x | | | x | | | | |
| Japan | x | x | x | x | x | | | | | x |
| Korea | x | x | | x | x | x | x | | | |
| Mexico | x | x | x | x | x | x | x | x | x | x |
| Norway | x | | x | | | x | x | | | |
| Portugal | x | | | x | x | | | | | |
| Spain | x | x | x | x | x | | | | | |
| Sweden | | x | | x | | x | x | x | x | x |
| Total OECD | 9 | 10 | 8 | 13 | 9 | 10 | 5 | 5 | 4 | 4 |

*Note*: Only shows OECD countries which have introduced gender budgeting.
Data for the United States are not available; Information on data for Israel: http://dx.doi.org/10.1787/888932315602.
*Source:* OECD (2018), OECD Budget Practices and Procedures Survey, Question 34, OECD, Paris.

### *Gender information published alongside the budget*

Nine of the 17 OECD countries that have introduced gender budgeting also publish information alongside the annual budget to help inform budget oversight. This often takes the form of a "gender statement". In at least two thirds of the cases, this information includes: a general statement on gender objectives (7 OECD countries); gender impact analysis of specific budget measures (7) and information on spending allocated to gender equality projects (6). Just 3 countries publish gender impact analysis of the budget as a whole (Canada, Mexico and Spain).

**Table 6.6. Gender information published alongside the budget**

| | General statement on gender objectives | Progress statement | Information on spending allocated to gender equality projects | Gender impact analysis of specific budget measures | Gender impact analysis of budget as a whole |
|---|---|---|---|---|---|
| Canada | x | x | | x | x |
| Iceland | | | | x | |
| Japan | x | | x | | |
| Korea | x | x | x | x | |
| Mexico | x | x | x | x | x |
| Norway | x | x | | x | |
| Portugal | x | | x | | |
| Spain | x | x | x | x | x |
| Sweden | | | x | x | |
| **Total** | **7** | **5** | **6** | **7** | **3** |

*Note*: Only shows OECD countries which publish gender information alongside the budget.
Data for the United States are not available; Information on data for Israel: http://dx.doi.org/10.1787/888932315602.
*Source:* OECD (2018), OECD Budget Practices and Procedures Survey, Question 34, OECD, Paris.

## *6.3.3. Support for the implementation of gender budgeting*

Over half of OECD countries that have introduced gender budgeting have standard guidelines from the CBA on implementation (Austria, Belgium, Canada, Iceland, Ireland, Israel, Italy, Korea, Mexico, Norway, Spain, Sweden), general and/or specific gender-disaggregated data (Austria, Canada, Chile, Finland, Germany, Iceland, Japan, Korea, Mexico, Norway, Portugal, Spain, Sweden), training and capacity development (Austria, Canada, Chile, Iceland, Ireland, Italy, Japan, Korea, Spain, Sweden) and an annual budget circular with instructions related to gender budgeting (Austria, Belgium, Canada, Iceland, Israel, Korea, Mexico, Spain, Sweden).

Support for implementation has changed over time across OECD countries that have introduced gender budgeting. In some cases, there has been a reduction in the percentage of OECD countries which have various support elements in place. This is likely to be influenced by a number of countries having recently introduced gender budgeting and not yet having had time to fully embed the practice.

**Figure 6.5. Support for implementing gender budgeting (2016 and 2018)**

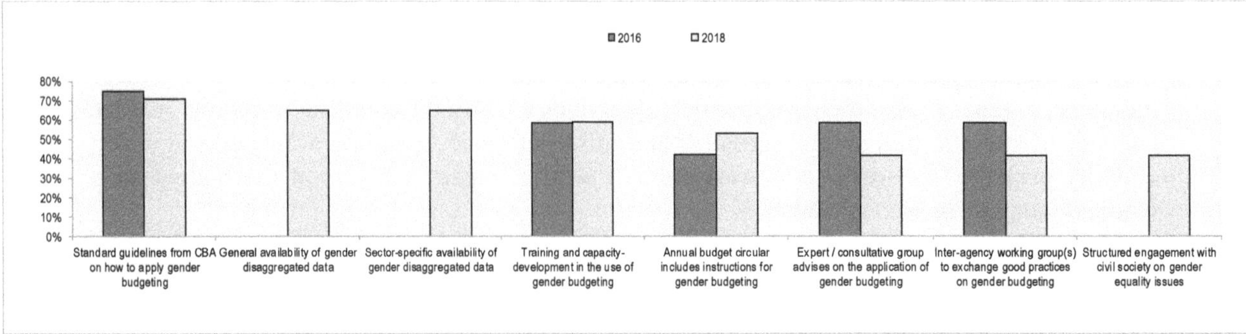


*Note*: Only shows data for OECD countries that have introduced gender budgeting. Data for 2016 is not availabe for all variables; 2018 data for the United States are not available; Information on data for Israel: http://dx.doi.org/10.1787/888932315602.
*Sources:* OECD (2018), OECD Budget Practices and Procedures Survey, Question 35, OECD, Paris; OECD (2016), OECD Gender Budgeting Survey, Question 3.2, OECD, Paris

StatLink http://dx.doi.org/10.1787/888933947027

### *6.3.4. First pass at a composite indicator on Gender budgeting*

OECD countries are at various stages of implementing gender budgeting: for most countries, gender budgeting is still in its early stages of development. The OECD's first pass at a gender budgeting composite index is designed to facilitate policy-makers and the public in tracking the progress of gender budgeting over time, focusing upon the governance framework, operational tools and supportive environment that is in place. The composite index contains 15 variables that cover information across these measures (see Annex B for further information). The weightings used emphasise the operational tools of implementing gender budgeting (40%), followed by the governance framework and the supportive environment (each 30%).

Countries that receive a high score have created a comprehensive gender budgeting framework with key governance aspects in place, a wide range of tools applied across the budget cycle, and wide-ranging institutional supports for the practice. However, this index does not measure how successfully any given system of gender budgeting operates. Success is better evaluated by examining the extent to which the government's approach by allocating resources is helping achieve overarching gender objectives.

Countries have been categorised as having an advanced gender budgeting practice (score 0.9 or above), a mainstreamed gender budgeting practice (score between 0.5 and 0.9), an introductory gender budgeting practice (score between 0.2 and 0.5) or a threshold gender budgeting practice, where there is no or limited gender budgeting in place (score of 0 to 0.2). The index provides that Spain, Mexico, Korea, Japan, Iceland, Sweden, Canada, Austria, and Norway all have successfully attained a level of gender budgeting practice that can be categorised as "mainstreamed", (Figure 6.6), although no country yet qualifies as "advanced practice".

The OECD's composite indicator on gender budgeting will be further refined over time in order to ensure it captures the elements that underpin a comprehensive gender budgeting framework.

**Figure 6.6. Composite indicator on gender budgeting**

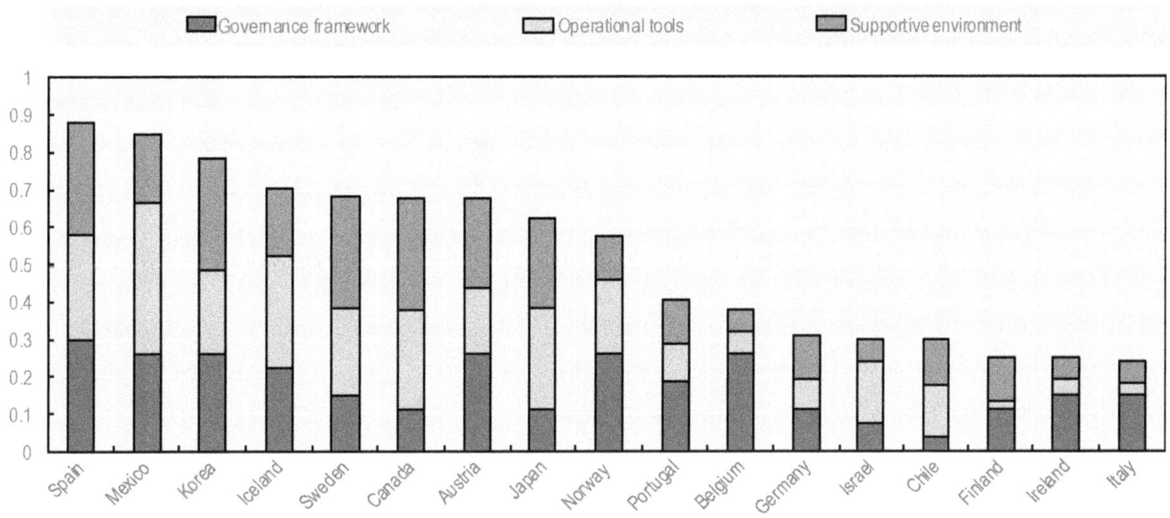


Note: Only shows data for OECD countries that have introduced gender budgeting.
Data for the United States are not available; Information on data for Israel: http://dx.doi.org/10.1787/888932315602.
*Source: OECD (2018), OECD Budget Practices and Procedures Survey, OECD, Paris.*

StatLink http://dx.doi.org/10.1787/888933947046

## References


OECD (2016), *2015 OECD Recommendation of the Council on Gender Equality in Public Life*, OECD Publishing, Paris, https://doi.org/10.1787/9789264252820-en.

OECD (2017), Recommendation of the Council on Open Government, Paris, www.oecd.org/gov/Recommendation-Open-Government-Approved-Council-141217.pdf

OECD (2017), *OECD Budget Transparency Toolkit: Practical Steps for Supporting Openness, Integrity and Accountability in Public Financial Management*, OECD Publishing, Paris, https://doi.org/10.1787/9789264282070-en.

# 7. Quality of public expenditures: Budgeting for performance, results and value-for-money

*Countries use a range of processes to control the quality and impact of public expenditures, in addition to the amount of spending. These processes include spending reviews, performance budgeting and evaluation procedures. The survey results underline the continuing difficulties in making effective use of these instruments and in demonstrating their impact on budgetary decision-making. Spending reviews are now in regular use in the majority of OECD countries, and serve both in identifying areas for potential savings, and to improve alignment of public expenditure with strategic and political priorities. Assessing the tangible impact of spending review is hampered by data issues, however promising new approaches emphasise the 'directional' approaches of aligning such revsiews with thematic priorities and with a framework of 'public value'. Performance budgeting is increasingly prevalent but involves significant additional data and information requirements while the direct input to policy making remains sometimes insufficiently visible. Approaches of developing "strategic dashboards" to manage the flow of information to desinion makers, and encouraging routine use of performance information by programme managers arein keeping with the aspirations of performance budgeting. Evaluation processes have yet to demonstrate a close linkage to budgetary decision-making.More clearly structured approaches and policies on evaluation and establishing closer connections between ex-ante and ex-post evlauations, appear to point the way forward.*

## 7.1. Introduction

The budget is perhaps the key strategic tool through which governments can deliver their policy objectives and satisfy the expectations of voters. At the same time, a well-managed budget process serves as an important 'reality check' on political and societal ambitions, stimulating debate on fiscal policy, discipline and trade-offs between competing spending priorities. However, the process of aligning spending with the government's policy priorities is challenging for several reasons. First, budget discussions tend to focus on new or incremental spending, with much less attention paid to ongoing commitments that result from past spending decisions. Second, spending decisions are often made with poor information on what the expected results of spending are, or in the absence of an evaluation of the effectiveness of past spending. Third, the inherently political nature of the budget means that detailed spending decisions are often driven by narrow or near-term interests that often run counter to higher level government policy objectives.

Over the past decade or so OECD governments have developed a range of tools designed to strengthen the alignment of detailed budget decision making with government policy and strategy at key points in the budget cycle. This chapter focuses primarily on three of these tools; 1) spending reviews, 2) performance budgeting and 3) programme evaluation, while also making reference to other non-budgetary processes that are closely linked to strategic budgeting, namely strategic planning and public sector performance management.

## 7.2. Spending reviews

Spending reviews are widely used as a strategic budgeting tool in OECD countries with all but six countries reporting that they conduct spending reviews either annually or periodically. Figure Figure 7.1 shows a steady trend towards the use of spending reviews between 2011 and 2018.

**Figure 7.1. Adoption of spending reviews 2011 - 2018**

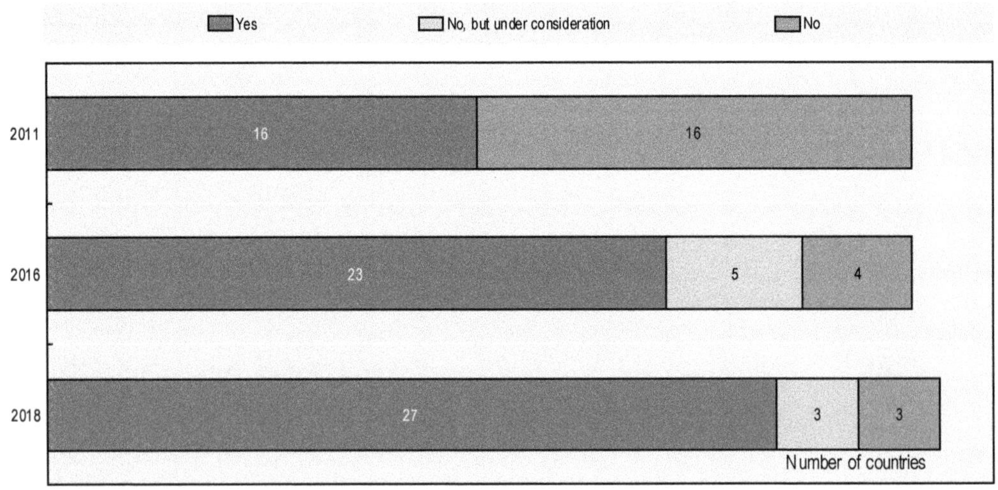


*Notes*: 2018 data for Israel and the United States are not available; Information on data for Israel: http://dx.doi.org/10.1787/888932315602.
*Source*: OECD (2018), OECD Performance Budgeting Survey, Question 36, OECD, Paris.

StatLink http://dx.doi.org/10.1787/888933947065

The main objective of spending reviews is to increase the fiscal space available to government to finance its policy priorities. Governments have made use of this tool to carry out budget consolidation, cutting less effective spending while safeguarding key spending priorities and to reprioritise expenditure, helping governments to align spending with key policy priorities. A key characteristic of most spending reviews, which differentiates them from other budgeting tools, is that they systematically analyse baseline expenditures to identify scope for savings. This contrasts with the normal focus in the budget on competing demands for incremental increases in spending.

**Figure 7.2. Use of spending reviews by country**

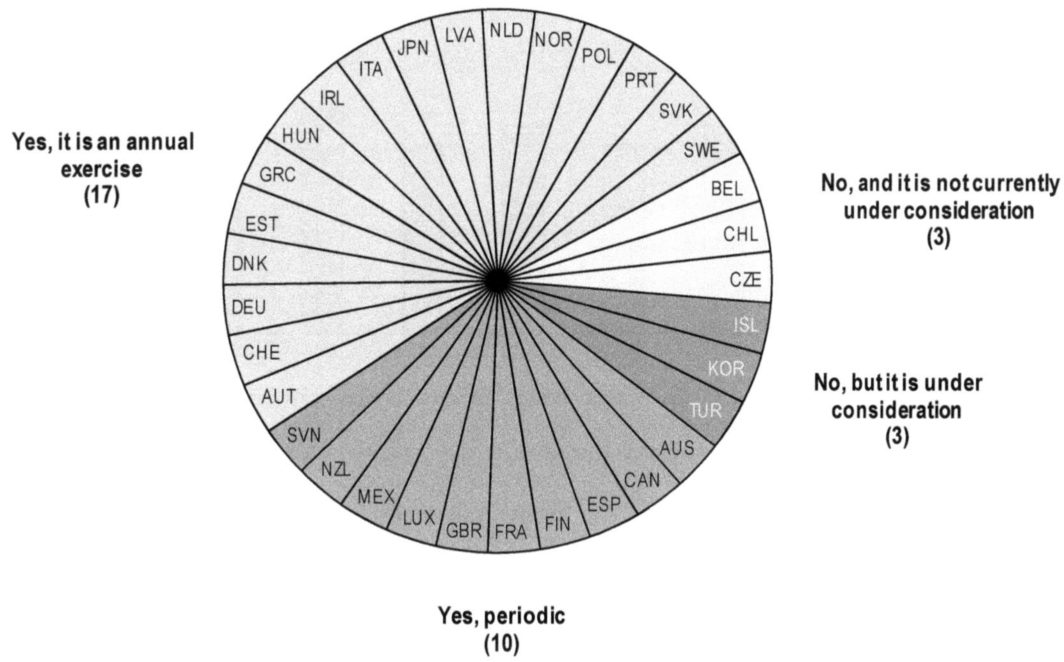


*Notes*: 2018 data for Israel and the United States are not available; Information on data for Israel: http://dx.doi.org/10.1787/888932315602.
*Source*: OECD (2018), OECD Performance Budgeting Survey, Question 36, OECD, Paris.

StatLink http://dx.doi.org/10.1787/888933947084

Spending reviews are resource-intensive exercises and so are not typically applied annually to all expenditures. The approach to spending reviews varies widely across the OECD as illustrated in Figure 7.3. A number of countries such as Denmark, the Netherlands and Germany conduct limited spending reviews of selected spending programmes each year. Their purpose is to improve spending efficiency, reprioritise spending within a limited area and improve the efficiency of administration. In contrast the UK and Ireland have used comprehensive spending reviews, carried out every few years, to identify savings across the whole of government and redirect resources towards priority programmes and objectives. Such reviews are initiated with the objective of aligning the budget to the government's policy priorities and its wider fiscal objectives. Typically, they take place in response to the election of a new government (e.g. 2010, 2015) or between elections (2007,

2013) to take account of changes to the economy or the government's approach to specific policy issues in the intervening period. More recently Ireland has transitioned from periodic "comprehensive reviews of expenditure", which assisted during the budgetary consolidation and recovery period 2009-2014, towards a rolling series of reviews that can feed into the budgetary process each year. Spending reviews in Canada have been modified in scope to become a more regular feature of budgetary governance.

**Figure 7.3. Prevalence of different types of spending review**

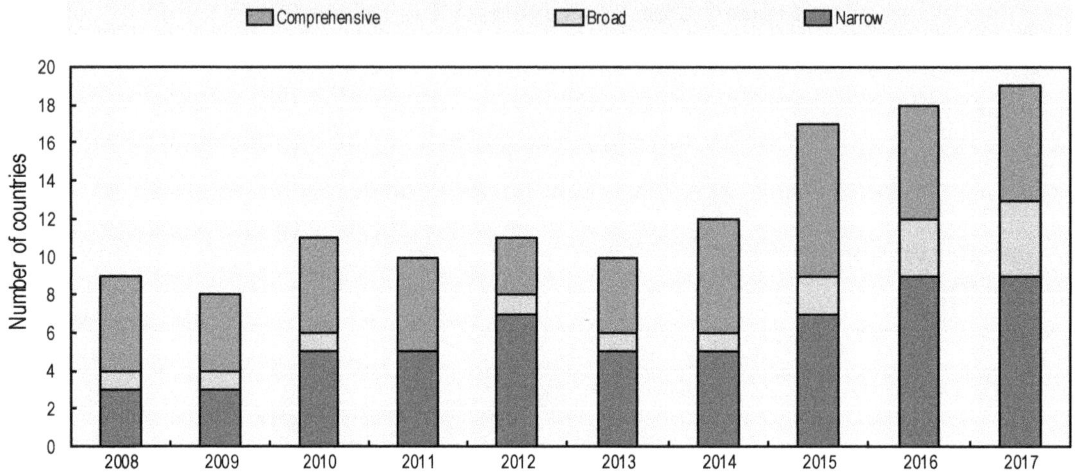


*Notes:* 2018 data for Israel and the United States are not available; Information on data for Israel: http://dx.doi.org/10.1787/888932315602.
*Source*: OECD (2018), OECD Performance Budgeting Survey, Question 39, OECD, Paris.

StatLink http://dx.doi.org/10.1787/888933947103

### *7.2.1. Effectiveness of spending reviews*

The results of the 2018 survey show that OECD countries view spending reviews as an effective tool for strategic budgeting. A large majority of countries report that the objectives of spending reviews have been substantially met, with a very small number reporting that the objectives were largely unmet. However, the data also points to an important gap in assessment, with a large number of countries reporting that the results of spending reviews had not been assessed (see Figure 7.4).

**Figure 7.4. Effectiveness of spending reviews**

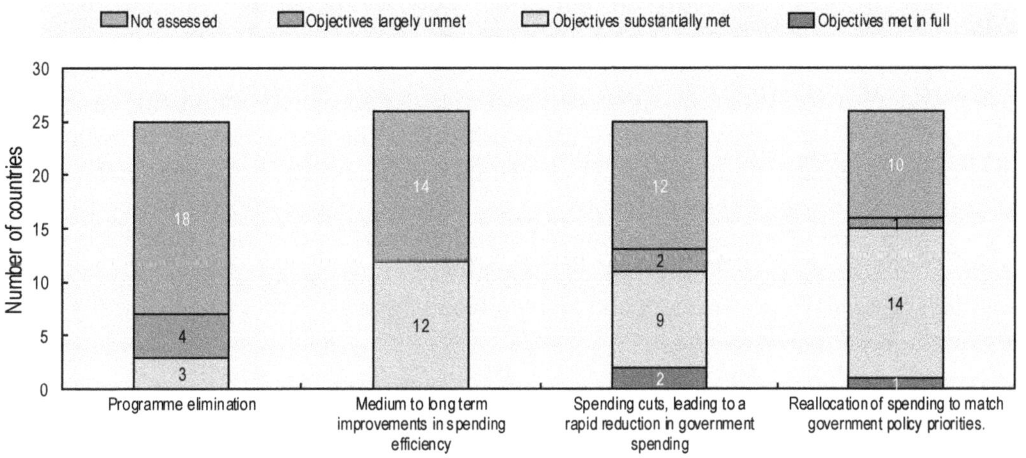


*Notes:* 2018 data for Israel and the United States are not available; Information on data for Israel: http://dx.doi.org/10.1787/888932315602.
*Source*: OECD (2018), OECD Performance Budgeting Survey, Question 42, OECD, Paris.

StatLink http://dx.doi.org/10.1787/888933947122

**Figure 7.5. Main challenges for the implementation of spending reviews**

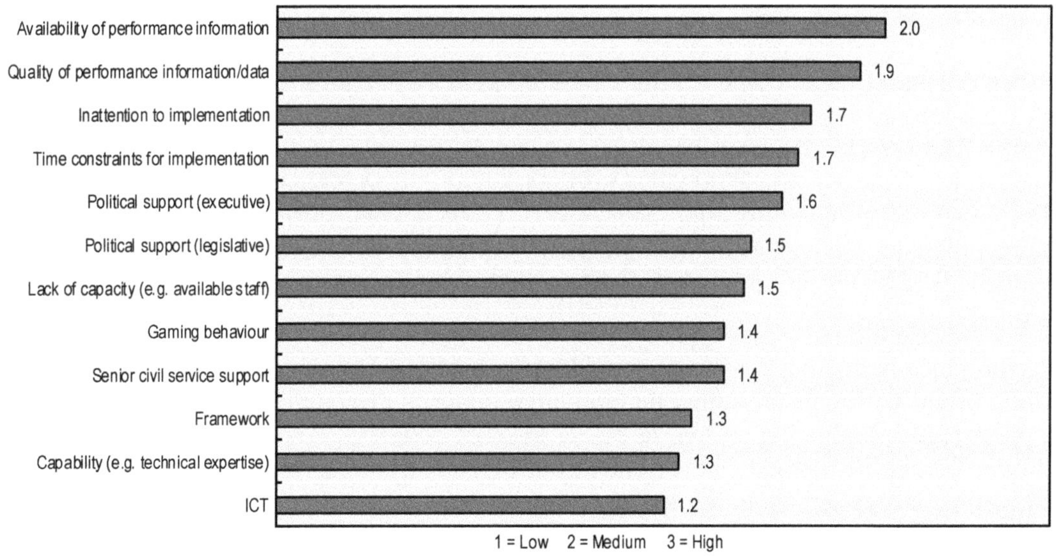


*Notes:* Data for Israel and the United States are not available; Information on data for Israel: http://dx.doi.org/10.1787/888932315602.
*Source*: OECD (2018), OECD Performance Budgeting Survey, Question 43, OECD, Paris.

StatLink http://dx.doi.org/10.1787/888933947141

The top two challenges in implementing spending reviews are the absence of performance data and its poor quality. Such information is critical in enabling budget analysts to make informed decisions about the effectiveness of different types of expenditure. The fact that spending reviews are normally carried out in a compressed time frame is also a constraint on effective implementation, while the survey results also point to the need to strengthen follow up on implementation of spending review recommendations.

### *7.2.2. Notable innovations in spending review practices*

Canada and the UK offer two noteworthy examples of recent developments in spending reviews. Canada's *Policy on Results* (2016) prioritised the achievement of results across government by enhancing transparency on which resources are allocated to achieve them and through better use of evidence including use of performance information and spending reviews. As a result, Canada has introduced spending reviews focused on thematic areas of spending, such support for innovation, management of fixed assets. These reviews look at spending across all of government and apply a results-driven, rather than a fiscally-driven, approach to spending assessment.

In 2017 the UK government published a review[1] led by Sir Michael Barber that introduced the concept of a "Public Value Framework". The Framework assesses the likelihood of value being maximised in any given area of spending and produces recommendations for improving the processes through which inputs are turned into outcomes, thereby maximising public value and delivering improvements to people's lives. Such an approach focuses not only on potential for value creation, but also whether or not the conditions are in place to realise that value. It emphasises the importance of sound planning, citizen engagement and highlights the importance of changing cultures and behaviours within government. Application of the public value framework is being piloted in 2018, with a view to incorporating it in to future budget planning rounds if successful.

## 7.3. Performance budgeting

A performance budget can be defined broadly as "any budget that represents information on what agencies have done or expect to do with the money provided to them" (Schick, 2003). The OECD also uses a longer working definition, which states that performance budgeting is "the use of performance information to inform budget decisions, whether as a direct input to budget allocation decisions or as contextual information and/or inputs to budget planning, as well as to instil greater transparency and accountability throughout the budget process, by providing information to the public on performance objectives and results".

Performance budgeting practices are widespread in OECD countries (see Figure 7.6). In 2018, initial survey results show that the large majority of countries have some variant of a performance budgeting system in place. In most countries a consistent methodology is applied across the whole of government, but in a small number of countries performance budgeting is applied in a limited way for major line ministries. Countries that have introduced performance budgeting since the previous survey in 2016 include Belgium and Hungary.

**Figure 7.6. Is there a performance budgeting framework in place?**

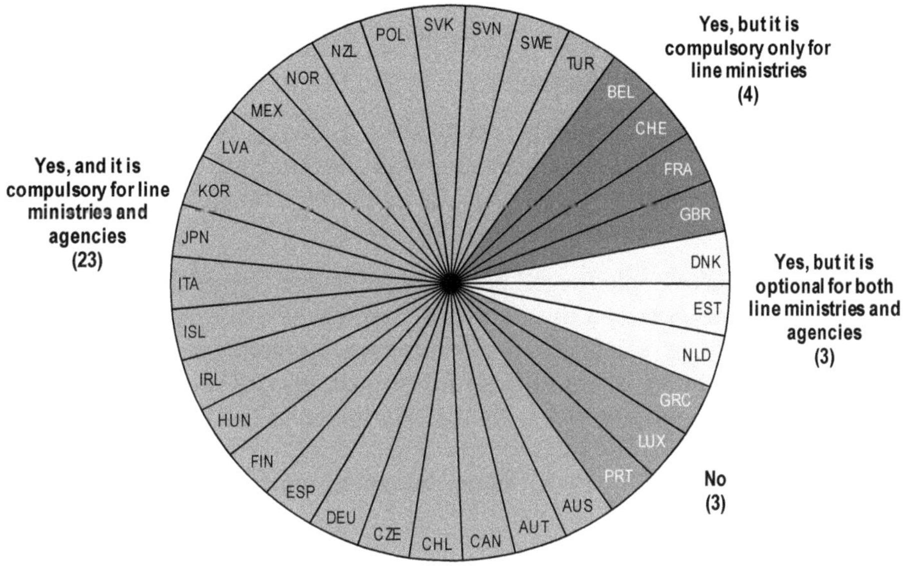


*Notes:* Data for Israel and the United States are not available; Information on data for Israel: http://dx.doi.org/10.1787/888932315602.
*Source*: OECD (2018), OECD Performance Budgeting Survey, Question 5, OECD, Paris.

StatLink http://dx.doi.org/10.1787/888933947160

The OECD identifies four models of performance budgeting. These broadly reflect the differing strength of the links between budgeting and performance data in different countries and also the extent to which performance budgeting has a top-down or a bottom-up management perspective.

1. **Presentational performance budgeting**

   This shows outputs, outcomes and performance indicators separately from the main budget document. This is relatively easy to achieve and is appropriate where the objective is limited to demonstrating that budget allocations and actual expenditures are responsive to government's strategic objectives and policy priorities. On the other hand by separating performance and budget data it is harder to relate the two.

2. **Performance-informed budgeting**

   This includes performance metrics within the budget document and involves re-structuring of budget document on the basis of programmes. This approach requires considerable effort to achieve and is appropriate for governments that want to achieve more ambitious goals such as re-prioritisation of expenditure linked to performance and increased devolution of budget control to programme managers. This is the form of performance budgeting that many OECD countries have adopted.

3. **Managerial performance budgeting**

Managerial performance budgeting is a variant on performance informed budgeting. In this approach the focus is on managerial impacts and changes in organisational behaviour, achieved through combined use of budget and related performance information. This depends on a performance culture existing within government that will take time to establish if it does not already exist.

4. **Direct performance budgeting**

   Direct performance budgeting establishes a direct link between results and resources, usually implying contractual type mechanisms that directly link budget allocations to the achievement of results, implying a budgetary response to over or under-achievement of performance objectives.

OECD countries that have implemented performance budgeting are divided approximately into equally proportions between the first three approaches (see Figure 7.7). No OECD country identifies itself as using direct performance budgeting as a general approach. However, there are examples where funding for limited types of service, such as payments to health providers for specificservices, are directly linked to performance.

**Figure 7.7. Performance budgeting approaches**

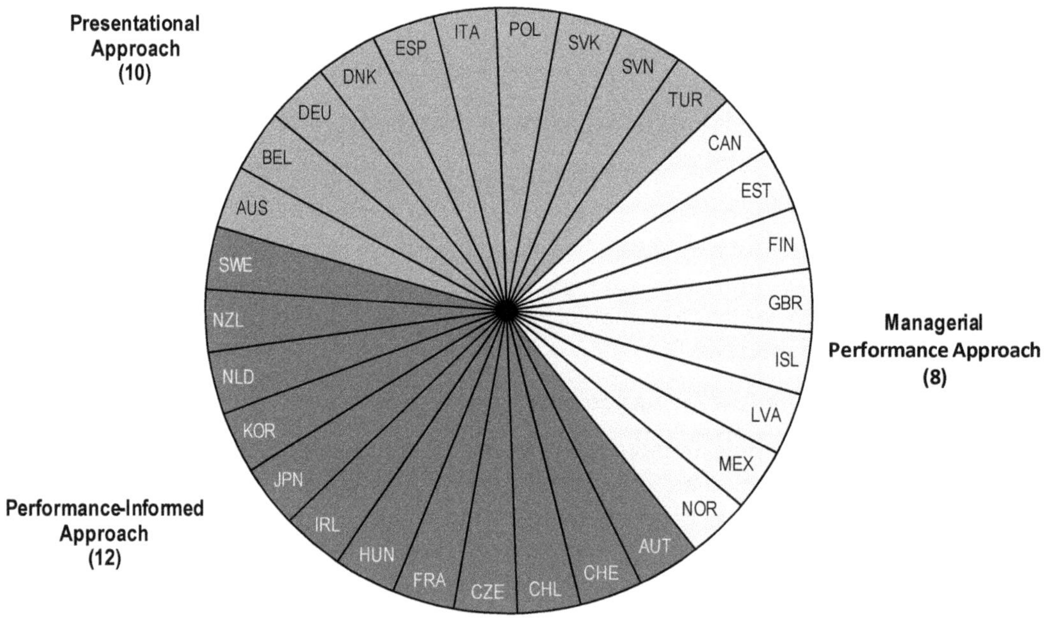


*Notes:* Greece, Luxembourg and Portugal indicated to not have a performance budgeting framework in place. Data for Israel and the United States are not available; Information on data for Israel: http://dx.doi.org/10.1787/888932315602.
*Source*: OECD (2018), OECD Performance Budgeting Survey, Question 5a, OECD, Paris.

StatLink http://dx.doi.org/10.1787/888933947179

While there has been widespread adoption of performance budgeting across the OECD the impact on performance has been more limited than was hoped, and countries have continued to refine their approaches. Countries' overall assessment of the impact that performance budgeting has had on management of public finances is shown in Figure 7.8 below. These results suggest that performance budgeting has had most impact as a communication tool, increasing transparency around the budget, enabling parliament and citizens to understand the objectives of public spending and the results achieved. On the other hand the impacts in terms of improving resource allocation, promoting performance culture and helping government to achieve cross-cutting objectives have been more limited.

**Figure 7.8. Expected and actual benefits from introducing performance budgeting**

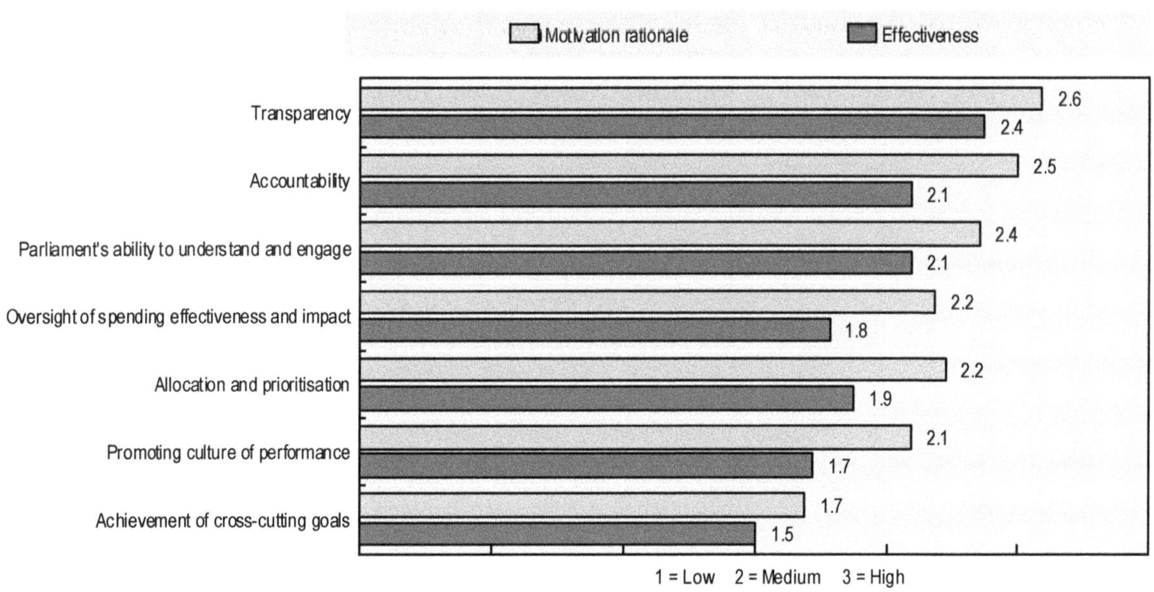


*Notes:* Data for Israel and the United States are not available; Information on data for Israel: http://dx.doi.org/10.1787/888932315602.
*Source*: OECD (2018), OECD Performance Budgeting Survey, Questions 15 and 16, OECD, Paris.

StatLink http://dx.doi.org/10.1787/888933947198

In every category the achievement has fallen short of the original expectations. The shortfall is most notable in respect of promoting accountability and instilling a culture of performance. Compared with the results of the 2016 survey it is notable that the 2018 results are stronger for strengthening parliamentary engagement, but weaker in respect of resource allocation, oversight and promoting culture of performance.

Consistent with these results the 2018 survey also shows that countries see the biggest benefits from performance budgeting in terms of non-quantifiable improvements. They also show a high level of disagreement with the proposition that performance budgeting has led to no perceptible improvement with only four countries "somewhat" agreeing.

While these results suggest a modest level of benefit averaged across the OECD, countries individually report very different levels of impact and satisfaction. Countries that stand out in terms of their positive assessment of the benefits of performance budgeting include Iceland, , Austria, Latvia, New Zealand and Korea. At the other end of the scale countries that report poor results include the Czech Republic, Italy and Poland.

Despite many years of experience of using performance budgeting, OECD countries continue to report significant challenges in operating the systems well and realising the expected benefits. Figure 7.9 below shows how OECD countries rank different challenges in operating performance budgeting systems.

**Figure 7.9. Main challenges in implementation of performance budgeting**

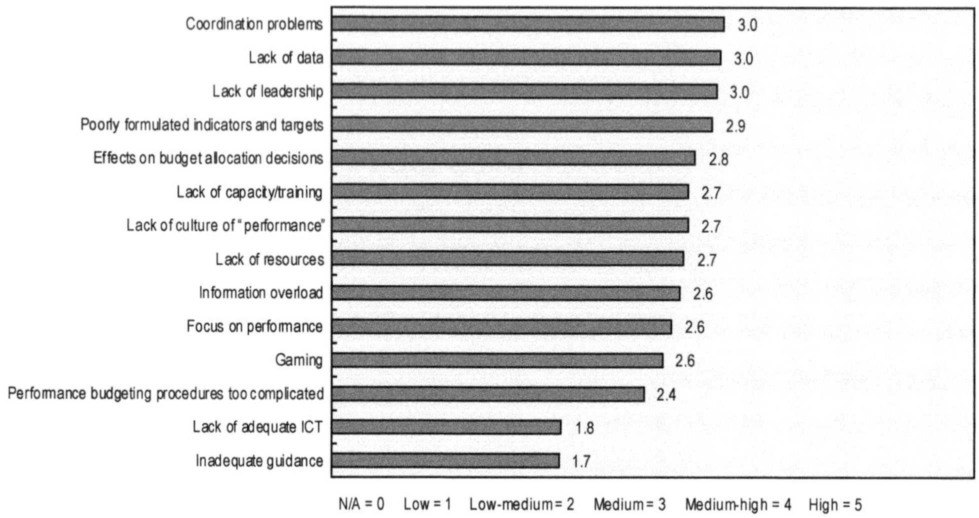


*Notes:* Data for Greece and Portugal are not availabe for performance budgeting implementation challenges. Data for Israel and the United States are not available; Information on data for Israel: http://dx.doi.org/10.1787/888932315602.

*Source*: OECD (2018), OECD Performance Budgeting Survey, Question 22, OECD, Paris.

StatLink http://dx.doi.org/10.1787/888933947217

## *7.3.1. Notable practices in performance budgeting*

France offers an example of strong links between key performance indicators established at national level and budgets. France's organic budget law *(Loi organique relative aux lois de finances (LOLF))* groups expenditures by "missions" that bring together related programmes that are associated with high level policy objectives and performance indicators. Recent reforms have additionally focused on streamlining the indicators to make them clearer to parliamentarians and the public; France enacted a law in 2015 requiring the Government to present wealth and well-being indicators other than GDP to promote debate on policy impacts. Based on the LOLF system the French government is developing a strategic dashboard using a limited set of internationally comparable indicators, including:

## *7.3.2. Economic development indicators such as FDI (OECD) and Doing Business (World Bank).*

- Social progress indicators, such as healthy life expectancy at 65 by gender (OECD), percentage of 18-24 year olds with no qualification who are not in training (France Stratégie/Eurostat) and poverty gaps (World Bank).
- Sustainable development indicators such as greenhouse gas emissions per unit of GDP (European Energy Agency/Eurostat).

To address the issue of poor quality of performance information in 2015 the Department of Finance in Australia issued Guidance on Developing Good Performance Information

(RMG 131). The key focus of the guidance, and subsequent Quick Reference Guide (July 2016) is to support the development of good performance reporting, including:

- creating a common understanding of an entity's purposes and the activities through which those purposes are achieved,
- identifying a mix of quantitative and qualitative measures that demonstrates the effectiveness with which purposes are achieved,
- selecting appropriate methods to collect and analyse performance information, and
- presenting performance information to tell a clear and accurate performance story.

A system of advice and assurance also supports entities in setting their performance information. For example, Finance supports entities in drafting performance documentation, each entity's audit committee reviews the appropriateness of its performance measures, and the Australian National Audit Office (ANAO) conducts periodic audits of the system.

Management of performance information is a challenge for all OECD countries. Balancing the need for effective communication, which favours clarity and brevity, with the need for sufficiently detailed information to provide programme managers with a sufficiently detailed understanding to inform operational decision making, is a continuing challenge. Notable developments in this area include introducing greater selectivity in the presentation of performance information, especially to senior managers, including identification of priority goals (for example the practice of identifying "Agency Priority Goals" in the United States) and the practice of developing dashboards to provide concise information to senior managers reporting progress in terms of progress in budget implementation and in moving towards performance targets.

A common issue in performance budgeting is that some of the government's most important strategic policy objectives relate to complex or "wicked" issues. For example, reducing the rate of death from road accidents might require multiple actions in areas ranging from road design and construction, policing, vehicle standards and inspection, to public education and awareness etc. To ensure that activities are effectively co-ordinated to deliver high level outcomes requires inter-agency co-ordination and monitoring. The United States offers an example of institutionalised mechanisms to promote co-ordination around cross-agency goals.

**Box 7.1. United States – Co-ordination of cross–agency priority goals**

The GPRA Modernization Act of 2010 (GPRAMA) requires the Office of Management and Budget (OMB) to co-ordinate with agencies to develop cross-agency priority (CAP) goals, which are 4-year outcome-oriented goals covering a number of complex or high-risk management and mission issues. Examples of CAP goals and goal statements.

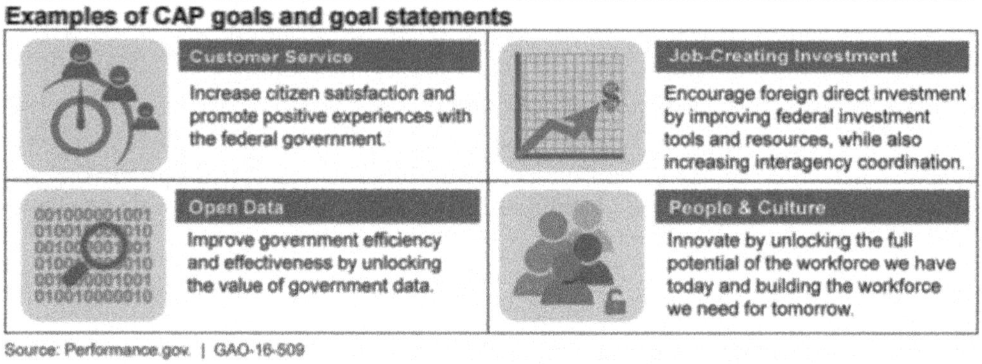


OMB and the Performance Improvement Council (PIC) have introduced a goal governance structure that includes agency leaders, and regular senior-level reviews on CAP goal progress. CAP goal teams reported to the US Government Accountability Office (GAO) that the CAP goal designation increased leadership attention and improved inter-agency collaboration on these issues.

### *7.3.3. Towards OECD Good Practices in Performance Budgeting*

Drawing on the analyses and discussions of the past decade and more at the SBO and its Network on Performance & Results, and reflecting the findings of the 2016 and 2018 Surveys of Performance Budgeting, Evaluation and Spending Review, the OECD has developed Good Practices which codify the key lessons that have been identified. The Good Practices are summarised in Box 7.2 below.

**Box 7.2. OECD Good Practices for Performance Budgeting**

Arising from the work of the OECD Working Party of the Senior Budget Officials (the SBO) and its Network on Performance and Results, the OECD has developed Good Practices for Performance Budgeting.

**1. The rationale and objectives of performance budgeting are clearly documented and reflect the interests of key stakeholders.**

- The rationale, objectives and approach to performance budgeting are set out in a strategic document such as an organic budget law or public financial management reform programme.
- The interests and priorities of multiple stakeholders in the budget cycle are reflected in the objectives and design of the performance budgeting system.

- Performance budgeting is championed by political leaders, with support from senior officials.
- The introduction of performance budgeting is supported by regulations and guidelines.

**2. Performance budgeting aligns expenditure with the strategic goals and priorities of the government.**

- Budget proposals are systematically linked to relevant development plans, government programme commitments and other statements of strategic direction and priority.
- Multi-year budget frameworks provide realistic and reliable fiscal parameters for the preparation of performance budgets.
- The achievement of complex objectives, requiring inter-ministerial collaboration, is supported by the central government's co-ordination of activities and budgets.

**3. The performance budgeting system incorporates flexibility to handle the varied nature of government activities and the complex relationships between spending and outcomes.**

- The type and volume of performance information required varies based on the nature of the programme.
- Government uses a mix of performance measures, reflecting the multi-dimensional nature of performance in the public sector.
- Programme structures are aligned with the administrative responsibilities and service delivery functions of ministries and agencies.
- Expenditure classification and control frameworks are revised to facilitate programme management and promote accountability for results.

**4. Government invests in human resources, data and other infrastructure needed to support performance budgeting.**

- The Central Budget Authority builds capacity, internally and within line ministries, to manage and operate the performance budgeting system.
- The CBA regularly reviews and adjusts the operation of the performance budgeting system to improve its performance.
- Performance measurement systems are progressively improved to provide quality data on a reliable basis.
- Performance data is governed and managed as a strategic asset, with the objective of ensuring that the data is discoverable, interoperable, standardised and accessible in timely manner.

**5. Performance budgeting facilitates systematic oversight by the legislature and civil society, reinforcing the government's performance orientation and accountability.**

- The annual budget and expenditure reports presented to the legislature contain information about performance targets and the level of achievement.

- The supreme audit institution carries out performance audits, including tests of the accuracy and reliability of reported performance.
- Parliament, supported by the SAI, scrutinises performance-based budgets and financial reports, holding ministers and senior public managers accountable in the event of poor performance or misrepresentation.
- Budget and expenditure data is published in machine-readable and accessible formats

**6. Performance budgeting complements other tools designed to improve performance orientation, including programme evaluation and spending reviews.**

- *Ex ante* appraisal of new spending programmes is used to strengthen programme design including key performance indicators, and to facilitate processes of monitoring and *ex post* evaluation.
- *Ex post* evaluations of major spending programmes are carried out on a rolling basis and the findings are systematically fed back into the budget preparation process.
- Spending reviews are used in conjunction with performance budgeting to review the justification for spending and to identify budgetary savings that can be redirected to support priority goals.

**7. Incentives around the performance budgeting system encourage performance-oriented behaviour and learning.**

- The centre of government promotes a management culture that focuses on performance.
- Performance measurement encourages comparison and competition between similar entities as a means of improving effectiveness and efficiency in service provision.
- Identified individuals and teams are responsible and accountable for the achievement of performance goals.
- Managers organise structured internal discussions to review financial and operational performance regularly through the year.
- Responses to programme under-performance emphasise learning and problem solving, rather than individual financial rewards and penalties.

*Source*: OECD (forthcoming). Note that the Good Practices are subject to further amendment and refinement during the process of finalisation and quality-assurance.

## 7.4. Evaluation

The effectiveness of public spending, and the extent to which taxpayers receive value for money, are matters of continuing concern to governments and the public. OECD governments have developed a variety of tools to evaluate the quality of public spending. Programme evaluation should ideally take place at the stage of policy/programme design (*ex ante*) and at an advanced stage of implementation or completion (*ex post*). The results of both ex ante and ex post evaluations, and of performance audits should feed back into the strategic budget decision-making process and, at the same time, boost transparency and accountability for the management of stewardship of public funds.

Compared to other aspects of strategic budgeting the evaluation function is less centrally regulated and, in most countries, less systematically applied. Few countries have a centrally regulated process for conducting evaluations. Figure 7.10 shows the governance of spending evaluation and notably the dominant role played by line ministries and agencies as compared with the central budget authority and the very small role typically played by government evaluation services and the legislature. Note that the supreme audit institution plays a substantial role in relation to *ex post* reviews. Governments also often rely on external consulting firms and academics to carry out evaluation in order to ensure timely delivery and access specific skills.

**Figure 7.10. Governance of *ex ante* and *ex post* evaluation**

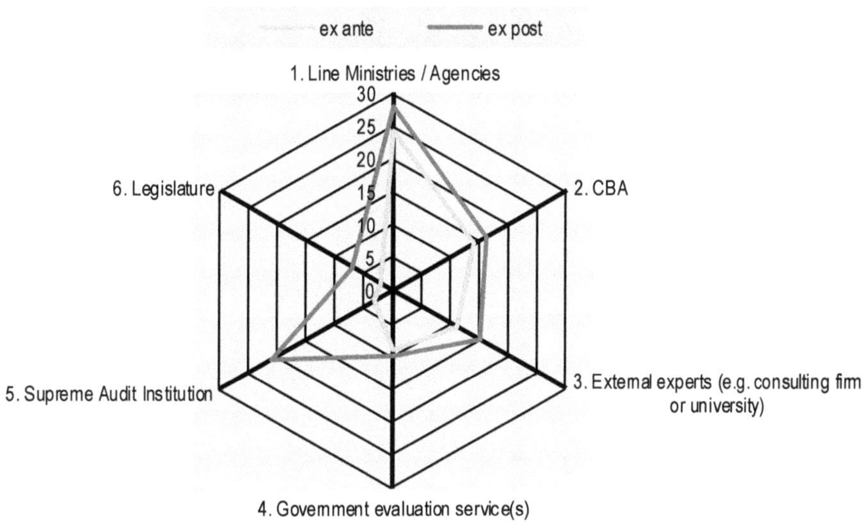


*Notes:* Data for Israel and the United States are not available; Information on data for Israel: http://dx.doi.org/10.1787/888932315602.
*Source*: OECD (2018), OECD Performance Budgeting Survey, Question 30, OECD, Paris.

StatLink http://dx.doi.org/10.1787/888933947236

What is involved in *ex ante* assessment varies substantially. In many countries *ex ante* assessment is understood to cover both ex ante budget impacts of proposed policies and can also cover regulatory impact assessment, which may or may not examine the long term budgetary impact of regulatory initiatives. In others there are separate procedures for appraising long-term capital investment projects. In a few countries all of these are processes of *ex ante* assessment and appraisal are covered by one set of guidelines (the "Green Book" in the case of the UK).

The range of issues covered in *ex post* evaluation varies widely as shown in Table 7.1. Certain countries including Canada, Japan and Spain mandate coverage of a comprehensive set of issues in their evaluations. In contrast Chile and Korea have a strong focus on issues of policy and programme design and programme management, while countries such as Slovenia and the UK focus more on programme effectiveness and efficiency.

**Table 7.1. Issues covered in programme evaluation**

| | Policy design | Programme design including choice of indicators, targets etc. | Programme management | Programme effectiveness | Programme efficiency | Programme accountability |
|---|---|---|---|---|---|---|
| Australia | ⊗ | ⊗ | ⊗ | ⊗ | ⊗ | ⊗ |
| Austria | ⊗ | ⊗ | ⊗ | ⊙ | ⊗ | ⊖ |
| Canada | ⊗ | ⊙ | ⊙ | ⊙ | ⊙ | ⊙ |
| Chile | ⊗ | ⊗ | ⊗ | ⊗ | ⊗ | ⊠ |
| Czech Republic | ⊗ | ⊗ | ⊗ | ⊗ | ⊗ | ⊖ |
| Denmark | ⊠ | ⊗ | ⊗ | ⊠ | ⊠ | ⊠ |
| Estonia | ⊖ | ⊙ | ⊖ | ⊗ | ⊖ | ⊗ |
| Finland | ⊗ | ⊗ | ⊗ | ⊗ | ⊗ | ⊗ |
| France | ⊗ | ⊠ | ⊗ | ⊙ | ⊗ | ⊖ |
| Germany | ⊗ | ⊗ | ⊗ | ⊗ | ⊗ | ⊗ |
| Hungary | ⊗ | ⊗ | ⊗ | ⊗ | ⊗ | ⊙ |
| Iceland | ⊠ | ⊠ | ⊖ | ⊖ | ⊖ | ⊠ |
| Ireland | ⊗ | ⊗ | ⊗ | ⊗ | ⊗ | ⊗ |
| Japan | ⊙ | ⊙ | ⊙ | ⊙ | ⊙ | ⊙ |
| Korea | ⊙ | ⊙ | ⊙ | ⊗ | ⊖ | ⊖ |
| Latvia | ⊗ | ⊗ | ⊗ | ⊗ | ⊗ | ⊗ |
| Luxembourg | ⊖ | ⊗ | ⊗ | ⊗ | ⊗ | ⊗ |
| Mexico | ⊖ | ⊗ | ⊗ | ⊖ | ⊖ | ⊗ |
| Netherlands | ⊙ | ⊙ | ⊗ | ⊙ | ⊙ | |
| New Zealand | ⊗ | ⊖ | ⊖ | ⊗ | ⊖ | ⊠ |
| Norway | ⊖ | ⊗ | ⊗ | ⊖ | ⊗ | ⊗ |
| Poland | ⊗ | ⊗ | ⊗ | ⊗ | ⊗ | ⊗ |
| Portugal | ⊠ | ⊠ | ⊠ | ⊠ | ⊠ | ⊠ |
| Slovak Republic | ⊗ | ⊗ | ⊗ | ⊗ | ⊗ | ⊗ |
| Slovenia | ⊖ | ⊗ | ⊖ | ⊗ | ⊗ | ⊗ |
| Spain | ⊗ | ⊙ | ⊙ | ⊙ | ⊙ | ⊙ |
| Sweden | ⊖ | ⊖ | ⊖ | ⊖ | ⊖ | ⊖ |
| Switzerland | ⊙ | ⊙ | ⊗ | ⊙ | ⊙ | ⊗ |
| United Kingdom | ⊖ | ⊖ | ⊖ | ⊗ | ⊗ | ⊗ |
| **Key** | **Total** | | | | | |
| ⊖ Occasionally | 7 | 3 | 6 | 4 | 6 | 5 |
| ⊗ Usually | 15 | 16 | 18 | 16 | 16 | 14 |
| ⊙ Always | 4 | 7 | 4 | 7 | 5 | 4 |
| ⊠ Never | 3 | 3 | 1 | 2 | 2 | 5 |

*Notes:* Data for Belgium, Greece, Italy and Turkey are not availabe for programme evaluation issues / scope of evaluation.

Data for Israel and the United States are not available; Information on data for Israel: http://dx.doi.org/10.1787/888932315602.

*Source*: OECD (2018), OECD Performance Budgeting Survey, Question 31, OECD, Paris.

StatLink http://dx.doi.org/10.1787/888933947654

## *7.4.1. Impact of evaluations*

Compared to spending reviews the impact of evaluation processes on budget decision making is low, especially at the macro level (see Figure 7.11). Although it could be anticipated that evaluation findings would influence budget allocation decisions at the level of the Central Budget Authority, in practice this is where the influence is least, perhaps reflecting the decentralised nature of the evaluation process itself. Even at the programme level, where the impact is greatest, the impact level overall is rated between low and medium. The single most important problem preventing evaluations having impact is the absence of any formal mechanism to consider evaluation findings in the budget process, followed by insufficient bureaucratic and political interest in the evaluation findings.

**Figure 7.11. Impact of evaluation processes on budget decision making**

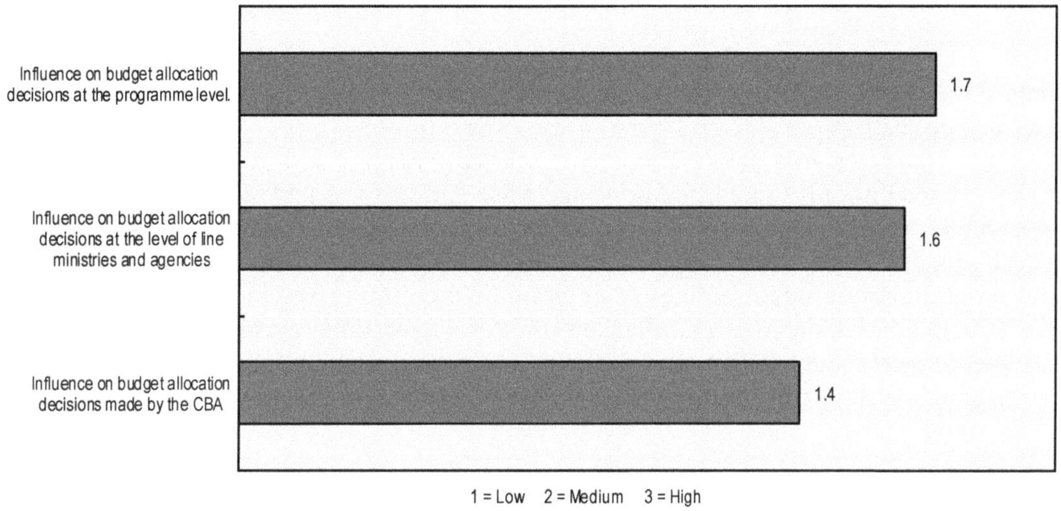


*Notes*: Data for Australia, Denmark, Greece, Italy, Turkey, Portugal and Turkey are not availabe for the impact of evaluation processes on budget decision making.
Data for Israel and the United States are not available; Information on data for Israel: http://dx.doi.org/10.1787/888932315602.
*Source*: OECD (2018), OECD Performance Budgeting Survey, Question 34, OECD, Paris.

StatLink http://dx.doi.org/10.1787/888933947255

## *7.4.2. Notable practices in evaluations*

Chile's budget legislation (State Financial Administration Law) provides a strong legal framework supporting a systematic approach to both *ex ante* and *ex post* evaluation of spending programmes. Parliament and the CBA are closely involved in the annual selection of programmes to be evaluated, there is clear central guidance on the conduct of evaluations and there is legal requirement that the results of programme evaluations are considered as part of budgetary process.

The Government of Canada has had policies governing programme evaluation in its departments and agencies since 1977. The most recent, the Policy on Results, no longer requires comprehensive evaluation coverage of all direct programme spending every five years (as required by the Previous Policy on Evaluation). Rather, building from the premise that all spending and programmes should be evaluated periodically, departments build an evaluation schedule based on risk and other needs. Departments are required to make public not only their planned evaluations, but rationales for programmes and spending that will not be evaluated. The Policy on Results has introduced other new elements into the federal evaluation function including the ability for the Secretary of the Treasury Board of Canada to initiate an evaluation exercise.

In Korea the programme evaluation process seeks to measure the relevance, efficiency, and effectiveness of a programme. The In-depth Evaluation of Budgetary Programme institutionalised the in-depth evaluation process as part of the performance budgeting system. Every year, an evaluation panel is created for each of the group of cross-cutting programmes selected for evaluation. Panel members mostly come from public research institutes and universities and since many stakeholders are involved in any given programme, the evaluation panel holds frequent meetings to collect inputs and feedback. The completed evaluation reports are considered by the central budget office, which decides whether to reflect these results in resource allocation changes or programme consolidation. Line ministries are required to report back with their follow-ups.

## 7.5. The Performance Continuum: Towards an integrated approach to evaluation, spending review and performance management

As this chapter has illustrated, countries make use of a wide variety of tools and techniques in order to assess whether public expenditures are achieving their objectives in a cost-effective manner. The tools range from *ex ante* evaluation and appraisal of new policies and programmes, through routines of programme monitoring and budgetary reporting, to retrospective assessment as a normal part of the policy-making cycle. These processes are complemented by deeper dives less directly linked to the annual budget cycle, in the form of spending reviews that examine the baseline of expenditures, and in-depth evaluations of key programmes.

However, as the analysis in this chapter highlights, the total impact of these various approaches is unclear, and in most OECD countries their application is disjointed – a fact exacerbated by the distribution of roles among different ministries and different policy communities and by the widely-varying timeframes and reporting horizons that apply to the different tools.

If the various strategic tools available to policy-makers are to have a substantial impact on resource allocation it would seem that a more connected approach is needed, involving coordinated use of the different tools and connecting the analysis of performance from a budgeting perspective to the monitoring of the effectiveness of government activity as a whole. This subject is proposed as a future topic of enquiry and analysis for the SBO Network on Performance and Results, in the first instance. This analysis can usefully draw upon the notable country examples that are outlined in this chapter; and can build upon the points of intersection of these instruments across the policy cycle. The ultimate aim is to help policy-makers understand how the various tools can complement one another as part of the continuum of evaluative and performance information that imbues the policy cycle, drawing concrete messages about where public policies are achieving their impacts, and informing the continual debate about policy trade-offs, opportunity costs and optimisation of value for public money.

Among the dimensions to be considered in developing this ‘performance continuum’ are:

- Strengthening links between strategic planning and budgeting, thereby providing a politically-validated agenda of national performance and budget realignment, in support of which the various evaluative tools can be organised and aligned. This would help to ensure coherence between the strategic setting of government objectives from a centre of government perspective, and the resources allocations that are aligned to help deliver these objectives from a budgetary standpoint.
- Expanding the available evidence base on performance, including identifying indicators that reflect citizen experience, connect with well being measurement and actual outcomes and making use of social media and other information resources , such as open and/or administrative data, that can gain traction with the public– in

contrast, perhaps, to inward-facing bureaucratic processes of cost-benefit analysis, programme evaluation etc.

- Learning how countries can better disseminate the results of the programme evaluation and of the more technical activities mentioned above, making the results publicly available in a format that citizens will understand.
- Engaging the other key public institutions, including the parliament, and the related bodies in charge of evalaution and budgeting that are attached to Parliament in some countries and the supreme audit institution, to pay an active role in strengthening evaluation, and promoting a culture of performance and accountability.
- Promoting results oriented behaviour based on evidence of performance and dissemination of information about 'what works', so that performance budgeting can benefit from an "Evidence Informed Policy Approach", drawing on experiences in the UK, US and Nordic countries.
- Shared learning and integration of approaches across different communities – policy, budgetary, regulatory, as well as economists and expert communities in the various fields, such as health, education or the environment – to boost the effectiveness of these tools. The joint SBO-Health Network offers a good example of a fruitful multidisciplinary approach to these issues.

## Note

[1] Delivering better outcomes for citizens: practical steps for unlocking public value; HM Treasury 2017

## References

Barber. M (2017), *Delivering better outcomes for citizens: practical steps for unlocking public value*, HM Treasury, https://assets.publishing.service.gov.uk/government/uploads/system/uploads/attachment_data/file/660408/PU2105_Delivering_better_outcomes_for_citizens_practical_steps_for_unlocking_public_value_web.pdf

Darville, P. (2017), Results-Based Budgeting: The Chilean Experience. Presentation to the OECD Senior Budget Officials Network on Performance and Results, http://www.oecd.org/gov/budgeting/D2-AM%20-%20Session%206%20-%20P.%20Darville%20-%20Chile.pdf

de Vries, E. (2017), Canada: Recent Experience with Reviews; Presentation to the OECD Senior Budget Officials Network on Performance and Results, https://www.slideshare.net/OECD-GOV/spending-reviews-erik-de-vries-canada

Kennedy F. and J. Howlin (2017), Spending reviews in Ireland – Learning from experience, OECD Journal on Budgeting, vol 2016/2, https://www.oecd-ilibrary.org/governance/spending-reviews-in-ireland-learning-from-experience_budget-16-5jg30cchf0g0

French Ministry of Finance (2015), Website on performance (managed by the Budget Directorate) (2015), Some documents in English. www.performance.gouv.fr.

Moynihan, D. and I. Beazley (2016), *Toward Next Generation Performance Budgeting*, World Bank, Washington D.C., https://openknowledge.worldbank.org/bitstream/handle/10986/25297/9781464809545.pdf?sequence=2

Schick, A. (2003), "The Performing State: Reflection on an Idea Whose Time Has Come but Whose Implementation Has Not", *OECD Journal on Budgeting*, vol. 3/2, https://doi.org/10.1787/budget-v3-art10-en.

Schick, A. (2003), "The role of fiscal rules in budgeting", *OECD Journal on Budgeting,* vol. 3/3, https://doi.org/10.1787/budget-v3-art14-en.

Vammalle, C. and A. Ruiz Rivadeneira (2017), "Budgeting in Chile", *OECD Journal on Budgeting*, vol. 16/3, https://doi.org/10.1787/budget-16-5jfw22b3c0r3.

US Government Accountability Office (2016), Managing for Results, GAO-15-509, www.gao.gov/assets/680/677368.pdf

# 8. Capital budgeting, Infrastructure Governance and PPPs

*Having a sound capital budgeting framework is essential to ensuring that the budget meets national development needs in a cost-effective and coherent manner. The OECD Principles of Budgetary Governance highlight four key elements towards certifying this objective: 1) the grounding of capital investment plans in objective appraisal of economic capacity gaps, infrastructural development needs and sectoral/social priorities; 2) the prudent assessment of costs and benefits of such investments, affordability, relative priority among various projects, and overall value for money; 3) the evaluation of investment decisions independently of the specific financing mechanism; and 4) the development and implementation of a national framework for supporting public investment (OECD, 2015).*

*This chapter gives a snapshot of OECD practices for capital budgeting and how they compare with these principles using the OECD Infrastructure Governance Framework and the OECD Principles of Public Governance of Public-Private Partnership (PPP).*

## 8.1. Capital Budgeting Framework

A robust and clear institutional framework is essential to ensure a well-functioning capital budgeting system. Most countries reported that line ministers are the main actors responsible for evaluating infrastructure needs (77%), deciding the delivery mode (59%), monitoring project execution (63%), as well as prioritising and approving infrastructure projects (48%). Some countries also identify the Central Budget Authority (CBA) as a key actor, particularly for project prioritisation (30%) and approval (41%). Some countries (23%) identified Supreme Audit Institutions (SAI) as the main actor responsible for ex-post evaluation (Table 8.1. ).

While many countries did not identify Central Infrastructure/ PPP Units a the primary body responsible for most of these functions, they were identified as actors performing a complementary role.

The way capital expenditure is integrated in the overall budget process has different advantages and disadvantages. While full integration between current and capital expenditure can improve planning, facilitate co-ordination and increase flexibility, separate budgets can ensure that mandatory items such as entitlements do not crowd out discretionary items such as capital investment (Posner, 2009). Governments need to be aware of the inherent challenges of their system in order to certify that proper mechanisms are in place to face them. If a government decides to submit capital and current budgets separately, it will need to strengthen the selection mechanisms of capital projects to make certain that line ministries better integrate their capital and current expenditure decisions. If it decides for a unified budget, it should make sure that it is also accompanied by guidelines or fiscal rules as well as the political will to limit government borrowing that finances current expenditure (Burger and Hawkesworth, 2013).

Most OECD countries have achieved a certain degree of integration of their current and capital budgets. Of the countries surveyed, 50% reported that capital and current expenditure are submitted and considered in an integrated way during the budget preparation process. In addition, in 23% of the countries surveyed, capital and current expenditure requests are submitted together by line ministers during the budget preparation phase, but the decision process is managed in a separate way (Figure 8.1). For example in the UK, capital expenditure is defined in Spending Reviews conducted every five years, with annual capital budget allocation by department.

In 27% of the countries surveyed, line ministries are required to separate their capital from operating budget requests and the process for deciding upon capital and operating budget requests are distinct (Figure 8.2). For example in Greece capital expenditure is budgeted under the Public Investment Programme (PIP) managed by the Ministry of Economy and Development. The PIP is voted every year by the Parliament along with the ordinary budget. Similarly, in Slovenia capital expenditure is budgeted under the Development Programmes Plan (DPP). The DPP contains public investments projects financed by the central government together with other financing sources (e.g. EU financing).

There is great variation between the ways surveyed countries fund multi-year capital projects. While 39% of countries reported to budget requests funding for the entire cost of multi-year project up-front, 35% reported to budget requests funding incrementally each year until the project is completed. Meanwhile, 12% of countries, reported to have another type of budgeting approach (Figure 8.2). In particular, Australia, Chile and Switzerland have a combined approach. Other countries, such as Ireland and Luxemburg have a separate medium-term capital plan. In Israel and New Zealand there are no general rules and funding is determined on a case by case basis.

**Table 8.1. Institutional framework of infrastructure governance/public procurement system**

| | Evaluation of infrastructure needs | Prioritisation of all infrastructure/capital projects | Deciding whether PPPs or TIP* are more adequate | Project approval | Monitoring project execution | *Ex post* evaluations |
|---|---|---|---|---|---|---|
| Australia | ⊗ | ⊗ | ⊗ | ⊗ | ⦿ | ⦿ |
| Austria | ⦿ | ◬ | ⦿ | ⦿ | ⦿ | ■ |
| Chile | ⦿ | ⦿ | ⦿ | ⦿ | ⦿ | ⦿ |
| Czech Republic | ⦿ | ⦿ | ⦿ | ⊗ | ■ | ■ |
| Denmark | ⦿ | ⦿ | ⦿ | ⦿ | ⦿ | ⦿ |
| Estonia | ⦿ | ⦿ | ⊗ | ⊗ | ⦿ | ■ |
| France | ⦿ | ⦿ | ⦿ | ⦿ | ⦿ | ⦿ |
| Germany | ⦿ | ⊗ | ⦿ | ⦿ | ◬ | ■ |
| Greece | ⦿ | ⦿ | ◬ | ◬ | ◬ | ⦿ |
| Hungary | ⊗ | ⦿ | ⦿ | ⊗ | ⊖ | ⊖ |
| Ireland | ⦿ | ⦿ | ⦿ | ⦿ | ⦿ | ⦿ |
| Israel | ⦿ | ◬ | ⊖ | ⊗ | ◬ | ◬ |
| Italy | ⦿ | ⦿ | ⦿ | ⦿ | ⦿ | ⦿ |
| Japan | ⦿ | ⊗ | ⦿ | ⦿ | ⦿ | ⦿ |
| Luxembourg | ⦿ | ⊗ | ⊗ | ⊗ | | |
| Mexico | ⊗ | ⊗ | ⊗ | ⊗ | ⦿ | ⊖ |
| Netherlands | ⦿ | ⦿ | ⦿ | ⦿ | ⦿ | ◬ |
| New Zealand | ⦿ | ⊗ | ⊗ | ⦿ | ⦿ | ⦿ |
| Norway | ⦿ | ⦿ | ⦿ | ⊗ | ◬ | ◬ |
| Portugal | ⦿ | ◬ | | | | |
| Slovak Republic | | | ⊗ | ⊗ | | ■ |
| Slovenia | ⦿ | ⊠ | ⦿ | ⦿ | ⦿ | |
| Spain | ⦿ | ⦿ | ⦿ | ⦿ | ⦿ | ⦿ |
| Sweden | ◬ | ◬ | ◬ | | ◬ | ◬ |
| Switzerland | ⦿ | ⦿ | ⦿ | ⦿ | ⦿ | ■ |
| Turkey | ⦿ | ⊗ | ◬ | ⊗ | ⦿ | ⦿ |
| United Kingdom | ◬ | ⊗ | ⦿ | ⊗ | ⦿ | ⦿ |
| **Key - Primary Institution responsible** | **Total** | | | | | |
| ⦿ Line Ministries | 21 | 13 | 16 | 13 | 17 | 12 |
| ⊗ Central Budget Authority | 3 | 8 | 6 | 11 | 0 | 0 |
| ⊖ Central Infrastructure/ PPP Unit | 0 | 0 | 1 | 0 | 1 | 2 |
| ■ Supreme Audit Institution | 0 | 0 | 0 | 0 | 1 | 6 |
| ◬ Others | 2 | 4 | 3 | 1 | 5 | 4 |
| ⊠ Activity not performed | 0 | 1 | 0 | 0 | 0 | 0 |

*Notes*: Answers refer to primary institution responsibility. If responsibilities are shared, other institutions are not further listed; Data for Greece refers to one primary institution on national level only (primary instituions on regional level are not reflected).
Data for Belgium, Canada, Finland, Iceland, Korea, Latvia, Poland and the United States are not available; Information on data for Israel: http://dx.doi.org/10.1787/888932315602.
*Source*: OECD (2018), OECD Survey of Capital Budgeting and Infrastructure Governance, Question 1, OECD, Paris.

StatLink http://dx.doi.org/10.1787/888933947673

**Figure 8.1. Distinction between capital and current expenditure requests**

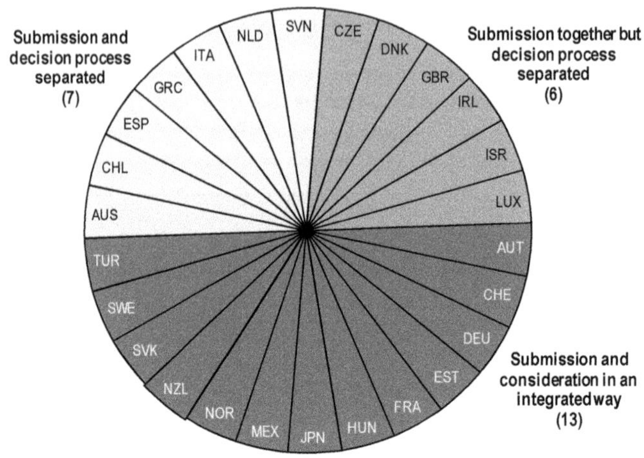


*Notes*: In Germany capital and current expenditures are outlined separately in the budget, but negotiated and decided in an integrated way.
Data for Portugal are not available for this question; Data for Belgium, Canada, Finland, Iceland, Korea, Latvia, Poland and the United States are not available; Information on data for Israel: http://dx.doi.org/10.1787/888932315602.
*Source*: OECD (2018), OECD Survey of Capital Budgeting and Infrastructure Governance, Question 5, OECD, Paris.

StatLink http://dx.doi.org/10.1787/888933947274

**Figure 8.2. Budgeting of multi-year capital projects**

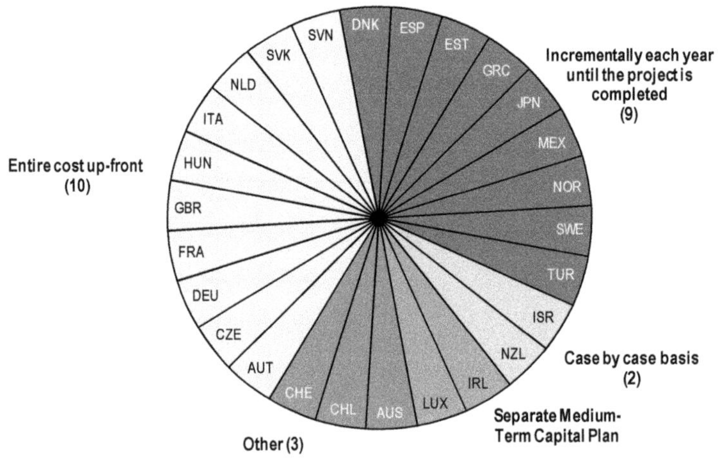


*Notes*: In Norway budget requests funding incrementally each year but the system includes authorisation for the executive to plan and implement large capital projects based on the entire cost up-front.
Data for Portugal are not available for this question; Data for Belgium, Canada, Finland, Iceland, Korea, Latvia, Poland and the United States are not available; Information on data for Israel: http://dx.doi.org/10.1787/888932315602.
*Source*: OECD (2018), OECD Survey of Capital Budgeting and Infrastructure Governance, Question 5a, OECD, Paris.

StatLink http://dx.doi.org/10.1787/888933947293

## 8.2. Strategic planning and prioritisation

High quality infrastructure is one of the backbones for achieving long-term inclusive development. Nevertheless, infrastructure projects often fail to meet their timeframe, budget, and service delivery objectives. This is often due to shortcomings in the country's governance framework for infrastructure. Good governance of infrastructure promotes not only value for money, affordability and enhanced infrastructure productivity, but helps to make the right projects happen in a manner that is trusted by users and citizens.

Successful governance of infrastructure demands a clear regulatory and institutional framework, robust co-ordination and sustainable performance throughout the life cycle of the asset, as well as a comprehensive preparation phase, including overall strategic planning, open and transparent prioritisation mechanism and decision processes that are based on affordability and cost efficiency (OECD, 2017). However, designing a clear and coherent strategic vision is difficult. This is essentially due to the complex nature of infrastructure policy that needs to address multiple and potentially contradictory objectives, such as growth, productivity, affordability, inclusive development and environmental objectives.

Strategic long-term planning is a key element for successful infrastructure development. More than half of OECD countries reported to have an overall long-term strategic infrastructure vision that cuts across all sectors. This is a new practice in some countries such as Luxembourg and Norway. Likewise, the Slovak Republic reported that the office of the Prime Minister is currently preparing a national infrastructure plan. Thirty-seven percent of surveyed countries reported to have both an overall infrastructure plan as well as long-term plans at the sector level. Co-ordination between these instruments is essential to ensure a clear strategic vision for infrastructure. The same amount of the surveyed countries reported to have only infrastructure plans at the sector level. Most of these countries only have long-term plans for certain sectors (e.g. roads, railways, energy, housing, health). Only Estonia and Sweden reported not having any type of long-term strategic plan (Figure 8.3).

Motivations for long-term strategies are heterogeneous across countries and heavily depend on the development aims and economic conditions. Transport bottlenecks, demography, and regional development imbalances are the most common drivers of strategic infrastructure plans in OECD surveyed countries (Figure 8.4)

In complement to the long-term vision, governments should also identify a short list of priority projects, taking into account the opposing policy goals, existing infrastructure needs and budget constraints. More than half of the countries surveyed identify such short-list of priority projects, either in an overall short list (26%), in multiple shortlists prepared by each sector (26%), or through an alternative mechanism (19%) (Figure 8.5). In most of the cases these priority lists refers only to the national level. Japan, Denmark, Mexico, New Zealand, Slovak Republic, Slovenia, Spain and the United Kingdom informed that they do not have a process to short-list priority projects.

The most important element for projects that get on the short list are strong results of the cost-benefit analysis, followed by the project's part of the long term strategic plan and strong political backing (Figure 8.6). Other important criteria include the project's functional fit with other infrastructure assets and its importance for the development of a particular sector. Less important are strong popular backing; the private sector's interest; and market failures. External funding from the EU or other donors is the least important factor for most OECD countries; however, for some countries (i.e. Estonia, Greece and the Slovak Republic) this was identified as a very relevant criterion.

**Figure 8.3. Existence of long-term strategic infrastructure plans**

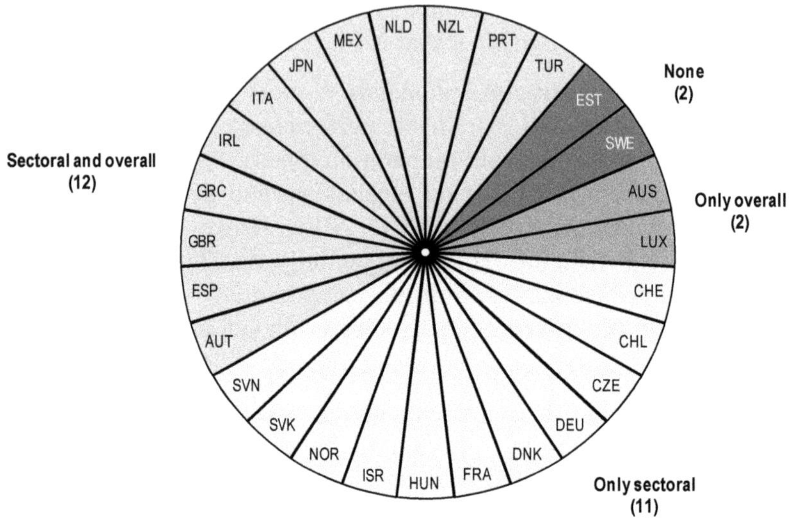


*Notes*: Data for Belgium, Canada, Finland, Iceland, Korea, Latvia, Poland and the United States are not available; Information on data for Israel: http://dx.doi.org/10.1787/888932315602.
*Source*: OECD (2018), OECD Survey of Capital Budgeting and Infrastructure Governance, Questions 8 and 9, OECD, Paris.

StatLink http://dx.doi.org/10.1787/888933947312

**Figure 8.4. Key drivers of the current overall strategic infrastructure plan**

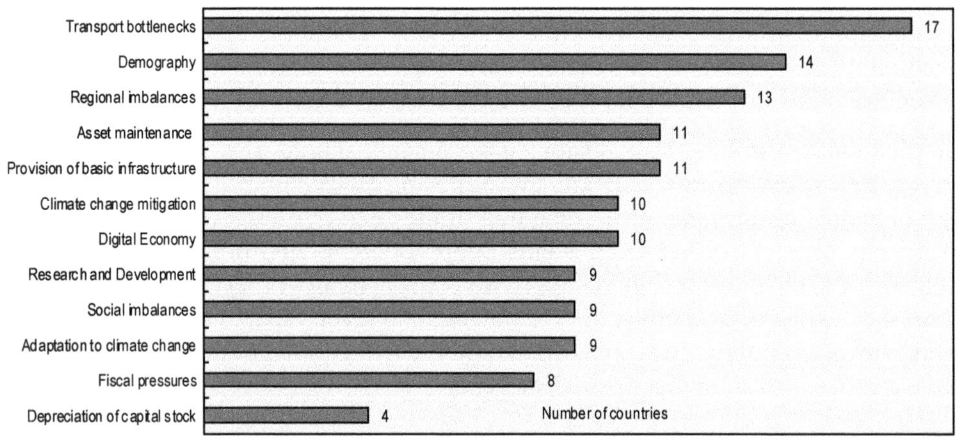


*Notes*: Data for Belgium, Canada, Finland, Iceland, Korea, Latvia, Poland and the United States are not available; Information on data for Israel: http://dx.doi.org/10.1787/888932315602.
*Source*: OECD (2018), OECD Survey of Capital Budgeting and Infrastructure Governance, Question 8b, OECD, Paris.

StatLink http://dx.doi.org/10.1787/888933947331

**Figure 8.5. Prioritisation process for infrastructure projects**

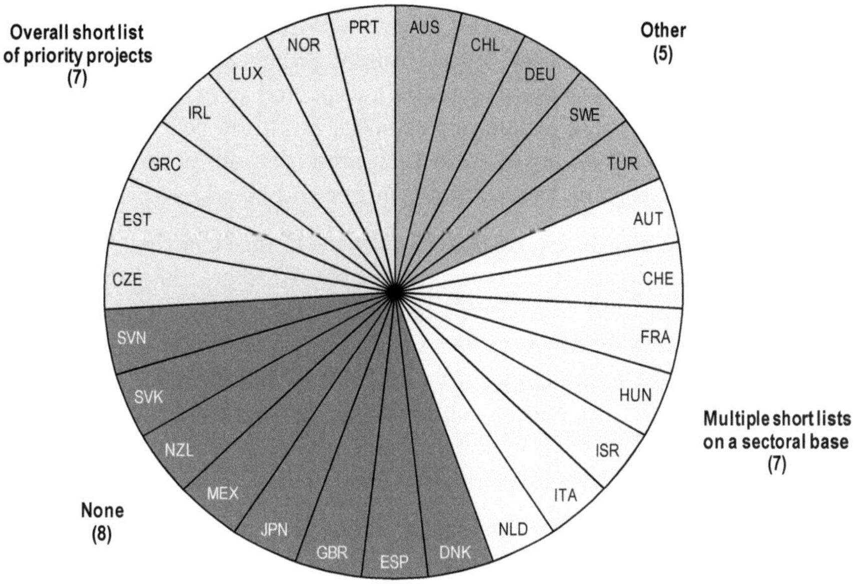


*Note*: Data for Belgium, Canada, Finland, Iceland, Korea, Latvia, Poland and the United States are not available; Information on data for Israel: http://dx.doi.org/10.1787/888932315602.
*Source*: OECD (2018), OECD Survey of Capital Budgeting and Infrastructure Governance, Question 11, OECD, Paris.

StatLink http://dx.doi.org/10.1787/888933947350

**Figure 8.6. Criteria for project prioritisation and approval**

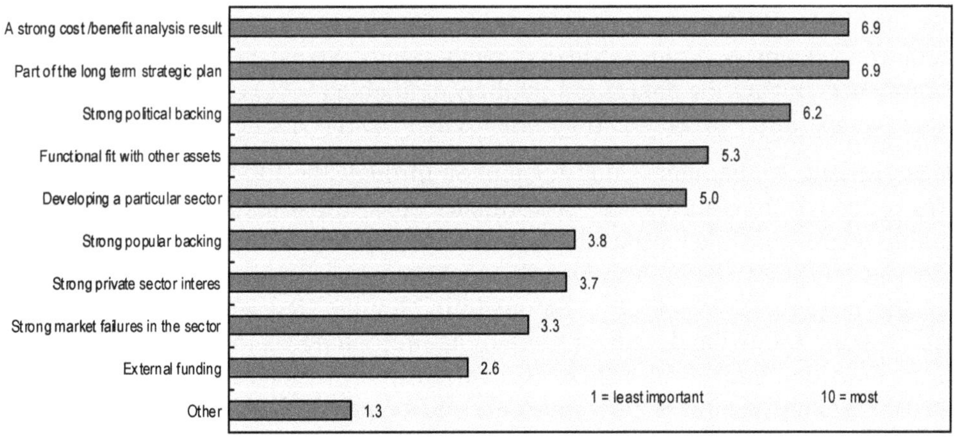


*Notes*: The graph reflects average ranking points.
Data for Belgium, Canada, Finland, Iceland, Korea, Latvia, Poland and the United States are not available; Data for France, Hungary, Israel, Portugal, Slovenia and Spain are not available for this question and hence not taken into account for the average ranking points; Information on data for Israel: http://dx.doi.org/10.1787/888932315602.
*Source*: OECD (2018), OECD Survey of Capital Budgeting and Infrastructure Governance, Question 12, OECD, Paris.

StatLink http://dx.doi.org/10.1787/888933947369

## 8.3. Key practices for value-for-money assessment

In principle, the general assessment of costs and benefits of an investment should be the driving force for the prudent evaluation of investment decisions (OECD, 2015). Value for money (VfM) can be defined as what a government judges to be an optimal combination of quantity, quality, features and price (i.e. cost), expected over the whole of the project's lifetime. In a nutshell, the value-for-money concept could be described as the balance of interests of citizens, both as taxpayers and recipients of public services to establish the highest overall societal return on investment (Burger and Hawkesworth, 2011).

VfM can be measured in absolute cost-benefit terms (Do the benefits exceed the costs?) or in relative terms (Is one form of delivery more cost-effective than the other – see next section). In many cases, VfM is assessed using a combination of quantitative (such as cost/benefit analysis) and qualitative tools. A majority of surveyed countries conduct both absolute and relative VfM assessments for either all of the projects or for those projects above a certain threshold, no matter whether the projects are delivered via PPPs or traditionally procured (Figure 8.7). In some, countries, such as Slovakia and Austria VfM assessments are only compulsory for some line ministries (e.g. railways in Austria).

There are several techniques for assessing value for money. Cost-benefit analysis (including total cost of ownership during the life-cycle) is the most popular approach (89%), followed by net present value (70%) and cash-flow estimates over the project cycle (70%). The popularity of cost-benefit studies reflects the results from previous surveys (OECD, 2014) and (OECD, 2017). About half of the countries also use other tools, including internal rate of return, analysis of the willingness of users to pay, or business case methodology. In many cases these VfM assessments are assessed by combined approaches. Denmark for example, calculates and reports the socio-economic value and conducts business cases. Norway follows an alternative approach assessing all PPP projects and all large investment projects (over NOK 750 million) within a general quality assurance scheme.

Results for VfM assessments are not, however, routinely made publicly available. Only five countries (Denmark, France, Mexico, Netherlands, Sweden) fully publish the results, while in most countries the data is not publicly available (44%) or only made available to the extent compatible with commercial sensitivity (36%) (OECD, 2018).

It can be difficult to maintain value for money through the lifecycle of the asset, which requires effective monitoring of performance of infrastructure. In most countries, institutions are responsible for the development and delivery of infrastructure, not for "after sales service" (OECD, 2017). Although the preparation and construction phases inevitably require the majority of resources, responsibility for the assessment and monitoring of projects over the following decade or more of its lifespan needs to be clearly allocated. To do so, in most countries (69%) there is a formal policy ensuring that the relevant line ministry or agency conducts performance assessment of each project, which is either centrally mandated (31%) or falls under the department's responsibility (38%) (Figure 8.8.

Equally, in most countries (70%), asset conditions are monitored on a regular basis in order to assess the impacts of ageing infrastructure on service levels and maintenance need (OECD, 2018). In some cases, new technologies, such as drones (in the case of Denmark) have made the monitoring task significantly cheaper and easier. To ensure VfM through the life cycle, project design should also take environment and climatic impacts into account. In most countries (85%), a monitoring, reporting and verification (MRV) process is in place to ensure compliance resulting from environmental impact assessments throughout the life cycle. Fewer countries have set up MRV processes for compliance with climate impact assessments (44%) or mitigation measures (48%), and risk assessments (41%), or climate adaptation measures (33%). Additionally, the Netherlands works with a nation-wide monitoring programme for climate risk management (OECD, 2018).

**Figure 8.7. Formal process/legal requirement for absolute (A and B) and relative (C and D) value for money in infrastructure projects**

(A) PPPs

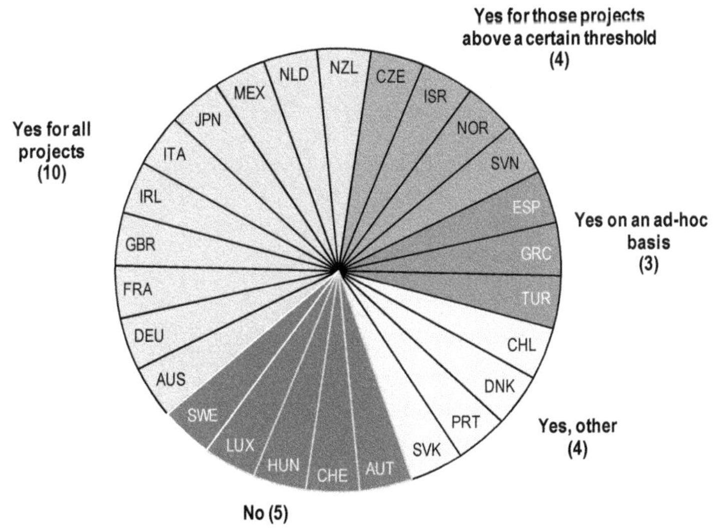


(B) TIPs

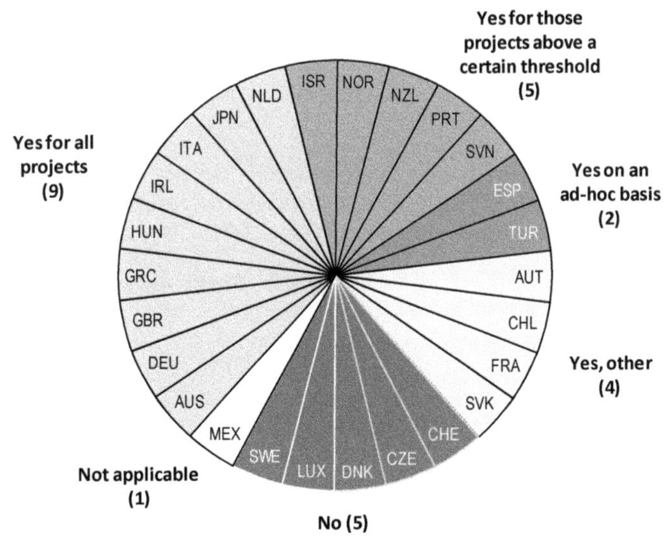


StatLink http://dx.doi.org/10.1787/888933947388

(C) PPPs

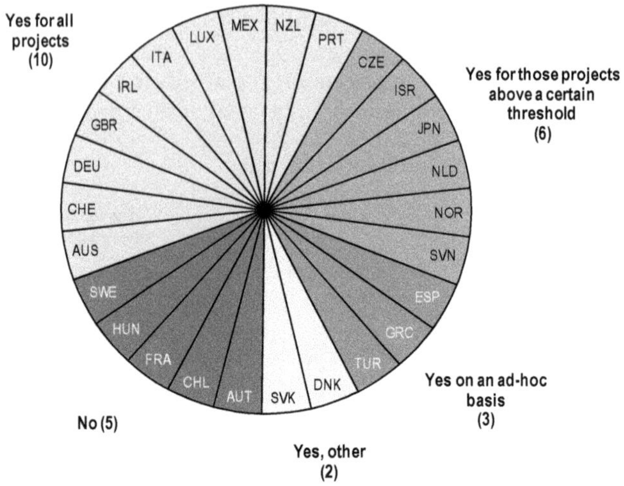


(D) TIPs

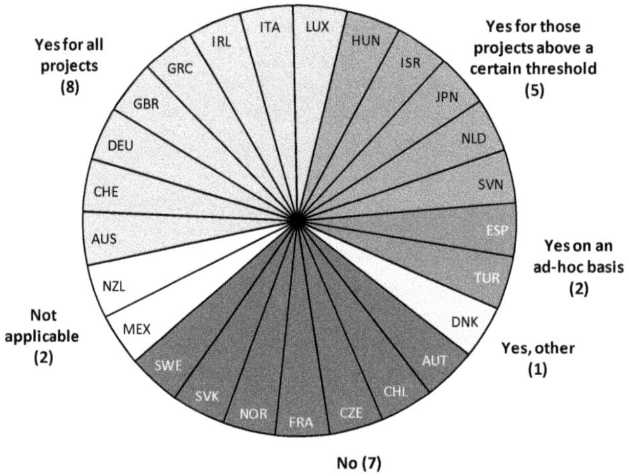


StatLink http://dx.doi.org/10.1787/888933947388

*Notes:* A. The data for Portugal is referring to central government and SOE's PPPs only. In Denmark, there is a formal process that ensures that the VfM analysis is being conducted, so the politicians make their decision on an informed basis. But in the end it is a political decision which infrastructure project is realised and which is not realised; B. France has a mandatory cost benefit analysis for all government projects. Portugal does not cover PPPs at regional or local level; C. In Switzerland, there is a formal obligation to consider PPPs if suitable (=more efficient/effective).

Data for Belgium, Canada, Finland, Iceland, Korea, Latvia, Poland and the United States are not available; Data for Estonia are not available for this question (PPPs and TIPs); Data for Portugal are not available for this question (TIPs); Information on data for Israel: http://dx.doi.org/10.1787/888932315602.

*Source*: OECD (2018), OECD Survey of Capital Budgeting and Infrastructure Governance, Question 34, OECD, Paris.

**Figure 8.8. Formal Policy for implementation of performance assessment of each project**

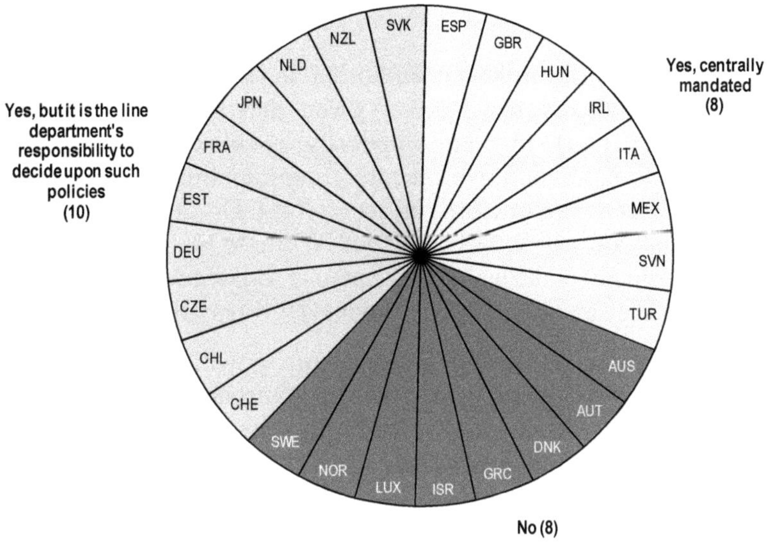


*Note*: Data for Belgium, Canada, Finland, Iceland, Korea, Latvia, Poland and the United States are not available; Data for Portugal are not available for this question; Information on data for Israel: http://dx.doi.org/10.1787/888932315602.
*Source*: OECD (2018), OECD Survey of Capital Budgeting and Infrastructure Governance, Question 44, OECD, Paris.

StatLink http://dx.doi.org/10.1787/888933947426

## 8.4. Public Private Partnership (PPP) Practices

Despite a growing proportion of infrastructure services that have been delivered through PPPs in the last decade, current levels of infrastructure investment taking place through PPPs is still moderate. Most OECD countries (83%) reported to have between 0% and 5% of public sector infrastructure investment taking place through PPPs in the last 3 years (Figure 8.9), including Sweden with only one project in the recent 3 years. In Australia and New Zealand the share lies between 5% and 10%. Only in a few countries is this share higher than 10%, including Italy and Netherlands (10%-15%), and in the case of Chile above 20% (OECD, 2017). Most countries have no restrictions with regard to the sectors that can make use of PPPs. However, most commonly, PPPs are used in transport (road, rail, port) and public buildings.

Given the complexity of PPPs and their relative infrequent use, PPP units can concentrate critical skills to ensure value for money. However, while the overall share of countries with dedicated PPP units has remained relatively stable in the last decade (OECD, 2010[8], OECD, 2016[9]; OECD, 2018[7]) developments across countries have been distinctive. In several countries, new PPP Units have been built up, while closed in others (Czech Republic, Canada) as their mandate is considered to have been fulfilled, or responsibilities transferred. In Italy, for example, responsibilities have been assigned to the planning department at the Presidency of the Council of Ministers. For Switzerland different units within the departmental structure of the Ministry of Finance assist the line Ministries regarding PPPs. Some countries like the UK or Slovak Republic have additional units within specific line ministries to ensure that specific expertise in the relevant sectoral area can be supplied. In other cases, independent statutory infrastructure bodies were created with a broader mandate to prioritise and progress nationally significant infrastructure, such as Infrastructure Australia. Currently, about 65% of the countries entertain dedicated units for PPPs (Table 8.2).

Where central government has the relevant authority, it should consider allowing sub-national governments to prudently use PPPs – given that the relevant capacities are available at the sub-national level. In a large majority of countries (73%) PPP units or Infrastructure Units at sub-national governments (municipalities, regions, states) are allowed to design and run infrastructure projects (OECD, 2018). In practice, this opportunity is taken on distinctively across countries. While in New Zealand and Sweden, sub-national governments do not make use of this capacity, other countries, such as Canada, deliver 95% of their PPPs via subnational governments (Infrastructure Canada, 2018).

The contingent fiscal liabilities, as well as of long-term government commitments that often come with PPP contracts demand a prudent and transparent management of PPPs. For example, the decision to invest in a new infrastructure asset should be separated from the decision on how to procure and finance the project, as done in the majority of the countries (62%)(Figure 8.10). Many countries use value for money assessments between delivery modes in order to ensure that procedures, such as special subsidies, accounting rules, etc. or simply traditions do not unduly favour certain types of delivery modalities. However, only 50% do so systematically[1]. Additionally, in 70% of countries surveyed, the CBA is required to systematically[2] approve PPP projects of line ministries, only slightly more than for traditionally procured projects (65%) (OECD, 2018).

**Figure 8.9. Percentage of public sector infrastructure investment (value) through PPPs in the recent 3 years**

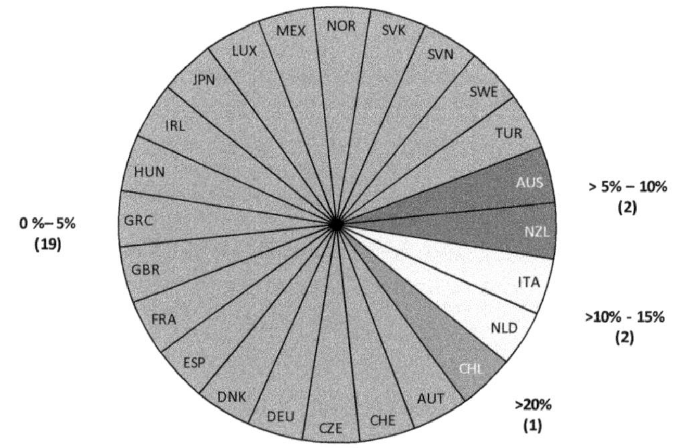


*Notes*: Switzerland noted that the exact value would depend on the definition of PPPs.
Data for Belgium, Canada, Finland, Iceland, Korea, Latvia, Poland and the United States are not available; Data for Estonia, Israel and Portugal are not available for this question; Information on data for Israel: http://dx.doi.org/10.1787/888932315602.
*Source*: OECD (2018), OECD Survey of Capital Budgeting and Infrastructure Governance, Question 58, OECD, Paris.

StatLink http://dx.doi.org/10.1787/888933947445

**Figure 8.10. Investment decision in a new infrastructure asset**

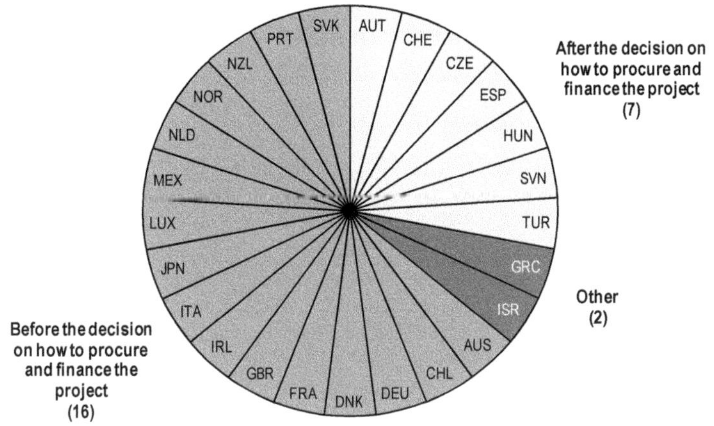


*Note*: This question is not applicable to Sweden. Italy answered yes, in general. But it could be possible for example to have unsolicited proposals.

Data for Belgium, Canada, Finland, Iceland, Korea, Latvia, Poland and the United States are not available; Data for Estonia are not available for this question; Information on data for Israel: http://dx.doi.org/10.1787/888932315602.

*Source*: OECD (2018), OECD Survey of Capital Budgeting and Infrastructure Governance, Question 39, OECD, Paris.

StatLink http://dx.doi.org/10.1787/888933947464

**Table 8.2. Existence of a dedicated unit for public-private partnerships (PPP)**

| | No | Yes, within the departmental structure of the Ministry of Finance | Yes, as a separate agency answering to the Minister of Finance | Yes, within the departmental structure of a line ministry | Yes, as a separate agency answering to a line ministry | Yes, other unit |
|---|---|---|---|---|---|---|
| Australia | | | | x | | |
| Austria | x | | | | | |
| Chile | | | | x | | |
| Czech Republic | x | | | | | |
| Denmark | x | | | | | |
| Estonia | | | | | | |
| France | | | x | | | |
| Germany | | x | | | x | |
| Greece | | | | x | | |
| Hungary | x | | | x | | |
| Ireland | | x | x | x | x | |
| Israel | | x | x | | | |
| Italy | | | | | | x |
| Japan | | | x | | | |
| Luxembourg | x | | | | | |
| Mexico | | x | | | | |
| Netherlands | x | | | | | |
| New Zealand | | x | | | | |
| Norway | x | | | | | |
| Portugal | | x | | | | |
| Slovak Republic | | x | | x | | |
| Slovenia | x | | | | | |
| Spain | x | | | | | |
| Sweden | x | | | | | |
| Switzerland | | | | | | x |
| Turkey | x | | | | | |
| United Kingdom | | | x | | | |
| Total | **11** | **7** | **5** | **6** | **2** | **2** |

*Note*:; In Turkey, although there is no PPP unit in traditional means, there is the High Planning Council (HPC) which approves the PPP projects and the Ministry of Development which is conducting the secretariat of HPC is acting like a PPP unit in many regards.
Data for Belgium, Canada, Finland, Iceland, Korea, Latvia, Poland and the United States are not available; Data for Estonia is not available for this question.
Information on data for Israel: http://dx.doi.org/10.1787/888932315602.
*Source*: OECD (2018), OECD Survey of Capital Budgeting and Infrastructure Governance, Question 59, OECD, Paris.

## Notes

[1] All projects or projects above a certain threshold.

[2] All projects or projects above a certain threshold.

## References


Burger, P. and I. Hawkesworth (2013), "Capital budgeting and procurement practices", *OECD Journal on Budgeting*, Vol. 131, http://dx.doi.org/10.1787/16812336. [2]

Burger, P. and I. Hawkesworth (2011), "How To Attain Value for Money: Comparing PPP and Traditional Infrastructure Public Procurement", *OECD Journal on Budgeting* 11. [5]

Infrastructure Canada (2018), *Public Private Partnerships in Cananda.* [10]

OECD (2018), *OECD Survey of Capital Budgeting and Infrastructure Governance.* [9]

OECD (2017), *Gaps and Governance Standards of Public Infrastructure in Chile: Infrastructure Governance Review*, OECD Publishing, Paris, http://dx.doi.org/10.1787/9789264278875-en. [11]

OECD (2017), *Getting Infrastructure Right: a framework for better governance*, OECD Publishing, Paris. [3]

OECD (2016), *OECD dataset on the Governance of Infrastructure*, https://qdd.oecd.org/subject.aspx?Subject=GOV_INFRG. [8]

OECD (2015), "Recommendation of the Council on Budgetary Governance", *Public Governance and Territorial Development Directorate.* [4]

OECD (2014), *The challenges and applications of cost-benefit analysis (CBA) for the preliminary feasibility study of capital investments, Government at a Glance 2015 Database*, http://qdd.oecd.org/subject.aspx?Subject=17375f7e-fc6c-4a5f-. [6]

OECD (2010), *Dedicated Public-Private Partnership Units: A Survey of Institutional and Governance Structures*, OECD Publishing, Paris, http://dx.doi.org/10.1787/9789264064843-en. [7]

Posner, P. (2009), "Public-private Partnerships: The relevance of budgeting.", *OECD Journal on Budgeting*, Vol. Volume 2009/1, pp. 49-74. [1]

Schick, A. (2003), "The Role of Fiscal Rules in Budgeting", *OECD Journal on Budgeting*, Vol. 3/3, https://dx.doi.org/10.1787/budget-v3-art14-en. [12]

# Annex 8.A. Chapter 8 annex

### Annex Table 8.A.1. Steps taken at the beginning of the project development to ensure that the design takes environment and climatic impact into account

| | Envrionmental impact assessment | Climate impact assessment? GHG emissions model (baseline calculations) been created to estimate the project's potential emissions | Actively targeting mitigation measures to climate change | Risk assessment how project could be jeopardized by climate change and natural hazard | Actively targeting adaptation measures to climate change |
|---|---|---|---|---|---|
| Australia | x | | | | |
| Austria | x | x | x | x | x |
| Chile | x | | x | x | x |
| Czech Republic | x | x | x | | |
| Denmark | x | x | x | x | x |
| France | x | x | x | | |
| Germany | x | | | x | |
| Greece | x | x | x | x | x |
| Hungary | x | | | x | |
| Ireland | x | x | x | x | x |
| Israel | x | x | x | | |
| Italy | x | x | x | | |
| Japan | x | | | | |
| Mexico | x | | x | x | x |
| Netherlands | x | x | x | x | |
| Norway | x | | | | |
| Portugal | x | | | | |
| Slovak Republic | x | | | | |
| Slovenia | x | | | | |
| Spain | x | | | | x |
| Sweden | x | x | x | x | x |
| Switzerland | x | x | | | |
| United Kingdom | x | x | x | x | x |
| **Total** | **23** | **12** | **13** | **11** | **9** |

*Note*: Data for Belgium, Canada, Finland, Iceland, Korea, Latvia, Poland and the United States are not available; Data for Estonia, Luxembourg, New Zealand and Turkey are not available for this question; Information on data for Israel: http://dx.doi.org/10.1787/888932315602.

*Source*: OECD (2018), OECD Survey of Capital Budgeting and Infrastructure Governance, Question 29, OECD, Paris.

**Annex Table 8.A.2. CBA approval for capital/infrastructure projects of line ministries**

| | PPPs | TIPs |
|---|---|---|
| Australia | ◉ | ⊗ |
| Austria | ⊗ | ⊗ |
| Chile | ◉ | ◉ |
| Czech Republic | ◉ | ◉ |
| Denmark | ⊗ | ⊗ |
| Estonia | ◉ | ◉ |
| France | ◉ | ⊠ |
| Germany | ⚠ | ⚠ |
| Greece | ⊠ | ⊠ |
| Hungary | ⊠ | ◉ |
| Ireland | ⊠ | ⊠ |
| Israel | ◉ | ◉ |
| Italy | ⊖ | ⊖ |
| Japan | ◉ | ◉ |
| Luxembourg | ◉ | ⊗ |
| Mexico | ◉ | ◉ |
| Netherlands | ⊗ | ⊗ |
| New Zealand | ⊠ | ⊠ |
| Norway | ⊗ | ⊗ |
| Portugal | ⚠ | |
| Slovak Republic | ⊗ | ⊗ |
| Slovenia | ◉ | ⚠ |
| Spain | ⊗ | ⊗ |
| Sweden | ⊗ | ⊗ |
| Switzerland | ⊠ | ⊠ |
| Turkey | ◉ | ⚠ |
| United Kingdom | ◉ | ◉ |
| **Key** | **Total** | |
| ◉ Yes for all projects | 12 | 8 |
| ⊗ Yes for those projects above a certain threshold | 7 | 9 |
| ⊖ Yes on an ad-hoc basis | 1 | 1 |
| ⚠ Yes, other | 2 | 3 |
| ⊠ No | 5 | 5 |

*Note*: Data for Belgium, Canada, Finland, Iceland, Korea, Latvia, Poland and the United States are not available;; Information on data for Israel: http://dx.doi.org/10.1787/888932315602.
*Source*: OECD (2018), OECD Survey of Capital Budgeting and Infrastructure Governance, Question 7, OECD, Paris.

**Annex Table 8.A.3. Capital budgeting process and environmental/ climate costs and benefits**

| | Presentation of information |
|---|---|
| Australia | ⊗ |
| Austria | ⊗ |
| Chile | ⊠ |
| Czech Republic | ■ |
| Denmark | ⊖■ |
| Estonia | ⊖ |
| France | ■ |
| Germany | ⊗ |
| Greece | ⊖ |
| Hungary | ⊠ |
| Ireland | ■ |
| Israel | ⊖■ |
| Japan | ⊖ |
| Luxembourg | ⊖■ |
| Mexico | ⊗⊖ |
| Netherlands | ■ |
| New Zealand | ⊖ |
| Norway | ⦿⊗ |
| Portugal | ■ |
| Slovak Republic | ■⊠ |
| Spain | ■ |
| Switzerland | ⊠ |
| United Kingdom | ⚠ |

| Key | | Total |
|---|---|---|
| ⦿ | Addressed in the longer-term fiscal planning document | 1 |
| ⊗ | Included as background information in the budget document | 5 |
| ⊖ | Measured and taken into account to determine resource allocation during the budgetary process | 8 |
| ■ | Studied only at the project base level | 10 |
| ⚠ | Other | 1 |
| ⊠ | Not included | 4 |

*Note*: Data for Belgium, Canada, Finland, Iceland, Korea, Latvia, Poland and the United States are not available; Data for Italy, Slovenia, Sweden and Turkey are not available for this question; Information on data for Israel: http://dx.doi.org/10.1787/888932315602.

*Source*: OECD (2018), OECD Survey of Capital Budgeting and Infrastructure Governance, Question 28, OECD, Paris.

# 9. Country Profiles

*The following country notes summarise how OECD countries apply public financial management practices in their national context. The country notes show that, while approaches are varying and distinctive, the OECD principles of budgetary governance continue to provide a useful frame of reference for considering how budgeting systems should be considered, and that the various themes of modern Public Financial Management (PFM) are inter-connected and mutually supportive.*

*Annex A at the end of the chapter contains the full country data that was used for the country profiles graphs A, C and D.*

## Budgetary Governance in Practice: Australia

### *Economic context*

Australia's economy will continue growing at a robust pace. Business investment outside the mining sector will pick up, with exports boosted as new resource-sector capacity comes on stream. The strengthening labour market and household incomes will sustain private consumption, and inflation and wages will pick up gradually.

### *Fiscal policy plans*

The medium-term fiscal strategy aims to achieve budget surpluses, on average, over the course of the economic cycle. The strategy is underpinned by the following policy elements: investing in a stronger economy by redirecting government spending to quality investment; maintaining strong fiscal discipline by controlling expenditure to reduce the government's share of the economy (with a falling government expenditure-to-GDP ratio); supporting revenue growth through a strong economy while maintaining a sustainable tax burden with a cap on the tax receipts-to-GDP ratio; stabilising and then decreasing net debt over time. The budget repair strategy is designed to deliver sustainable budget surpluses building to at least 1% of GDP as soon as possible, consistent with the medium-term fiscal strategy.

**A: Fiscal Balance and Public Debt**

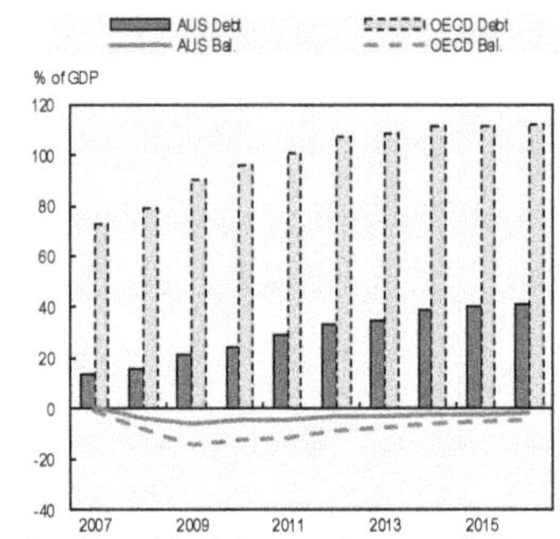


*Note:* The graph is referring to general government fiscal balance and general government gross debt as defined in the OECD National Accounts Statistics.

*Source*: OECD National Accounts Statistics (database); Eurostat Government finance statistics (database).

**B: Fiscal Policy Plans**

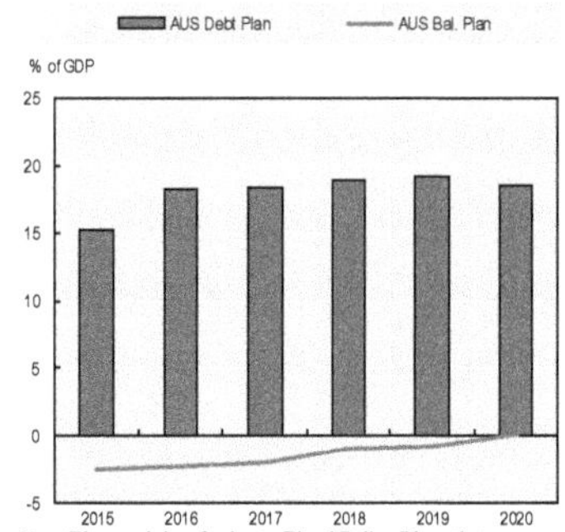


*Note:* The graph is referring to Fiscal Policy Plans that are implemented and/or officially announced as of November 2017 and as indicated by the country. Actual results in graph A may differ as the Fiscal Policy Plans are prepared by the country beforehand and as the Debt and Balance Plan reported by the country are based on the country's own definition; Data for Australia are referring to federal government. Australia's debt plan is a plan for net debt.

*Source:* 2018 OECD Fiscal Plans and Budgeting Framework Survey.

**C: Public Investment**

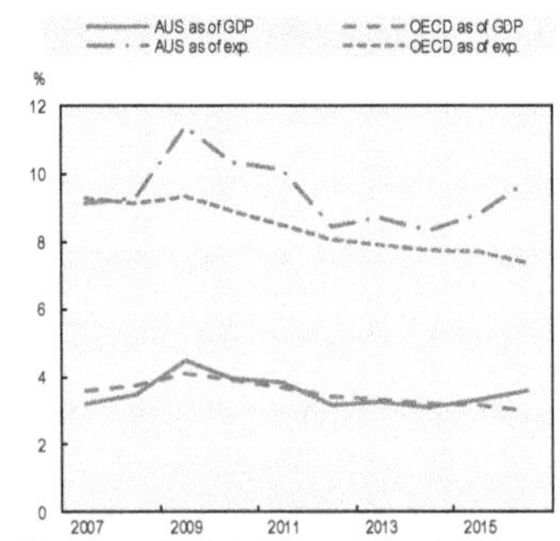


*Note:* The graph is referring to government investment as a percentage of GDP and as a share of total government expenditures.

*Source*: OECD National Accounts Statistics (database).

**D: Expenditure by function (2016)**

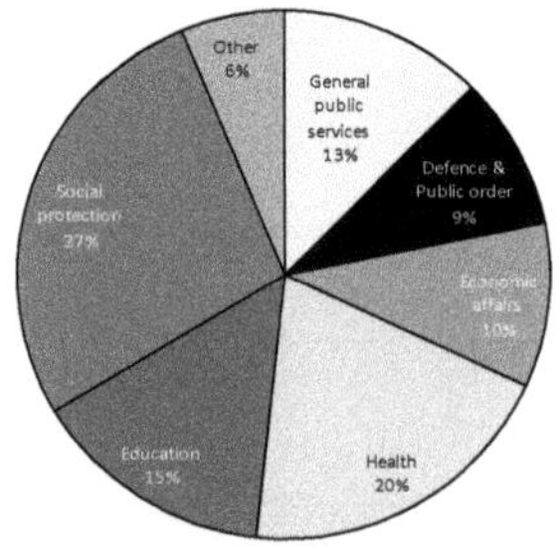


*Source:* OECD National Accounts Statistics (database); Eurostat Government finance statistics (database). Data for Australia are based on Government finance statistics provided by the Australian Bureau of Statistics.

### *Developments in budgetary governance*

Recent reforms in Australia have included a strong focus on improving the use and impact of performance information.

The Parliament's analytical capacity has been significantly enhanced since the establishment of the Parliamentary Budget Office in 2012. The PBO is mandated to "inform the parliament by providing independent and non-partisan analysis of the budget cycle, fiscal policy and the financial implications of proposals." In addition to policy costings, the PBO costs election platforms.

Budget transparency is generally high and Australia was an early adopter of accruals methodology. Distributional analyses of the budget are not produced. Australia was an originator of gender-responsive budgeting, although these approaches are not currently employed at the national level.

**Central Budget Authority**

Shared between the Department of the Treasury and the Department of Finance.

Weblinks: www.treasury.gov.au and www.finance.gov.au
Also see www.budget.gov.au

**Legal Framework**

The Constitution lays out the requirements for legislative authorisation of all spending and taxation. Other aspects of budgeting are covered in legislation such as the Charter of Budget Honesty Act (1998) which sets out principles and requirements for government's management of fiscal policy and the Public Governance, Performance and Accountability Act (PGPA, 2013) which lays out a system of governance and accountability for public resources, with an emphasis on planning, performance and reporting. The PGPA Act is undergoing an independent statutory review in 2017-18.

**Budget coverage**

The executive's budget covers central government. Most public services are the primary responsibility of the states and territories. The national government collects most taxes in Australia, including on behalf of the states and territories, and is the main funder of the states and territories through specific purpose payments and general revenue assistance (mainly revenues raised from the Goods and Services Tax -GST). The Commonwealth Grants Commission annually recommends how the GST should be distributed to achieve horizontal fiscal equalisation.

| Budget cycle | |
|---|---|
| Budget circular | n/a |
| Pre-budget statement | n/a |
| Negotiations with line ministries | winter |
| Executive budget proposal | mid-May |
| Parliamentary vote on budget | 30 June |
| *Start of financial year* | *1 July* |
| In-year budget execution reports | monthly |
| Mid-year implementation report | November or December |
| *End of financial year* | *30 June* |
| Year-end financial statement | 30 September |
| Audited financial report | end November |
| Parliamentary accounting | end October |

**Australia's application of OECD budget principles "at a glance"**

| | | |
|---|---|---|
| 1. | Fiscal policy objectives | There are no legally binding fiscal rules in force but there is a political commitment to a balanced budget and debt reduction targets. There are upper limits on revenue and constraints on use of windfall revenues. |
| 2a. | Strategic alignment | Australia will deliver its first Voluntary National Review on the 2030 Agenda for Sustainable Development in July 2018. Different federal government agencies are responsible for each of the goals. |
| 2b. | MTEF | The government publishes its fiscal strategy and prepares estimates for the budget year and the following three financial years. This is done on a rolling basis. The MTEF does not provide expenditure ceilings. |
| **3.** | **Capital and infrastructure** | **Infrastructure Australia prioritises and progresses nationally significant infrastructure. It develops 15-year rolling Infrastructure Plans with national and state priorities. There are distinct processes for deciding on capital and operating budget requests. PPP and infrastructure projects must demonstrate absolute and relative VFM.** |
| 4. | Transparency and accessibility | The budget and related reports are published along with official summaries for policymakers, citizens' guides, and open data. No impact assessments are published. |
| 5a. | Parliamentary engagement | The parliament does not have a Budget Committee and committees in the lower house play little role. Committees in the upper house hold estimates hearings. By convention the legislature approves the budget (or Appropriations Bill No. 1) without amendment. *Ex post* oversight is conducted by the joint Public Accounts Committee. The Parliamentary Budget Office has significantly increased analytical capacity. |
| 5b. | Inclusive public / civic debate | Limited engagement of policy stakeholders in budget cycle. Government does issue a public call for proposals in the pre-budget phase and may consult relevant groups during the development of policy proposals. |
| **6.** | **Financial reporting and accounting** | **The budget and appropriation bills are prepared on both a cash and accrual basis, as are the financial reports.** |
| 7. | Budget execution | Single treasury fund is mandatory for all revenues and expenditures of central government. Sound budget execution is primarily the responsibility of line ministries who can reallocate items within an "outcome", and can carry-over unused funds or appropriations, within limits. There are no supplementary budgets. |
| **8a.** | **Performance budgeting** | **Performance information is reported in portfolio budget statements at the outcome and programme level and presented to Parliament. Performance information is produced primarily for purposes of accountability and transparency, although it also supports management-level decision making on the delivery of programmes and services, and, to a lesser extent, strategic decision-making on the allocation of resources.** |
| 8b. | Evaluation and VFM | |
| 9. | Fiscal risk and long-term sustainability | CBA produces projections covering a 10-year fiscal outlook that are updated twice a year.. A Statement of Risks is published in the budget update. There is a contingency reserve or allowance included in aggregate expenditures. Also, an Intergenerational Report is produced at least every 5 years that includes 40 year projections and assesses the long-term sustainability of current government policies, including the financial implications of demographic change. |
| 10. | Quality assurance and audit | CBA consults independent central bank before finalising its economic forecasts to underpin the Budget. The Parliamentary Budget Office reports on fiscal risks and long-term fiscal sustainability and carries out policy and election platform costings. Independent SAI established in primary legislation that audits government financial report. |

*Note*: Rows in **bold** represent notable international practice.

# Budgetary Governance in Practice: Austria

## *Economic context*

Following strong rebounds in investment and exports, economic activity in Austria is set to remain buoyant through 2018 and, to a lesser extent, 2019. Unemployment will continue to decline and labour market participation will rise further, in particular for women and older workers. Inflation remains higher than in other euro area countries, mainly driven by prices in sectors that are little exposed to international trade.

## *Fiscal policy plans*

The Austrian government has identified its medium-term budgetary objectives and priorities as: sustainable, secure, growth-oriented and sound budgetary policy at all governmental levels in order to open additional fiscal leeway for the future. The key objective is to create room for implementing tax relief measures with a view towards lowering the tax ratio to 40% of GDP. An additional target is to comply fully with the EU Stability and Growth Pact and other EU-related criteria (e.g. maintain a structural deficit of 0.5% of GDP).

**A: Fiscal Balance and Public Debt**

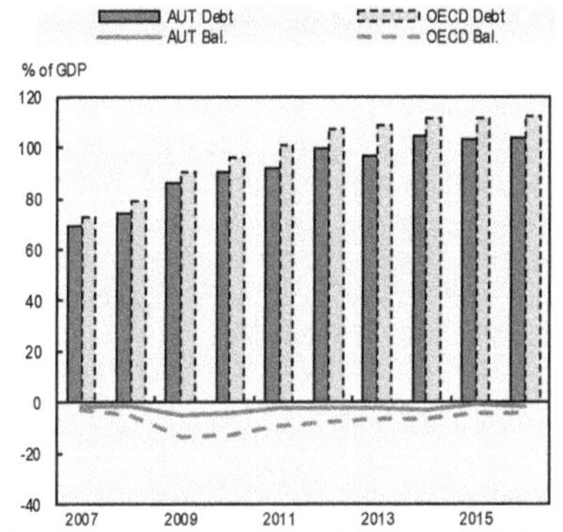


*Note:* The graph is referring to general government fiscal balance and general government gross debt as defined in the OECD National Accounts Statistics.

*Source:* OECD National Accounts Statistics (database); Eurostat Government finance statistics (database).

**B: Fiscal Policy Plans**

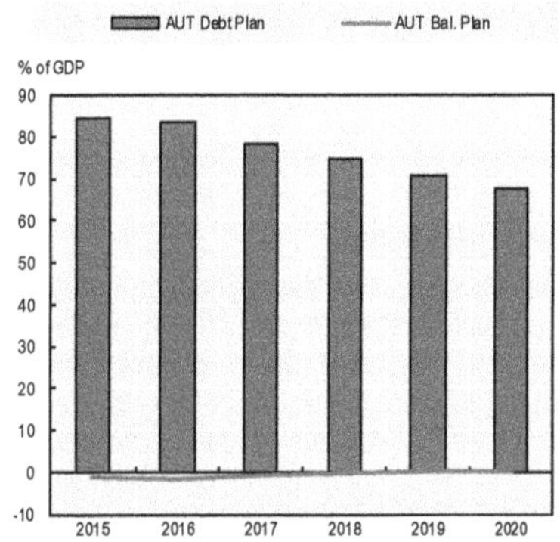


*Note:* The graph is referring to Fiscal Policy Plans that are implemented and/or officially announced as of November 2017 and as indicated by the country. Actual results in graph A may differ as the Fiscal Policy Plans are prepared by the country beforehand and as the Debt and Balance Plan reported by the country are based on the country's own definition.

*Source:* 2018 OECD Fiscal Plans and Budgeting Framework Survey

**C: Public Investment**

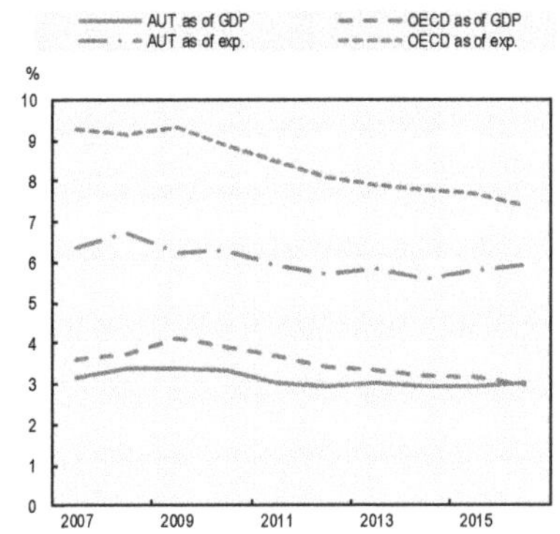


*Note:* The graph is referring to government investment as a percentage of GDP and as a share of total government expenditures.

*Source*: OECD National Accounts Statistics (database).

**D: Expenditure by function (2016)**

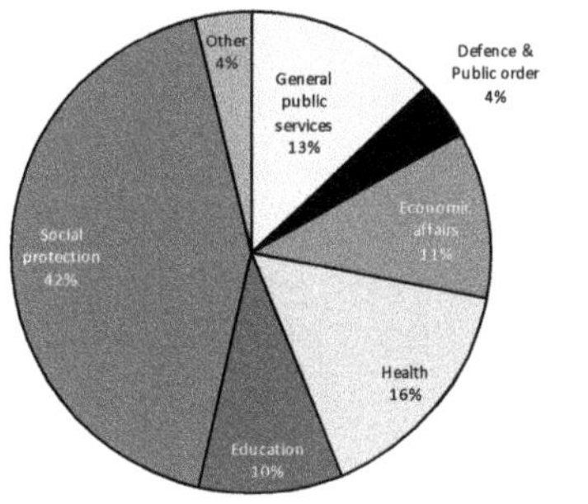


*Source:* OECD National Accounts Statistics (database); Eurostat Government finance statistics (database).

### *Developments in budgetary governance*

Since 2009, Austria has undertaken a carefully-considered and ambitious series of modern budgeting reforms which are designed to achieve a number of objectives, including increased flexibility, transparency and performance. A first phase in 2009 introduced a medium term expenditure framework (*Bundesfinanzrahmengesetz,* BFRG) with legally binding expenditure ceilings covering four years ahead on a rolling basis. In 2013, a second phase introduced changes to the budget structure, replacing detailed appropriations with global budgets below the chapter level for more flexibility for line ministries for in-year re-allocations. Furthermore, performance budgeting has been introduced as an integral element of the Austrian federal budget reform; and gender budgeting is implemented in a systematic manner as one distinct element of this overall approach. Moreover, a dual approach to financial reporting and budgeting was implemented, involving both cash and accrual accounting and budgeting in parallel. The Parliamentary Budget Office plays a particular role in helping parliamentarians to engage constructively with the performance and budgetary information.

| Central Budget Authority |
|---|
| Federal Ministry of Finance (Directorate General - Budget and Public Finances)<br>Directorate General - Budget and Public Finances<br>Weblink: https://english.bmf.gv.at/ |

| Legal Framework |
|---|
| The foundational principles for public financial management are anchored in the constitution such as the form and structure of the annual budget and the MTEF. The Organic Budget Law (introduced 2009) set out the main characteristics of the budget and budget procedures. In April 2018, the Budget Law was amended to foresee that the MTEF is presented together with the annual budget, in order to avoid budget debates twice a year and frequent changes of the MTEF. |

| Budget coverage |
|---|
| The executive's budget proposal applies to central government. The national budgetary co-ordination between the Federal Government, states and municipalities is regulated in the Austrian Stability Pact (ÖStP). The Austrian system is characterised by significant vertical fiscal imbalances, and Subnational Governments depend largely on federal transfers, even after the 2017 Fiscal Equalisation Law (Finanzausgleichsgesetz, FAG). As a first step towards aligning spending and financing responsibilities at different administrative levels, the *Länder* are granted autonomy concerning the rate of an already existing payroll tax, a contribution to housing subsidies, currently set at 1% of the payroll, from 2018 onwards. |

| Budget cycle | |
|---|---|
| Budget circular | March |
| Pre-budget fiscal policy statement[2] | N/A |
| Negotiations with line ministries | Summer |
| Executive budget proposal | October[3] |
| Parliamentary vote on budget | November |
| *Start of financial year* | *1 Jan.* |
| In-year budget execution reports | monthly |
| Mid-year implementation report | April and Sept.[4] |
| *End of financial year* | *31 Dec.* |
| Year-end financial statement | June |
| Audited financial report | 30 June |
| Parliamentary accounting | July - September |

[2]The EU-related Stability Programme Update (SPU) currently serves as the main pre-budget fiscal report (April)

[3] Latest 10 weeks before start of the fiscal year

[4] Mid-year implementation report are produced twice a year: April 30 (January-April) and September 30 (January-September)

| | | |
|---|---|---|
| | | **Austria's application of OECD budget principles "at a glance"** |
| 1. | Fiscal policy objectives | Austria's top-down budgeting is anchored at national level by the Austrian Stability Pact 2012, a constitutional treaty between various levels of government which is ratified by all levels of government, which allows for a structural deficit of up to 0.45% for the general government from 2017 onwards. |
| 2a. | Strategic alignment | No formal, structured link to Coalition Agreement or to SDGs. The MTEF is accompanied by a strategy report giving information about priorities. |
| 2b. | MTEF | 4-year rolling ceilings; legally-grounded, consistent with fiscal rules; ceilings are adjusted annually. Parliamentary approval is necessary; the multi-year expenditure ceilings however have not yet become established as fixed and normative upper limits and are adjusted regularly. |
| 3. | Capital and infrastructure | Capital and current expenditure are submitted and considered in an integrated way. The budget requests funding for the entire cost of multi-year project up-front. Project approval of capital expenditure projects above certain thresholds require approval by the Ministry of Finance. |
| 4. | Transparency and accessibility | 7 out of 8 Core Budget Reports are produced and publicly available. 6 of 12 ancillary reports, of which 4 are publicly available. The budget documentation supplied by the Federal Ministry of Finance is comprehensive, in particular on performance information. |
| 5a. | Parliamentary engagement | Comprehensive reporting of the administration to Parliament. The Parliamentary Budget Office (est. 2012) provides strong support to the Budget Committee with technical budget expertise for parliamentary scrutiny. |
| 5b. | Inclusive public / civic debate | Short hearings of experts on the overall federal budget in the Budget Committee. No citizens' guides are produced in addition to the budget documents. Limited opportunities for citizens and civil-society groups to engage with the budgetary process. |
| **6.** | **Financial reporting and accounting** | **The budget is prepared on cash and accrual basis (budgeting and accounting) to meet the constitutional requirement of obtaining a "true and fair view". The parallel presentation of both cash and accruals information is advanced practice, although information is not yet not used to its full potential.** |
| 7. | Budget execution | Single treasury fund is mandatory. The budget structure allows for flexibility for line ministries around in-year reallocations. The Ministry of Finance has still a strong oversight role in budget execution, in particular for projects with substantial financial impacts. |
| **8a.** | **Performance budgeting** | **Austria's distinctive system of gender budgeting is well integrated within the performance budgeting framework and rates highly in international comparison.** |
| **8b.** | **Evaluation and VFM** | **Austria's outcome-oriented impact assessments apply both *ex post* and *ex ante*, and in a broadly uniform manner across regulatory policy and budgetary policy measures. Spending reviews are being gradually introduced by the Federal Ministry of Finance as an additional tool of budgetary analysis and flexibility. As a first step spending reviews are used for identifying efficiency and effectiveness potentials.** |
| 9. | Fiscal risk and long-term sustainability | Austria also introduced long-term fiscal projections of up to 30 years to provide a long-term perspective for budget planning. Each line ministry has its own risk management for the budget and reports to the MoF which collects all the reporting in the central budget risk management. Furthermore there is a more general risk report (Governance Risk Compliance Report) which covers a wide range of risks. |
| 10. | Quality assurance and audit | The independence of the Court of Auditors (*Rechnungshof*) has its legal basis in the constitution. Its responsibilities cover compliance control on public spending, financial audits, and performance audit. |

*Note*: Rows in **bold** represent notable international practice.

## Budgetary Governance in Practice: Belgium

### *Economic context*

Belgium has made progress in implementing the structural reforms announced since the beginning of 2015, notably in the area of pensions, competitiveness and taxation. Against this background, economic growth increased in 2017 and is projected to stabilise at 1.7% in 2018 and 2019. Although private consumption was an important driver of growth in recent years, it is Government[5] and private investment that are now projected to support growth. Employment growth is projected to remain solid and lead to further declines in the unemployment rate, to 6.6% in 2019.

### *Fiscal policy plans*

Belgium's strong record of large primary fiscal surpluses was undone by the crisis, and progress in reducing high public debt has been slower since then. Belgium's general government deficit is however progressively narrowing, from 2.5% of GDP in 2016 to 1.0% in 2017. Debt fell at 103.1% of GDP in 2017. To ensure sustainability, the Government will continue efforts to balance the budget across all levels of government, with gradual reduction in spending while safeguarding fiscal revenues.

**A: Fiscal Balance and Public Debt**

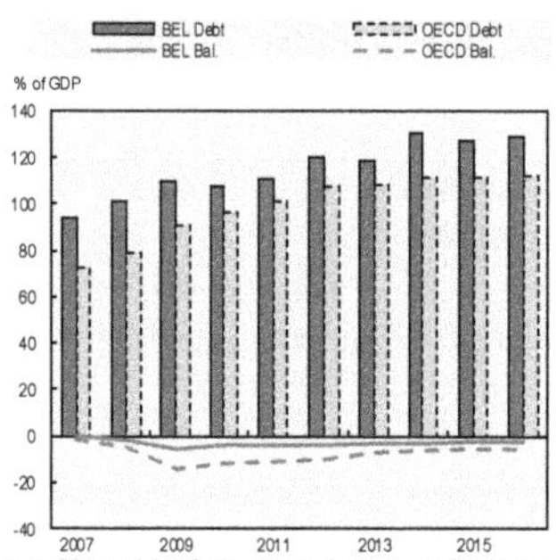


*Note* : The graph is referring to general government fiscal balance and general government gross debt as defined in the OECD National Accounts Statistics.

*Source* : OECD National Accounts Statistics (database); Eurostat Government finance statistics (database).

**B: Fiscal Policy Plans**

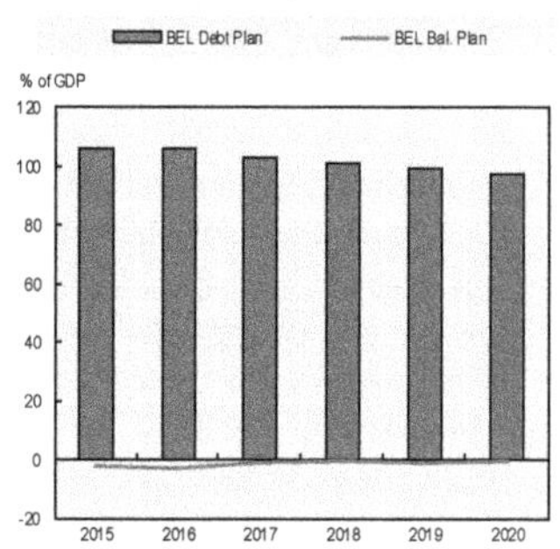


*Note* : The graph is referring to Fiscal Policy Plans that are implemented and/or officially announced as of November 2017 and as indicated by the country. Actual results in graph A may differ as the Fiscal Policy Plans are prepared by the country beforehand and as the Debt and Balance Plan reported by the country are based on the country's own definition; Data for Belgium are referring to federal government + social security.

*Source* : 2018 OECD Fiscal Plans and Budgeting Framework Survey

**C: Public Investment**

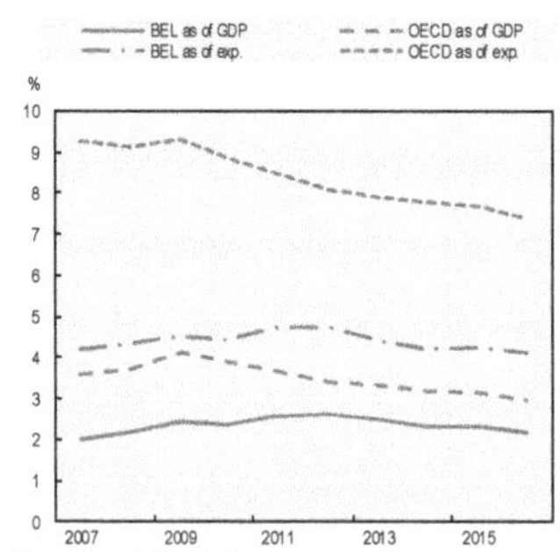


*Note:* The graph is referring to government investment as a percentage of GDP and as a share of total government expenditures.

*Source* : OECD National Accounts Statistics (database).

**D: Expenditure by function (2016)**

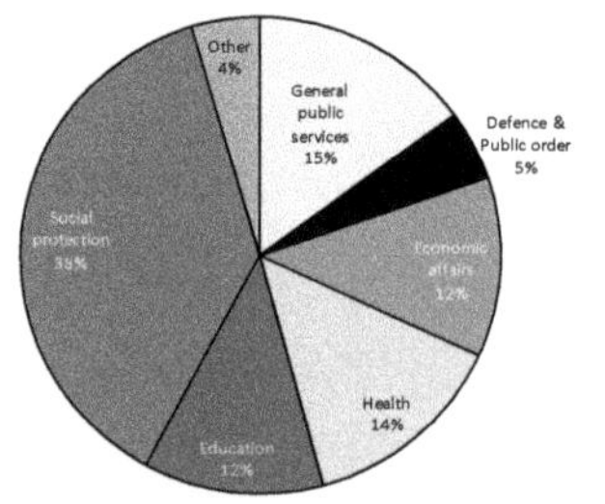


*Source:* OECD National Accounts Statistics (database); Eurostat Government finance statistics (database).

[5] A national strategic investment pact is expected to support potential growth.

### *Developments in budgetary governance*

Belgium's federal structure of government allots budgetary governance between the central/federal government, autonomous regions and communities. This has often led to complex budgetary arrangements across governmental systems making economic and budgetary consensus difficult to achieve. To address this challenge, the governments adopted a co-operation agreement in 2013 to outline individual budget targets to be supervised and monitored by the High Council of Finance.

Gender budgeting is practiced in accord with the 12 January 2007 law requiring "the integration of the gender perspective into the whole of its policies, measures, budgetary preparations and actions". Line ministries are required to account for the gender dimension on resource allocation preparation in conjunction with the interdepartmental co-ordination group (chaired by the Institute for the equality of women and men) which formulates a consistent strategy across the federal government.

| Central Budget Authority |
|---|
| Federal Public Service (FPS) Policy and Support, DG Budget and Policy Evaluation.[6] |
| Weblink: https://bosa.belgium.be/en.belgium.be/en |

| Legal Framework |
|---|
| The Belgian Constitution (article 170-181) provides foundational principals for public financial management. The executive is required to submit annual expenditure and revenue plans for scrutiny and approval by the legislature. |
| Processes for the division of roles and responsibilities, authorisation of spending, reporting, the use of contingency reserve funds, and requirements for auditing are also stipulated in laws and regulations. |

| Budget coverage |
|---|
| The federal budget applies to the federal level of government. Budgets for the autonomous regions & communities of Belgium are managed by their respective governments. |

| Budget cycle | |
|---|---|
| Budget circular | December |
| Pre-budget fiscal policy statement | October |
| Negotiations with line ministries | May |
| Executive budget proposal | October |
| Parliamentary vote on budget | December[7] |
| *Start of financial year* | *1 Jan.* |
| In-year budget execution reports | Budget balance reports |
| Mid-year implementation report | March/April (*at middle of the month*) |
| *End of financial year* | *31 Dec.* |
| Year-end financial statement | January |
| Audited financial report | October |
| Parliamentary accounting | October |

[6] Formerly *Federal Public Service Budget and Management Control*, the FPS Policy & Support was set up on 1 March 2017 following the 'redesign' of the federal government in the agreement of 1 October 2014

[7] Both Tax and Expenditure Policy measures must be voted upon by 31 December.

| Belgium's application of OECD budget principles "at a glance" | | |
|---|---|---|
| 1. | Fiscal policy objectives | Implementation of EU Fiscal rules. The 2013 Co-operation Agreement has allowed defining individual budget targets for central/federal government, autonomous regions and communities. |
| 2a. | Strategic alignment | No formal alignment tools or procedures in place to the Coalition Agreement. |
| 2b. | MTEF | No formal MTEF in place. The coalition agreement sets out medium-term strategic plans of the government; each new government must submit medium-term fiscal policy objectives. |
| 3. | Capital and infrastructure | Financially integrated with general budget; carryover and overspending proposals subject to legislative approval; High Council of Finance has to examine investment behaviour of local authorities; Central government proposing a *Strategic Investment Pact* to catalyse PPP investment. |
| 4. | Transparency and accessibility | All core budget reports are publicly available but budget impact analyses are not published. Budget data is downloadable. |
| 5a. | Parliamentary engagement | Strong engagement by Parliament along all parts of budgetary approval process; notably the Finance and Budget Committee. Parliament has unrestricted ability to amend budget, though restrictions are placed on placing conditions to the budget (e.g. earmarks). |
| 5b. | Inclusive public / civic debate | Limited public consultation and engagement with stakeholders in the budget cycle. Line ministries are consulted in budget formulation and policy development; no participatory budgeting and no engagement from minority & marginalised groups from decision-making process. |
| 6. | Budget accounting and financial reporting | Modified cash and commitment basis for budgeting and reporting. Accrual financial statements are also prepared at year-end. Budget and year-end financial statements cover all federal government entities. |
| 7. | Budget execution | Single treasury fund for all revenues and expenditures in federal government (with some exceptions) with budget execution primarily a responsibility of line ministries. Carry-over not permitted to line ministries (with some exceptions); Supplementary budgets require parliamentary approval (three supplemental budgets enacted in the past 5 FYs). |
| **8a.** | **Performance budgeting** | **Gender budgeting is practiced in accord with the 12 January 2007 law requiring "the integration of the gender perspective into the whole of its policies, measures, budgetary preparations and actions".** |
| 8b. | Evaluation and VFM | Individual line ministries are tasked to develop their own performance budgeting framework CBA monitors performance of line ministries/agencies. |
| 9. | Fiscal risk and long-term sustainability | Long-term sustainability report prepared every 3 years (European Commission); No framework for fiscal risk identification; however the explanatory document of the budget proposal must contain a sensitivity analysis; There is contingency reserve for foreseen expenditure (not yet decided/publicly announced) |
| 10. | Quality assurance and audit | The Court of Audit (SAI) provides compliance control on public spending, audits of government financial reports, and quality control and audits over government performance. High Council of Finance monitors targets set by Federal, Regional, and Community Governments. |

*Note*: Rows in **bold** represent notable international practice.

# Budgetary Governance in Practice: Canada

## *Economic context*

Strong economic growth in Canada has been led by household consumption, which should slow as rapid job growth and wealth effects from house price appreciation abate. Earlier robust export increases have weakened substantially, in part because of the stronger Canadian dollar. Consumer price inflation is expected to reach 2% in 2019, as remaining spare capacity is exhausted and exchange rate effects dissipate.

## *Fiscal policy plans*

Canada's budgetary policy is focused on smart, targeted investments that will help create the conditions required to foster economic growth and grow the middle class. The government's expressed view is that fiscal policy has an important role to play in delivering stronger economic growth today and in expanding the economy's growth potential over the long term, while maintaining Canada's low-debt advantage.

**A: Fiscal Balance and Public Debt**

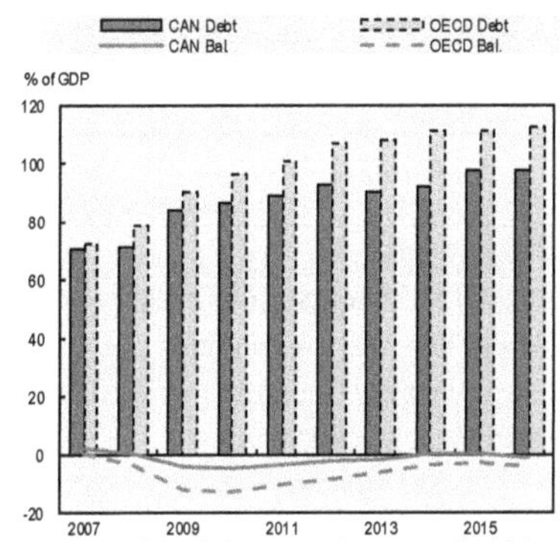


*Note*: The graph is referring to general government fiscal balance and general government gross debt as defined in the OECD National Accounts Statistics.

*Source:* OECD National Accounts Statistics (database); Eurostat Government finance statistics (database).

**B: Fiscal Policy Plans**

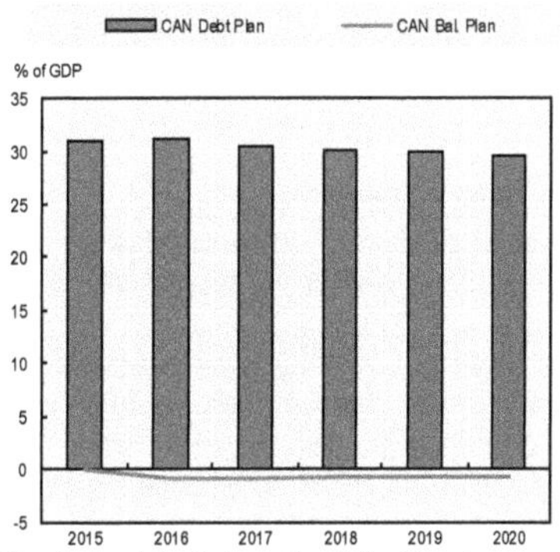


*Note*: The graph is referring to Fiscal Policy Plans that are implemented and/or officially announced as of November 2017 and as indicated by the country. Actual results in graph A may differ as the Fiscal Policy Plans are prepared by the country beforehand and as the Debt and Balance Plan reported by the country are based on the country's own definition; Data for Canada are referring to central/federal government; Canada's debt plan is a net debt measure; total liabilites less total financial and non-financial assets.

*Source:* 2018 OECD Fiscal Plans and Budgeting Framework Survey

**C: Public Investment**

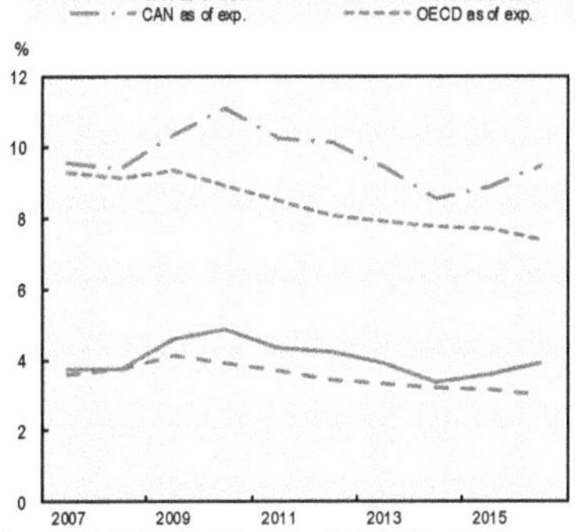


*Source:* OECD National Accounts Statistics (database).
*Note:* The graph is referring to government investment as a percentage of GDP and as a share of total government expenditures.

### *Developments in budgetary governance*

Although there are no legally binding fiscal rules in force but as of Budget 2017, the Government of Canada's fiscal objective is to balance the need to make targeted investments to support economic growth while preserving Canada's low-debt advantage for current and future generations.

Canada is particularly strong in the area of citizen engagement during the budget process, with the government seeking the views of stakeholders, businesses, NGOs and the public on what budget priorities should be during pre-budget consultations. Recent initiatives to improve budgetary governance include a commitment to improve fiscal transparency and the introduction of a new long-term capital infrastructure plan.

Canada also introduced gender budgeting in 2016, and the draft budget proposal now includes gender-based analysis of budgetary measures. A Gender Results Framework was also introduced in 2018, to guide policies included in Budget 2018 and future budgets[8].

| Central Budget Authority |
|---|
| Department of Finance and Treasury Board Secretariat (TBS).<br><br>Weblinks: www.fin.gc.ca and www.canada.ca/en/treasury-board-secretariat.html |

| Legal Framework |
|---|
| Constitutional conventions and Constitution Acts provide the principles for the relationship between the executive and the legislative branches at federal level. The Constitution Act (Chapters VI and VIII) stipulates the principal provisions for Parliament's budgetary powers, including for the adoption of appropriation and tax bills, and for approving public debt. The Financial Administration Act defines the responsibilities of the Treasury Board and the Ministry of Finance. In general, new budgeting procedures are introduced by Cabinet decision, rather than by new statutes or major modifications to existing statutes. This reflects the strong unwritten powers enjoyed by Cabinets and Cabinet committees in Westminster countries. |

| Budget coverage |
|---|
| The executive's budget applies to central government. The coverage of the budget is not defined in law. By convention, the executive departments can propose changes in the institutional units comprising "federal government". |

| Budget cycle | |
|---|---|
| Budget circular | Sept/Oct |
| Pre-budget fiscal policy statement | n/a |
| Negotiations with line ministries | n/a |
| Executive budget proposal | Feb/Mar |
| Parliamentary vote on budget | No set date |
| *Start of financial year* | *1 Apr.* |
| In-year budget execution reports | Monthly |
| Mid-year implementation report | Oct/Nov |
| *End of financial year* | *31 Mar* |
| Year-end financial statement | By 31Dec |
| Audited financial report | By 31Dec |
| Parliamentary accounting | Within a year |

[8] For more information on gender budgeting in Canada, see OECD (2018), *Gender Equality in Canada: Mainstreaming, Governance and Budgeting*, OECD Publishing, Paris, https://doi.org/10.1787/9789264301108-en.

**Canada's application of OECD budget principles "at a glance"**

| | | |
|---|---|---|
| **1.** | **Fiscal policy objectives** | **There are no legally binding fiscal rules in force but as of Budget 2017, the fiscal objective is to balance the need to make targeted investments to support economic growth while preserving Canada's low-debt advantage for current and future generations.** |
| 2a. | Strategic alignment | The medium-term priorities of the government are set out in the Speech from the Throne at the start of each parliamentary session. |
| **2b.** | **MTEF** | **The MTEF is operated through adoption of a 5-year horizon for budgetary projections (revenues, expenses, budgetary balance). The planning horizon can be longer for expenses such as defence or infrastructure funding. Ceilings are adjusted annually.** |
| 3. | Capital and infrastructure | The government has a long-term capital infrastructure plan – Investing in Canada (2016). Legislation has been passed for an Infrastructure Bank to work with the private sector to increase infrastructure investment. |
| **4.** | **Transparency and accessibility** | **In 2015 the government committed to raise the bar for openness and transparency. Canada's Open Government Commitments (2016-2018) set out four priority areas including fiscal transparency. Most budget data is provided in open data format.** |
| 5a. | Parliamentary engagement | The parliamentary budget process can be divided into the pre-budget consultation process and the approval process. The Finance Committee examines the *ex ante* budget. Standing committees examine estimates that fall within their mandate. However, no committee co-ordinates overall scrutiny of the estimates. Amendment powers are very limited. |
| **5b.** | **Inclusive public / civic debate** | **The government seeks the views of the public on budget priorities during pre-budget consultations. It introduced gender budgeting in 2016 and publishes a gender impact assessment of the budget. It also publishes a citizen's guide to the year-end budget execution report.** |
| 6. | Budget accounting and financial reporting | The budget is prepared on an accrual basis. The government has presented its financial statements on a full accrual accounting basis since 2003. Monthly updates on spending and revenue are published in the Fiscal Monitor. Departments publish quarterly financial statements. |
| 7. | Budget execution | Single treasury fund is mandatory for all revenues and expenditures of central government. Appropriations can be reallocated between votes with the approval of the Treasury Board. Supplementary estimates ask the parliament to approve funding for new initiatives. |
| 8a. | Performance budgeting | Departmental Results Frameworks for each department and agency provide the structure for performance reporting. Departmental Plans and Departmental Results Reports form the foundation of Canada's departmental monitoring structure. |
| **8b.** | **Evaluation and VFM** | **All grant and contribution programmes must be evaluated every five years. The Office of the Auditor General also conducts performance audits of departments and agencies. Spending reviews focus on eliminating poorly targeted and inefficient programmes, wasteful spending, and ineffective and obsolete government initiatives.** |
| 9. | Fiscal risk and long-term sustainability | Potential fiscal risks are included in the Economic and Fiscal Update. The government and the Parliamentary Budget Office both publish a long-term fiscal sustainability report. |
| **10.** | **Quality assurance and audit** | **The Office of the Auditor General audits conducts performance audits, audits of financial statements and financial audits. A Parliamentary Budget Office was established in 2008 to provide independent analysis to parliament on the budget, the estimates and other documents. Its mandate was expanded in 2017 to include election costings.** |

*Note*: Rows in **bold** represent notable international practice.

## Budgetary Governance in Practice: Chile

### *Economic context*

GDP growth is projected to strengthen to around 3% in 2018-19, supported by improving external demand, a more accommodative monetary policy and mining investment. As exports and investment pick up, the labour market will strengthen, reducing income disparities and stimulating private consumption. Increasing aggregate demand and a stabilising exchange rate will bring back inflation towards target.

### *Fiscal policy plans*

The fiscal policy strategy is to reduce the structural deficit by approximately one quarter of a percentage point of the GDP each year, measured with comparable structural parameters from one year to the next from 2016 until 2018.

The fiscal policy of Chile is based on the concept of Central Government Structural Balance (Cyclically Adjusted Balance - CAB). In basic terms, the Structural Balance concept involve estimating the fiscal revenue that would obtained as a net of the impact of the economic cycle, spending only the amount that would be compatible with this level of revenue and a previously defined target. The current fiscal goal is to reduce the Structural Deficit by approximately 0.2% of the GDP each year from 1.8% in 2018 to 1% in 2022. There is no escape clause involved.

**A: Fiscal Balance and Public Debt**

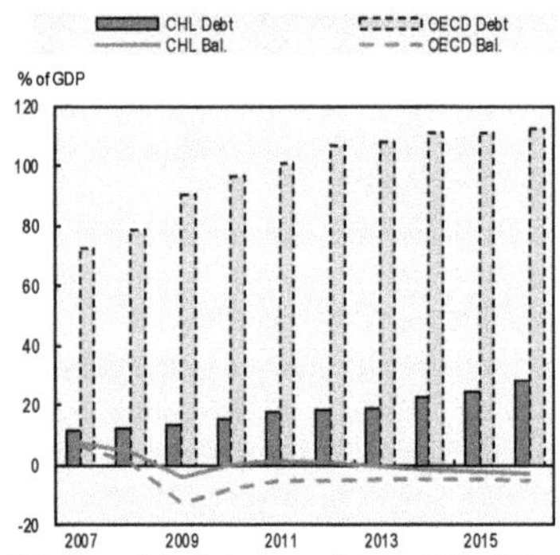


*Note* : The graph is referring to general government fiscal balance and general government gross debt as defined in the OECD National Accounts Statistics.
*Source:* OECD National Accounts Statistics (database); Eurostat Government finance statistics (database).

**D: Expenditure by function (2016)**

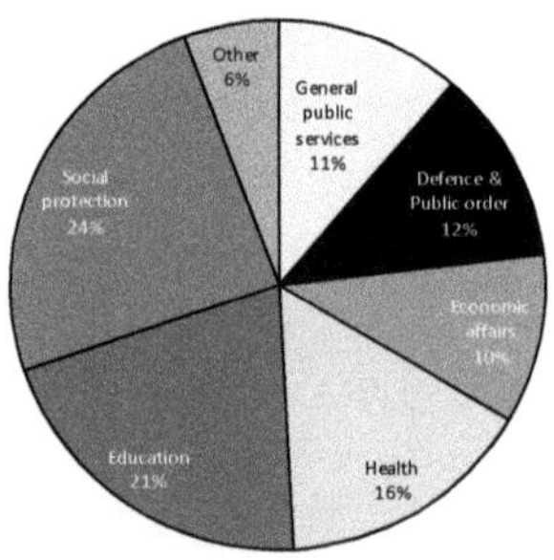


*Source:* OECD National Accounts Statistics (database); Eurostat Government finance statistics (database).

### *Developments in budgetary governance*

Chile's budget system has achieved outstanding results in terms of fiscal sustainability, economic growth, and reduction of extreme poverty. Chile's commitment to fiscal discipline is exemplified by a structural fiscal rule and the operation of a fiscal stabilisation fund whereby surpluses are saved during good economic times and drawn down during more challenging times. Fiscal risks are clearly identified and a detailed report on contingent liabilities is published each year.

Chile has a robust evaluation and control system, providing a great amount of performance information. This system is designed to support performance management in general. Evaluations have broad objectives with a heavy emphasis on improvements in policy, process and management. However, this evaluation system is not integrated into budget planning.

The Congress has built up some capacity regarding the budget in the last decade with a new Permanent Joint Committee on the Budget and the creation of a Budget Advisory Unit. However, the role of Congress in the budget discussions in Chile is still rather limited.

| Central Budget Authority |
|---|
| Ministry of Finance/Economy<br><br>Weblink: www.dipres.cl |

| Legal Framework |
|---|
| The Constitution lays out the requirements for legislative authorisation of spending and taxation, as well as the roles and responsibilities of the Legislature and the Executive in the budget process. Other aspects of budgeting are covered in legislation such as the Organic Decree-Law for the Financial Administration of the State (1975) and the Fiscal Responsibility Law (2006). The Government has prepared a draft bill to create an Autonomous Fiscal Council in Chile |

| Budget coverage |
|---|
| The national budget document applies to the central government, including ministries, public agencies, and social security funds. As a unitary country, local authorities have limited revenue-raising power and must run balanced budgets. |

| Budget cycle | |
|---|---|
| Budget circular | June |
| Pre-budget fiscal policy statement | October |
| Negotiations with line ministries | July/August |
| Executive budget proposal | 30 September |
| Parliamentary vote on budget | 30 November |
| *Start of financial year* | *1 Jan.* |
| In-year budget execution reports | Monthly |
| Mid-year implementation report | July |
| *End of financial year* | *31 Dec.* |
| Year-end financial statement | 30 January |
| Audited financial report | May |
| Parliamentary accounting | April/May |

| Chiles's application of OECD budget principles "at a glance" | | |
|---|---|---|
| **1.** | **Fiscal policy objectives** | **Chile's commitment to fiscal discipline is exemplified by a structural fiscal rule and the operation of a fiscal stabilisation fund whereby surpluses are saved during good economic times and drawn down during more challenging times.** |
| 2a. | Strategic alignment | The CBA has a leadership role in promoting alignment between annual budgets and medium-term plans/priorities |
| 2b. | MTEF | In 2000, Chile started maintaining baseline projections of government revenue and expenditures for the next three years. Projections are only presented to the Congress and shared with line ministries at a very aggregate level. |
| 3. | Capital and infrastructure | Well-institutionalised social evaluation process. The Ministry of Finance has played an important role as gatekeeper by ensuring that the projects undertaken are affordable. Chile has also been successful in mobilising private financing for infrastructure development. |
| 4. | Transparency and accessibility | Chile has all core budget reports; independent reviews of macroeconomic and fiscal assumptions are not produced; budget circular and pre-budget fiscal policy statement are produced but are not publicly available. Basic online accessibility tools; citizen's guides are prepared for both budget proposal and budget approved by Congress. |
| 5a. | Parliamentary engagement | The role of Congress in the budget discussions in Chile is rather limited. Congress may only decrease expenditure proposed by the executive; it may not increase or reallocate expenditures.<br>Budget oversight is carried out by a joint Special Budget Committee with an equal number of members from each Chamber. The Joint Committee has a specialist advisory unit of four. Discussions are underway within the Congress on establishing a congressional budget office to further enhance its analytical capacity. |
| 5b. | Inclusive public / civic debate | The role of civil society has increased but focus on budgetary issues is very limited. No participatory budgeting and no specific mechanisms in place to seek the views of people from minority communities and/or marginalised groups. |
| 6 | Budget accounting and financial reporting | There have been major improvements in Chile's accounting system during the last decade – moving from a cash basis system to a fully accrual basis system of financial reporting. In 2010, Chile formally started a process to prepare the adoption of International Public Sector Accounting Standards (IPSAS). |
| 7. | Budget execution | Single treasury fund mandatory for all central government revenues and expenditures; except for major public-service funds (e.g. social security, healthcare, and the Reserved Law of Copper). All expenditure must be pre-approved by the Comptroller-General in order to ensure their legality. Budget reallocations within year are frequent, and mainly driven and approved by the Budget Office. |
| 8a. | Performance budgeting | Performance information plays a role in spending decisions; however, resources are related either to proposed future performance or to performance results in an indirect manner. Performance reports are made available to the Congress and the public. |
| 8b. | Evaluation and VFM | Chile has a robust evaluation and control system. It is not well integrated into budget planning. Evaluations have broad objectives with emphasis on policy, process and management. |
| **9.** | **Fiscal risk and long-term sustainability** | **Fiscal risks are clearly identified and a detailed report on contingent liabilities is published each year.**<br>The budget incorporates a contingency reserve (as high as 7.8% of total expenditures) to fund legislation that the Congress may enact after the introduction of the budget. |
| 10. | Quality assurance and audit | Constitutionally-independent SAI provide financial audit; limited role in performance audit or governance systems audit.<br>Chile's Fiscal Advisory Council established in 2013 has limited institutional independence. In June 2018, the Government sent to Congress a new bill giving the council a legal status, more independence and resources. |

*Note*: Rows in **bold** represent notable international practice.

# Budgetary Governance in Practice: Czech Republic

## *Economic context*

Strong growth in the Czech Republic is expected to continue in 2018 and 2019, driven by robust private demand and a dynamic external sector. Increasing wages will support household consumption and low interest rates will boost capital investment. Historically low unemployment is likely to push inflation above the central bank's 2% target.

## *Fiscal policy plans*

The Act on Fiscal Responsibility (2017) defines the fiscal rule based on the medium term objective (MTO), which is a structural deficit of 1% of GDP. On-going effective debt and liquidity management (increasing the number of entities subjects which must operate accounts under the National Bank) is contributing positively to expenditure on debt service. The planned deficit for the state budget and state funds must not exceed the value set under the fiscal rule.

**A: Fiscal Balance and Public Debt**

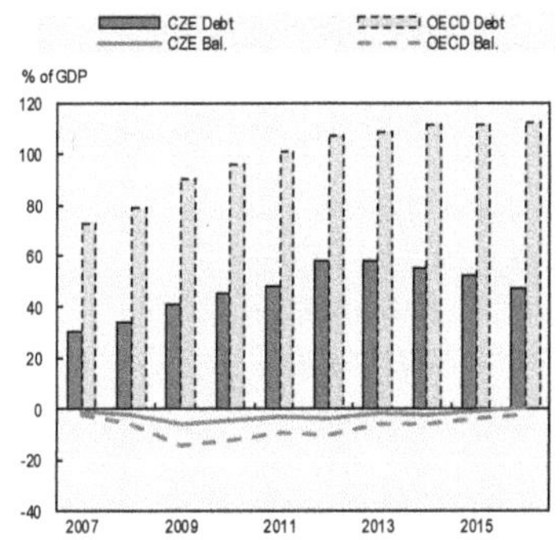


*Note*: The graph is referring to general government fiscal balance and general government gross debt as defined in the OECD National Accounts Statistics.

*Source:* OECD National Accounts Statistics (database); Eurostat Government finance statistics (database).

**B: Fiscal Policy Plans**

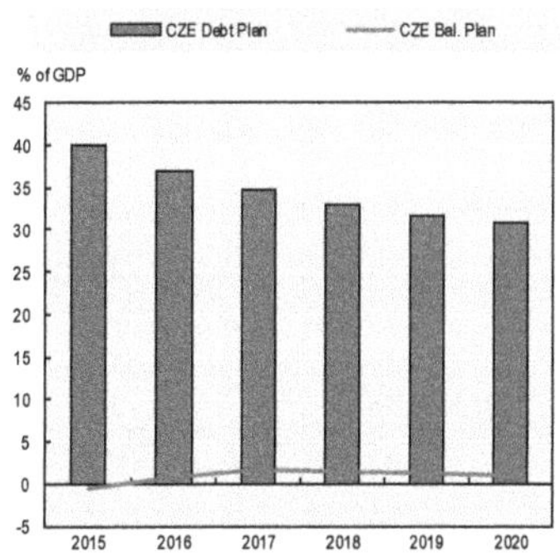


*Note*: The graph is referring to Fiscal Policy Plans that are implemented and/or officially announced as of November 2017 and as indicated by the country. Actual results in graph A may differ as the Fiscal Policy Plans are prepared by the country beforehand and as the Debt and Balance Plan reported by the country are based on the country's own definition; Data are referring to general government.

*Source:* 2018 OECD Fiscal Plans and Budgeting Framework Survey.

**C: Public Investment**

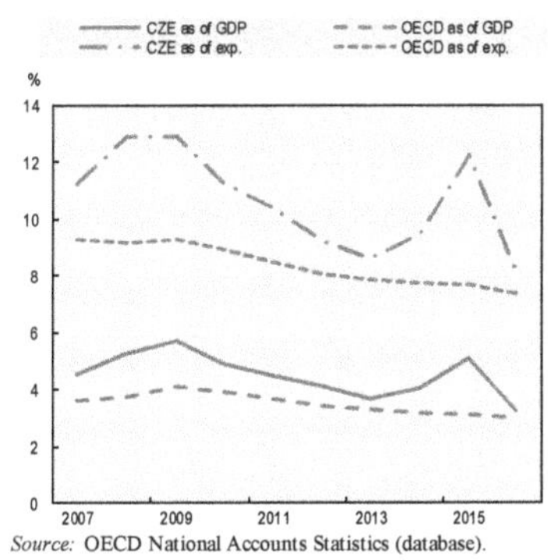


*Source:* OECD National Accounts Statistics (database).

*Note:* The graph is referring to government investment as a percentage of GDP and as a share of total government expenditures.

**D: Expenditure by function (2016)**

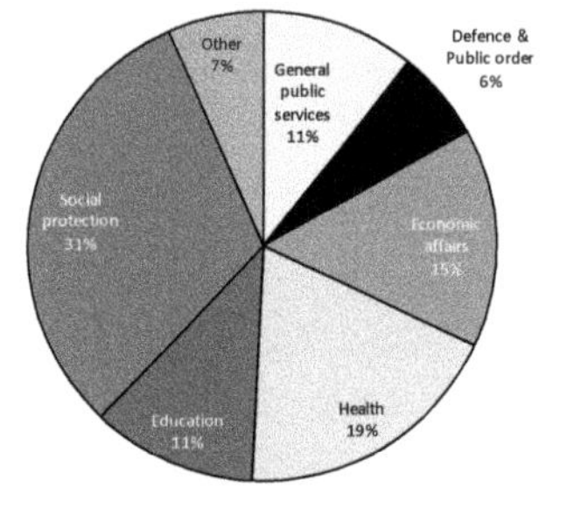


*Source:* OECD National Accounts Statistics (database); Eurostat Government finance statistics (database).

*Developments in budgetary governance*

The Czech economy performed well in the aftermath of the financial crisis of 2008 and the euro area crisis. Nevertheless, the government introduced essential changes in several areas of its institutional budget framework in order to strengthen its fiscal position. Major reforms implemented in the period 2010 to 2012 included;

**Top-down budgeting:** The principles of performance budgeting were introduced in central government units, initially on a voluntary basis.

**Budget approval process:** The budget approval process was adapted to the European Semester, the EU budget surveillance procedures, and fiscal and structural policy co-ordination within the EU.

**Budget execution practices:** Major upgrade of the Treasury system, including new IT support, streamlining the central government's cash management across all levels of government. The budgetary information system is divided into four subsystems: 1) state accounts, 2) payment system, 3) budget formulation, and 4) budget performance.

| Central Budget Authority |
|---|
| Ministry of Finance, State Budget Department.<br><br>Weblink: www.mfcr.cz/en/about-ministry/organisation-chart/section-06-public-budgets/dept-11-state-budget-department |

| Legal Framework |
|---|
| Act on Budget Rules 218/2000. In 2017 a Fiscal Responsibility Act, (23/2017), implemented crucial provisions of the EU Council Directive (EU) 2011/85 into Czech Law. |

| Budget cycle | |
|---|---|
| Pre-budget fiscal policy statement | April |
| Budget circular | May |
| Negotiations with line ministries | Feb-September |
| Executive budget proposal | September |
| Parliamentary vote on budget | December |
| *Start of financial year* | *1 Jan.* |
| In-year budget execution reports | monthly |
| Parliamentary vote on budget | March |
| Mid-year implementation report | October |
| *End of financial year* | *31 Dec.* |
| Year-end financial statement | April |
| Audited financial report | September |
| Parliamentary scrutiny of audited financial report | March/April (year+2) |

| Budget coverage |
|---|
| The national budget applies to almost all public spending; a unitary country; local authorities have limited revenue-raising power. Local governments are independent under the Constitution and can run budget surpluses or deficits. |

| Czech Republic's application of OECD budget principles "at a glance" | | |
|---|---|---|
| 1. | Fiscal policy objectives | EU fiscal rules are in force, and translated into local legislation in the form of the 2017 Budget Responsibility Act. |
| 2a. | Strategic alignment | No formal, structured link to national plan, Government programme or to SDGs |
| 2b. | MTEF | 3-year MTEF; based in law; consistent with fiscal rules and adjusted each year. |
| 3. | Capital and infrastructure | Selection of investment projects is driven by political support, but also by strategic plan priorities and economic needs analysis.<br>Capital expenditure requests are submitted for the total project costs and the processes for deciding on capital budgets are distinct.<br>In –depth appraisal and evaluation is applied to public private partnerships but not to traditional investment projects; |
| 4. | Transparency and accessibility | Annual budget is accessible online in downloadable format; Pre-Budget Statement, Mid-Year Review and citizens' budget are published, but with some delay. |
| **5a.** | **Parliamentary engagement** | **Clear, structured engagement by parliamentary committees, notably the budget committee of the Chamber of Deputies.**<br>**Parliament has unrestricted powers to amend the budget;**<br>Independent office for evaluation of fiscal and macro-economic projections is established and operational. |
| 5b. | Inclusive public / civic debate | Government meetings with important stakeholder groups, including minority groups, represented by various councils. |
| 6. | Budget accounting and financial reporting | Cash budgeting ; comprehensive coverage;<br>Cash and commitment reporting;<br>General government reporting (matching EU-requirements); no whole-of-government reporting. |
| 7. | Budget execution | Single treasury account covering central government operations.<br>Carry-over from year to year with few restrictions.<br>Limited budget flexibility for ministries with MOF authorisation required above a 10% threshold.<br>Supplementary budgets require advance parliamentary approval |
| 8a. | Performance budgeting | Performance-informed budgeting; budget document includes output targets alongside financial allocations in a dedicated part of the budget document;<br>Annual performance report, but not linked to over-arching performance framework or accountability mechanisms |
| 9. | Fiscal risk and long-term sustainability | The National Budgetary Council assesses the fiscal impact of government measures and prepares a report on the long term sustainability of public finances. The long term sustainability analysis is published annually in the Convergence Programme, every 3 years in the Ageing Report and the Fiscal Sustainability Report and every 5 years a report is produced on sustainability in relation to changes in the statutory retirement age. |
| **10.** | **Quality assurance and audit** | **Independent fiscal council assesses compliance with fiscal rules and comments on the government's fiscal policy stance (Committee for Budgetary Forecasts).**<br>**Constitutionally-independent SAI conducts financial compliance and performance audits that examine programme efficiency and effectiveness.** |

*Note*: Rows in **bold** represent notable international practice.

## Budgetary Governance in Practice: Denmark

### *Economic context*

After reaching 2.2% in 2017, GDP growth in Denmark is projected to return to a pace of 2% in 2018 and 2019, supported by robust domestic demand. Wages and inflation are expected to rise as labour resources become increasingly scarce.

### *Fiscal policy plans*

The main fiscal policy objective is a consolidation of the public finances. The strategy includes a targeted structural deficit of 0.1% of GDP by 2020 and a goal of structural balance by 2025.

**A: Fiscal Balance and Public Debt**

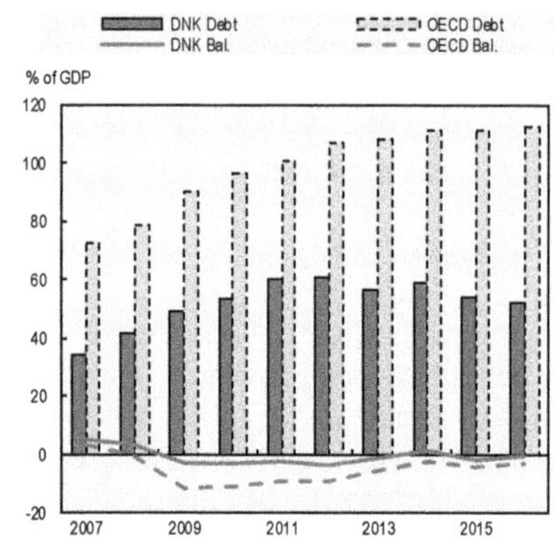


*Note*: The graph is referring to general government fiscal balance and general government gross debt as defined in the OECD National Accounts Statistics.

*Source:* OECD National Accounts Statistics (database); Eurostat Government finance statistics (database).

**B: Fiscal Policy Plans**

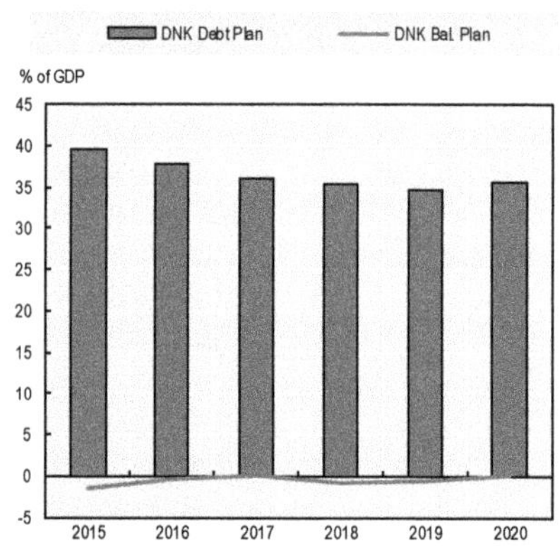


*Note*: The graph is referring to Fiscal Policy Plans that are implemented and/or officially announced as of November 2017 and as indicated by the country. Actual results in graph A may differ as the Fiscal Policy Plans are prepared by the country beforehand and as the Debt and Balance Plan reported by the country are based on the country's own definition; Data are referring to general government.

*Source:* 2018 OECD Fiscal Plans and Budgeting Framework Survey.

**C: Public Investment**

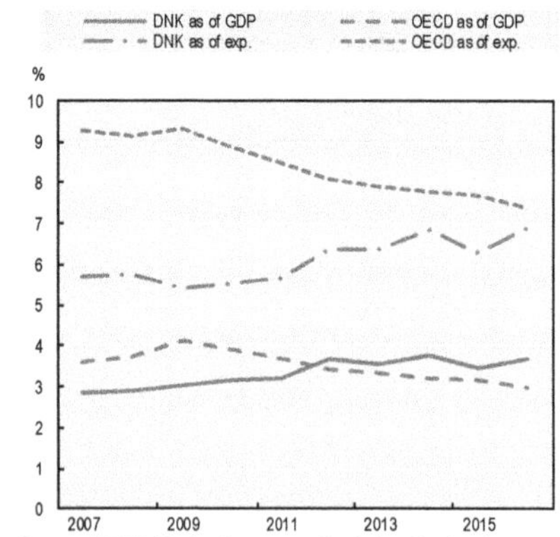


*Source:* OECD National Accounts Statistics (database).
*Note:* The graph is referring to government investment as a percentage of GDP and as a share of total government expenditures.

**D: Expenditure by function (2016)**

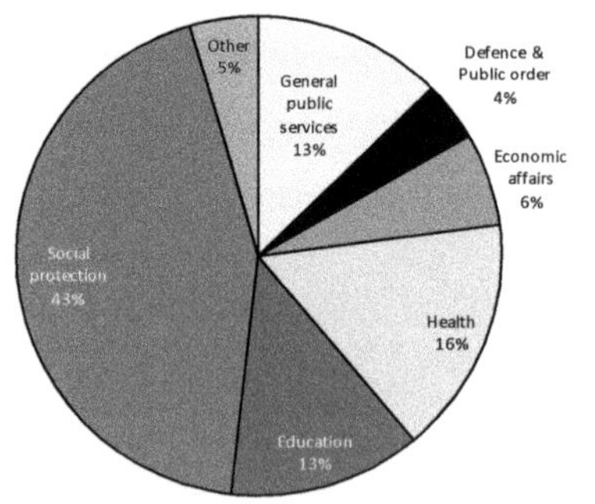


*Source:* OECD National Accounts Statistics (database); Eurostat Government finance statistics (database).

### *Developments in budgetary governance*

By the introduction of the Budget Law from 2012, the structural budget balance as the key measure in planning and monitoring fiscal policy was fixed by law. The Budget Law also introduced binding and multiannual expenditure ceilings for central government, municipalities and regions, respectively, starting from 2014.

Performance information is reported on a voluntary basis for both line ministries and agencies. The Danish experiences of using performance indicators primarily concern the management process and do not play a significant role in decision making on allocations. Performance information is presented with budgeting documents or other government documents as background information for the purposes of accountability and dialogue with legislators and citizens on public policy issues and government direction. The performance framework is not aligned with the SDG, which are covered by a separate action plan for implementation.

Parliamentary power is strong and the legislature has unrestricted powers to amend the budget. Specialised staff of the Budget Committee is available to parliamentarians for specialised advice. Public consultation and engagement are not formalised in the context of the budgetary process. However, public institutions engage independently in different types of informal arrangements to include stakeholders in the process.

| Central Budget Authority |
|---|
| Federal Ministry of Finance<br><br>Weblink: www.fm.dk |

| Legal Framework |
|---|
| The Constitution as well as the Budget Law (introduced 2012), includes foundational principles for budget procedures, including legislative authorisation, audit and reporting. Provisions related to the use of contingency reserve funds, environmental issues, off-budget expenditures and public employment provisions have no formal basis. |

| Budget coverage |
|---|
| The executive's budget proposal applies to central government. With the introduction of the 2012 Budget Law, the annual financial agreement between the government and the Danish regions and municipalities must comply with the expenditure ceilings for sub-national levels of government. Within these limits, these levels of government maintain their autonomy in determining levels of service. |

| Budget cycle | |
|---|---|
| Budget circular | March |
| Pre-budget fiscal policy statement[9] | n/a |
| Negotiations with line ministries | Mar- May |
| Executive budget proposal | August |
| Parliamentary vote on budget | December |
| *Start of financial year* | *1 Jan.* |
| In-year budget execution reports | quarterly |
| Mid-year implementation report | August |
| *End of financial year* | *31 Dec.* |
| Year-end financial statement | March |
| Audited financial report | February |
| Parliamentary accounting | March |

9 The EU-related Stability Programme Update (SPU) serves as the main pre-budget fiscal report.

**Denmark's application of OECD budget principles "at a glance"**

| | | |
|---|---|---|
| 1. | Fiscal policy objectives | With the Budget Law from 2012 a structural budget deficit limit has been adopted. The annual structural deficits must not exceed 0.5% of GDP. This way, the structural budget balance as the key measure in planning and monitoring fiscal policy has been fixed by law. |
| 2a. | Strategic alignment | The MoF promotes the alignment between the annual budgetary allocations, and the medium-term strategic plans and priorities of the government that are set out in the government programme and National Development Plan. |
| **2b.** | **MTEF** | **4-year rolling ceilings; legally-grounded. Ceilings are initially permanent, but can be altered in case of certain events as described in the Budget Law. If expenditure ceilings are exceeded, the expenditure ceiling for the following year reduced correspondingly.** |
| 3. | Capital and infrastructure | Capital and current expenditure requests are submitted jointly by line ministries, but the process for deciding upon capital and operating budget requests are distinct. The budget requests funding incrementally each year until the project is completed. There is a formalised understanding that the total project budget is approved for the project's long-term need. There are no overall long term strategic infrastructure plans, but sectoral plans exist. |
| 4. | Transparency and accessibility | 6 out of 8 core budget reports, of which 4 are publicly available; 8 of 9 ancillary reports, of which 7 are publicly available. Citizen guides are available for the MTEF and mid-year implementation report. Social impact assessments are published together with fiscal reforms or can be requested by the parliament; user friendly on-line budget data portal. |
| 5a. | Parliamentary engagement | Unrestricted power to approve and amend the budget. Specialised staff of the Budget Committee is available to parliamentarians for specialised advice. |
| 5b. | Inclusive public / civic debate | Ministry of Finance does not arrange public hearings or focus groups in the context of the budgetary process. Stakeholder engagement can take place informally. Budget Finance Committee Meetings are sometimes open to the public. |
| 6. | Budget accounting/ financial reporting | The budget is prepared on an accrual basis. |
| 7. | Budget execution | There is a mandatory single treasury fund with no exceptions. Up to a certain limit line ministers can re-allocate funds within their own budget envelope. Supplementary budgets are produced and publically available. |
| 8a. | Performance budgeting | The national performance budgeting framework is optional for both line ministries and agencies. |
| 8b. | Evaluation and VFM | There are no legally binding requirements for evaluation of programmes *ex ante*. The SAI and ministries use performance information for evaluation and scrutiny of performance. Spending reviews are an annual exercise. |
| **9.** | **Fiscal risk and long-term sustainability** | **The Danish Economic Council annually assesses long-term fiscal sustainability. Long term economic projections include a medium term planning horizon up to 2025 and projections on a technical basis towards 2100. Long-term fiscal projections generally revised two times a year.** |
| 10. | Quality assurance and audit | The Rigsrevisionen, the Danish National Audit Office, provides compliance control on public spending and financial audit, but has a limited role in performance audit. |

*Note*: Rows in **bold** represent notable international practice.

# Budgetary Governance in Practice: Estonia

## *Economic context*

After exceeding 4% in 2017, economic growth in Estonia is projected to decline to 3% by 2019. Public and private investment should recover from past low levels, notably supported by resumed disbursement of EU funds. High wage growth, due to the tightening labour market, will sustain private consumption. While this poses a risk to competitiveness, export growth will remain strong.

## *Fiscal policy plans*

Countercyclical or neutral fiscal policy is a main fiscal policy direction. The medium-term budgetary objective (MTO) of the Government is a general government structural deficit is not exceeding 0.5% of GDP.

**A: Fiscal Balance and Public Debt**

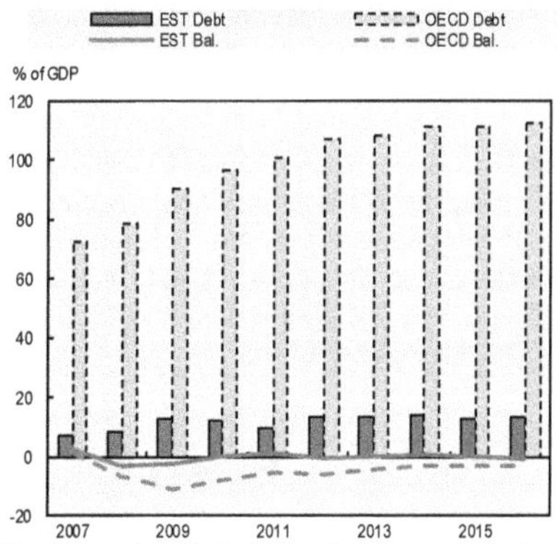


*Note*: The graph is referring to general government fiscal balance and general government gross debt as defined in the OECD National Accounts Statistics.

*Source:* OECD National Accounts Statistics (database); Eurostat Government finance statistics (database).

**B: Fiscal Policy Plans**

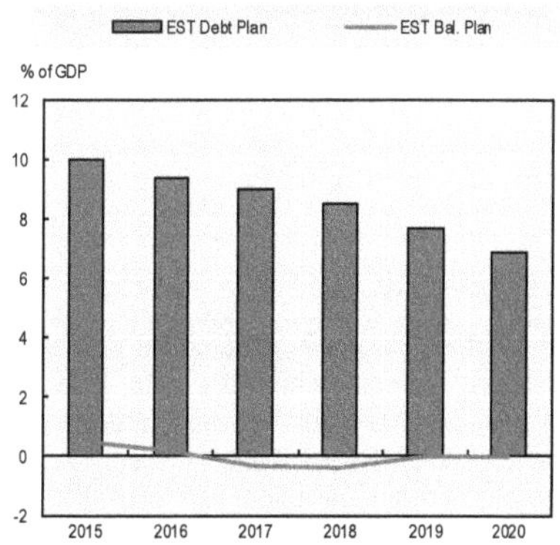


*Note*: The graph is referring to Fiscal Policy Plans that are implemented and/or officially announced as of November 2017 and as indicated by the country. Actual results in graph A may differ as the Fiscal Policy Plans are prepared by the country beforehand and as the Debt and Balance Plan reported by the country are based on the country's own definition; Estonia's fiscal balance is shown as structural balance; Data are referring to general government.

*Source*: 2018 OECD Fiscal Plans and Budgeting Framework Survey

**C: Public Investment**

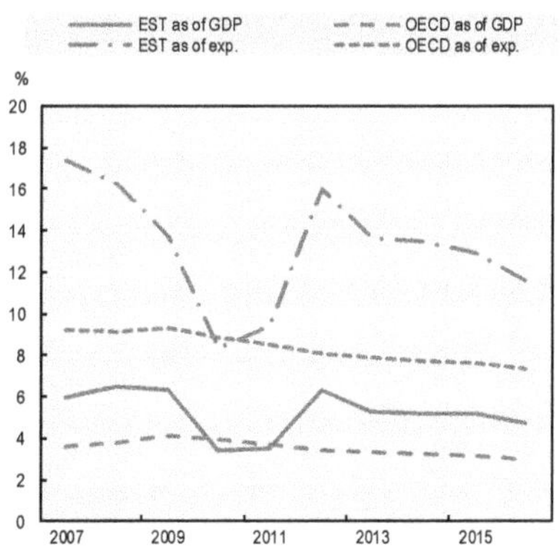


*Source:* OECD National Accounts Statistics (database).
*Note:* The graph is referring to government investment as a percentage of GDP and as a share of total government expenditures.

**D: Expenditure by function (2016)**

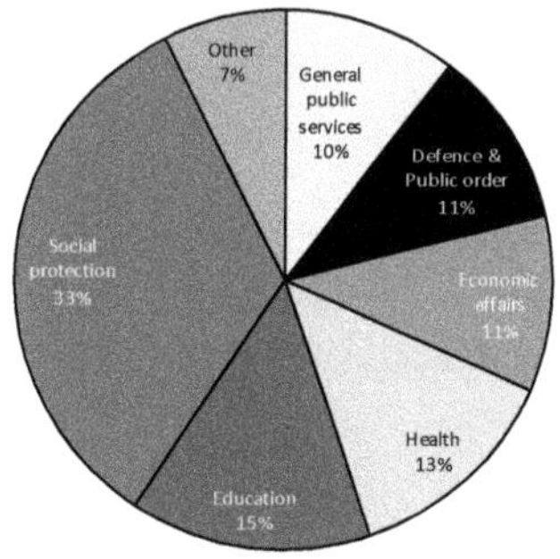


*Source:* OECD National Accounts Statistics (database); Eurostat Government finance statistics (database).

### *Developments in budgetary governance*

Since independence in 1991, Estonia has been at the forefront of institutional reform in the area of financial management. Budget formulation is divided into two distinct stages: strategic planning and preparation of the annual budget that is submitted to Parliament.

Estonian fiscal policy has centred for a long time on the budget balance rule. In 2014 a balanced-budget rule in structural terms was written into the State Budget Act. Other changes to strengthen Estonia's fiscal framework and enable compliance with the EU Fiscal Stability Treaty included the introduction of correction and compensation mechanisms and Estonia's Fiscal Council, which is attached to the Central Bank. According to the Treaty of the Fiscal Council, it must provide an assessment of government's economic and fiscal forecast, medium-term budgetary strategy and of achievement of the structural budget balance objective.

| Central Budget Authority |
|---|
| State Budget Department and Fiscal Policy Department in Ministry of Finance<br><br>Weblink: www.rahandusministeerium.ee/en/state-budget-and-economy |

| Legal Framework |
|---|
| Budget procedures are put into practice in accordance with the Constitution of the Republic of Estonia and the State Budget Act. The former lays out the requirements for the form and structure of the annual budget, the roles and responsibilities of the legislature and executive in the budget process, the medium term expenditure framework, requirements for legislative authorisation of tax reforms, rules for use of contingency funds, what happens when the budget is not approved, and public employment provisions. Other aspects of budgeting are covered in regulation such as requirements for legislative authorisation of spending and audit (internal and external). There is no formal basis for provisions relating to the inclusion of environmental issues and management and reporting relating to off-budget expenditures. |

| Budget coverage |
|---|
| The executive's budget applies to central government. The coverage of the budget is generally comprehensive. There are two extra-budgetary funds, i.e. the Health Insurance Fund and the Unemployment Insurance Fund. Both funds are mostly financed by earmarked taxes (the social tax and the unemployment insurance tax). The funds are each ruled by a Board that is exempt from ministerial responsibility. However, both funds are included in general government balance calculations in the explanatory note to the draft budget and the State Budget Strategy as well as in the final accounts. |

| Budget cycle | |
|---|---|
| Budget circular | N/A |
| Pre-budget fiscal policy statement | April |
| Negotiations with line ministries | March-April |
| Executive budget proposal | October |
| Parliamentary vote on budget | December |
| *Start of financial year* | *1 Jan* |
| In-year budget execution reports | Monthly |
| Mid-year implementation report | August |
| *End of financial year* | *31 Dec* |
| Year-end financial statement | March |
| Audited financial report | July |
| Parliamentary accounting | September |

| Estonia's application of OECD budget principles "at a glance" | | |
|---|---|---|
| 1. | Fiscal policy objectives | Estonian fiscal policy has centred for a long time on the budget balance rule, and in 2014 this was written into the State Budget Act. To take better account of the economic cycle and its impact on tax revenues, the requirement for the annual budget balance is set in structural terms. |
| **2a.** | **Strategic alignment** | **Estonia has in place a strategic planning process that culminates in the adoption of the State Budget Strategy. This outlines the priorities of the government and associated funding plans for the next four years. It is approved by government and then presented to the parliament.** |
| **2b.** | **MTEF** | **The State Budget Strategy presents projections and targets for the main aggregates of government finances for the next four years based on the MoF's macroeconomic scenario. It plays a guiding role in the annual budget process.** |
| 3. | Capital and infrastructure | The annual budget strategy sets out planned capital investments. Capital and current expenditure requests are submitted during the budget process and decisions on these requests are taken together. |
| 4. | Transparency and accessibility | Reporting is in line with international transparency standards. Although no citizen's budget is produced, Estonia has a high level of transparency in relation to financial reporting, as all important data are released on the website of the MoF after only a short delay. |
| 5a. | Parliamentary engagement | Parliament receives the draft budget law in October, ahead of the first reading debate. It is discussed at the Finance Committee in October-December. The committee considers the draft law within a few weeks before each of the three readings in the plenary. The legislature may make amendments but cannot change the total surplus/deficit proposed. |
| 5b. | Inclusive public / civic debate | Limited engagement of civil society stakeholders in the budget cycle. |
| **6.** | **Budget accounting and financial reporting** | **Accrual accounting was introduced in 2004 and accrual-based budgeting was introduced as part of changes to the State Budget Act in 2014. The budget has been prepared on an accruals basis since 2017.** |
| 7. | Budget execution | Single treasury fund is mandatory for all revenues and expenditures of central government. |
| 8a. | Performance budgeting | Performance budgeting was first introduced in 2004. There is a government unit responsible for developing and overseeing these procedures. The framework includes general guidelines and definitions and standard templates for reporting performance information. Performance budgeting reforms are currently being implemented and will be finalised in 2020. |
| 8b. | Evaluation and VFM | *Ex ante* evaluation must be undertaken for all new major primary laws and sectoral development plans. A mid-term and *ex post* evaluation plan is decided by the government. In 2016, Estonia started conducting regular spending reviews to improve budget efficiency and create fiscal space for new priorities. In 2017, a spending review process was institutionalised in the State Budget Act. |
| 9. | Fiscal risk and long-term sustainability | MoF produces projections covering 41-50 years that are revised annually and is in charge of identifying and assessing fiscal risks during the economic forecasting process. No assessment of fiscal risks is produced; however there is a counter-cyclical stabilisation fund and a long-term reserve fund. |
| 10. | Quality assurance and audit | The Estonia Fiscal Council, which is attached to the Central Bank, was established in 2014. According to the Treaty of the Fiscal Council, it must provide an assessment of government's economic and fiscal forecast, medium-term budgetary strategy and of achievement of the structural budget balance objective. The National Audit Office of Estonia is also established as part of the constitution and undertakes financial and performance audits. |

*Note*: Rows in **bold** represent notable international practice.

## Budgetary Governance in Practice: Finland

### *Economic context*

Boosted by exports, output growth in Finland will remain strong in 2018-19 but is likely to slow somewhat, as private consumption softens due to the impacts of wage moderation and rising inflation on household real incomes. Investment in construction is also set to decelerate, but export demand and the implementation of some major industrial projects will support business investment.

### *Fiscal policy plans*

The fiscal policy objective is to bring living on credit to an end in 2021. The Government also aims to cover the EUR 10 billion sustainability gap through actions instantly enhancing the general government finances, measures supporting growth and employment, and reforms strengthening general government finances. In addition to the debt target the Government has set targets for central government (deficit no more than 0.5% of GDP), local government (deficit no more than 0.5% of GDP) and the social security funds (earnings-related pension funds surplus 1% and other social security funds financial standing 0% of GDP) during the parliamentary term (until 2019).

A: Fiscal Balance and Public Debt

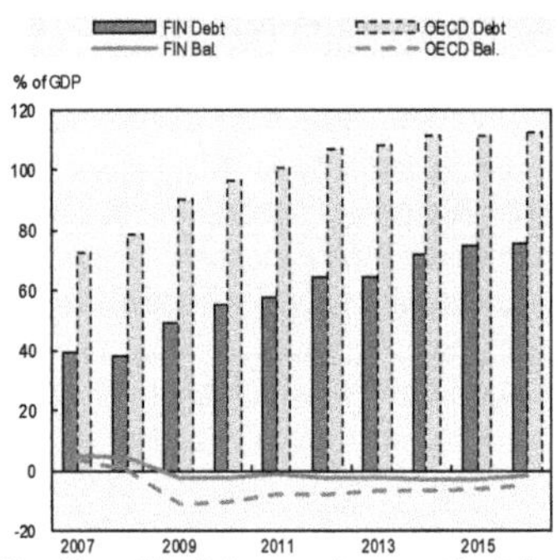


*Note:* The graph is referring to general government fiscal balance and general government gross debt as defined in the OECD National Accounts Statistics.

*Source:* OECD National Accounts Statistics (database); Eurostat Government finance statistics (database).

B: Fiscal Policy Plans

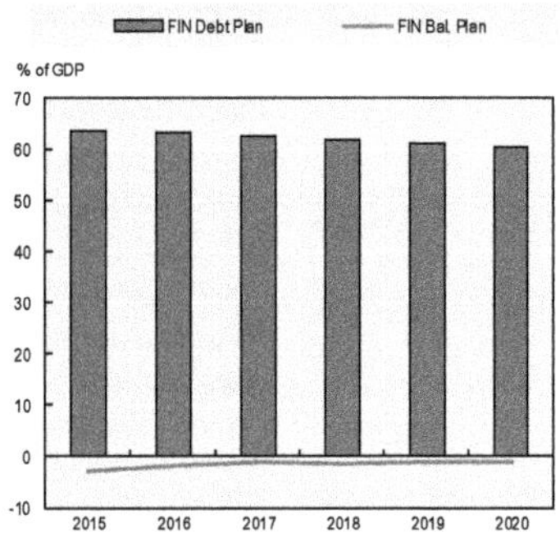


*Note*: The graph is referring to Fiscal Policy Plans that are implemented and/or officially announced as of November 2017 and as indicated by the country. Actual results in graph A may differ as the Fiscal Policy Plans are prepared by the country beforehand and as the Debt and Balance Plan reported by the country are based on the country's own definition; Data are referring to general government.

*Source:* 2018 OECD Fiscal Plans and Budgeting Framework Survey.

C: Public Investment

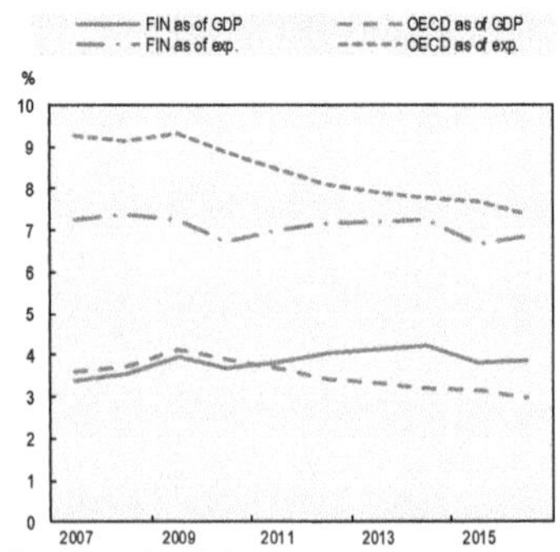


*Note:* The graph is referring to government investment as a percentage of GDP and as a share of total government expenditures.

*Source*: OECD National Accounts Statistics (database).

D: Expenditure by function (2016)

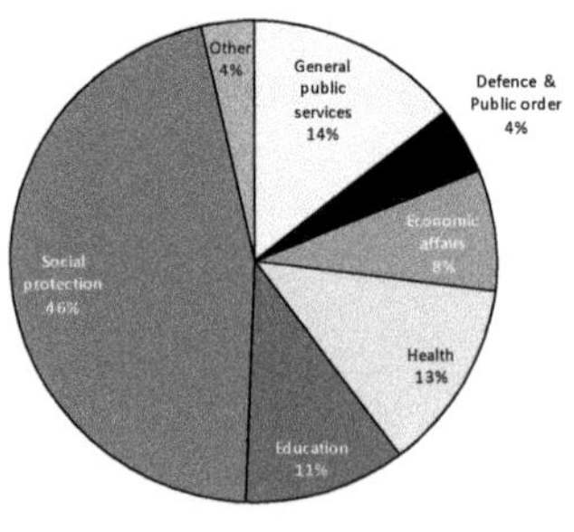


*Source:* OECD National Accounts Statistics (database); Eurostat Government finance statistics (database).

### *Developments in budgetary governance*

The Finnish budget framework is characterised by a spending limits system that has been in use in central government finances since 1991. The spending limit system was reformed in 2003 but remains well respected and spending limits are never exceeded.

Recent budgetary developments include the development of fiscal oversight. The National Audit Office (Fiscal Policy Function) gained responsibility for reviewing compliance against fiscal objectives in 2012 and the Economic Policy Council - in charge of fiscal policy assessment - was established in January 2014 in charge of fiscal policy assessment.

A participative approach to budgeting has not yet been integrated into the budget procedures.

| Central Budget Authority |
|---|
| Budget Department at Ministry of Finance<br><br>Weblink: http://vm.fi/en/departments |

| Legal Framework |
|---|
| Extensive budget-related provisions are contained in the written constitution, which has an entire chapter devoted to state finances. It defines the form and structure of the annual budget as well as the roles and responsibilities of different stakeholders and requirements for legislative authorisation. The *State Budget Act* also contains provisions in these areas and gives legal underpinning to the MTEF. It also states that "provisions concerning the stages of and procedures to be followed in the preparation of the budget proposal may be issued by government decree". Thus, the State *Budget Decree 1992* and *Parliament Rules of Procedure* specify these rules in more detail, setting the budget calendar and specifying the content of ministerial budget submissions. |

| Budget coverage |
|---|
| The executive's budget applies to central government. The budget documentation discloses all central government revenue, expenditures, and financing by ministries, agencies, extra budgetary funds, and social security funds. A few entities classified as extra budgetary funds are not included in the budget documentation but they are included in the general government reports.<br><br>The MTEF establishes spending limits for central government. These cover most budgetary central government expenditure but not for example tax expenditure and extra budgetary funds. |

| Budget cycle | |
|---|---|
| Budget circular | May |
| Pre-budget fiscal policy statement | April |
| Negotiations with line ministries | August |
| Executive budget proposal | September |
| Parliamentary vote on budget | December |
| *Start of financial year* | *1 Jan* |
| In-year budget execution reports | N/A |
| Mid-year implementation report | N/A |
| *End of financial year* | *31 Dec* |
| Year-end financial statement | April |
| Audited financial report | May |
| Parliamentary accounting | May |

| Finland's application of OECD budget principles "at a glance" | | |
|---|---|---|
| **1.** | **Fiscal policy objectives** | **In addition to EU fiscal rules, Finland has a system of national fiscal rules in place: an expenditure rule which sets a cap for central government spending for the electoral period which has been complemented by balanced budget and deficit targets.** |
| 2a. | Strategic alignment | The Government Programme sets out fiscal objectives and the spending limits for the four-year-period. |
| **2b.** | **MTEF** | **Finland introduced the medium-term perspective into the process of budgetary planning in the mid-1990s. It now has a well-established MTEF which has been in place since 2003 and sets global expenditure ceilings for central government at the start of each four year parliamentary term, updated annually. Spending limits are never exceeded.** |
| 3. | Capital and infrastructure | All major investment projects are subject to open and competitive tender and medium-term obligations are disclosed, but not all cost-benefit analyses are published before approval. |
| 4. | Transparency and accessibility | A citizen's guide is produced in relation to the budget proposal and the approved budget. The budget proposal, the approved budget, supplementary budgets and year-end budget execution reports are also available in open data format. |
| 5a. | Parliamentary engagement | The parliament discusses pre-budget fiscal policy and must approve the annual budget. Budget legislation is referred to the Finance Committee and its report is used as a basis for the vote on the budget, taken in a single plenary session. The parliament has unlimited powers of amendment. |
| 5b. | Inclusive public / civic debate | A participative approach to budgeting has not yet been integrated into the budget procedures. |
| 6. | Budget accounting and financial reporting | Finland employs accruals to differing degrees in its budgeting and financial reporting functions. The annual financial report is on full accrual basis whereas the budget operates on a mixture of cash and accrual basis. |
| 7. | Budget execution | The Government does not use a treasury fund but a consolidated account that is administered by the State Treasury. |
| 8a. | Performance budgeting | Performance agreements between sector ministries and their agencies form the core of the system. They are morally, not legally, binding; document of mutual understanding. Budget documentation contains targets for and reports on the outputs and outcomes. |
| 8b. | Evaluation and VFM | There is a general aim and recommendation to have agencies evaluated on approximately four to six year intervals. In addition to agency evaluations, there are policy evaluations, which are in certain areas a statutory requirement. |
| 9. | Fiscal risk and long-term sustainability | Reports on fiscal risks and long-term fiscal sustainability are publicly available, but are not presented in parliament. |
| 10. | Quality assurance and audit | The National Audit Office (Fiscal Policy Function) reviews compliance against fiscal objectives. The Economic Policy Council was established in January 2014 in charge of fiscal policy assessment. |

*Note*: Rows in **bold** represent notable international practice

# Budgetary Governance in Practice: France

## *Economic context*

Economic growth in France rebounded in 2017 and is expected to remain robust in 2018-19, thanks to stronger external demand, a recovery in tourism, robust business confidence and job creation. Cuts in business taxes and labour market reforms are expected to further support investment and employment.

## *Fiscal policy plans*

Since 2016, France has been running large deficits. However, in 2017, France's fiscal deficit fall below the EU's 3% limit for the first time in a decade. Building on the momentum, the new Government has set a medium-term objective for general government structural balance at -0.4% of potential GDP in 2022. Fiscal objectives are expected to be achieved through significant cuts in public spending, following a spending review exercise covering the whole of the general government, and a substantial tax relief package that is expected to generate substantial economic growth.

**A: Fiscal Balance and Public Debt**

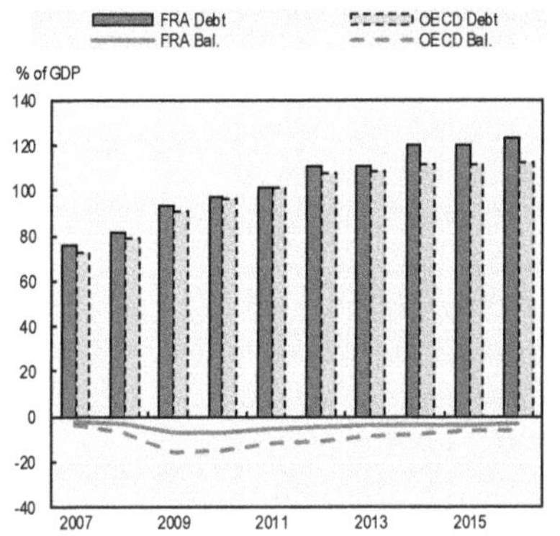


*Note*: The graph is referring to general government fiscal balance and general government gross debt as defined in the OECD National Accounts Statistics.

*Source:* OECD National Accounts Statistics (database); Eurostat Government finance statistics (database).

**B: Fiscal Policy Plans**

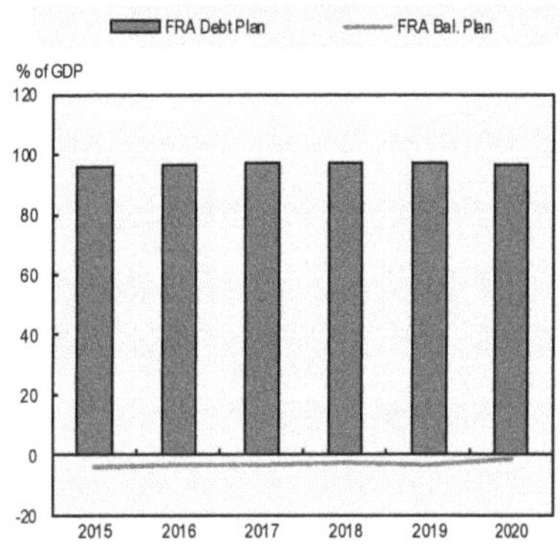


*Note:* The graph is referring to Fiscal Policy Plans that are implemented and/or officially announced as of November 2017 and as indicated by the country. Actual results in graph A may differ as the Fiscal Policy Plans are prepared by the country beforehand and as the Debt and Balance Plan reported by the country are based on the country's own definition; Data are referring to general government.

*Source:* 2018 OECD Fiscal Plans and Budgeting Framework Survey.

**C: Public Investment**

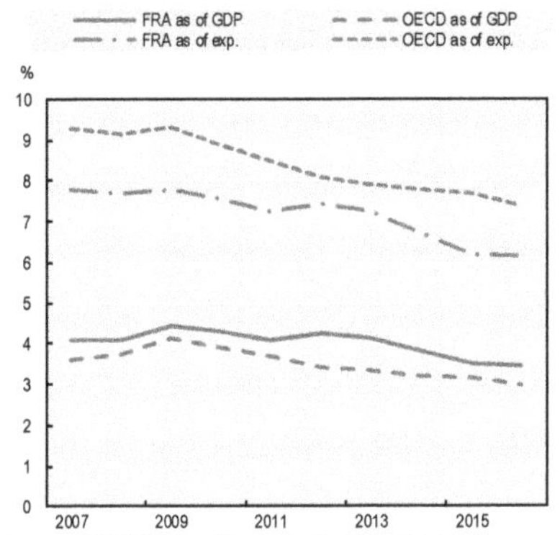


*Source:* OECD National Accounts Statistics (database).
*Note:* The graph is referring to government investment as a percentage of GDP and as a share of total government expenditures.

**D: Expenditure by function (2016)**

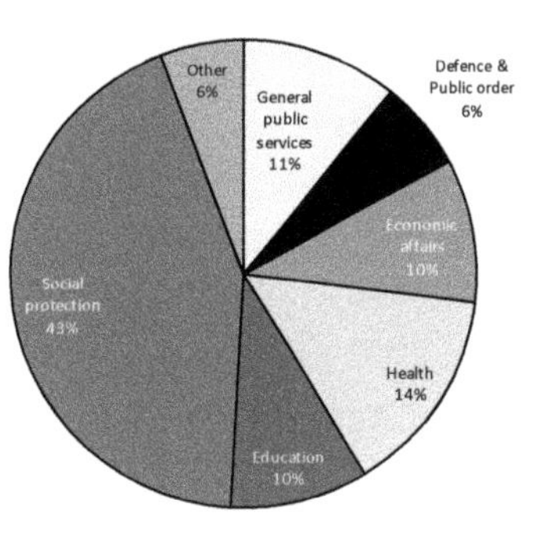


*Source:* OECD National Accounts Statistics (database); Eurostat Government finance statistics (database).

### *Developments in budgetary governance*

Two waves of reforms in 2006 and 2012 have profoundly transformed France's budgetary framework. In more recent years, changes have therefore been limited and consisted mostly in refining and improving existing budgetary governancearrangements. For example, State expenditure rules have been revised in 2018, to improve their coverage. Also, performance objectives and indicators are being streamlined in order to improve their legibility for Parliament.

Very recently, France started working on developing tools for highlighting resources allocated to core Government policies on gender equality and prevention climate change and outcomes achieved. In particular, France joined the Paris Collaborative on Green Budgeting which calls on governments to align their policy processes with environmental and climate targets.

| Central Budget Authority |
|---|
| Ministry of Finance, Directorate of the Budget<br><br>Weblink: www.performance-publique.budget.gouv.fr/ |

| Budget coverage |
|---|
| The State budget covers all line ministries and a number of independent administrative bodies. Social security and public agencies have separate budgets. |

| Legal Framework |
|---|
| Foundational principles for public financial management are stipulated in the Constitution and provided by the Organic Law № 2001-692 of 1 August 2001 relating to finance laws.<br><br>Processes for the division of roles, responsibilities, reporting, and medium-term expenditure framework are also stipulated in the Organic Law № 2012-1403 of 17 December 2012 on the programming and governance of public finances. |

| Budget cycle | |
|---|---|
| Budget proposals by line ministries | April |
| Pre-budget fiscal policy statement | June |
| Executive budget proposal | October |
| Parliamentary vote on budget | December |
| *Start of financial year* | *1 Jan.* |
| In-year budget execution reports | Monthly |
| Mid-year implementation report | June |
| *End of financial year* | *31 Dec.* |
| Publication of year-end reports | May[10] |
| Audited financial report | May[11] |
| Parliamentary accounting | June |

[10] The consolidated, central government year-end are issued before 1. June.

[11] The audit report on the consolidated, central government end-year reports is published before 1 June.

| France's application of OECD budget principles "at a glance" | | |
|---|---|---|
| 1. | Fiscal policy objectives | Laws on the Programming of Public Finances provide for a medium-term objective (OMT) for general government structural balance and detail the planned public financial trajectory to converge towards this objective. |
| 2a. | Strategic alignment | The leadership role in promoting alignment between medium-term plans and annual budgets belongs to the Directorate of the Budget, based on priorities defined at political level. |
| 2b. | MTEF | Targets for total spending of each level of general government are set for a three or five-year period in Laws on the Programming of Public Finances. Targets are "operationalised" into a set of expenditure rules. |
| 3. | Capital and infrastructure | Capital expenditure is integrated in the State budget and identified as a category of public expenditure. There is a codified process for ensuring absolute value for money from infrastructure projects (PPPs). |
| 4. | Transparency and accessibility | All core budget reports are publicly available. Budget data is available in downloadable form (e.g. spreadsheet). |
| 5a. | Parliamentary engagement | Engagement of Parliament is focused on the budget approval stage. Parliament has ability to amend budget if it doesn't change the total deficit or surplus proposed by the Executive. |
| 5b. | Inclusive public / civic debate | Limited public consultation and engagement with stakeholders in the budget cycle. |
| **6.** | **Budget accounting and financial reporting** | **Commitment, cash and accrual accounting and monthly budget reports throughout the accounting cycle.** |
| 7. | Budget execution | A Treasury Single Account is used for all central government and local government entities. Flexibility measures are codified with clear criteria (emergencies and/or ceilings); appropriations can be frozen by the Ministry of Finance; at least one supplementary budget per year. |
| **8.** | **Performance budgeting** | **Both summary and detailed information on performance objectives, indicators and results for each Government programme is published each year for accountability purpose.** |
| 9. | Fiscal risk and long-term sustainability | Several fiscal risks are managed by the Ministry of Finance and other stakeholders, but they are not systematically measured and disclosed. Fiscal sustainability is assessed only as part of European Union Aging Report exercise. |
| 10. | Quality assurance and audit | The Court of Audit ("*Cour des Comptes*") effects compliance control on public spending, audits of government financial reports, and quality control and audits over government performance. The High Council for Public Finances underpins the quality of macro-economic forecasts |

*Note*: Rows in **bold** represent notable international practice.

## Budgetary Governance in Practice: Germany

### *Economic context*

Growth in Germany is projected to ease somewhat but still remain solid and employment is set to expand further. Stronger activity in the euro area is boosting exports and business investment, but euro appreciation and higher wages may dent competitiveness. Low unemployment and wage gains underpin private consumption, but are also raising consumer price inflation. Low interest rates and strong housing demand, partly due to immigration, sustain residential investment. The current account surplus will fall somewhat, but will still remain high.

### *Fiscal policy plans*

The fiscal policy objective is to adopt a balanced budget containing no new debt to contribute to bringing Germany's debt-to-GDP ratio below 60% by 2020. Fiscal policy priorities are forward-looking investment, education and research and security.

**A: Fiscal Balance and Public Debt**

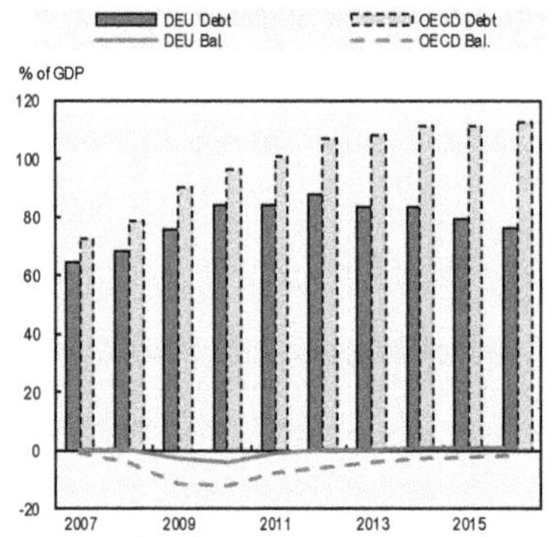


*Note*: The graph is referring to general government fiscal balance and general government gross debt as defined in the OECD National Accounts Statistics.

*Source:* OECD National Accounts Statistics (database); Eurostat Government finance statistics (database).

**B: Fiscal Policy Plans**

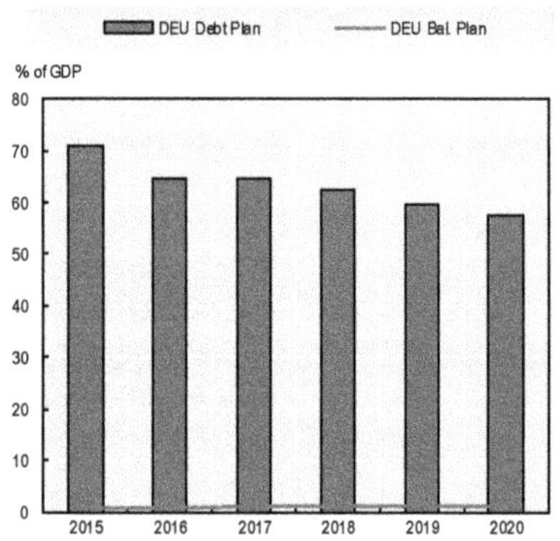


*Note:* The graph is referring to Fiscal Policy Plans that are implemented and/or officially announced as of November 2017 and as indicated by the country. Actual results in graph A may differ as the Fiscal Policy Plans are prepared by the country beforehand and as the Debt and Balance Plan reported by the country are based on the country's own definition; Data are referring to general government.

*Source:* 2018 OECD Fiscal Plans and Budgeting Framework Survey.

**C: Public Investment**

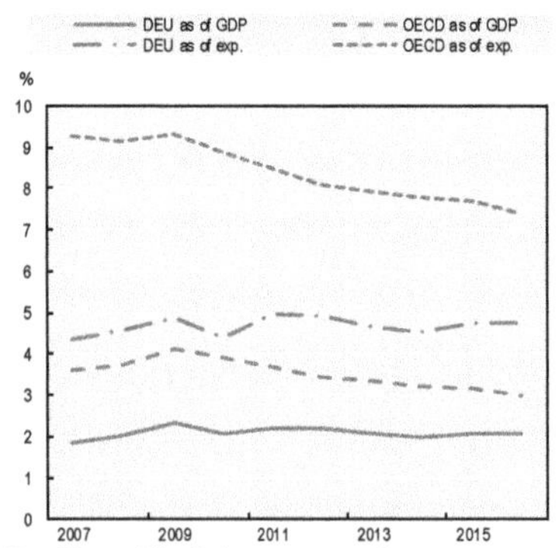


*Note:* The graph is referring to government investment as a percentage of GDP and as a share of total government expenditures.

*Source*: OECD National Accounts Statistics (database).

**D: Expenditure by function (2016)**

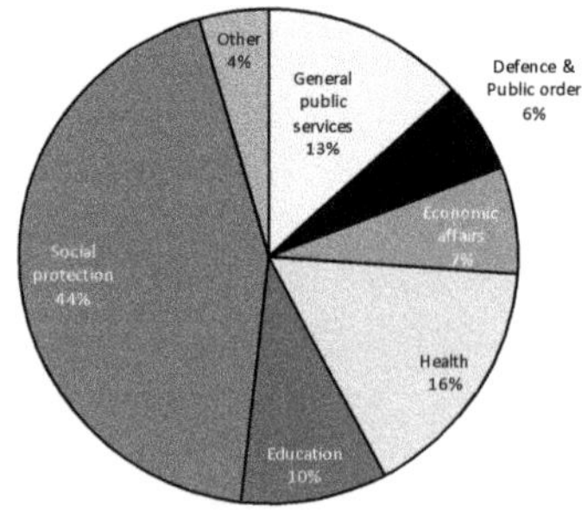


*Source:* OECD National Accounts Statistics (database); Eurostat Government finance statistics (database).

### *Developments in budgetary governance*

Germany's top-down approach to budgeting, introduced in 2010 to help ensure compliance with the debt-brake fiscal rule, involves a structured annual cycle.

Parliamentary engagement is particularly strong: the Budget Committee actively scrutinises the executive budget proposal, including through rapporteurs who lead the examination of ministry-specific allocations, and the power to revise allocations or 'block' (i.e. set conditions to) particular budget lines.

Performance budgeting is not a feature of budgeting in Germany although measures have been taken to clarify the broader strategic context of budget allocations. Since 2014/15, a spending review mechanism has been introduced to improve flexibility and responsiveness in the budget system, in line with recommendations from the 2014 OECD Budget Review of Germany.

Germany still uses a cash-centric system of financial reporting and budgeting at the federal level, although some *Länder*[12] (and almost all municipalities[13]) now use an accruals basis for financial reporting.

| Central Budget Authority |
|---|
| Federal Ministry of Finance<br><br>Weblink: www.bundesfinanzministerium.de |

| Budget coverage |
|---|
| The federal budget applies to the federal level of government. A National Stability Pact between the federal government and the highly-autonomous regions *(Länder)*, and associated Stability Council, manages multi-level fiscal coordination. |

| Legal Framework |
|---|
| Constitution (Basic Law) includes foundational principles for public financial management; a Budgetary Principles Act and Federal Budget Code further specify the comprehensive budgeting framework. |

| Budget cycle | |
|---|---|
| Budget circular | March[14] |
| Pre-budget fiscal policy statement[15] | April |
| Negotiations with line ministries | spring |
| Executive budget proposal | Summer |
| *Start of financial year* | *1 Jan.* |
| In-year budget execution reports | monthly |
| Mid-year implementation report | - |
| *End of financial year* | *31 Dec.* |
| Year-end financial statement | April |
| Audited financial report | November |
| Parliamentary accounting | December |

[12] 3 out of 16

[13] 75%

[14] The "benchmark figures decision" of government is notified to line ministries as a basis for budget preparation

[15] The EU-related Stability Programme Update (SPU) serves as the main pre-budget fiscal report.

**Germany's application of OECD budget principles "at a glance"**

| | | |
|---|---|---|
| **1.** | **Fiscal policy objectives** | **Debt brake (cyclical balance rule with corrective mechanism) in constitutional Basic Law; supplemented by EU fiscal rules.** |
| 2a. | Strategic alignment | No formal, structured link to Coalition Agreement or to SDGs |
| 2b. | MTEF | Elements of a MTEF, although budgeting is managed in a "top down" manner within medium term fiscal constraints, while also allowing opportunities for political re-prioritisation. |
| 3. | Capital and infrastructure | Financially integrated with general budget and MTEF; also subject to distinct planning and reporting mechanisms;<br>Grounding in economic and infrastructure needs appraisal;<br>Well-developed appraisal and evaluation mechanisms;<br>Targeted use of PPPs using well-developed methodologies |
| 4. | Transparency and accessibility | All core budget reports; 4 of 12 ancillary reports;<br>Limited impact assessments showing incidence of budget measures; Basic online accessibility tools; no citizen's budget. |
| **5a.** | **Parliamentary engagement** | **Strong engagement by Budget Committee of parliament, including rapporteur-led scrutiny of ministry allocations and right to revise proposed allocations.**<br>**No specific administrative support for parliamentary scrutiny.** |
| 5b. | Inclusive public / civic debate | Limited engagement of policy stakeholders in budget cycle. Line ministries include consultative mechanisms in policy development. |
| 6. | Budget accounting and financial reporting | Cash budgeting; comprehensive coverage; cash reporting; all based on accounting standards on federal level and for the *Länder* from a dedicated standard setting body. General government reporting (EU-related); no whole-of-government reporting |
| 7. | Budget execution | Single treasury fund covers 74% of public spending; also health and social security fund. Sound budget execution is primarily the responsibility of line ministries, who receive their full budgetary allocation on 1 January. IT system facilitates ongoing monitoring and management against monthly cash profiles.<br>Limited budget carry-over from year to year; mainly for capital;<br>Well-specified virement rules; MOF authorisation only by exception;<br>Supplementary budgets require advance parliamentary approval |
| 8a. | Performance budgeting | No performance-related budgeting; budget chapters include some narrative information to provide a policy context for allocations. |
| 8b. | Evaluation and VFM | Monitoring and evaluation within line ministries;<br>Targeted spending review introduced in 2014. |
| 9. | Fiscal risk and long-term sustainability | No overall report on fiscal risk; multiple sectoral reports;<br>Long-term sustainability report prepared every 3 years;<br>No contingency or reserve funds |
| 10. | Quality assurance and audit | Extensive use of independent institutes in preparing economic forecasts. No national Independent Fiscal Institution, although technical body provides support to Stability Council (for multi-level fiscal co-ordination).<br>Constitutionally-independent SAI provides financial audit and gives additional advice; limited role in performance audit or governance systems audit. |

Note: Rows in **bold** represent notable international practice.

## Budgetary Governance in Practice: Greece

### *Economic context*

GDP growth in Greece is estimated to have reached 2.1% in 2018, and then peak to 2.5% in 2019. Investment will lead the recovery, responding to reduced policy uncertainty and gradually improving financial conditions. Exports should continue to increase, supported by rising external demand. Excess capacity is diminishing but remains exceptionally large, limiting price and wage pressures.

### *Fiscal policy plans*

The medium-term fiscal policy has three priorities: 1) further enhancement of fiscal reliability in order to restore trust in the medium-term perspectives of the economy and regain access to international capital markets, 2) the fair distribution of the cost of macroeconomic adjustment and the support of vulnerable households, 3) progressive adjustment of the fiscal policy mix in order to enhance productivity and retain a sufficient growth rate. The primary general government balance targets (in enhanced surveillance terms) for the coming years up to 2022 are set at 3.5% of GDP.

**A: Fiscal Balance and Public Debt**

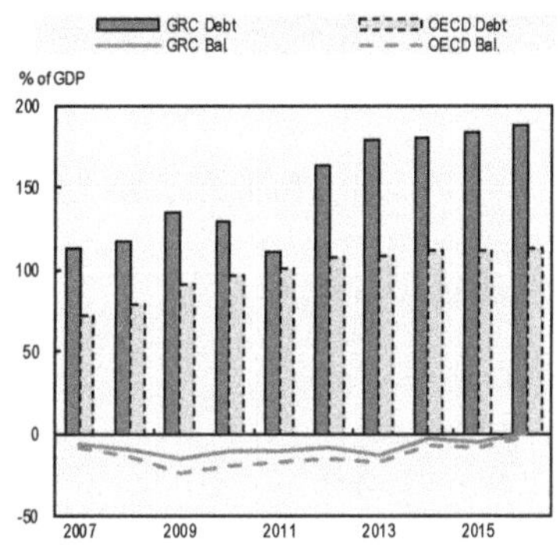


*Note* : The graph is referring to general government fiscal balance and general government gross debt as defined in the OECD National Accounts Statistics.

*Source:* OECD National Accounts Statistics (database); Eurostat Government finance statistics (database).

**B: Fiscal Policy Plans**

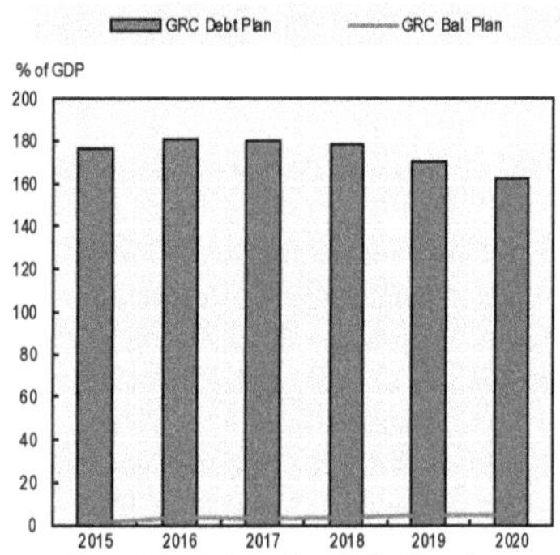


*Note* : The graph is referring to Fiscal Policy Plans that are implemented and/or officially announced as of November 2017 and as indicated by the country. Actual results in graph A may differ as the Fiscal Policy Plans are prepared by the country beforehand and as the Debt and Balance Plan reported by the country are based on the country 's own definition; Data are referring to general government.

*Source:* 2018 OECD Fiscal Plans and Budgeting Framework Survey.

**C: Public Investment**

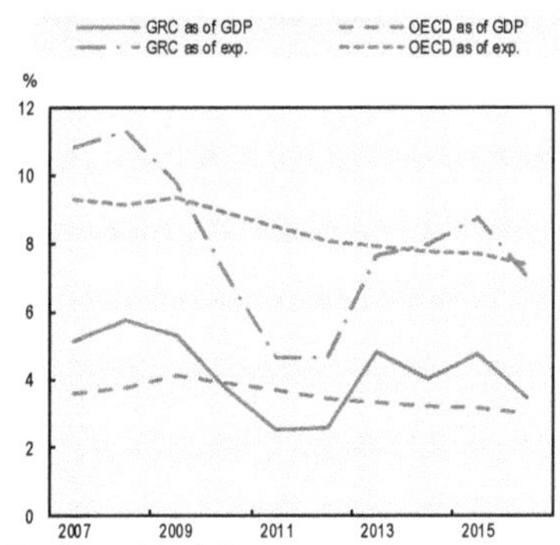


*Note:* The graph is referring to government investment as a percentage of GDP and as a share of total government expenditures.

*Source* : OECD National Accounts Statistics (database).

**D: Expenditure by function (2016)**

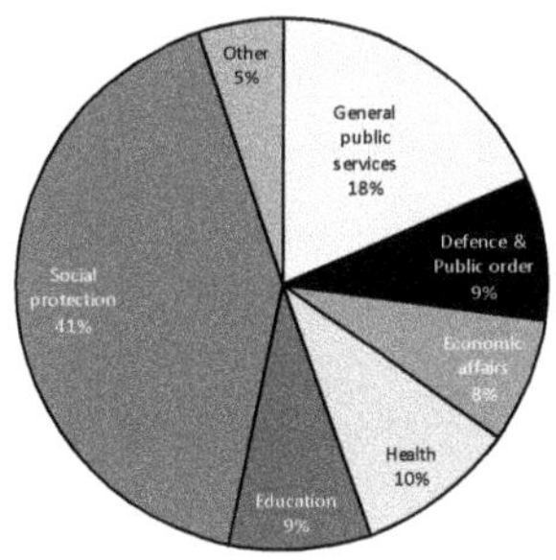


*Source:* OECD National Accounts Statistics (database); Eurostat Government finance statistics (database).

### *Developments in budgetary governance*

The public finance challenges in recent years have prioritised the need to address weaknesses in public financial management. A new Organic Budget Law introduced in 2014 transposed EU obligations into Greek law and introduced fiscal rules (a balanced budget rule, a debt rule, a convergence rule and correction mechanisms). This builds on the introduction of a Medium Term Fiscal Strategy in 2010.

Institutional reforms in recent years have also strengthened the fiscal framework in Greece. This includes the creation of a "Budget Bureau - General Directorate of Financial Services" in each spending ministry and the establishment of a Parliamentary Budget Office in 2010 and the Hellenic Fiscal Council in 2014.

There are still relatively low levels of budget transparency and parliamentary engagement in the budget process. There is also limited citizen engagement in the budget process and the government does not publish any citizen's budgets.

| Central Budget Authority |
|---|
| Ministry of Finance, and more specifically, the General Accounting Office.<br><br>Weblink: www.minfin.gr/ |

| Budget coverage |
|---|
| The executive's budget applies to the units of general government (central government, social security funds and local government). Public enterprises and organisations are not included, except budget transfers to these organisations. |

| Legal Framework |
|---|
| The Greek constitution sets out the roles and responsibilities of the legislature and the supreme audit institution in relation to the budget. A new organic budget law (Law 4270/2014 and its latest amendment Law 4549/2018) sets out the main characteristics of the budget and budget procedures. Other details are explained in Ministerial decisions and circulars. Presidential decrees and other legal provisions state the roles and responsibilities of each ministry and other public entities included in the budget. |

| Budget cycle | |
|---|---|
| Budget circular | By 31 May |
| Pre-budget fiscal policy statement | On 1st Monday in October |
| Negotiations with line ministries | May-November |
| Executive budget proposal | By 21 November |
| Parliamentary vote on budget | By 31 December |
| *Start of financial year* | *1 Jan.* |
| In-year budget execution reports | Monthly |
| Mid-year implementation report | n/a |
| *End of financial year* | *31 Dec.* |
| Year-end financial statement | By 30 June |
| Audited financial report | By 31 October |
| Parliamentary accounting | Within a year of receipt |

**Greece's application of OECD budget principles "at a glance"**

| | | |
|---|---|---|
| 1. | Fiscal policy objectives | Law 4270/2014 introduced fiscal rules in compliance with the EU fiscal framework. These include a budget balance rule which sets a floor for the structural budget, a debt rule, an adjustment path rule, and a correction mechanism. |
| 2a. | Strategic alignment | The annual state budget is accompanied by an explanatory report which sets out a description of the economic and fiscal strategy of the government. |
| **2b.** | **MTEF** | **A rolling Medium Term Fiscal Strategy Framework was introduced in 2010. Medium-term expenditure ceilings are set at the ministerial level for four years and are binding for the two first years. It is sent to parliament for approval. The annual budgets that follow have to respect the binding balance targets and the spending ceilings.** |
| 3. | Capital and infrastructure | The Public Investment Program (PIP) is a discrete category of the State Budget that includes mainly capital expenditure and is managed by the Ministry of Economy and Development. Capital and current expenditure requests are submitted separately by line ministries and the process for deciding upon these budget requests are distinct. |
| 4. | Transparency and accessibility | For most budget documents, official summaries are prepared for decision makers. There has also been some focus given to open data initiatives in recent years. Most budget reports and budget data are now available in downloadable form. |
| 5a. | Parliamentary engagement | The parliament receives a final budget proposal at least 40 days before the start of the fiscal year. It is examined by the Standing Committee on Economic Affairs and then debated and voted on in parliament plenary. Although parliamentary budget oversight is limited, it has been strengthened in the last decade through the introduction of amendment powers in 2008 and the establishment of the Parliamentary Budget Office in 2010. |
| 5b. | Inclusive public / civic debate | The Ministry of Finance holds meetings with key stakeholder during the budgetary process but there is no framework for citizen engagement and the government does not produce citizen's budgets. |
| 6. | Budget accounting and financial reporting | The budget is prepared on a modified cash basis. However, there are plans to transition from accounting on a modified cash basis to accrual accounting. |
| 7. | Budget execution | A single treasury fund is used. |
| 8a. | Performance budgeting | There is no performance budgeting framework in place., although the transition to performance budgeting is currently planned for by the General Accounting Office. |
| 8b. | Evaluation and VFM | There is limited capacity for evaluation and performance audits which provide information on value for money. |
| 9. | Fiscal risk and long-term sustainability | The Medium Term Fiscal Strategy is accompanied by an explanatory note that contains an analysis of public debt sustainability and the main sources of risk to the government fiscal forecasts. Long-term fiscal projections are undertaken for the pension system every three years by the National Actuarial Authority. |
| 10. | Quality assurance and audit | The constitution sets out that the Hellenic Court of Audit is the supreme audit institution. It focuses on compliance and financial audit. Law 4270/2014 established the Hellenic Fiscal Council with responsibility for assessing the macroeconomic and fiscal projections and compliance with fiscal rules. |

*Note*: Rows in bold represent notable international practice.

## Budgetary Governance in Practice: Hungary

### *Economic context*

The recent strong economic performance in Hungary is projected to continue in 2018, before softening somewhat in 2019. Investment remains a main driver with the resumed disbursement of EU structural funds and domestic and foreign firms responding to capacity constraints. Solid private consumption growth will be underpinned by continued strong real wage and employment increases. However, rising inflation is expected to harm cost competitiveness and increasingly constrain exports.

### *Fiscal policy plans*

For the next years, Hungary's budgetary priorities are to keep the deficit ratio permanently below 3% of GDP and reduce it further to reach the gradual reduction of public debt in line with domestic and EU fiscal rules. The government aims to achieve long-term sustainability through balanced economic growth, boosting employment and improving competitiveness and supporting families.

**A: Fiscal Balance and Public Debt**

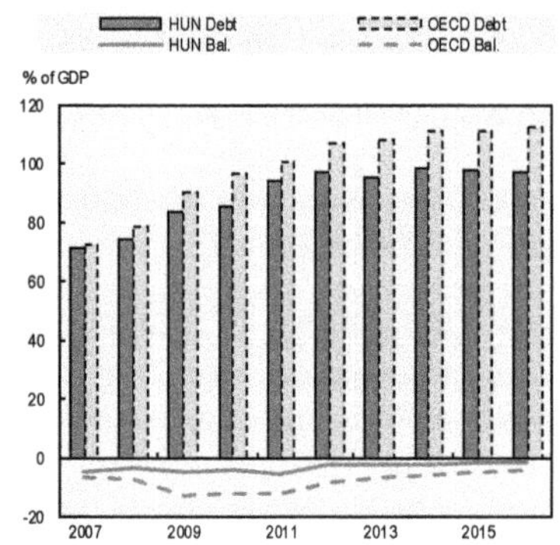


*Note*: The graph is referring to general government fiscal balance and general government gross debt as defined in the OECD National Accounts Statistics.

*Source:* OECD National Accounts Statistics (database); Eurostat Government finance statistics (database).

**B: Fiscal Policy Plans**

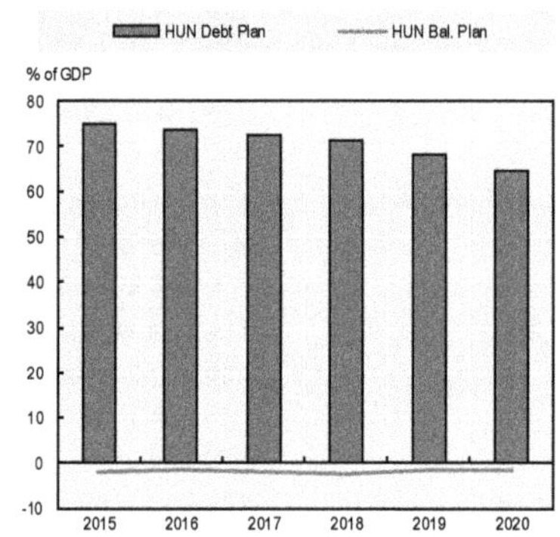


*Note*: The graph is referring to Fiscal Policy Plans that are implemented and/or officially announced as of November 2017 and as indicated by the country. Actual results in graph A may differ as the Fiscal Policy Plans are prepared by the country beforehand and as the Debt and Balance Plan reported by the country are based on the country's own definition.

*Source:* 2018 OECD Fiscal Plans and Budgeting Framework Survey.

**C: Public Investment**

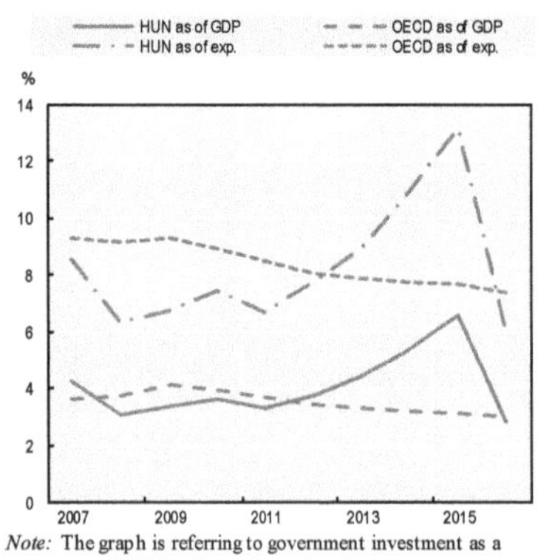


*Note:* The graph is referring to government investment as a percentage of GDP and as a share of total government expenditures.

*Source*: OECD National Accounts Statistics (database).

**D: Expenditure by function (2016)**

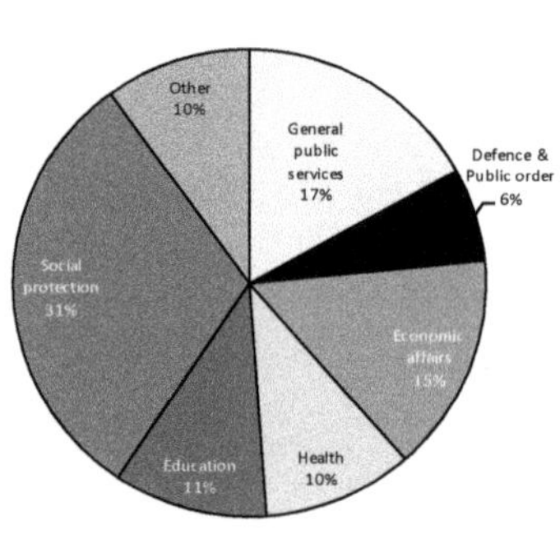


*Source:* OECD National Accounts Statistics (database); Eurostat Government finance statistics (database).

### *Developments in budgetary governance*

Hungary has no official national performance framework in place. However, there is a centrally-determined framework for linking sectoral output objectives with national outcome goals, including the use of routine and standardised use of international benchmarks to assess performance across various areas. Furthermore, the national statistical authority - on its own initiative - presents a clear set of statistical indicators on national performance.

In 2014, a reform of operational rules of the National Assembly aimed to improve the transparency of the budgetary approval process and to enhance predictability of budgetary planning. Additional reforms to enhance budget transparency, openness and accessibility were introduced in 2017.

The Hungarian Fiscal Council provides analytical support to Parliamentarians with regards to budgetary issues. The council furthermore needs to give its consensus for the adoption of the budget bill before the final vote ("veto right") to ensure its conformity with the constitutional debt rule.

| Central Budget Authority |
|---|
| Ministry of Finance<br><br>Weblink: www.kormany.hu/en/ministry-for-national-economy |

| Budget coverage |
|---|
| The executive's budget proposal applies to the federal level of government. Counties are not allowed to levy taxes. Municipalities have limited revenue-raising power. SNG are responsible for their own financial management and must run balanced budgets. |

| Legal Framework |
|---|
| Constitution includes foundational principles, roles and responsibilities of the Legislature and the Executive in the budget process as well as for audits by the SAI. Key aspects of the budget process (eg. MTEF, and legislative authorisation of spending) are furthermore specified by law. |

| Budget cycle | |
|---|---|
| Budget circular | April |
| Pre-budget fiscal policy statement[16] | December |
| Negotiations with line ministries | Spring |
| Executive budget proposal | April |
| Parliamentary vote on budget | December[17] |
| *Start of financial year* | *1 Jan.* |
| In-year budget execution reports | monthly |
| Mid-year implementation report | July |
| *End of financial year* | *31 Dec.* |
| Year-end financial statement | September |
| Audited financial report | September |
| Parliamentary accounting | October |

[16]The EU-related Stability Programme Update (SPU) currently serves as the main pre-budget fiscal report.

[17] By law, Legislature must vote until December. In practice, the final parliamentary votes take place in June or July.

| Hungary's application of OECD budget principles "at a glance" | | |
|---|---|---|
| **1.** | **Fiscal policy objectives** | **The debt target lies at 50% of GDP. As long as state debt exceeds this threshold, the National Assembly may only adopt an Act on the central budget which provides for state debt reduction in proportion to the GDP. The budget deficit must be below the 3% of GDP. The Hungarian Fiscal Council has veto power to stop the final approval of the budget in case of serious breach of the debt reduction rule.** |
| 2a. | Strategic alignment | The Government promotes the alignment between the annual budgetary allocations and the medium-term strategic plans, set out in government programme (December), and in the Convergence Programme and National Reform Programme. |
| 2b. | MTEF | 3-year rolling ceilings; legally-grounded overall public spending medium-term limits. Approval by Cabinet. |
| 3. | Capital and infrastructure | Capital and current expenditure are submitted and considered in an integrated way. The budget requests funding for the entire cost of multi-year project up-front. Based on feasibility studies, capital expenditures are included in the budgeting process. |
| 4. | Transparency and accessibility | All core budget reports are publicly available; 8 of 9 ancillary reports, of which 7 are publicly available. A number of impact assessments are published, including on gender and environment. Citizen's guides are available for several of the key budget documents. However, there is room to increased information on the Executive's Budget Proposal, including a Citizen's budget. |
| 5a. | Parliamentary engagement | Power to approve and amend the budget. A vote on the budget is however not considered a vote of confidence. |
| 5b. | Inclusive public / civic debate | Public meetings are held in Parliament. Formal hearings of key stakeholder and public roundtables. Budget-related consultation includes inputs from minority communities groups, and there are some opportunities for private consultations of civil society with the government and line ministries. |
| 6. | Budget accounting and financial reporting | The budget is prepared on both cash and accrual. The monthly financial report was reformed in 2017, providing more details in more a user-friendly format. |
| 7. | Budget execution | Single treasury fund is mandatory for all revenues and expenditures of central government, with no exceptions. In case of chapter-managed appropriations, line ministers can re-allocate funds within their own budget envelope, otherwise up to a certain limit. Supplementary budgets are produced and publically available. |
| 8a. | Performance budgeting | There is no national performance framework. |
| 8b. | Evaluation and VFM | There are legally binding requirements for *ex ante* evaluation of programmes that deemed important or sensitive. Spending reviews are an annual exercise. |
| **9.** | **Fiscal risk and long-term sustainability** | **The CBA produces long-term fiscal projections that span between 41 and 50 years and are updated every year. The long-term projections are specifically linked to the budgetary priorities for the improvement of demographic situation of the country. Contingency funds are in place for unforeseen expenditure (e.g. natural disasters), for policy reserves and a counter-cyclical stabilisation fund.** |
| 10. | Quality assurance and audit | The State Audit Office of Hungary has its legal basis for independence based in the constitution. Its responsibilities with regard to the year-end financial reporting include compliance control on public spending and audit of government financial report. However, it has a limited role in performance audit. |

Note: Rows in **bold** represent notable international practice.

# Budgetary Governance in Practice: Iceland

## *Economic context*

Growth in Iceland is expected to ease but remain robust; the economy is approaching capacity limits. Household consumption will increase on the back of continued labour immigration and rising wages in 2018 but slowdown in 2019. Business investment will decline after completion of several large projects. Unemployment has reached its lowest level since the 2008-09 economic and financial crisis and will continue to fall slightly. Revenues from exports and tourism are expected to decline from the strong levels reached in 2017.

**A: Fiscal Balance and Public Debt**

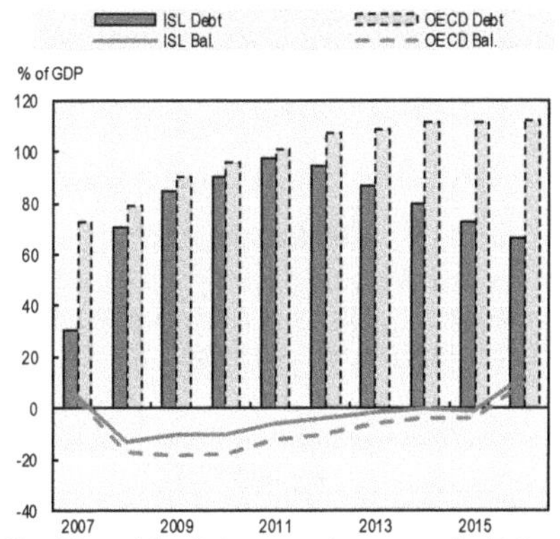


*Note*: The graph is referring to general government fiscal balance and general government gross debt as defined in the OECD National Accounts Statistics.

*Source:* OECD National Accounts Statistics (database); Eurostat Government finance statistics (database).

**B: Fiscal Policy Plans**

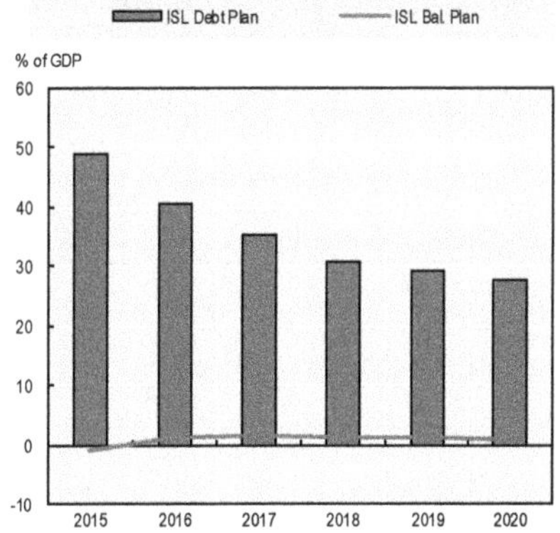


*Note*: The graph is referring to Fiscal Policy Plans that are implemented and/or officially announced as of November 2017 and as indicated by the country. Actual results in graph A may differ as the Fiscal Policy Plans are prepared by the country beforehand and as the Debt and Balance Plan reported by the country are based on the country's own definition; Data are referring to general government.

*Source:* 2018 OECD Fiscal Plans and Budgeting Framework Survey.

**C: Public Investment**

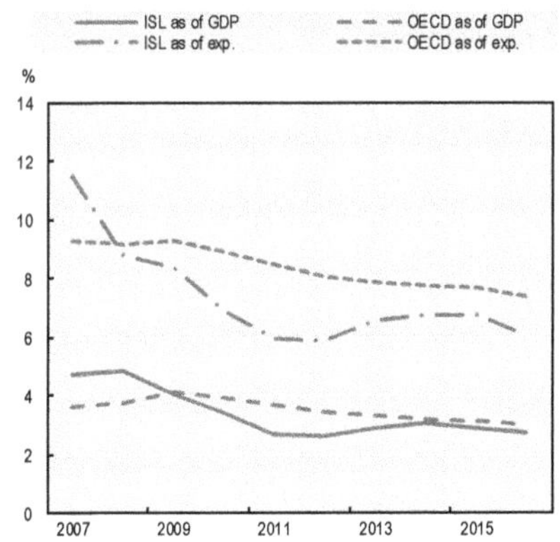


*Note:* The graph is referring to government investment as a percentage of GDP and as a share of total government expenditures.

*Source*: OECD National Accounts Statistics (database).

**D: Expenditure by function (2016)**

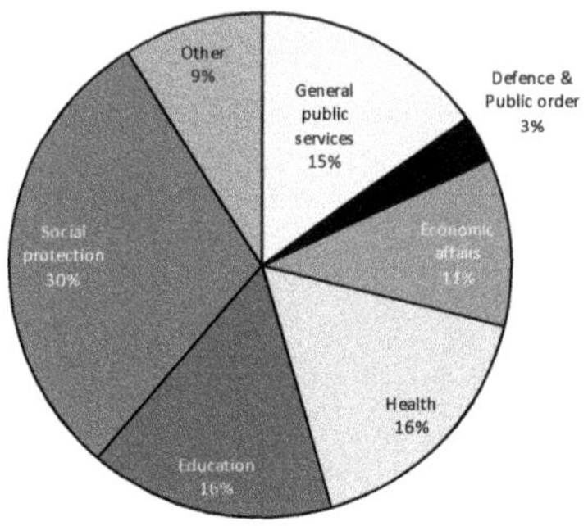


*Source:* OECD National Accounts Statistics (database); Eurostat Government finance statistics (database).

### *Developments in budgetary governance*

A new Organic Budget Law was introduced in Iceland in 2016 providing for a reformed fiscal framework with three fiscal rules and multi-year fiscal planning. It requires the publication of a Five-year Fiscal Policy Statement every five years and a Fiscal Strategy and Budget Bill on an annual basis. The new fiscal framework is more goal orientated, taking Iceland towards performance budgeting.

The law also introduced an independent fiscal institution in the form of a Fiscal Council. Its role is to provide independent opinion on the extent to which proposed fiscal policy aligns with the fundamental values and fiscal rules in the legislation.

Gender budgeting was also a major element of the 2016 budget reforms. The Finance Minister, in consultation with the Minister responsible for gender equality, leads the formulation of a gender budgeting programme, which is taken into account in the drafting of the budget bill. The budget bill must also outline its effects on gender equality targets.

| Central Budget Authority |
|---|
| Ministry of Finance and Economic Affairs.<br><br>Website: www.stjornarradid.is/raduneyti/fjarmala-og-efnahagsraduneytid/skipulag/skrifstofa-opinberra-fjarmala/ |

| Legal Framework |
|---|
| Legislation provides for the form and structure of the budget as well as what happens when the budget is not approved by the start of the fiscal year, the medium-term expenditure framework and audit rules and requirements. The current Organic Budget Law came into force on 1 January 2016 (Public Finance Act 123/2015). The roles and responsibilities of the legislature and the executive in the budget process are stipulated in internal rules. There is no formal basis for the roles and responsibilities of the different parts of the Executive in budget formulation and execution. |

| Budget coverage |
|---|
| According to the new Organic Budget Law, the budget will consolidate all entities controlled by the State – that is the ministries, public agencies, social security funds, and State-owned enterprises. |

| Budget cycle | |
|---|---|
| Budget circular | |
| Pre-budget fiscal policy statement | n/a |
| Negotiations with line ministries | |
| Executive budget proposal | September |
| Parliamentary vote on budget | December |
| *Start of financial year* | *1 Jan.* |
| In-year budget execution reports | Quarterly |
| Mid-year implementation report | |
| *End of financial year* | *31 Dec.* |
| Year-end financial statement | By 1 June |
| Audited financial report | |
| Parliamentary accounting | |

**Iceland's application of OECD budget principles "at a glance"**

| | | |
|---|---|---|
| 1. | Fiscal policy objectives | The Law on Public Finance provides for three fiscal rules. The net lending/borrowing over a five year period should always be positive and the annual deficit below 2.5% of GDP. Total liabilities must be lower than 30% of GDP. If the debt ratio exceeds 30%, the excess should be reduced in every three year period by at least 5% per year. |
| 2a. | Strategic alignment | Each new government must publish a policy statement and strategy for the next five years. The Policy Statement and the Strategy reflects the government's objectives and emphasis concerning the economic policy effect of public finances, tax policy, and prioritisation of spending. |
| 2b. | MTEF | The Minister of Finances lays a MTEF before parliament no later than 1 April each year. This sets out expenditure ceilings for the 34 expenditure areas for the next five years. |
| 3. | Capital and infrastructure | The use of Public-Private Partnerships (PPPs) is rare in Iceland. Municipal governments are responsible for local infrastructure. There have been calls for central government and the municipalities to better co-ordinate investment plans. |
| 4. | Transparency and accessibility | Iceland's current reporting framework, based primarily on the Financial Reporting Act of 1997, is relatively advanced and requires the reporting of an operating statement, a balance sheet, and a cash flow statement. Another strength is the close alignment of budgets and financial statements. |
| 5a. | Parliamentary engagement | Parliament debates the budget bill in three readings. Between readings the Budget Committee reviews the budget bill. The Parliament may make amendments to the budget if it does not change the total deficit/surplus. |
| 5b. | Inclusive public / civic debate | Gender budgeting was introduced in 2015. The Finance Minister, in consultation with the Minister responsible for gender equality, leads the formulation of a gender budgeting programme, which is taken into account in the drafting of the budget bill. The budget bill must also outline its effects on gender equality targets. |
| **6.** | **Budget accounting and financial reporting** | **Iceland was one of the first countries to introduce accrual concepts in budgeting. The budget and year-end statements are prepared on an accrual basis, subject to a number of modifications. Both the budget and financial statements are composed of all key statements and disclosures, as required by international standards, except for the statement of changes in net assets.** |
| 7. | Budget execution | Each Minister must regularly monitor the finances in their area of responsibility and seek ways to ensure that spending does not exceed the budget. Ministers may change the allocation of appropriations across categories as long as the decision is explained to the relevant head of the department with at least six weeks notice. |
| 8a. | Performance budgeting | The 2015 Organic Budget Law requires ministers to formulate and submit five year policy statements setting out targets, including quality and service targets, and explaining how these will be achieved. Budgeting is now more goal orientated and Iceland is working towards performance budgeting. |
| 8b. | Evaluation and VFM | |
| 9. | Fiscal risk and long-term sustainability | Each minister must regularly assess long-term financial sustainability in their own areas of responsibility and notify the Finance Minister of risk factors and how to deal with them. The Finance Minister makes the Government and the Budget Committee at parliament aware of these. |
| 10. | Quality assurance and audit | The Icelandic National Audit Office (INAO) undertakes financial and performance audit. A Fiscal Council was set up in 2016 to provide independent opinion on the extent to which proposed fiscal policy aligns with the fundamental values and fiscal rules in the legislation. |

Note: Rows in **bold** represent notable international practice.

## Budgetary Governance in Practice: Ireland

### *Economic context*

The Irish economy is projected to keep growing robustly, as domestic demand is set to remain solid. As the labour market tightens, wage pressures will continue to be strong and are projected to feed into higher inflation. Output is expected to expand at a slower pace than in past years due to already high labour costs and high external uncertainty, including about the future impact of Brexit on the Irish economy.

### *Fiscal policy plans*

The government's fiscal policy objective is to achieve the Medium Term Budgetary Objective of a balanced budget in structural terms. This objective is being targeted for the current fiscal year (2018).

**A: Fiscal Balance and Public Debt**

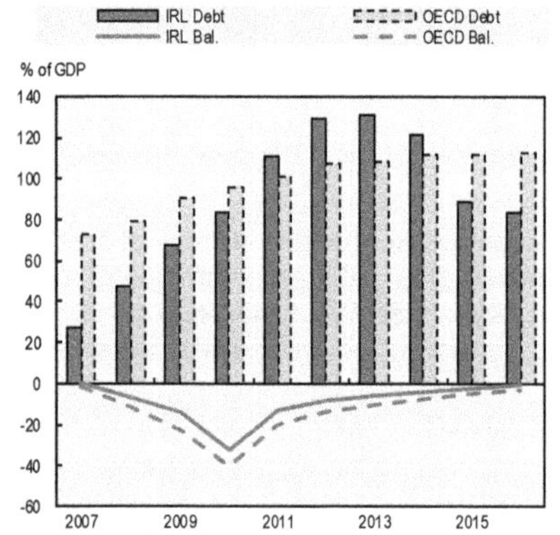


*Note:* The graph is referring to general government fiscal balance and general government gross debt as defined in the OECD National Accounts Statistics.

*Source:* OECD National Accounts Statistics (database); Eurostat Government finance statistics (database).

**B: Fiscal Policy Plans**

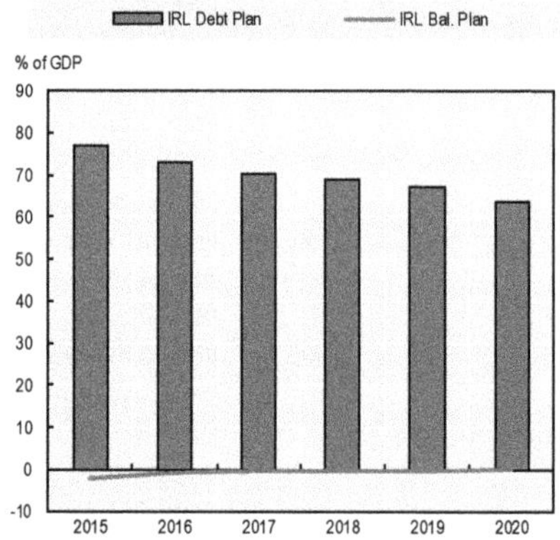


*Note*: The graph is referring to Fiscal Policy Plans that are implemented and/or officially announced as of November 2017 and as indicated by the country. Actual results in graph A may differ as the Fiscal Policy Plans are prepared by the country beforehand and as the Debt and Balance Plan reported by the country are based on the country's own definition; Data are referring to general government.

*Source:* 2018 OECD Fiscal Plans and Budgeting Framework Survey.

**C: Public Investment**

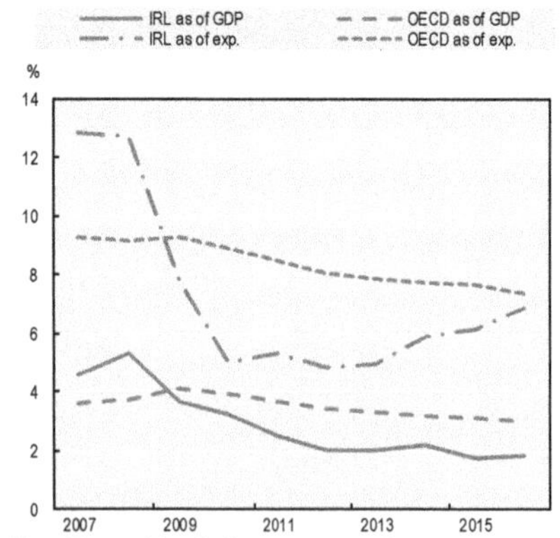


*Note:* The graph is referring to government investment as a percentage of GDP and as a share of total government expenditures.

*Source* : OECD National Accounts Statistics (database).

**D: Expenditure by function (2016)**

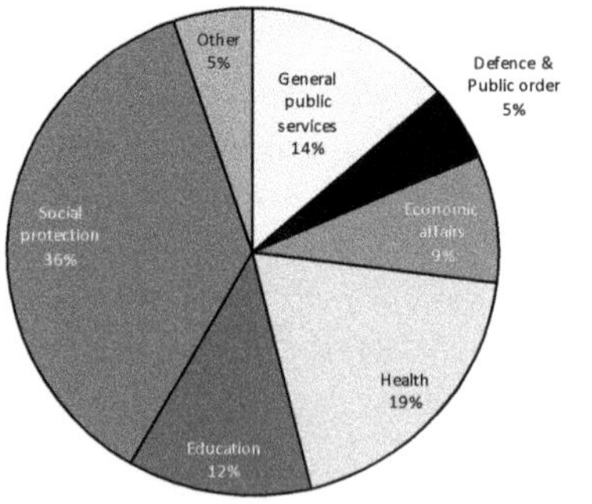


*Source:* OECD National Accounts Statistics (database); Eurostat Government finance statistics (database).

### *Developments in budgetary governance*

Against a background of major fiscal retrenchment, Ireland introduced structural economic reforms and broad-based budgetary reforms, notably from 2010-11. Since then, there have been further innovations in parliamentary engagement, including enhanced committee scrutiny and the establishment of an Irish Parliamentary Budget Office, drawing upon recommendations from the 2015 OECD Review of Parliamentary Engagement in Budgeting: Ireland.

Ireland's budget calendar has also been developed to promote a more "whole of year" approach; pre-budget deliberations are informed by a multi-stakeholder National Economic Dialogue in June. A pre-budget Economic Statement is published with perspectives on available fiscal resources.

The system of periodic spending review, instituted in 2011, has moved towards ongoing, rolling review processes. Ireland's has advanced, integrated systems for distributional analysis of budgetary measures, including incidence by household type and income levels. Gender budgeting reforms are in their initial stages.

| Central Budget Authority |
|---|
| Shared between the Department of Finance (macro-fiscal and tax policy) and the Department of Public Expenditure and Reform (expenditure policy). Since 2017 these Departments, while remaining distinct, are led by the same government minister.<br><br>Weblinks: www.finance.gov.ie and www.per.gov.ie |

| Legal Framework |
|---|
| No over-arching legal framework for budgeting: a combination of broad constitutional precepts, legislation in specific areas and established convention reflecting the Westminster tradition of government; all synthesised in an administrative reference code ("Public Financial Procedures"). |

| Budget coverage |
|---|
| The national budget applies to almost all public spending; a unitary country, local authorities have limited revenue-raising power and must run balanced budgets. |

| Budget cycle | |
|---|---|
| Pre-budget fiscal policy statement | July |
| Budget circular | July |
| Negotiations with line ministries | September |
| Executive budget proposal | October |
| Parliamentary vote on budget | December[18] |
| *Start of financial year* | *1 Jan.* |
| In-year budget execution reports | monthly |
| Parliamentary vote on budget | March[19] |
| Mid-year implementation report[20] | July |
| *End of financial year* | *31 Dec.* |
| Year-end financial statement | March |
| Audited financial report | September |
| Parliamentary accounting | February *(year+2)* |

[18] The Finance Bill which deals with tax policy is enacted by end-December.

[19] Parliamentary votes on the Estimates (granting interim legal authority to spend) take place in March-June of the financial year; final legal appropriation takes place in December of that year via the annual Appropriation Act.

[20] The Mid-year Expenditure Report is published since 2016; it covers only the expenditure side of the budget.

| Ireland's application of OECD budget principles "at a glance" | | |
|---|---|---|
| 1. | Fiscal policy objectives | EU fiscal rules are in force, including Fiscal Responsibility Act |
| 2a. | Strategic alignment | The fiscal plans are anchored to the Programme for Partnership Government. |
| 2b. | MTEF | 3-year rolling ceilings; legally-grounded, consistent with fiscal rules; ceilings are adjusted each year |
| **3.** | **Capital and infrastructure** | **Financially integrated with general budget and MTEF; also subject to distinct planning and reporting mechanisms;**<br>**Grounding in economic and infrastructure needs appraisal;**<br>**Well-developed appraisal and evaluation mechanisms;**<br>**Targeted use of PPPs using well-developed methodologies** |
| 4. | Transparency and accessibility | All core budget reports; 4 of 12 ancillary reports;<br>Advanced distributional analyses showing incidence of budget measures; Basic online accessibility tools; no citizen's budget. |
| 5a. | Parliamentary engagement | Clear, structured engagement by parliamentary committees, notably the budget oversight committee and public accounts committee;<br>No power to amend, or recommend amendments, to budget proposal;<br>Irish Parliamentary Budget Office established in 2017 |
| 5b. | Inclusive public / civic debate | Structured consultation with policy stakeholders via "National Fiscal Forum"; good engagement of year-round budget cycle |
| 6. | Budget accounting and financial reporting | Cash budgeting ; comprehensive coverage;<br>accruals reporting (adapted from IPSAS);<br>General government reporting (EU-related);<br>no whole-of-government reporting |
| 7. | Budget execution | Single treasury fund (Central Fund or "Exchequer") covers 74% of public spending; also Social Insurance and other funds;<br>Limited budget carry-over from year to year; mainly for capital;<br>Well-specified virement rules; MOF authorisation generally required;<br>Supplementary budgets require advance parliamentary approval |
| 8a. | Performance budgeting | Performance-informed budgeting; budget document includes output targets alongside financial allocations;<br>Annual performance report showing key deliverables of each ministry; not yet linked to over-arching performance framework or accountability mechanisms |
| **8b.** | **Evaluation and VFM** | **Monitoring and evaluation within line ministries;**<br>**Periodic spending review has now transitioned to rolling system of spending evaluations led by CBA;**<br>**Economic and evaluation service provides added professional capacity** |
| 9. | Fiscal risk and long-term sustainability | Fiscal risk matrix included in economic outlook;<br>Long-term sustainability report prepared every 5 years;<br>Sovereign wealth fund; no other contingency or reserve funds although a "rainy day fund" is proposed as a future reform |
| 10. | Quality assurance and audit | Independent fiscal council endorses official forecasts, assesses compliance with fiscal rules and comments on fiscal policy stance.<br>Constitutionally-independent SAI provide financial audit; limited resources for performance audit or governance systems audit. |

*Note*: Rows in **bold** represent notable international practice.

# Budgetary Governance in Practice: Israel

## *Economic context*

Economic growth in Israel is projected to strengthen to above 3.25% in 2018 and 2019. Domestic demand will be supported by accommodative fiscal and monetary conditions, the development of new gas fields and higher wage increases due to the persistence of low unemployment. With the somewhat stronger external environment, exports are also picking up as the shekel has stabilised at least temporarily.

## *Fiscal policy plans*

The government's fiscal policy goal is to reduce the fiscal deficit in the upcoming years by approximately 0.25% of GDP each year up until 1.5%; reaching a debt-to-GDP ratio of 50% and keeping government expenditures as percentage of GDP broadly stable.

**A: Fiscal Balance and Public Debt**

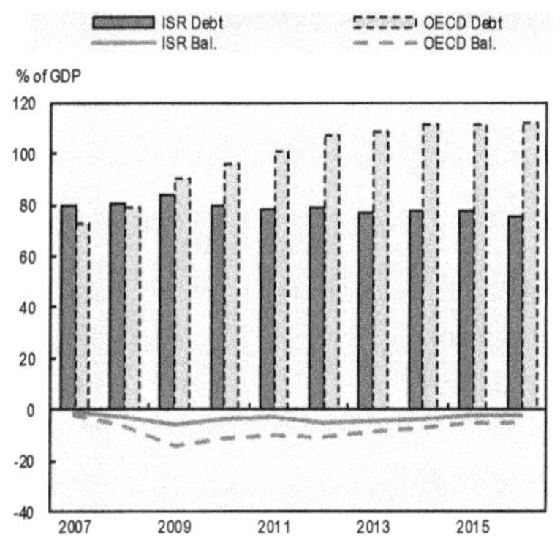


*Note*: The graph is referring to general government fiscal balance and general government gross debt as defined in the OECD National Accounts Statistics.

*Source:* OECD National Accounts Statistics (database); Eurostat Government finance statistics (database).

**B: Fiscal Policy Plans**

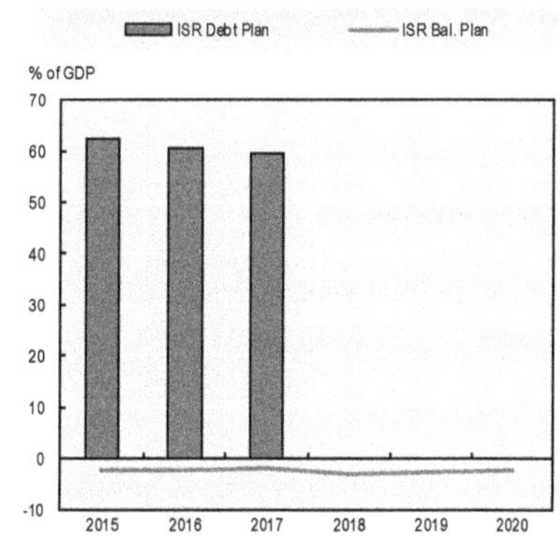


*Note*: The graph is referring to Fiscal Policy Plans that are implemented and/or officially announced as of November 2017 and as indicated by the country. Actual results in graph A may differ as the Fiscal Policy Plans are prepared by the country beforehand and as the Debt and Balance Plan reported by the country are based on the country's own definition; Data are referring to general government.

*Source:* 2018 OECD Fiscal Plans and Budgeting Framework Survey.

**C: Public Investment**

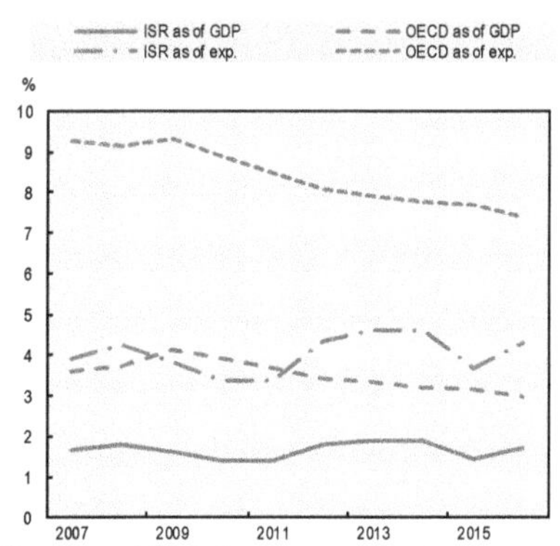


*Note:* The graph is referring to government investment as a percentage of GDP and as a share of total government expenditures.

Source: OECD National Accounts Statistics (database).

Information on data for Israel: http://dx.doi.org/10.1787/888932315602.

**D: Expenditure by function (2016)**

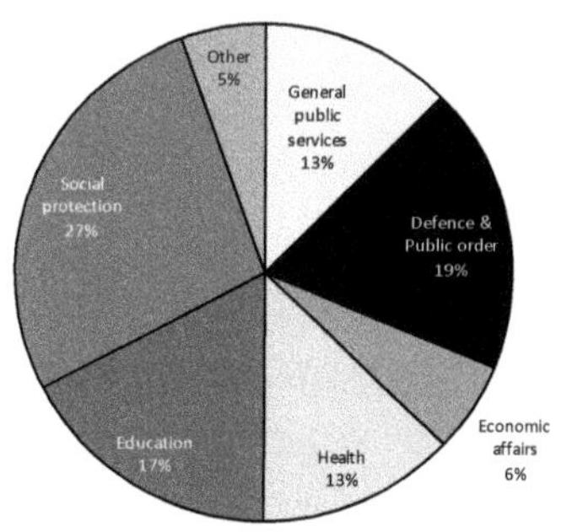


*Source:* OECD National Accounts Statistics (database); Eurostat Government finance statistics (database).

### *Developments in budgetary governance*

Israel has a distinctive system of biennial rather than annual budgeting, in place since 2009. This involves the government submitting a budget proposal for the two upcoming fiscal years[21].

Israel does not have independent institutions (such as a fiscal council or Supreme Audit Institution) on the same model as other OECD countries, although some objective, professional inputs to the budget process are in place including a new 'consensus methodology' to support the Chief Economist's economic forecasts and assumptions.

Israel does not publish distributional impacts of budget measures although there are some advanced elements of gender budgeting.

| Central Budget Authority |
|---|
| Ministry of Finance<br><br>Weblink: http://mof.gov.il/en/pages/default.aspx |

| Legal Framework |
|---|
| The Basic Law sets out fundamental requirements regarding submission of the state budget to the Knesset (or a designated committee), with other key details to be prescribed by law. |

| Budget coverage |
|---|
| The budget document covers central government. Israel has a single tier of local government: while a process of fiscal decentralisation is underway, the level of overall public spending managed by local authorities is small in international terms. However, local authorities implement around 60% of overall public investment. |

| Budget cycle | |
|---|---|
| Budget circular | early June |
| Pre-budget statement | n/a |
| Negotiations with line ministries | summer |
| Executive budget proposal | early November |
| Parliamentary vote on budget | end-December |
| *Start of financial year* | *1 January* |
| In-year budget execution reports | |
| Mid-year implementation report | n/a |
| *End of financial year* | *31 December* |
| Year-end financial statement | end-April |
| Audited financial report | end-April |
| Parliamentary accounting | n/a |

[21] In early 2018, the budget proposal was submitted and approved in respect of 2019 only, due to the scheduled general election in 2019.

| Israel's application of OECD budget principles "at a glance" | | |
|---|---|---|
| **1.** | **Fiscal policy objectives** | **The fiscal rules set a maximum budget deficit target (currently 1.5% of GDP), and an expenditure growth limit (currently 2.75% p.a. in real terms). The government has also set a debt target of 50% of GDP. A "Numerator" rule was introduced in 2016 as an additional constraint, limiting the government's ability to incur new spending commitments without identifying a funding source.** |
| 2a. | Strategic alignment | The budget allocations do not make explicit the alignment with medium-term governmental objectives. |
| 2b. | MTEF | Since 2015, the executive's budget proposal includes a detailed triennial plan to inform the continuity of policy development. The triennial plan may be revised in subsequent budget proposals. |
| 3. | Capital and infrastructure | Capital budgeting is mostly initiated and governed via the line ministries. At present there is no long-term strategic infrastructure plan currently in place, at central level. A central PPP unit provides guidance on this mode of capital procurement and delivery. |
| 4. | Transparency and accessibility | Key budget reports are published, and there have been improvements over recent years in the provision of open budget data. The Ministry of Finance has a web app to provide full details of the annual budget, including details of execution. |
| 5a. | Parliamentary engagement | The Knesset has authority over the annual budget. Its Finance Committee is a powerful and prestigious body that exercises significant *de facto* control over budgetary management. |
| 5b. | Inclusive public / civic debate | Limited opportunities for the general public and civil-society bodies to engage with the budgetary process. |
| 6. | Financial reporting and accounting | A cash basis is used for budgeting and reporting. |
| 7. | Budget execution | Large discretion is available to the Ministry of Finance, with oversight from the Knesset's Finance Committee, to adjust and reallocate the budget during the year. In recent years, the transparency of this process has been improved, and reforms are ongoing aimed at reducing the need for budgetary changes within the year. Line ministries may reallocate within their budgets only with approval of the Ministry of Finance. |
| 8a. | Performance budgeting | n/a |
| 8b. | Evaluation and VFM | n/a |
| 9. | Fiscal risk and long-term sustainability | Fiscal risks are taken into account by the Chief Economist in the context of preparing official forecasts and determining policy assumptions. |
| 10. | Quality assurance and audit | Economic forecasts are prepared by the Chief Economist in the Ministry of Finance; formerly these forecasts had been prepared by the Ministry's budget bureau.<br>The State Comptroller and Ombudsman is established under the Basic Law and its functions include efficiency audit and integrity audit. |

*Note*: Rows in **bold** represent notable international practice.

## Budgetary Governance in Practice: Italy

### *Economic context*

GDP growth in Italy is projected to edge down to 1% in 2018 and 2019. Private consumption will continue to be the main driver of the recovery, which will continue to broaden to investment and exports. Employment gains will buttress household disposable income. Tax incentives and rising external demand will support business investment and export growth. Excess capacity is narrowing but consumer price inflation and wage pressures will remain muted.

### *Fiscal policy plans*

Based on announcements by the Italian government in September 2018 and a budget law approved in December 2018, the government deficit is forecast to reduce to 2% of GDP in 2020 and 1.8% in 2021. More specifically: balancing of budgets corresponds to the medium-term objective, that is the structural balance determined using the criteria established in EU Law; targets are set on the budget balance in terms of general government net borrowing, as defined for the purposes of the excessive deficit procedure in the EU Treaty.

**A: Fiscal Balance and Public Debt**

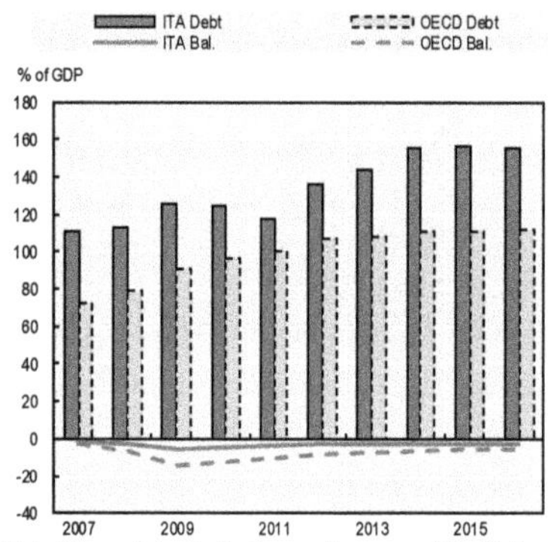


*Note*: The graph is referring to general government fiscal balance and general government gross debt as defined in the OECD National Accounts Statistics.

*Source:* OECD National Accounts Statistics (database); Eurostat Government finance statistics (database).

**C: Public Investment**

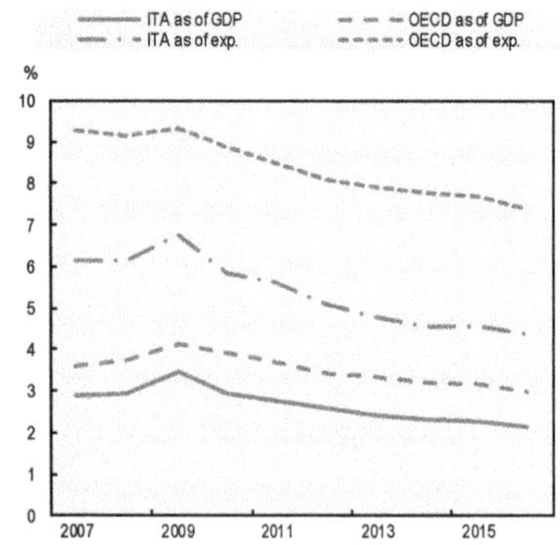


*Note:* The graph is referring to government investment as a percentage of GDP and as a share of total government expenditures.

*Source*: OECD National Accounts Statistics (database).

**D: Expenditure by function (2016)**

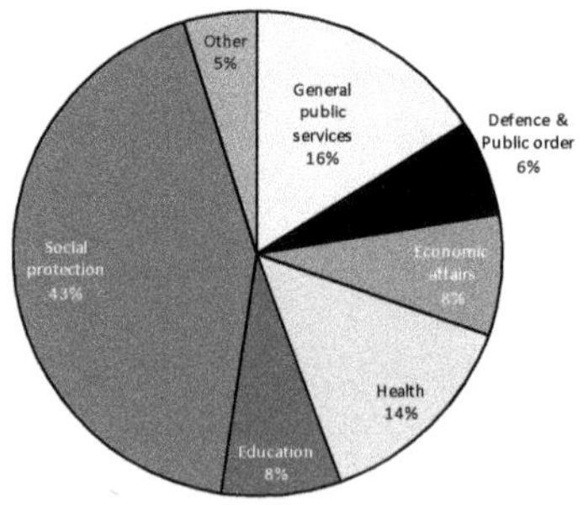


*Source:* OECD National Accounts Statistics (database); Eurostat Government finance statistics (database).

### *Developments in budgetary governance*

Important changes were enacted in 2012, with the objective of ensuring balanced budgets and debt sustainability. The 2012 Law also helped ensure compliance with the EU fiscal compact and the excessive deficit procedure.

In 2014 Italy established an independent Parliamentary Budget Office to assist legislators in scrutinising economic forecasts and budget proposals. The PBO endorses the accuracy of official economic forecasts, monitors compliance with fiscal rules and constitutional provisions related to the budget and comments on the governments overall fiscal stance and specific budget related policy proposals.

In 2016 Italy began to introduce gender budgeting. Following a pilot exercise in 2017, the methodology was further developed in 2018. Also in 2016 Italy introduced a requirement that the DEF contain well-being objectives and indicators, including environmental sustainability, economic equality, health, education etc.

**Central Budget Authority**

The State General Accounting Department within the Ministry of Economy and Finance is the Central Budget Authority. Developing the executive's budget proposal is the shared responsibility of the CBA and the Presidency of the Council of Ministers.

Weblink: www.rgs.mef.gov.it

**Legal Framework**

Provisions on public finance and debt are included in the Italian constitution (articles 81 and 97). There are also EU treaty obligations with respect to public finance. How these constitutional provisions and treaty obligations are fulfilled is set out in national legislation. Key laws governing public finance are Law 196/2009 and Law 243/2012).

**Budget coverage**

Italy is a unitary state, and the national budget is comprehensive in coverage. At the same time Italy has a high level of fiscal decentralisation. The fiscal federalism law of 2009 granted greater fiscal autonomy to the regions. However, in practice, the central government has imposed a balanced-budget rule on local government budgets due to the need for overall fiscal consolidation.

**Budget cycle**

| | |
|---|---|
| Pre-budget fiscal policy statement | September |
| Budget circular | May |
| Negotiations with line ministries | July |
| Executive budget proposal | October |
| Parliamentary vote on budget | December[22] |
| *Start of financial year* | *1 Jan.* |
| In-year budget execution reports | monthly |
| Parliamentary vote on budget | December |
| Mid-year implementation report[23] | June |
| *End of financial year* | *31 Dec.* |
| Year-end financial statement | May |
| Audited financial report | June |
| Parliamentary scrutiny of audited financial report | July onwards |

[22] The Finance Bill which deals with tax policy is enacted by end-December.

| Italy's application of OECD budget principles "at a glance" | | |
|---|---|---|
| 1. | Fiscal policy objectives | EU fiscal rules are in force, also balanced budget and debt sustainability provisions in the Italian constitution. |
| 2a. | Strategic alignment | The Budget is closely linked to the Economic and Financial Document (DEF) that is developed each year. In addition to fiscal parameters it includes national outcomes and well-being goals. |
| 2b. | MTEF | Basis in law, 3-year ceilings adjusted on an annual rolling basis |
| **3.** | **Capital and infrastructure** | **Cost benefit analysis is mandated in law to prioritise investment decisions, assess project designs and monitor project implementation. Actual practice is uneven.** |
| 4. | Transparency and accessibility | Italy provides a substantial amount of budget information to the public. The core budget reports are publicly available in a downloadable format and the government publishes a citizens' guide to the budget, although the information provided in this is limited. |
| **5a.** | **Parliamentary engagement** | **Clear, structured engagement by the Chamber of Deputies (Budget, Treasury and Planning Committee), the Senate (Committee on Economic Planning and the Budget) and sectoral committees.**<br>**Parliament frequently recommends amendments to budget proposals.**<br>**An independent Parliamentary Budget Office was established in 2014.** |
| 5b. | Inclusive public / civic debate | Italy does not have processes for direct public participation in the budget process. |
| 6. | Budget accounting and financial reporting | Cash budgeting; comprehensive coverage; cash and commitment reporting; general government reporting (EU-related); no whole-of-government reporting. |
| 7. | Budget execution | Budget execution is controlled centrally by MEF using the SICOGE system. The SICOGE system provides RGS with detailed control of budget execution in central offices of line ministries; territorial offices of ministries are gradually being pulled into the system.. RGS operates territorial offices which are responsible for the disbursement of central government funds at lower levels of government.<br>Italy operates a single treasury account system through the Banca d'Italia. Over 95% of the transactions are made through the on-line payment services.<br>Ministries have very limited flexibility to reallocate budget resources. Budgets are approved by parliament based on programmes. Reallocation is possible within a programme, but even this is subject to constraints. |
| 8a. | Performance budgeting | Presentational performance budgeting oriented towards transparency and dialogue between government and parliament and citizens, supported by provisions in the organic budget law; a law on performance based management (150/2009) in the public sector remains largely unimplemented.<br>Annual performance reporting is linked to objectives and indicators in the National Reform Programme and measures of equitable and sustainable well-being (BES). |
| 8b. | Evaluation and VFM | There is no requirement to evaluate programmes on a systematic basis. However, there are legal requirements for *ex ante* and *ex post* regulatory impact analysis provides similar information.<br>Spending reviews are carried out regularly and have very recently been formally integrated into annual budget cycle, replacing ad hoc spending reviews. |
| 9. | Fiscal risk and long-term sustainability | Annual forecasts of long term public finances and analysis of fiscal sustainability and risks are included in the Economic and Financial Document (EFD.) |
| 10. | Quality assurance and audit | Independent PBO endorses official forecasts, assesses compliance with fiscal rules and comments on fiscal policy stance.<br>A constitutionally-independent SAI carries out compliance audits and financial audits, following international auditing standards. It also provides a quality assurance and audit function in respect of performance information reported in the budget. |

Note: Rows in **bold** represent notable international practice.

## Budgetary Governance in Practice: Japan

### *Economic context*

Following a pick-up in economic growth in Japan to 1.5% in 2017, growth is projected to remain close to 1% in 2018 and 2019, despite a resumption of fiscal consolidation, as export growth remains robust. Employment is projected to peak in 2018 as the decline in the working-age population accelerates. Sustained above-potential growth will boost inflation to 1% in 2018 and around 1.5% in 2019 (excluding the impact of the increase in the consumption tax rate).

### *Fiscal policy plans*

The government aims to achieve a primary surplus of the central and local governments by 2025. Also, the government will seek to steadily reduce the public debt to GDP ratio at the same time.

**A: Fiscal Balance and Public Debt**

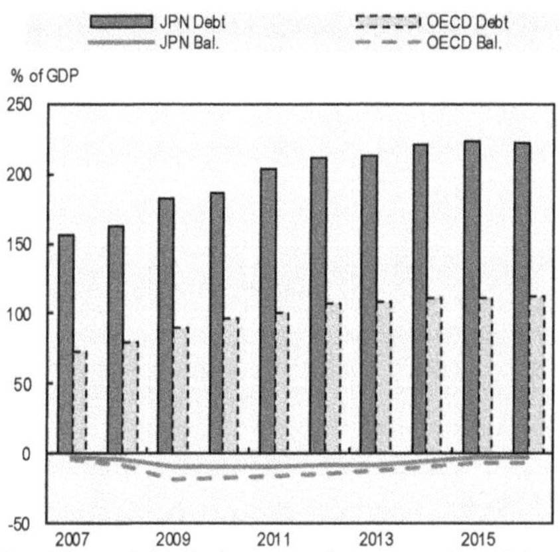


*Note*: The graph is referring to general government fiscal balance and general government gross debt as defined in the OECD National Accounts Statistics.

*Source:* OECD National Accounts Statistics (database); Eurostat Government finance statistics (database).

**C: Public Investment**

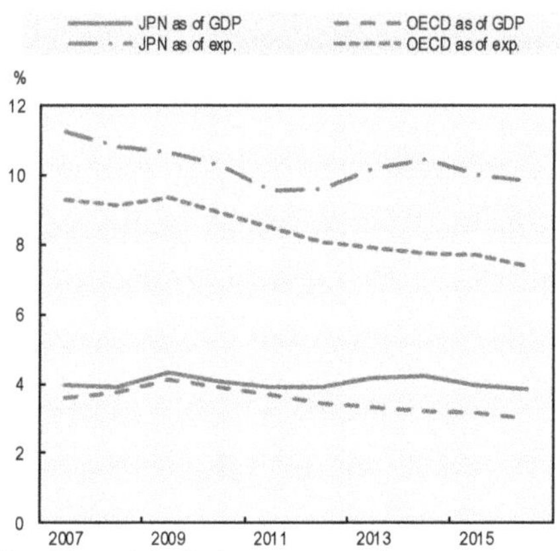


*Note:* The graph is referring to government investment as a percentage of GDP and as a share of total government expenditures.

*Source*: OECD National Accounts Statistics (database).

**D: Expenditure by function (2016)**

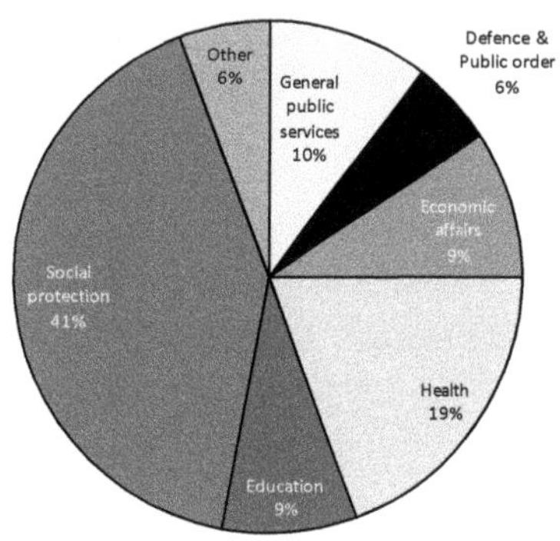


*Source:* OECD National Accounts Statistics (database); Eurostat Government finance statistics (database).

### *Developments in budgetary governance*

Settlement of Revenue and Expenditure of the national government is prepared every fiscal year based on the Public Finance Act in line with cash-basis accounting and single-entry accounting. In addition to the Settlement, "Financial Statements of the Government" is voluntarily prepared since FY2003 in line with accrual-basis accounting and double-entry accounting in order to enhance the transparency of financial situation.

The Council on Economic and Fiscal Policy, an advisory body to the Prime Minister made up of ministers, experts and the Governor of the Bank of Japan, has been playing a central role in shaping overall economic and fiscal policy. For example, this Council made the fiscal consolidation plans which were approved by the Japanese Cabinet. In order to ensure the progress of the fiscal consolidation plan, the Committee for Promoting the Integrated Economic and Fiscal Reforms under this Council (made up of academics, business leaders and experts) conducts a review and submits its report to the Council.

The government seeks to improve budget efficiency and effectiveness by utilising the PDCA cycle which is a kind of performance budgeting and also contributes to strategic policy planning. PDCA cycle consists of the following processes (Plan: Planning the budget, Do: Executing the budget, Check: Evaluating the budget execution in the context of achieving the policy agendas, Action: Making use of evaluation results for budget planning).

| Central Budget Authority |
|---|
| Ministry of Finance<br><br>Weblink: www.mof.go.jp/english/ |

| Legal Framework |
|---|
| Legal basis of the framework is established by the Constitution of Japan, the Public Finance Act and other related acts as well as by the Plan and other policy papers decided or approved by the Cabinet. |

| Budget coverage |
|---|
| The executive's budget proposal covers central government and year-end financial statements cover central government. |

| Budget cycle | |
|---|---|
| Budget circular | April |
| Pre-budget statement | December |
| Negotiations with line ministries | Sept-Dec |
| Executive budget proposal | January |
| Parliamentary vote on budget | March |
| *Start of financial year* | *April* |
| In-year budget execution reports | quarterly |
| Mid-year implementation report | |
| *End of financial year* | *March* |
| Year-end financial statement | July |
| Audited financial report | November |
| Parliamentary accounting | November |

**Japan's application of OECD budget principles "at a glance"**

| | | |
|---|---|---|
| 1. | Fiscal policy objectives | The government aims to achieve a primary surplus for central and local governments by FY2025. At the same time, the government seeks to steadily reduce the public debt to GDP ratio. |
| **2a.** | **Strategic alignment** | **The cabinet is important in determining National Development Plan that sets out the medium-term strategic plans and priorities and CBA and Prime Minister's Office has a leadership role in promoting alignment between annual budgets and medium-term plans/priorities.** |
| **2b.** | **MTEF** | **The 3-year MTEF that has a fixed period and not revised during the period. It is approved by the Cabinet and is internally monitored within government.** |
| 3. | Capital and infrastructure | The government usually conducts *ex ante* evaluation including cost-benefit analysis based on the Government Policy Evaluations Act. In addition, for example, the Ministry of Land, Infrastructure, Transport, and Tourism conduct *ex post* evaluation within 5 years after completing the projects. |
| 4. | Transparency and accessibility | All core budget reports are open data and budget data is available in downloadable form. The budget impact analyses are not published. |
| 5a. | Parliamentary engagement | The legislature has unrestricted powers to amend the budget. If the budget is not approved by the legislature before the start of the fiscal year, other interim measures are voted on by the legislature. |
| 5b. | Inclusive public / civic debate | In pre-budget proposal phase, public call for proposals and submissions are held in line ministries and in post-budget proposal phase, public hearings and consultations are held in the legislature. Participatory budgeting is not in place. |
| 6. | Financial reporting and accounting | The budget is prepared based on cash and/or commitment. The central government covers all main reports on public finance. |
| 7. | Budget execution | The single treasury fund is not used. The line ministries do not receive lump sum appropriations for operating expenditure, but they receive detailed operating expenditure. |
| 8a. | Performance budgeting | Japan seeks to improve budget efficiency and effectiveness by utilising the PDCA (Plan-Do-Check-Action) cycle which is a kind of performance budgeting and also contributes to strategic policy planning. |
| 8b. | Evaluation and VFM | The range of issues covered in *ex post* evaluation varies widely. It mandates coverage of a comprehensive set of issues in their evaluations. |
| 9. | Fiscal risk and long-term sustainability | Cabinet Office is primarily responsible the long-term fiscal projections which covers 6-10 years, are revised twice a year and incorporated into an overall direction of fiscal policy. The Fiscal System Council, which is the advisory body to the Minister of Finance on fiscal policy issues, conducted the "Long-term Projections on Japanese Public Finance in order to analyse the long-term sustainability and risk of Japanese public finance |
| 10. | Quality assurance and audit | Board of Audit of Japan takes on the supreme auditing. |

Note: Rows in **bold** represent notable international practice.

## Budgetary Governance in Practice: Korea

### *Economic context*

The rebound in international trade and greater fiscal support are projected to sustain output growth in Korea at around 3% through 2019, even though construction investment is projected to slow following tighter regulations on housing and mortgage lending. High household debt and weak employment growth continue to hold back private consumption. Inflation is projected to remain close to 2%, while the current account surplus will edge up to 6% of GDP.

### *Fiscal policy plans*

Key fiscal policies are to support job creation: increase public sector jobs, support private sector job creation, and develop a model for the job market focusing on job security and flexibility. In order to improve welfare to ensure wage-led growth, it will strengthen support for employment-friendly welfare, adopt childcare benefits, and raise basic pensions. In addition, key fiscal policies will promote innovation to help develop new growth engines which will support the 4th industrial revolution, build industry clusters for innovation, and develop innovative human resources.

A: Fiscal Balance and Public Debt

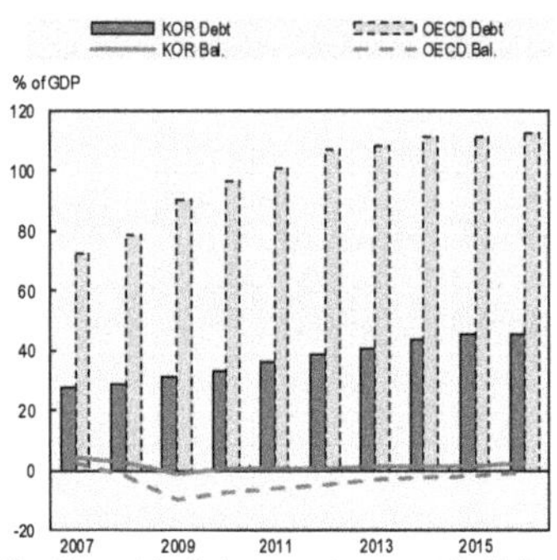


*Note*: The graph is referring to general government fiscal balance and general government gross debt as defined in the OECD National Accounts Statistics.

*Source:* OECD National Accounts Statistics (database); Eurostat Government finance statistics (database).

B: Fiscal Policy Plans

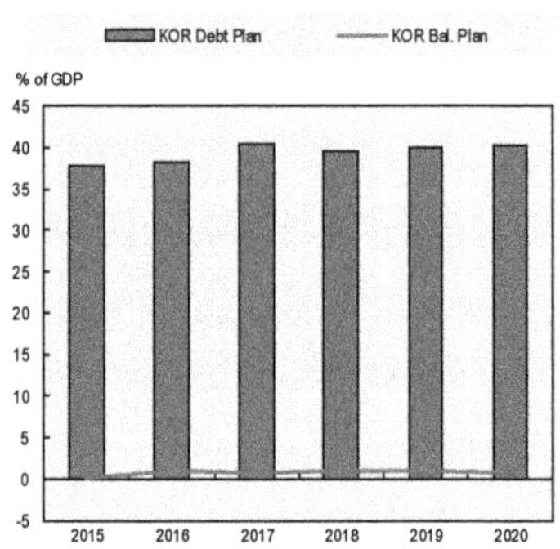


*Note*: The graph is referring to Fiscal Policy Plans that are implemented and/or officially announced as of November 2017 and as indicated by the country. Actual results in graph A may differ as the Fiscal Policy Plans are prepared by the country beforehand and as the Debt and Balance Plan reported by the country are based on the country's own definition; Data are referring to central/federal government.

*Source:* 2018 OECD Fiscal Plans and Budgeting Framework Survey.

C: Public Investment

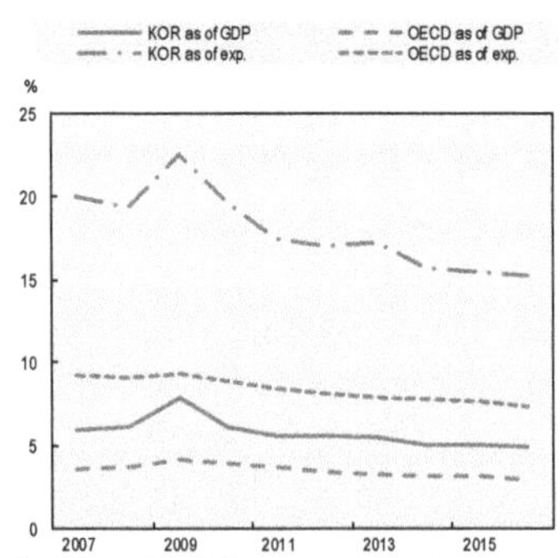


*Note:* The graph is referring to government investment as a percentage of GDP and as a share of total government expenditures.

*Source*: OECD National Accounts Statistics (database).

D: Expenditure by function (2016)

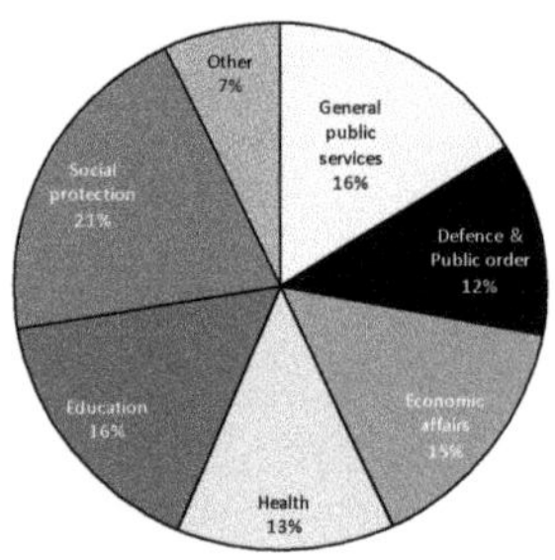


*Source:* OECD National Accounts Statistics (database); Eurostat Government finance statistics (database).

*Developments in budgetary governance*

From 2003 to 2007, major public finance reforms had been achieved; medium-term expenditure framework (National Fiscal Management Plan), top-down budgeting, performance management and digital budgeting and accounting system with the comprehensive overhaul of National Public Finance Law.

After the global financial crisis, the legal basis for long-term fiscal sustainability monitoring and systematic management of fiscal risk has been established through the amendment of the Enforcement Decree of the National Public Finance Law.

Recently, there has been an effort to enhance transparency and citizens' participation in the budgetary process by requiring the government to review the citizens' opinions and the result of the review may be applied in the budgetary process. Korea also has a number of gender budgeting elements in place.

| Central Budget Authority |
|---|
| Ministry of Economy and Finance<br><br>Weblink: http://english.moef.go.kr/ |

| Legal Framework |
|---|
| The roles and responsibilities of the legislature and requirement for legislative authorisation of spending and taxes are stipulated in the Constitution. National Public Finance Law stipulates the form and structure of the budget and the roles and responsibilities of the different parts of the executive and MTEF. |

| Budget coverage |
|---|
| The executive's budget proposal covers budgetary central government. |

| Budget cycle | |
|---|---|
| Budget circular | March |
| Pre-budget statement | n/a |
| Negotiations with line ministries | March-August |
| Executive budget proposal | 1 Sep. |
| Parliamentary vote on budget | 2 Dec. |
| *Start of financial year* | *1 Jan.* |
| In-year budget execution reports | Monthly |
| Mid-year implementation report | N.A. |
| *End of financial year* | *31 Dec.* |
| Year-end financial statement | 10 April |
| Audited financial report | 20 May |
| Parliamentary accounting | June |

**Korea's application of OECD budget principles "at a glance"**

| | | |
|---|---|---|
| 1. | Fiscal policy objectives | Medium-term fiscal plan sets out policy objectives (for the consolidated fiscal balance minus social security funds) is managed at a deficit of around 3.0% to GDP in 2018-22 medium-term fiscal periods. National debt target will be managed within early 40% to GDP in 2018-22 medium-term fiscal periods. |
| 2a. | Strategic alignment | MTEF set out the medium-term strategic plans and priorities of the government and CBA has a leadership role in promoting alignment between annual budgets and medium-term plans. |
| **2b.** | **MTEF** | **The 5 year MTEF is on a rolling basis framework and the ceilings are revised annually. The Ministry of Economy and Finance establishes guidelines for preparing MTEFs and holds a public hearing and open forum to hear opinions on MTEFs. MTEFs are approved by the Cabinet.** |
| 3. | Capital and infrastructure | Korea has an overall long-term strategic infrastructure plan that integrates both central and sub-national government. The Independent Infrastructure Commission is in charge of infrastructure governance. |
| 4. | Transparency and accessibility | Budget data is available in downloadable form. All core budget reports are publicly available. |
| 5a. | Parliamentary engagement | In case of an expenditure increase, executive consent is required. If the budget is not approved by the legislature before the start of the fiscal year, last year's budget takes effect on an interim basis. |
| **5b.** | **Inclusive public / civic debate** | **Participatory budgeting will be launched from 2019 in order to increase the public interest in the national budget and fiscal transparency. Citizens can suggest ideas for new projects and line ministries review the project and make them concrete in the form of a budget project. A representative group of citizens is organised to discuss and prioritise the participatory budget projects.** |
| 6. | Financial reporting and accounting | Financial statements are prepared on an accrual basis and the budget is prepared on a cash and/or commitment basis. |
| 7. | Budget execution | The use of a single treasury fund is mandatory for all revenues and expenditures of central government, except for special accounts that will be established by an Act when the country plans to operate a specific project or specialised fund for management. |
| 8a. | Performance budgeting | The Korean performance budgeting system has been focused on establishing a link between performance information and budget cuts, but recently its focus is shifting towards more performance improvement with more selective monitoring and evaluation. |
| 8b. | Evaluation and VFM | The programme evaluation process seeks to measure the relevance, efficiency, and effectiveness of a programme. The In-depth Evaluation of Budgetary Programme institutionalised the in-depth evaluation process as part of the performance budgeting system. Every year, an evaluation panel is created for each of the group of cross-cutting programmes selected for evaluation. Panel members mostly come from public research institutes and universities and since many stakeholders are involved in any given programme, the evaluation panel holds frequent meetings to collect inputs and feedback. The completed evaluation reports are considered by the central budget office, which decides whether to reflect these results in resource allocation changes or programme consolidation. Line ministries are required to report back with their follow-ups. |
| 9. | Fiscal risk and long-term sustainability | The Long-term fiscal outlook until 2060 was made for the first time in 2015 and MTEFs include fiscal risks analysis. |
| 10. | Quality assurance and audit | The board of audit and inspection of Korea is responsible for auditing of performance provided in year-end reports. |

*Note*: Rows in **bold** represent notable international practice.

# Budgetary Governance in Practice: Latvia

## *Economic context*

Economic growth in Latvia is projected to remain strong and broad-based. Exports are strengthening as prospects in EU countries and Russia are improving. Stronger exports and EU structural fund transfers are boosting investment. High wage growth will underpin household consumption. Unemployment is projected to fall only gradually due to skill and regional mismatches between workers and jobs. The current account deficit is projected to increase as strong domestic demand boosts imports.

## *Fiscal policy plans*

The fiscal policy strategy is based on a balanced budget during the economic cycle or general government structural budget deficit in the long term (MTO) shall not exceed 0.5% of GDP. It also entails the objective to achieve a sustainable economic breakthrough of the country - to provide a contribution through the fiscal policy measures for potential growth to increase from 3% to 5% of GDP by implementing tax reform measures. The fiscal objectives have been set to maintain the general government structural budget balance at -1.2% of GDP in 2018, -0.6% of GDP in 2019, and -0.4% of GDP in 2020.

A: Fiscal Balance and Public Debt

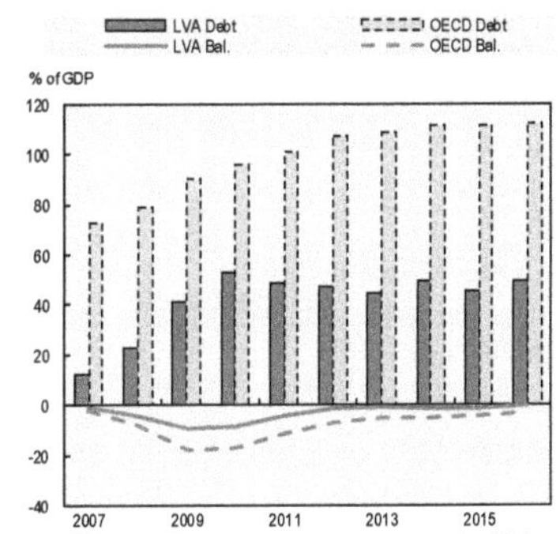


*Note*: The graph is referring to general government fiscal balance and general government gross debt as defined in the OECD National Accounts Statistics.

*Source:* OECD National Accounts Statistics (database); Eurostat Government finance statistics (database).

B: Fiscal Policy Plans

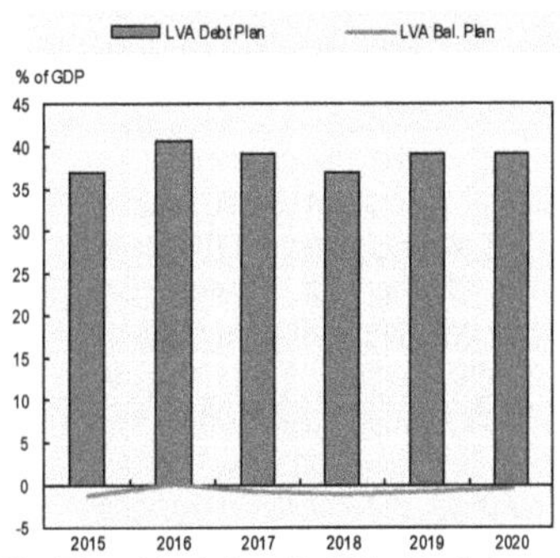


*Note*: The graph is referring to Fiscal Policy Plans that are implemented and/or officially announced as of November 2017 and as indicated by the country. Actual results in graph A may differ as the Fiscal Policy Plans are prepared by the country beforehand and as the Debt and Balance Plan reported by the country are based on the country's own definition;Data are referring to general government.

*Source:* 2018 OECD Fiscal Plans and Budgeting Framework Survey.

C: Public Investment

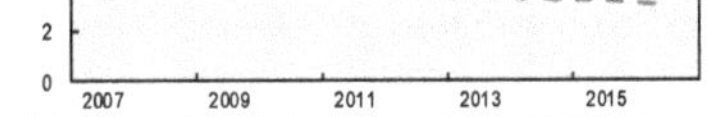


*Note:* The graph is referring to government investment as a percentage of GDP and as a share of total government expenditures.

*Source*: OECD National Accounts Statistics (database).

D: Expenditure by function (2016)

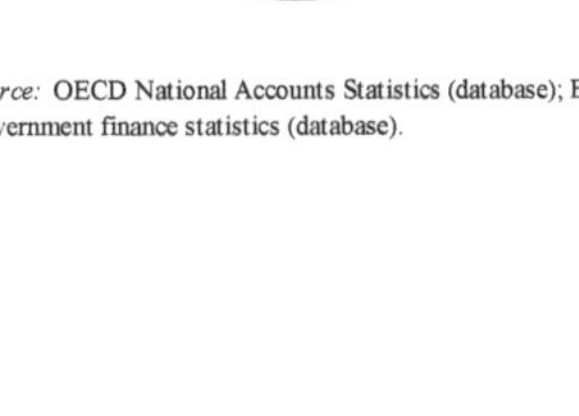


*Source:* OECD National Accounts Statistics (database); Eurostat Government finance statistics (database).

### *Developments in budgetary governance*

Latvia modernised its budgetary processes in advance of its membership of the euro area in 2014 and accession to the OECD in 2016, with a comprehensive range of reforms including fiscal rules, medium-term budgeting and an innovative approach to identifying and managing fiscal risk.

More recently, Latvia has focused on linking strategic planning documents with budgetary resources. The model of spending reviews introduced in 2016 aims to strengthen the resource re-allocation focus within the annual budgetary calendar: the spending reviews are given a statutory grounding in each spring semester, and lead to a dialogue with line ministries using available performance and evaluative indicators.

Latvia's strong tradition of open government is reflected in its approach to budget transparency which includes active budget communication, use of social media and data visualisation tools; as well as (since 2016) "scorecards" showing the link between resources and policy goals.

| Central Budget Authority |
|---|
| Ministry of Finance.<br><br>Weblink: www.fm.gov.lv |

| Legal Framework |
|---|
| The Constitution sets out basic requirements for parliamentary authorisation of the budget, based upon a proposal of the cabinet. The Law on Budget and Financial Management assigns the Minister for Finance the responsibility for bringing forward the annual package of budget bills, i.e. the Draft Medium Term Budget Framework Law and the Draft Annual State Budget Law. The Law on Fiscal Discipline (2013) provides for the implementation of EU fiscal rules, and includes provisions for taking account of fiscal risks. |

| Budget coverage |
|---|
| The executive's budget covers budgetary central government, i.e. the ministries and agencies. According to the conditions of the Law on Local government budgets and the Law on Budget and Financial Management, local governments approve their budgets. State institutions do not interfere in the process of local government budget drafting and execution. Main sources of revenues are personal income tax revenues, real estate tax (aprox. 64% in 2017) and other transfers including EU funds (aprox. 27% in 2017). |

| Budget cycle | |
|---|---|
| Pre-budget statement | end-April |
| Budget circular | mid-August |
| Negotiations with line ministries | September |
| Executive budget proposal | mid-October |
| Parliamentary vote on budget | December |
| *Start of financial year* | *1 January* |
| In-year budget execution reports | monthly |
| Mid-year implementation report | n/a |
| *End of financial year* | *31 December* |
| Year-end financial statement | July |
| Audited financial report | September |
| Parliamentary accounting | October |

**Latvia's application of OECD budget principles "at a glance"**

| | | |
|---|---|---|
| 1. | Fiscal policy objectives | The Law on Fiscal Discipline implements EU fiscal rules at the national level. This includes the medium-term objective of a balanced budget, debt limits and an expenditure growth rule. |
| 2a. | Strategic alignment | The Medium-Term Budget Framework Law (see below) takes account of national planning documents. There is no other particular mechanism for aligning political priorities and goals, decided by coalition partners in government, with medium-term resource allocation. |
| **2b.** | **MTEF** | **The annual Medium-Term Budget Framework Law provides for three-year rolling ceilings, which are compatible with the fiscal limits; the focus on the incoming year, and 'inheritance' of the other ceilings from year to year, are intended to give the framework a more binding character.** |
| 3. | Capital and infrastructure | n/a |
| 4. | Transparency and accessibility | High transparency: 6 of 7 core budget reports published (no mid-year report); 7 of 9 additional reports published (no pre-execution cash-flow profiles, no pre-election report). Citizen's guides are not presented, but transparency is helped via an interactive budget tool and data visualisation. |
| 5a. | Parliamentary engagement | The parliament (Saeima) has strong constitutional authority to decide the budget, and its approval is sought for the pre-budget fiscal position as well as the budget proposal. The practice of setting aside a contingency reserve within the budget proposal to respond to small allocation requests from deputies (so-called "deputy quotas") has been phased out, in order to promote more coherent and transparent approaches in resource allocation. |
| 5b. | Inclusive public / civic debate | No particular mechanisms for engaging with citizen or civil society groups or for involving marginalised groups within the budget cycle. |
| 6. | Financial reporting and accounting | Cash basis for both budgeting and budget execution, accrual basis for financial reporting and accounting. |
| 7. | Budget execution | The single treasury fund is used for all public expenditures and revenues, and execution is reported upon monthly. |
| 8a. | Performance budgeting | Well-developed system of performance information including "scorecards" making explicit the link between resources and policy goals. |
| **8b.** | **Evaluation and VFM** | **Spending reviews are now integrated within the resource-allocation considerations as part of the annual budget cycle.** |
| **9.** | **Fiscal risk and long-term sustainability** | **A Declaration of Fiscal Risks is annexed to the Medium-Term Budget Framework Law, based upon a fiscal risks register maintained by the Ministry of Finance in liaison with line ministries. A fiscal safety reserve (at least 0.1% of GDP) is calculated based upon the profile of risks.** |
| 10. | Quality assurance and audit | An independent Fiscal Discipline Council monitors compliance with the Fiscal Discipline Law, and gives an opinion on the adequacy of the fiscal safety reserve; and reports annually to the Saeima.<br>The State Audit Office is active in providing independent review not just of compliance and probity, and also but of the quality of the systems in place for planning, performance and budgetary governance more broadly. |

*Note*: Rows in **bold** represent notable international practice.

## Budgetary Governance in Practice: Luxembourg

### *Economic context*

Growth in Luxembourg is projected to strengthen significantly to 4% by 2019, boosted by dynamic domestic demand and growth in the domestic financial sector, which will foster exports. Wage growth, which is projected to pick up following automatic wage indexation at the beginning of the year, is a factor behind higher inflation. The unemployment rate is declining slowly, but, at around 6%, remains high, at least by Luxembourg standards.

### *Fiscal policy plans*

The government has limited the debt to GDP ratio below 30% of GDP and structural balance must not be below MTO. MTO was 0.5% in 2014 and 2015 and is now -0.5% of GDP.

**A: Fiscal Balance and Public Debt**

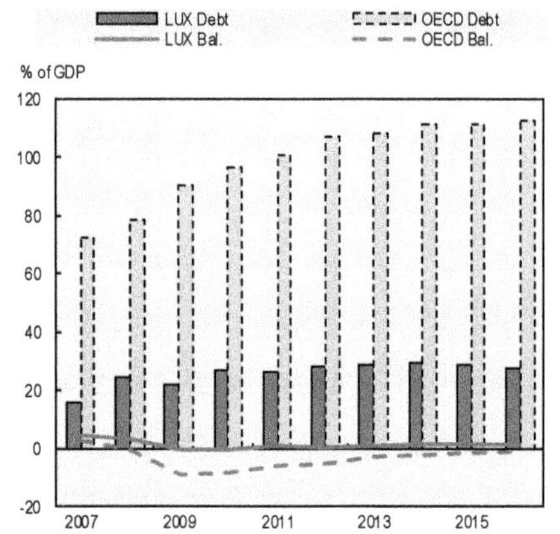


*Note*: The graph is referring to general government fiscal balance and general government gross debt as defined in the OECD National Accounts Statistics.

*Source:* OECD National Accounts Statistics (database); Eurostat Government finance statistics (database).

**B: Public Investment**

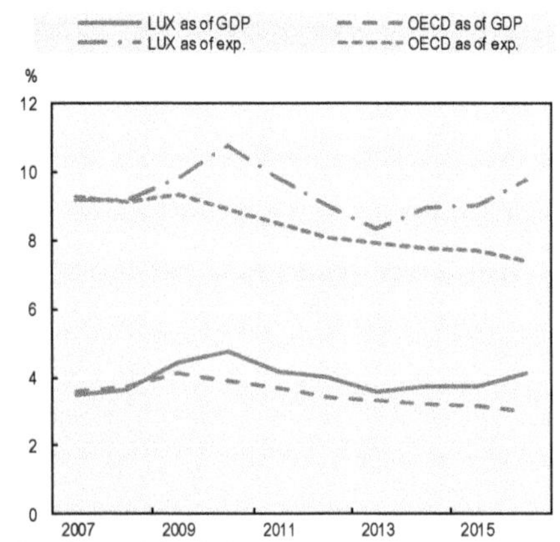


*Note:* The graph is referring to government investment as a percentage of GDP and as a share of total government expenditures.

*Source*: OECD National Accounts Statistics (database).

**C: Expenditure by function (2016)**

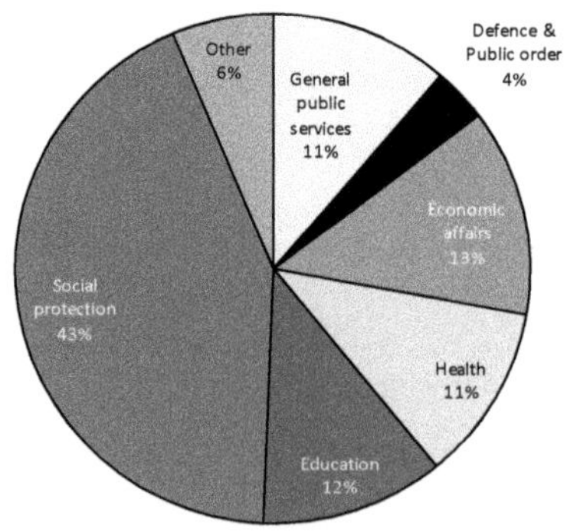


*Source:* OECD National Accounts Statistics (database); Eurostat Government finance statistics (database).

### *Developments in budgetary governance*

Recent developments in budgetary governance include the conduct of a comprehensive spending review in 2014, which generated significant savings through around 250 "savings measures" reported to Parliament.

Luxembourg also adopted new legislation in 2014 that established so-called multi-annual Laws for the programming of public finances *("Lois de programmation financière pluriannuelle*", or LPFP) and an independent fiscal council, the National Council of Public Finance ("*Conseil National des Finances Publiques*", or CNFP). Laws for the programming of public finances have profoundly modified the budgetary framework by setting multi-annual objectives in terms of nominal and structural deficits and public debts.

| Central Budget Authority |
|---|
| Finance Inspectorate (*Inspection Générale des Finances*, or IGF).<br><br>Weblink: https://igf.gouvernement.lu/en.html |

| Legal Framework |
|---|
| Five principles for budgeting are set in the Constitution. They are follows: annuality; unity; universality; non-earmarking; and specificity. |

| Budget coverage |
|---|
| Constitution (Basic Law) includes foundational The federal budget applies to the federal level of government. A National Stability Pact between the federal government and the highly-autonomous regions *(Länder)*, and associated Stability Council, manages multi-level fiscal co-ordination. |

| Budget cycle | |
|---|---|
| Budget circular to line ministries | April |
| Budget proposals by line ministries | Spring |
| Discussion of budget proposals by Finance Inspectorate and line ministries | June |
| Discussion by Government | Summer |
| Finalisation of budget proposal | September |
| Executive budget proposal | October |
| Parliamentary vote on budget | December |
| *Start of financial year* | *1 Jan.* |
| In-year budget execution reports | monthly |
| Mid-year implementation report | July |
| *End of financial year* | *31 Dec.* |
| Publication of year-end financial statements (*Loi portant règlement du compte général de l'exercice*) | July |
| Audited financial report | October |
| Parliamentary accounting | October |

| | Luxembourg's application of OECD budget principles "at a glance" | |
|---|---|---|
| 1. | Fiscal policy objectives | Political convention that the each new government sets out its fiscal policy objectives and targets at the start of its mandate. All governments have complied so far with the political convention of keeping public debt is expected to be below 30% of GDP. In addition, all governments comply with rules of the European Stability and Growth Pact (SGP), which requires a budget close to balance in the medium term and no deficit larger than 3% of GDP from year to year. |
| **2a.** | **Strategic alignment** | **The medium-term strategy is set out in three documents, the government programme, national development plan and the MTEF. The Finance Inspectorate insures alignment between these documents and the budget, which is also regularly discussed by the Cabinet.** |
| **2b.** | **MTEF** | **Indicative spending targets are set in multi-annual laws for the programming of public finances covering a four-year period. On this basis, ceilings for each ministry are defined internally, with which annual budget request are expected to be in line.** |
| 3. | Capital and infrastructure | The process for deciding upon capital and operating budget requests are distinct, but capital expenditure is provided for in the annual budget and in the multiannual financial programming law, under a separate chapter entitled "capital expenditure". |
| **4.** | **Transparency and accessibility** | **For all budget documents, official summaries are prepared for decision makers. Budget data is available in a downloadable form.** |
| 5a. | Parliamentary engagement | All budget documents prepared thorough the budget cycle are submitted to Parliament either for approval (e.g. the budget proposal) or for discussion (e.g. the long-term sustainability report). Budget documentation includes, among other information, comprehensive information on tax expenditures. Parliament has unrestricted powers to amend the budget. |
| 5b. | Inclusive public / civic debate | Luxembourg's professional chambers are required to provide a written opinion on the budget annually, which is around 100 pages long. |
| 6. | Budget accounting and financial reporting | The budget is prepared on a commitment (expenses and non-tax revenue) and cash (tax revenue) bases. The budget and financial report are established with a different coverage. The budget and year-end financial report cover the ministries and entities operating under their auspices. |
| **7.** | **Budget execution** | **Budget execution is monitored in monthly outturns prepared on commitment and cash bases. Limited flexibility exists (e.g. transfers between budget lines), hence very few supplementary budgets. A treasury single account is operated by the Treasury.** |
| 8a. | Performance budgeting | Luxembourg does not implement performance budgeting. |
| 8b. | Evaluation and VFM | Realisation of a comprehensive spending review in 2014, which generated significant savings thorough around 250 "savings measures" reported to Parliament. |
| 9. | Fiscal risk and long-term sustainability | Sustainability of public finances is assessed as part of the European Commission's Aging Report to the preparation of which Luxembourg's Social Security contributes. Fiscal risks are monitored by the Finance Inspectorate and independent fiscal institution. |
| 10. | Quality assurance and audit | The Court of Accounts reviews the internal control systems and performs compliance controls on a sample of revenue and expenditure operations. The CNFP assesses the public finances of Luxembourg (see new developments for more details). |

*Note*: Rows in **bold** represent notable international practice.

# Budgetary Governance in Practice: Mexico

## *Economic context*

Growth in Mexico remains above 2% despite an uncertain environment, fiscal consolidation and tighter monetary conditions. The economy will rebalance, with a higher contribution of exports and investment to growth while private consumption will be moderate. Construction activity will pick up from its historically low levels, reflecting reconstruction after the September 2018 earthquakes. Recent structural reforms and successful tenders in the energy sector are expected to boost private investment.

## *Fiscal policy plans*

In 2014 Mexico committed to undertake a fiscal consolidation path which included a pledge not to raise taxes or increase its debt. The time frame was stipulated in the 2014 plan and was updated for the 2017 fiscal year. The budget goal for 2017 was updated from a budgetary balance to a surplus goal of 0.1% of the GDP, and for 2018 onwards it is expected to have a budgetary balance. Regarding the Public Sector Borrowing Requirement (PSBR), the PSBR goal for 2017 was updated from 3.0% of GDP to 2.9% of GDP, and for 2018 onwards considered a 2.5% of GDP.

**A: Fiscal Balance and Public Debt**

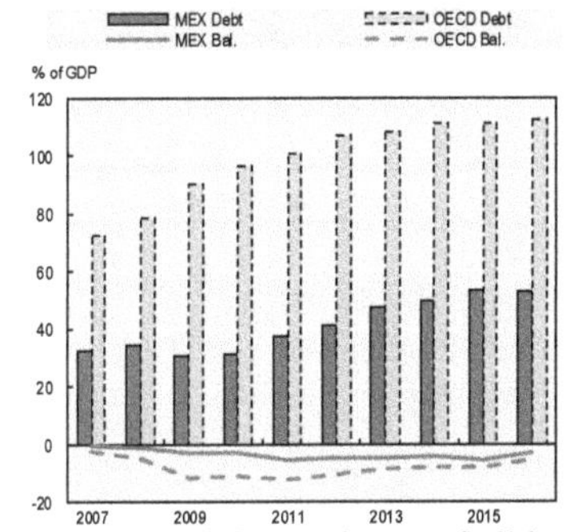


*Note*: The graph is referring to general government fiscal balance and general government gross debt as defined in the OECD National Accounts Statistics.

*Source:* OECD National Accounts Statistics (database); Eurostat Government finance statistics (database).

**B: Fiscal Policy Plans**

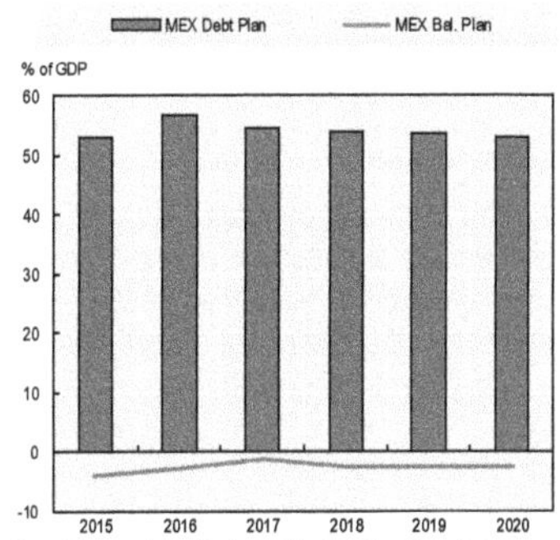


*Note:* The graph is referring to Fiscal Policy Plans that are implemented and/or officially announced as of November 2017 and as indicated by the country. Actual results in graph A may differ as the Fiscal Policy Plans are prepared by the country beforehand and as the Debt and Balance Plan reported by the country are based on the country's own definition;Data are referring to central/federal government.

*Source:* 2018 OECD Fiscal Plans and Budgeting Framework Survey.

**C: Public Investment**

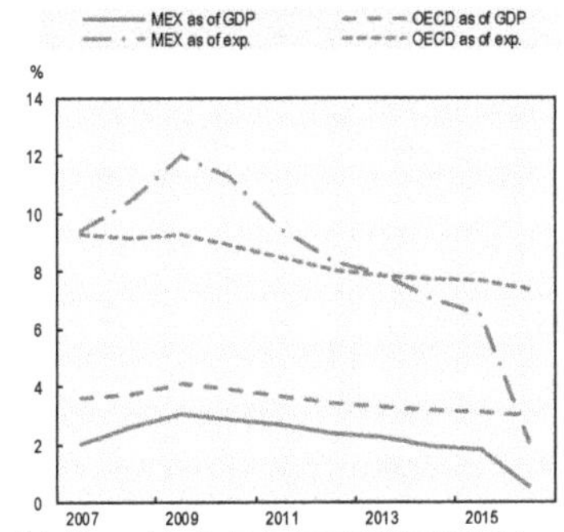


*Note:* The graph is referring to government investment as a percentage of GDP and as a share of total government expenditures.

*Source*: OECD National Accounts Statistics (database).

### *Developments in budgetary governance*

In 2013, the Federal Government proposed a transitory stimulus to support the economy and the implementation of the structural reform agenda. Since then, Mexico has committed to multi-year fiscal consolidation path that considers reaching a budget balance and public sector borrowing requirements of 2.5% of GDP for 2018.

The Budget and Public Accounts Committee of the Chamber of Deputies holds hearings on the expenditure budget and hears evidence from representatives from the Ministry of Finance. It also plays a co-ordinating role with sectoral committees submitting their proposals for amendments to be voted on by the Budget Committee before the Budget Committee votes to submit the whole budget to the plenary for approval. Legislative deliberations on the budget are open to the public and the media.

Performance information is used as a tool of performance management and accountability, rather than primarily as a tool of resource allocation. Programme design, management and accountability are often included as elements in the scope of evaluation. Not having a formal mechanism to consider evaluation findings in the resource allocation process is a key limitation for using evaluation evidence in the budget.

| Central Budget Authority |
|---|
| Ministry of Finance/Economy<br><br>Weblink: www.finmin.nic.in/bipa/mexico |

| Legal Framework |
|---|
| The Constitution lays out the form and structure of the annual budget, as well as the roles and responsibilities of the Legislature and the Executive in the budget process. Other aspects of budgeting are covered in the Federal Budget and Fiscal Responsibility Law (2006), and its regulatory decree (2006).<br><br>Other relevant legislation includes the Law for Fiscal Co-ordination (1978) which sets out rules to transfer resources to subnational governments, the Public Debt Law (1976) and the Audit and Accountability Law (2009). |

| Budget coverage |
|---|
| The federal budget applies to the federal level of government, including ministries, public agencies, social security funds, and state owned enterprises (SOEs). Fiscal relations across levels of government are managed by the Law for Fiscal Coordination (1978). |

| Budget cycle | |
|---|---|
| Budget circular | July |
| Pre-budget fiscal policy statement | September |
| Negotiations with line ministries | July/August |
| Executive budget proposal | September [24] |
| Parliamentary vote on budget | November |
| *Start of financial year* | *1 Jan.* |
| In-year budget execution reports | Monthly |
| Mid-year implementation report | September |
| *End of financial year* | *31 Dec.* |
| Year-end financial statement | April *(year+1)* |
| Audited financial report | June, October *(year+1)*, February *(year+2)* |
| Parliamentary accounting | October |

[24] Some of these dates change due to the electoral cycle

| Mexico's application of OECD budget principles "at a glance" | | |
|---|---|---|
| 1. | Fiscal policy objectives | Budget balance, debt, expenditure and revenue fiscal rules defined by law |
| 2a. | Strategic alignment | National Development Plan sets out medium-term strategic priorities of the government; The CBA has a leadership role in promoting alignment between annual budgets and medium-term plans/priorities. |
| 2b. | MTEF | No MTEF |
| 3. | Capital and infrastructure | Capital and current expenditure requests are submitted and approved in an integrated way. There is an overall long-term strategic infrastructure plan as well as sectoral infrastructure plans. There are formal processes for ensuring absolute and relative value for money. |
| **4.** | **Transparency and accessibility** | **All core budget reports and most ancillary reports are produced and made public; some impact assessments showing incidence of budget for individual measures; budget data is available in downloadable form; online data portal from the CBA that allows user-defined dynamic queries; budget citizen's guides available at different moments of the budget cycle, including Executive Budget Proposal, Approved Budget, Quarterly Reports and Year-End Report.** |
| 5a. | Parliamentary engagement | Congress has unrestricted powers to amend the budget. The vote on the Executive's budget proposal generally is considered a vote of confidence in the government. Expenditure without legislative approval is not allowed.<br><br>The *Centro de Estudios de las Finanzas Públicas* (CEFP) was established in 1998. In addition to the support provided by the CEFP, the Budget Committee also has its own staff to assist it, although they typically do not have the same level of technical expertise. |
| **5b.** | **Inclusive public / civic debate** | **Strong engagement of policy stakeholders in the budget cycle. Line ministries include consultative mechanisms in policy development; participatory budgeting in place.** |
| 6. | Budget accounting and financial reporting | The budgetary public revenues and expenditures statements are prepared on both accrual and cash basis. The Central Public Sector maintains coverage of all main reports on public finances. |
| 7. | Budget execution | Single treasury fund that is centrally controlled and the use of it is mandatory for all revenues and expenditures of the central government; Line ministers receive a lump -sum but with sub-limits. They can re-allocate funds within their own budget envelope but they need approval from the CBA in all cases.<br><br>Supplementary budgets do not require advance parliamentary approval.<br>Carry overs are not permitted |
| 8a. | Performance budgeting | Performance information is used as a tool of performance management and accountability, rather than primarily as a tool of resource allocation. |
| 8b. | Evaluation and VFM | Monitoring and evaluation within line ministries;<br>Comprehensive and sectoral reviews have been performed. However, they are not carried out every year. |
| **9.** | **Fiscal risk and long-term sustainability** | **Long-term fiscal risk projections are produced by the CBA every year; linkages to budgetary or fiscal policy of the government where they serve as the basis to formulate the multi-year fiscal consolidation path.**<br>**The Ministry of Finance manages and identifies fiscal risks while a different unit of the ministry attend to each type. There is a framework on fiscal risk identification and management. There are centrally defined criteria to decide which fiscal risk needs to be measured and monitored.**<br><br>**Public report prepared by CBA** |
| 10. | Quality assurance and audit | Constitutionally-independent Supreme Audit Institution (*Auditoria Superior de la Federacion*) that preforms compliance control, audit of government financial reports, quality control and audit over performance information. There is no Independent Financial Institution. |

*Note*: Rows in **bold** represent notable international practice.

## Budgeting Governance in Practice: The Netherlands

### *Economic context*

GDP growth in the Netherlands is projected to remain strong and broad-based in 2018 and 2019. Private consumption growth will peak in 2018, reflecting a strong labour market and a looser fiscal stance, before moderating in 2019. Growth in business investment should be vibrant, driven by improved economic sentiment and solid external demand. Wage growth and inflation are projected to rise gradually. The current account surplus is set to ease gradually but remain at a high level.

### *Fiscal policy plans*

The government follows a trend-based fiscal policy within the boundaries of European budgetary agreements, which are incorporated in Dutch law. The Dutch national budgetary framework includes a multi annual real expenditure ceiling, which is set at the start of the government period for at least as long as the government period (4 years). Macroeconomic stabilisation of the economy is supported via revenues and control of the total tax burden for citizens and businesses, using a revenue ceiling based on the policy-related increase in the tax burden.

A: Fiscal Balance and Public Debt

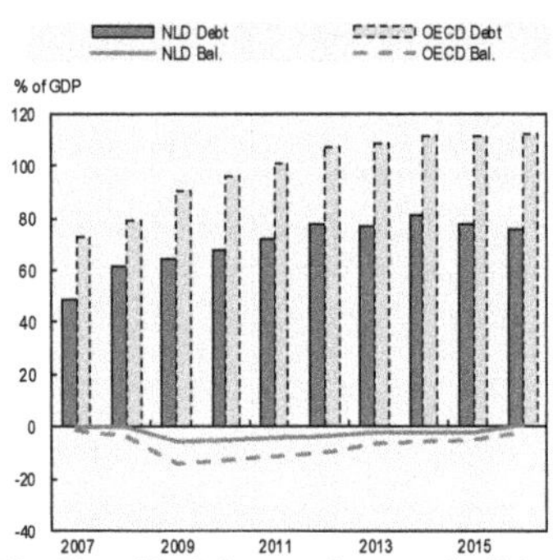


*Note*: The graph is referring to general government fiscal balance and general government gross debt as defined in the OECD National Accounts Statistics.

*Source:* OECD National Accounts Statistics (database); Eurostat Government finance statistics (database).

B: Fiscal Policy Plans

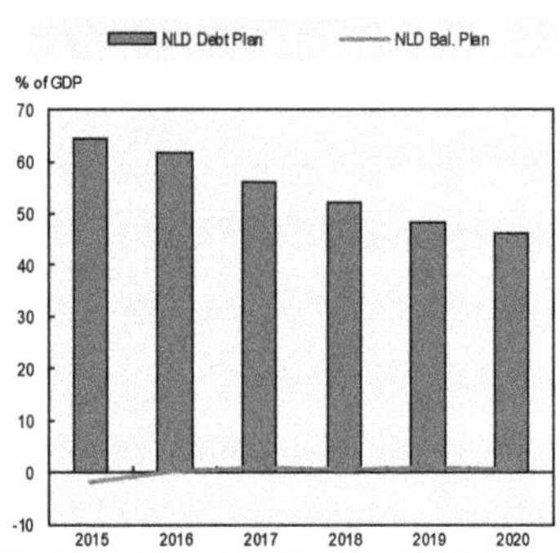


*Note*: The graph is referring to Fiscal Policy Plans that are implemented and/or officially announced as of November 2017 and as indicated by the country. Actual results in graph A may differ as the Fiscal Policy Plans are prepared by the country beforehand and as the Debt and Balance Plan reported by the country are based on the country's own definition.

*Source:* 2018 OECD Fiscal Plans and Budgeting Framework Survey.

C: Public Investment

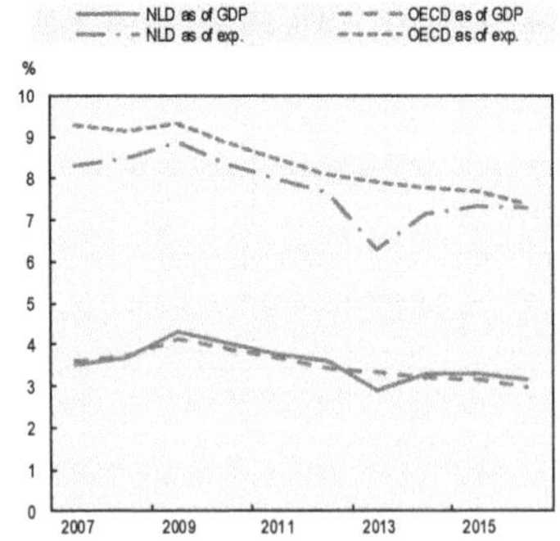


*Note:* The graph is referring to government investment as a percentage of GDP and as a share of total government expenditures.

*Source*: OECD National Accounts Statistics (database).

D: Expenditure by function (2016)

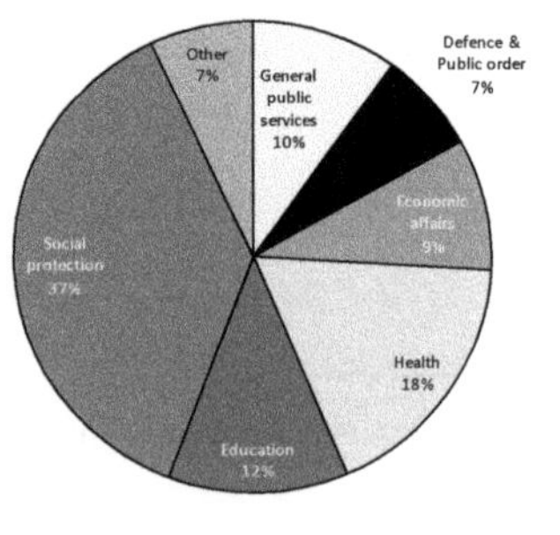


*Source:* OECD National Accounts Statistics (database); Eurostat Government finance statistics (database).

### *Developments in budgetary governance*

The Dutch budgeting system is designed to support the government in achieving its medium-term goals, and includes many elements of good practice across the various dimensions of budgetary governance. The medium-term expenditure framework is seen as an essential tool for implementing political priorities, and performance budgeting has been refined over the years into an advanced model with heterogeneous indicators and feedback connections to policy-making.

Transparency is high and the budget includes useful distributional analyses. Parliamentary engagement is strong. There are no particular mechanisms to foster public or civil society engagement in budgeting, and gender budgeting is not in place.

| Central Budget Authority |
|---|
| Ministry of Finance<br><br>Weblink: www.government.nl/ministries/ministry-of-finance |

| Budget coverage |
|---|
| The executive's budget covers central government. The local government level operates in a largely autonomous manner, but local tax-raising powers are limited and so this level is financed mainly from central government using a formula-based approach. |

| Legal Framework |
|---|
| The Dutch Constitution specifies that the budget is to be determined by law. The Law on Sustainable Government Finances (2013) applies EU fiscal rules within Dutch national law. |

| Budget cycle | |
|---|---|
| Budget circular | n/a[25] |
| Pre-budget statement | mid-March |
| Negotiations with line ministries | April-May |
| Executive budget proposal | mid-September |
| Parliamentary vote on budget | late December |
| *Start of financial year* | *1 January* |
| In-year budget execution reports | monthly |
| Mid-year implementation report | early June |
| *End of financial year* | *31 December* |
| Year-end financial statement | May |
| Audited financial report | May |
| Parliamentary accounting | May |

[25] The ministry spending ceilings, which typically feature in a budget circular, are in the Netherlands' case communicated at the start of each government's term of office

| | | The Netherlands' application of OECD budget principles "at a glance" |
|---|---|---|
| 1. | Fiscal policy objectives | EU fiscal rules are reflected in Dutch law. These rules are applied in a top-down manner to management of expenditures and revenues. At the start of each government term, a ministry-wide 'budget commission' advises on technical refinements to the rules and on the fiscal goal(s). |
| 2a. | Strategic alignment | Budgeting is strongly aligned with political processes and reflected in the Coalition Agreement. Performance budgeting indicators are aligned with government goals. |
| **2b.** | **MTEF** | **The multi-year real expenditure ceilings are fixed at the outset of each government and reflected in the Coalition Agreement. These ceilings are fixed, and do not change in response to revenue fluctuations, in order to provide a solid basis for budgetary management and policy planning.** |
| 3. | Capital and infrastructure | Capital management is handled via the line ministries, and project prioritisation is strongly linked to sectoral and national plans and to results of cost-benefit analysis. Central unit and departmental units in place for public-private partnerships. |
| 4. | Transparency and accessibility | High transparency with extensive budget reporting. Citizen's guides are not produced but information is summarised online and open data is used systematically. The budget includes distributional analyses based on household income, income inequality, and wellbeing. |
| 5a. | Parliamentary engagement | Strong parliamentary engagement in the annual budget process. The budget must, by law, be presented to parliament on the third Tuesday of September and the parliament has three months to consider and approve the various appropriation bills. The Finance Committee of the lower house considers fiscal aggregates and the sectoral committees of both houses consider the spending bills. Budget scrutiny is supported by a small Parliamentary Bureau for Research and Public Expenditure (the BOR). |
| 5b. | Inclusive public / civic debate | No particular mechanisms for engagement of civil society bodies and citizens directly in the budgetary process. |
| 6. | Financial reporting and accounting | Both cash and accruals methodologies are used, in both budgeting and appropriations. |
| 7. | Budget execution | Execution is closely monitored by each ministry's financial department, and communicated monthly to the Ministry of Finance. These monthly execution reports are not made public, but a report on budget execution is included in the budget-related memoranda (Spring and Autumn) submitted to parliament. |
| **8a.** | **Performance budgeting** | **Streamlined approach to performance budgeting, with different types of indicator selected in different sectors based on degree of government control.** |
| **8b.** | **Evaluation and VFM** | **Well-established system of line ministry evaluations and Ministry of Finance-led programme reviews ("spending reviews"), with independent chairing and "no-veto" rule to promote fresh thinking** |
| 9. | Fiscal risk and long-term sustainability | Good reporting on fiscal risk and long-term fiscal sustainability: the Ministry of Finance reports on its fiscal risk assessment; the CPB (see below) reports regularly on fiscal risks; a range of *ad hoc* commissions and agencies are tasked with identifying ad managing fiscal risks; and controls are in place regarding the incurring of contingent liabilities. |
| 10. | Quality assurance and audit | The CPB (Bureau for Economic Policy Analysis), established in 1945, is a functionally independent expert body that prepares official economic forecasts and prepares analyses on a variety of subjects. It also has a distinctive role in pre-election costing of political party commitments. More recently the Council of State *(Raad van State)* has been assigned functions of independent budgetary oversight, in compliance with EU requirements.<br>The Dutch Court of Audit is constitutionally established and *inter alia* plays an active role in performance audit. |

*Note*: Rows in **bold** represent notable international practice.

## Budgetary Governance in Practice: New Zealand

### *Economic context*

Economic growth in New Zealand should increase from 2.8% in the June quarter 2018 to a peak of 3.6% in the December 2019 quarter, as private consumption growth remains solid, increased government spending bolsters the economy, and both residential and business investment pick up. Growth is expected to slow to 2.5% by June 2022 as net migration inflows ease, and interest rates rise. Inflation is projected to remain relatively subdued at 1.4% in 2019.

### *Fiscal policy plans*

The government's Budget Responsibility Rules form the basis of its fiscal strategy. They are to deliver a sustainable operating surplus across an economic cycle, reduce the level of net core Crown debt to 20 per cent of GDP within five years of taking office in 2017, prioritise investments to address the long-term financial and sustainability challenges facing New Zealand, take a prudent approach to ensure expenditure is phased, controlled and directed to maximise its benefits to maintain expenditure to within the recent historical range of spending to GDP, and ensure a progressive taxation system that is fair, balanced and promotes the long-term sustainability and productivity of the economy. Gross debt is forecast to be 25.2% of GDP in 2021/22. Net core Crown debt (excluding NZS Fund and advances) is forecast to decline from 21.7% in 2016/17 to 19.1% in 2021/22.

**A: Fiscal Balance and Public Debt**

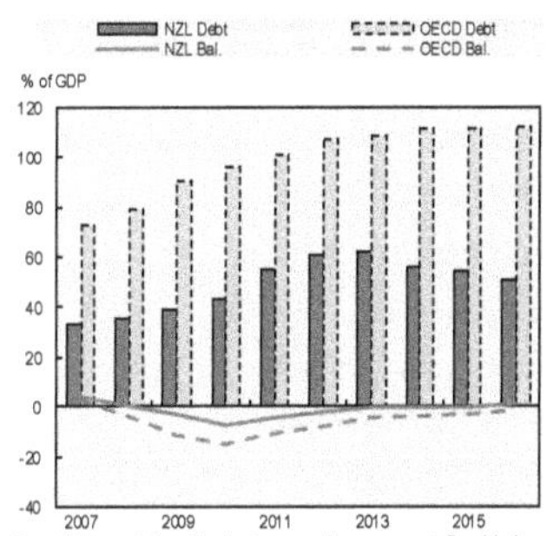


*Note*: The graph is referring to general government fiscal balance and general government gross debt as defined in the OECD National Accounts Statistics.

*Source:* OECD National Accounts Statistics (database); Eurostat Government finance statistics (database).

**B: Fiscal Policy Plans**

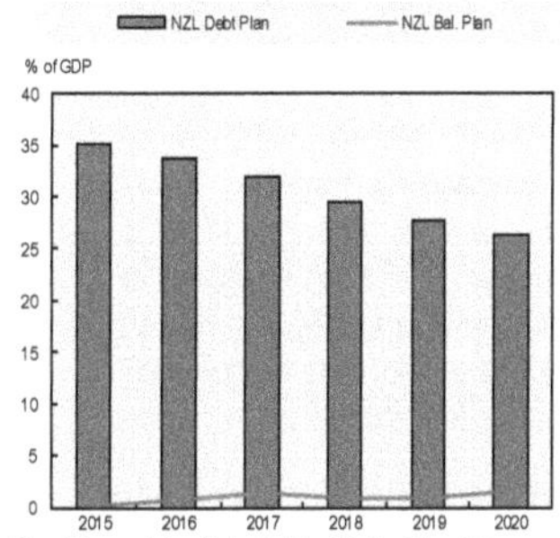


*Note*: The graph is referring to Fiscal Policy Plans that are implemented and/or officially announced as of November 2017 and as indicated by the country. Actual results in graph A may differ as the Fiscal Policy Plans are prepared by the country beforehand and as the Debt and Balance Plan reported by the country are based on the country's own definition.

*Source:* 2018 OECD Fiscal Plans and Budgeting Framework Survey.

**C: Public Investment**

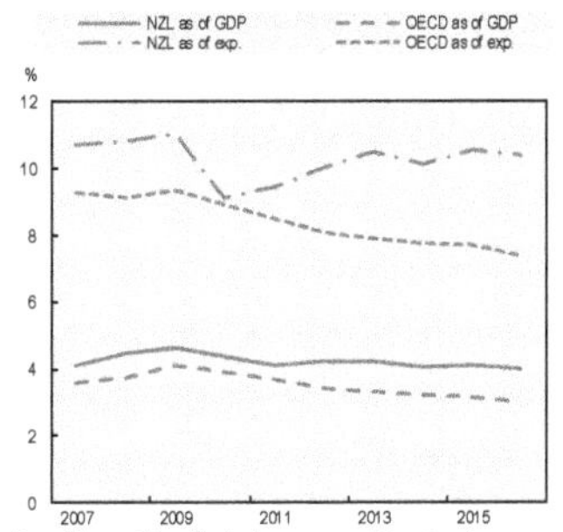


*Note:* The graph is referring to government investment as a percentage of GDP and as a share of total government expenditures.

*Source*: OECD National Accounts Statistics (database).

### *Developments in budgetary governance*

The Treasury is working to implement a Wellbeing Budget in 2019 that will broaden the Budget's focus beyond economic and fiscal policy by using the Treasury's Living Standards Framework to inform the Government's investment priorities and funding decisions. The Government is intending tp measure and report against a broader set of indicators to show a more rounded measure of success, as a country and as a Government. This will be supported by Budget processes that facilitate evidence-based decisions and deliver the Government's objectives in a cost-effective way.

New Zealand has for 25 years used the full suite of accrual accounting measures in its forecasts and budgetary decision-making.

In 2014, the New Zealand public sector moved from accounting standards based on IFRS to accounting standards based on IPSAS. Both forecast financial statements reported in the budget, and audited consolidated financial statements comply with these standards.

**Central Budget Authority**

The Treasury is the Central Budget Authority, covering both economic and financial policy functions. In preparing and communicating budget proposals the Treasury co-ordinates closely with Cabinet Ministers who have ultimate responsibility for determining overall budget parameters and ceilings for line ministries.

Weblink: www.treasury.govt.nz/

**Legal Framework**

The Public Finance Act 1989 provides the legal framework for the financial management system of the Government. The Act was substantially amended in 2004 and 2013. The budget process is detailed further in Treasury Instructions. Parliament's authority and role in relation to the budget is set out in the Constitution Act, and in parliamentary standing orders that have the force of law.

**Budget coverage**

New Zealand is a unitary state, and the national budget is comprehensive in coverage. Financial disclosure rules do not permit any off-budget expenditures.

| Budget cycle | |
|---|---|
| Pre-budget fiscal policy statement | December |
| Budget circular | December |
| Negotiations with line ministries | February |
| Executive budget proposal | May |
| Parliamentary vote on budget | August[26] |
| *Start of financial year* | *1 July.* |
| In-year budget execution reports | monthly |
| Parliamentary vote on budget | May |
| Mid-year implementation report | December |
| *End of financial year* | *30 June.* |
| Year-end financial statement | October |
| Audited financial report | October |
| Parliamentary accounting | October |

[26] The Finance Bill which deals with tax policy is enacted by end-December.

**New Zealand's application of OECD budget principles "at a glance"**

| | | |
|---|---|---|
| 1. | Fiscal policy objectives | Government is legally required to set out, in a public document, its medium term fiscal objectives. These include goals in respect of debt, operating balance, expenditure to GDP ratio, Tax to GDP ratio and government net worth. |
| **2a.** | **Strategic alignment** | **The budget is closely linked to the policy programme of the governing coalition. Budget inititiatives are assessed against the government policy priorities.** |
| 2b. | MTEF | Four-year MTEF, ceiling sets at ministry/agency level, adjusted on an annual rolling basis. The MTEF is fully integrated into the budget process and presented to the parliament as part of the budget package. |
| **3.** | **Capital and infrastructure** | **New capital expenditure is included in the budget spread over four fiscal years. Line agency budget proposals Integrate both operating and capital components.**<br>**Capital initiatives are evaluated competitively to determine which projects and initiatives should be included in the Budget package.** |
| 4. | Transparency and accessibility | New Zealand is a leader in the area of budget transparency and provides extensive budget information to citizens and the parliament. All major budget reports are publicly available in a downloadable format and the government publishes a citizens' guide to the budget. |
| 5a. | Parliamentary engagement | Parliamentary scrutiny of the Budget is undertaken through a clear, structured engagement on both the ex-ante expecations and the ex-post results is overseen by the Finance and Expenditure Committee of the House of Representatives.<br>Parliament has very limited power to amend executive budget proposals.<br>New Zealand does not have an independent fiscal institution. |
| 5b. | Inclusive public / civic debate | New Zealand does not have processes for direct public participation in the budget process. |
| **6.** | **Budget accounting and financial reporting** | **Budget is prepared on both cash and accrual bases; appropriation is accrual based; budget is comprehensive in coverage; forecasts and accounts are prepared on a whole of government accounting basis.** |
| 7. | Budget execution | Budget execution is controlled through a single treasury account that is used for all receipts and expenditures.<br>A separate imprest supply law is used to authorise spending in advance of parliamentary approval of the annual budget and to authorise new or reallocated spending in advance of the supplementary budget. |
| **8a.** | **Performance budgeting** | **Direct performance budgeting information is disclosed, making explicit links between budget allocations and the achievement of outputs or performance goals. Annual performance reporting includes reporting on progress towards achievement of strategic objectives and performance targets.** |
| 8b. | Evaluation and VFM | Line ministries take the lead on *ex ante* and *ex post, ex post* evaluation. Performance audits are carried out by the SAI. A Performance Improvement Framework and an Investor Credit Rating process are used to assess line ministries. Spending reviews regular but *ad hoc* with past reviews driven by Ministerial focus on deficit reduction and efficiency improvement. |
| 9. | Fiscal risk and long-term sustainability | The Treasury must produce long term fiscal projections over a 40-year period at least each four years. As part of the annual budget process, the government publishes a fiscal strategy that sets out its short term intentions and long term (10 year) objectives. Each economic and fiscal update provides information on risks to the outlook, alternative scenarios, fiscal sensitivities and specific fiscal risk information. |
| 10. | Quality assurance and audit | There is no independent fiscal institution.<br>The Auditor-General, a constitutionally independent SAI, audits all public entities either directly or using private sector audit firms. Audits cover both financial and performance statements. Reports also address cross-agency performance and outcomes, rather than just focusing on individual public entities. |

*Note*: Rows in **bold** represent notable international practice.

## Budgetary Governance in Practice: Norway

### *Economic context*

Output growth in the mainland economy in Norway is projected to be sustained by the expansion of private consumption and investment. Employment growth will further reduce the unemployment rate and consumer price inflation will gradually increase as the upturn in economic activity proceeds.

### *Fiscal policy plans*

The government is gradually phasing the revenues from the petroleum sector into the mainland economy. The petroleum revenues are transferred to a sovereign wealth fund. The expected real return from the investments made by the fund is spent over the budget. This means that over time the structural non-oil deficit in the central government budget shall be approximately in line with the fund's expected real return. Significant emphasis is placed on evening out economic fluctuations to contribute to sound capacity utilisation and low unemployment. The real return is estimated to be 3% of the value of the fund at the beginning of the fiscal year.

**A: Fiscal Balance and Public Debt**

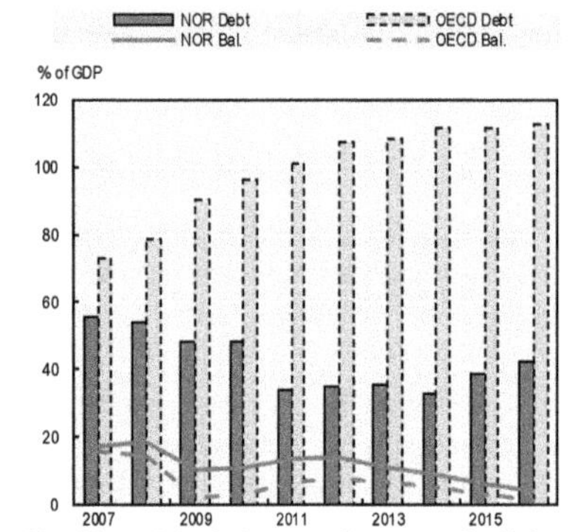


*Note*: The graph is referring to general government fiscal balance and general government gross debt as defined in the OECD National Accounts Statistics.
*Source:* OECD National Accounts Statistics (database); Eurostat Government finance statistics (database).

**C: Public Investment**

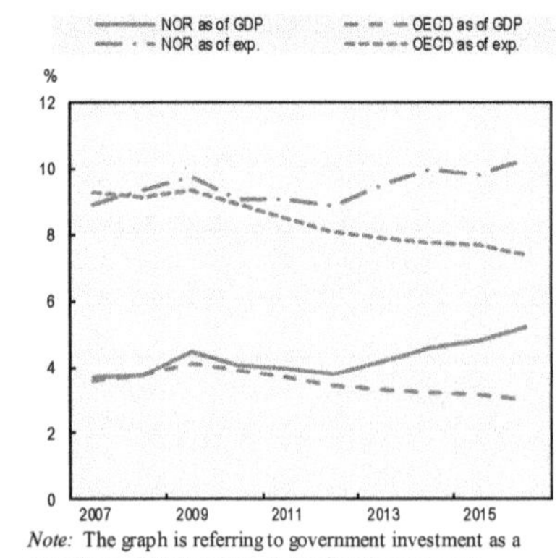


*Note:* The graph is referring to government investment as a percentage of GDP and as a share of total government expenditures.
*Source*: OECD National Accounts Statistics (database).

**D: Expenditure by function (2016)**

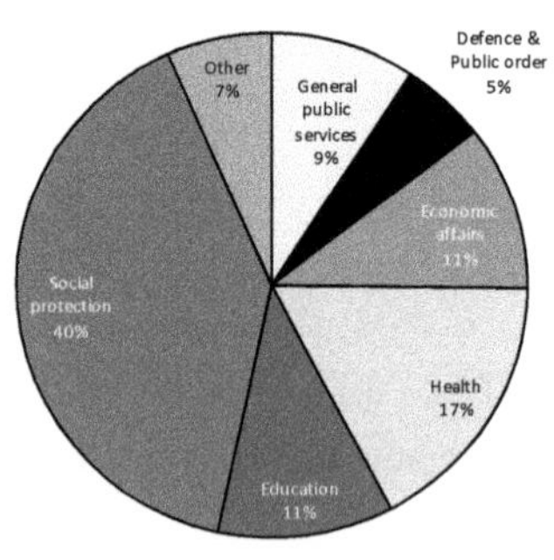


*Source:* OECD National Accounts Statistics (database); Eurostat Government finance statistics (database).

### *Developments in budgetary governance*

A resource-rich country, Norway focuses on disciplined management of the underlying budget while avoiding over-dependency on the country's oil wealth, which is stewarded via the Government Pension Fund Global (or oil fund), the largest sovereign wealth fund in the world with a value of over $1 trillion (as of May 2018). In recent years, the estimated rate of return from the oil fund – a figure which influences the permitted level of the public deficit – has been reduced from 4% to a more prudent 3% p.a.

Generally speaking, Norway has not followed international budgeting innovations, such as medium-term expenditure frameworks; although it has recently moved to introduce Public-Private Partnerships (PPPs) as a mode of infrastructure delivery. However, the project financing over the fiscal budget is designed to be largely independent of whether a particular project is organised as PPP or as traditional public procurement.

The process of developing the Fiscal Budget is structured and progressive, although not formally "semesterised". The parliament has a strong role in the budget approval process; however, parliamentary scrutiny of the audit report is delayed, by international standards.

**Central Budget Authority**

Ministry of Finance.

Weblink: www.regjeringen.no/en/dep/fin/id216/

**Legal Framework**

The Constitution of 1814 assigns authority to the parliament (*Storting*) for tax and expenditure matters. The annual budget procedure is based upon law adopted by the parliament; and in turn, administrative rules are in place within the framework of the legislation. The Government Pension Fund Act 2005 governs the administration and use of the oil fund.

**Budget coverage**

The executive's budget covers budgetary central government, i.e. government ministries and agencies. At sub-national level (municipalities and counties), there is a degree of tax-raising autonomy for locally-delivered services, but there is an over-arching requirement of budgetary balance.

**Budget cycle**

| | |
|---|---|
| Budget circular | December |
| Pre-budget statement | n/a |
| Negotiations with line ministries | spring |
| Executive budget proposal | early October |
| *Start of financial year* | *1 January* |
| In-year budget execution reports | monthly |
| Mid-year implementation report | mid-May |
| *End of financial year* | *31 December* |
| Year-end financial statement | April |
| Audited financial report | autumn |
| Parliamentary accounting | *in following year* |

**Norway's application of OECD budget principles "at a glance"**

| | | |
|---|---|---|
| **1.** | **Fiscal policy objectives** | **Budgetary drawdowns from the oil fund should over time reflect its expected real rate of return (recently reduced to 3% p.a.), and this rate in turn sets the allowable structural non-oil budget deficit.** |
| 2a. | Strategic alignment | No specific measures in place to promote alignment of budgets and national or sectoral plans other than two plenary discussions in the cabinet over the annual fiscal budget. |
| 2b. | MTEF | No MTEF in place |
| 3. | Capital and infrastructure | Capital budgeting is integrated within the main budget. Recent moves to introduce PPP modality into infrastructure provision. |
| 4. | Transparency and accessibility | Good budget transparency with 6 of 7 core budget reports in place (no pre-budget fiscal policy statement) and 7 of 9 additional budget reports. Systematic use of open data and a citizen's guide for the draft budget is available. |
| 5a. | Parliamentary engagement | Strong role for the parliament (*Storting*) in budgetary approval, with engagement of Standing Committee on Finance and Economic Affairs as well as other sectoral committees. No specific *ex ante* role in budgeting, and parliamentary scrutiny of the annual audit report does not take place until 1.3 years after the budget year. |
| 5b. | Inclusive public / civic debate | No particular measures in place for engaging civil society organisations or citizens directly within the budgetary process. |
| 6. | Financial reporting and accounting | Cash-based budgeting and reporting. The year-end report present the following statements: cash or commitment basis budget or appropriation outturn, balance sheet, income statement, statement of changes in net assets, budget execution statement and disclosures |
| 7. | Budget execution | All revenues and expenditures are managed via the single treasury fund. Carryovers are allowed for non-mandatory spending and within certain limits (5% of operational spending is transferable, investment appropriations may be transferred in total for two years) |
| 8a. | Performance budgeting | Performance budgeting for presentational and managerial purposes in place. |
| 8b. | Evaluation and VFM | Spending reviews and evaluations are used to inform the budget process each year. |
| 9. | Fiscal risk and long-term sustainability | Fiscal risks and long-term sustainability are discussed in annual national budgets. A long-term perspective report (white paper) is presented every four years discussing future challenges and options in the economy and the government's strategy for meeting them. |
| 10. | Quality assurance and audit | The Office of the Auditor General is established under the constitution.<br>There is no independent fiscal institution in place. |

*Note*: Rows in **bold** represent notable international practice.

# Budgetary Governance in Practice: Poland

## *Economic context*

GDP in Poland is estimated to have grown by 5.1% in 2018 but is projected to slow somewhat in 2019. Domestic demand is driving growth, underpinned by rising social transfers, an increasingly tight labour market and an investment recovery led by faster disbursements of EU structural funds. Inflation will gradually increase in line with accelerating wages.

## *Fiscal policy plans*

The fiscal policy objectives aim to maintain the sustainability of public finances while supporting inclusive growth. This requires, among others, a gradual progress towards achieving the medium term budgetary objective (in Poland - a structural deficit of 1% of GDP, set in accordance with the EU law). This is planned in the government's Convergence Programme of April 2018 for 2021. The public debt ceiling as well as additional prudential thresholds for the public debt-to-GDP ratio - 43%, 48%, 55%, 60% - are set in the Constitution of the Republic of Poland and in the Act on public finances.

**A: Fiscal Balance and Public Debt**

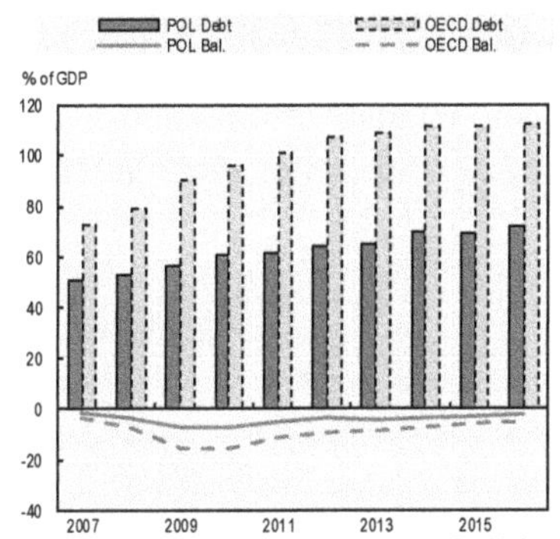


*Note*: The graph is referring to general government fiscal balance and general government gross debt as defined in the OECD National Accounts Statistics.

*Source:* OECD National Accounts Statistics (database); Eurostat Government finance statistics (database).

**B: Fiscal Policy Plans**

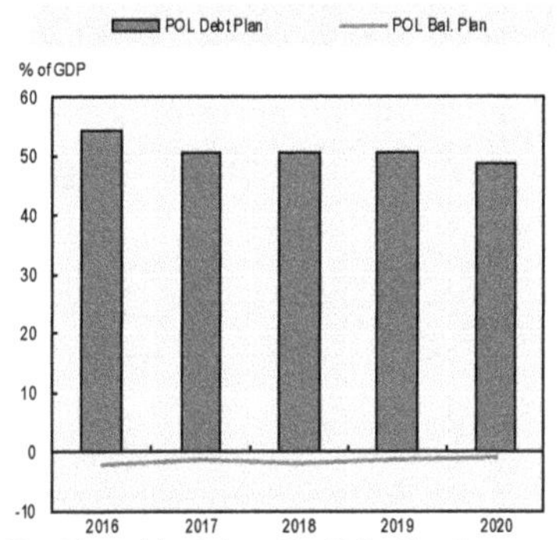


*Note*: The graph is referring to Fiscal Policy Plans that are implemented and/or officially announced as of November 2017 and as indicated by the country. Actual results in graph A may differ as the Fiscal Policy Plans are prepared by the country beforehand and as the Debt and Balance Plan reported by the country are based on the country's own definition; Data are referring to general government; No data available for 2015.

*Source:* 2018 OECD Fiscal Plans and Budgeting Framework Survey.

**C: Public Investment**

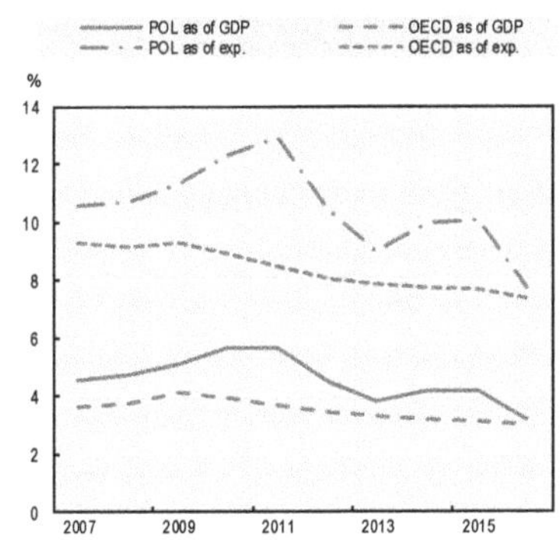


*Note:* The graph is referring to government investment as a percentage of GDP and as a share of total government expenditures.

*Source*: OECD National Accounts Statistics (database).

**D: Expenditure by function (2016)**

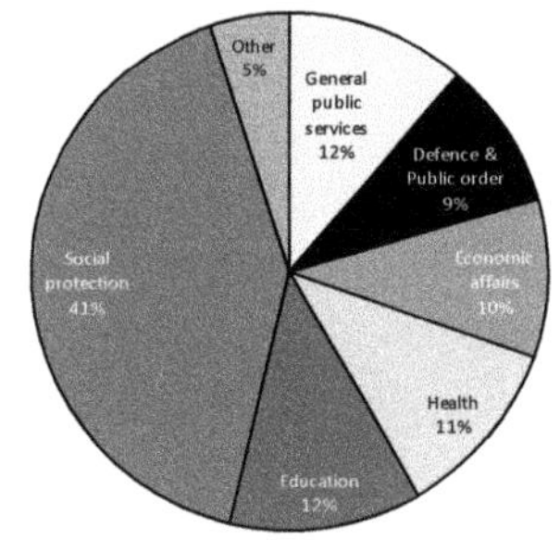


*Source:* OECD National Accounts Statistics (database); Eurostat Government finance statistics (database).

### *Developments in budgetary governance*

A stabilising expenditure rule, covering almost the entire general government, entered into force in 2013 and was applied for the first time to the budget of 2015. The aim of the rule is to ensure the stability of the public finances by stabilising the general government balance in the medium term at the level of medium-term budgetary objective (a structural deficit of 1% of GDP set in accordance with the EU law). Contrary to the constitutional debt rule, the expenditure rule imposes restrictions on public finances on an annual basis, not only after exceeding some thresholds and it enables the conduct of a counter-cyclical fiscal policy. The rule is equipped with a correction mechanism: the expenditure growth rate is reduced if public debt-to-GDP thresholds at 43% and 48% -calculated using average exchange rates and reduced by the value of State budget liquid funds- are exceeded.

In 2016 the Council of Ministers approved the principles of budget reform. The main objective of the planned reform is to introduce mechanisms to conduct and co-ordinate a responsible fiscal policy to facilitate, inter alia, long-term management of expenditure and fiscal space: 1) introduction of medium-term budgetary frameworks; 2) integration of annual and multi-annual planning processes; 3) redefinition of the role of the Council of Ministers, Minister of Finance and other members of the Council of Ministers in the budgetary process; 4) elimination of the existing dualism of expenditure classification and introduction of new division of the state budget and uniform performance-based classification (functional and programme-based classification); 5) improved data collection systems (budget reporting and financial reporting); and 6) institutionalisation and inclusion of public spending reviews in the budget process along with other mechanisms enhancing efficiency of public spending

| Central Budget Authority |
|---|
| Ministry of Finance |
| Weblinks: www.mf.gov.pl |

| Legal Framework |
|---|
| Constitution stipulates the important budgetary governance such as form and structure of budget, roles and responsibilities of executive and legislature. More detailed items are stipulated in Public Finance Act and regulation. |

| Budget coverage |
|---|
| The executive's budget proposal covers general government. |

| Budget cycle | |
|---|---|
| Budget circular | |
| Pre-budget statement | 15 June |
| Negotiations with line ministries | Feb-Sep. |
| Executive budget proposal | 30 Sep. |
| Parliamentary vote on budget | January |
| *Start of financial year* | *1 Jan.* |
| In-year budget execution reports | monthly |
| Mid-year implementation report | 10 Sep. |
| *End of financial year* | *31 Dec.* |
| Year-end budget execution report[27] | 31 May |
| Audited year-end budget execution | June |
| Parliamentary accounting | June |

[27] Poland does not elaborate financial statement (balance sheet etc.) at the level of central government or state/general government. However, it does elaborate and present to the legislature and SAI a year-end budget execution report.

| Poland's application of OECD budget principles "at a glance" | | |
|---|---|---|
| **1.** | **Fiscal policy objectives** | **The fiscal framework in Poland is based on a set of rules. At the level of the general government, it is a so-called stabilising expenditure rule, at the level of the domestic public finance sector it is a debt rule. The main objective of the debt rule is to prevent the public debt (calculated according to the Polish methodology) from breaching the ceiling of 60% of GDP. The expenditure rule is to ensure the stability of the Polish public finances by stabilising the general government balance in the medium term at the level of medium-term budgetary objective (a structural deficit of 1% of GDP).** |
| 2a. | Strategic alignment | The Ministry of Investment and Development sets out the Development Strategy and the Ministry of Finance has a leadership role in promotion alignment between annual budgets and medium-term plans/priorities |
| 2b. | MTEF | Medium-term planning (multi-year financial plan of the State) is formed every year and each time new figures are presented for the years covered under the plan. Budgetary objectives/ceilings in the Convergence programme are set for general government sector (e.g. debt) and, through stabilising expenditure rule, for expenditures of about 90% units of general government sector. |
| 3. | Capital and infrastructure | Capital and operating budgets are integrated and multi-year capital projects are usually financed in the form of multiannual programmes adopted by the Council of Ministers. |
| 4. | Transparency and accessibility | Budget data is available in downloadable form. Most of the core budget reports are open data except for the mid-year implementation report that is submitted to the Parliament, but not published. The impact analyses are not published. |
| 5a. | Parliamentary engagement | The Parliament may make amendments but only if it does not change the total deficit/surplus proposed by the Executive. If the budget is not approved by the legislature before the start of the fiscal year, the executive's budget proposal takes effect. |
| 5b. | Inclusive public / civic debate | In the pre-budget proposal phase, consultations take place within the Social Dialogued Council, comprising of representatives of the Government, trade unions and employers' association. There is no public consultation in post-budget proposal phase. |
| 6. | Financial reporting and accounting | The budget is prepared on cash and/or commitment basis. A year end budget execution report is prepared but there is no year-end financial statement as it is not applicable. |
| 7. | Budget execution | Government should use the single treasury fund except for major public-service funds. The line ministries receive detailed operating expenditure and can re-allocate funds within their budget. |
| 8a. | Performance budgeting | Performance information is presented with budgeting documents or other government documents but is included as background information. Performance information does not play a significant role in decision-making on allocations nor is it intended to do so. |
| 8b. | Evaluation and VFM | Poland initiated spending reviews implementation in 2014. In 2015, it completed three pilot public spending reviews in the policy areas of support to low-income families, housing policy and assessment of the expenditure baseline. The reviews are conducted annually on the basis of a prepared plan. |
| 9. | Fiscal risk and long-term sustainability | The long-term fiscal projection covers four years and are updated every year as part of the budget formulation process. The Ministry of Finance assesses a risk of significant deviation from EU rules and monitors the public debt level |
| 10. | Quality assurance and audit | Introduction of stabilising expenditure rule in 2013 resulted in the widening of the Supreme Audit Office's (NIK's) duties. NIK gives an opinion on compliance with the rule that is presented in its report on the implementation of the Budget Act. |

*Note*: Rows in **bold** represent notable international practice.

## Budgetary Governance in Practice: Portugal

### *Economic context*

Economic growth in Portugal is projected to remain above 2% in 2018 and 2019, driven by both domestic demand and exports. Consumption growth will remain solid in response to further declines in the unemployment rate and stronger wage growth. Investment will be supported by a pick-up in major export market growth and increased public investment. Increased exports will be matched by higher imports as a result of the pick-up in domestic demand, leaving the current account balance relatively unchanged.

### *Fiscal policy plans*

The strategy is to improve the fiscal sustainability and to continue the recent fiscal adjustments. The targets for the headline deficit is -1.4% of GDP for 2017, -1.1% of GDP for 2018, and the medium targets are: -0.3% of GDP in 2019, 0.4% of GDP in 2020, 1.3% of GDP in 2021. For debt-to-GDP ratio, it is estimated at 126.2% for 2017, 123.5% in 2018, 120% in 2019, 117.6% in 2020 and 109.4% in 2021.

**A: Fiscal Balance and Public Debt**

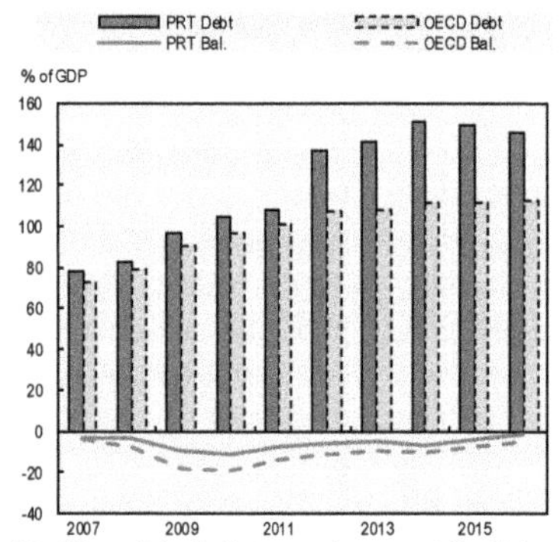


*Note*: The graph is referring to general government fiscal balance and general government gross debt as defined in the OECD National Accounts Statistics.

*Source:* OECD National Accounts Statistics (database); Eurostat Government finance statistics (database).

**B: Fiscal Policy Plans**

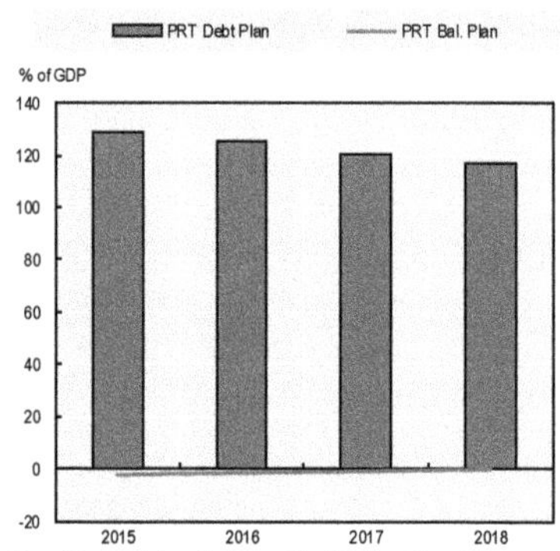


*Note*: The graph is referring to Fiscal Policy Plans that are implemented and/or officially announced as of November 2017 and as indicated by the country. Actual results in graph A may differ as the Fiscal Policy Plans are prepared by the country beforehand and as the Debt and Balance Plan reported by the country are based on the country's own definition; Data are referring to general government; No data available for 2019 and 2020.

*Source:* 2018 OECD Fiscal Plans and Budgeting Framework Survey.

**C: Public Investment**

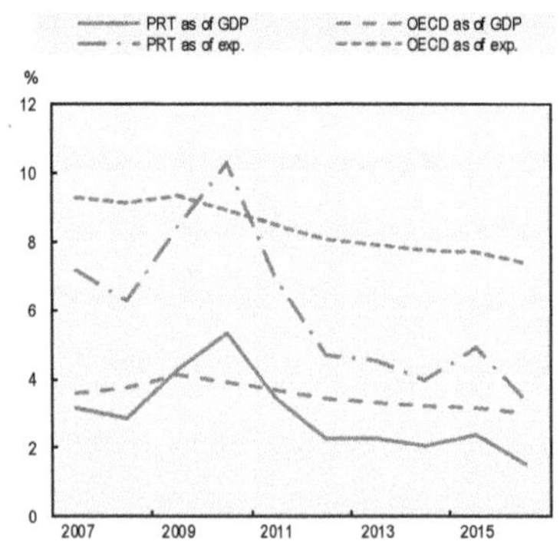


*Note:* The graph is referring to government investment as a percentage of GDP and as a share of total government expenditures.

*Source*: OECD National Accounts Statistics (database).

**D: Expenditure by function (2016)**

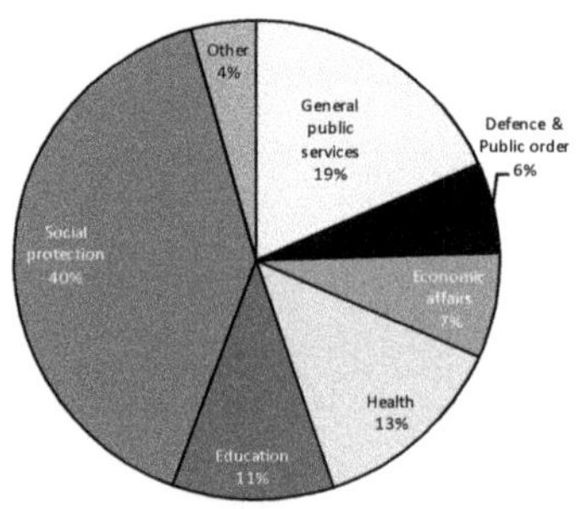


*Source:* OECD National Accounts Statistics (database); Eurostat Government finance statistics (database).

### *Developments in budgetary governance*

A new budgetary framework law (Law 151/2015 of 11 September), was adopted in 2015 to reinforce accrual accounting; further align major documents (e.g. the budget and the Stability Programme) with European fiscal surveillance requirements; increase responsibility for line ministries in budget execution; and reinforce programme and performance based budgeting.

The Portugal Participatory Budget (PPB) was introduced in 2017 as an opportunity for civil society to propose and vote on ideas for public investment of EUR 3 million in the areas of education and adult training, culture, science, agriculture and justice. In 2018, the PPB will comprise EUR 5 million and citizens will be able to propose ideas in all government areas. Portugal also has a wide range of participatory budgets at the local level with more than 80 on-going exercises.

| Central Budget Authority |
|---|
| Ministry of Finance. |
| Weblink: www.dgo.gov.pt |

| Legal Framework |
|---|
| The Constitution outlines the content, preparation and supervision of the budget. Other aspects of budgeting are covered in the budgetary framework law (latest version, Law 151/2015 of 11 September). |

| Budget coverage |
|---|
| The executive's budget covers general government. |

| Budget cycle | |
|---|---|
| Budget circular | April |
| Pre-budget fiscal policy statement | April |
| Negotiations with line ministries | April-Oct. |
| Executive budget proposal | 15. October |
| Parliamentary vote on budget | December |
| *Start of financial year* | *1 Jan.* |
| In-year budget execution reports | regularly |
| Mid-year implementation report | October |
| *End of financial year* | *31 Dec.* |
| Year-end budget execution report | April |
| Audited y/e budget execution report | n/a |
| Parliamentary accounting | November |

| Portugal's application of OECD budget principles "at a glance" | | |
|---|---|---|
| 1. | Fiscal policy objectives | In addition to the EU fiscal rules, an expenditure rule sets binding nominal expenditure ceilings by budget programme for the following year and indicative ceilings for the three following years. |
| 2a. | Strategic alignment | Only loose links between national framework and SDGs but Ministry of Foreign Affairs monitors the 17 SDGs and the National Statistical Institute makes information available when measurable. |
| 2b. | MTEF | The MTEF covers four years on a rolling basis with ceilings revised annually. |
| **3.** | **Capital and infrastructure** | **The budget process includes a Planning and Infrastructures Programme. Procurement under a PPP model is preceded by an analysis and proposal submitted through the PPP Unit.** |
| 4. | Transparency and accessibility | The budget is published with open data, data visualisation tools, and a citizens' guide. Distributional analyses are not published. |
| 5a. | Parliamentary engagement | The parliament holds a pre-budget debate but does not produce a report. Budget scrutiny is led by a budget committee which takes recommendations from sectoral committees into consideration. The legislature has unrestricted powers to amend the budget. Analytical support is provided by a specialised unit of around seven people. The legislature does not currently receive long-term sustainability analysis. |
| **5b.** | **Inclusive public / civic debate** | **Portugal is among only four countries that undertake participative budgeting on the national level.** |
| 6. | Budget accounting and financial reporting | Cash and/or commitment budgeting and reporting. |
| 7. | Budget execution | There is no single treasury fund; however there is a central treasury accounts system in which all general revenues are deposited. Central Government's entities revenues generally fall under the treasury unity regime, apart from certain exceptions approved annually. Social Security is separate. Line ministries and agencies have flexibility to reallocate funds, with prior approval of the Minister of Finance/Secretary of State for the Budget for certain categories of expenditure. |
| 8a. | Performance budgeting | Limited experience with performance budgeting. |
| 8b. | Evaluation and VFM | No programme evaluation requirements in place. There is an annual spending review process. |
| 9. | Fiscal risk and long-term sustainability | The Office of Planning, Strategy, Evaluation and International Relations in the Ministry of Finance produces projections covering up to five years and updated annually. The office is also responsible for identifying and managing overall fiscal risks. The Public Finance Council and parliamentary budget office also play a role identifying fiscal risks. There is a contingency reserve for unforeseen expenditure such as a natural disaster and for foreseen expenditure on policies not yet decided or announced. |
| 10. | Quality assurance and audit | The Public Finance Council assesses and endorses the macroeconomic forecasts and monitors the sustainability of fiscal policy and compliance with the fiscal rules. The parliamentary budget office provides complimentary analysis. Independent Court of Audit established in the Constitution audits government financial report. |

*Note*: Rows in **bold** represent notable international practice.

# Budgetary Governance in Practice: Slovak Republic

## *Economic context*

The Slovak economy will maintain its rapid expansion and growth and is projected to exceed 4% in 2018 and 2019. Low interest rates and strong labour market outcomes will fuel consumer spending. Unemployment has already fallen to record lows, and intensifying labour shortages will boost wage growth. Investment should pick up, supported by an improving business climate and new infrastructure investment. Exports will continue to benefit from the expansion in the automotive sector, allowing the current account to reach a modest surplus.

## *Fiscal policy plans*

In line with the government`s manifesto, balanced budget is to be achieved by 2020. The Budgetary rules Act was amended in line with Stability and Growth Pact and Two Pack. This act contains corrective mechanism in case of deviation from the trajectory of achieving the MTO. The Constitutional Act on budget responsibility also includes automatic corrective mechanisms if the debt exceeds the set levels.

**A: Fiscal Balance and Public Debt**

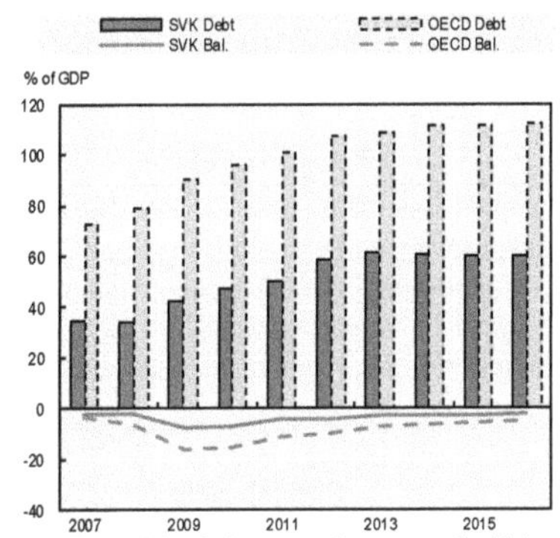


*Note*: The graph is referring to general government fiscal balance and general government gross debt as defined in the OECD National Accounts Statistics.

*Source:* OECD National Accounts Statistics (database); Eurostat Government finance statistics (database).

**B: Fiscal Policy Plans**

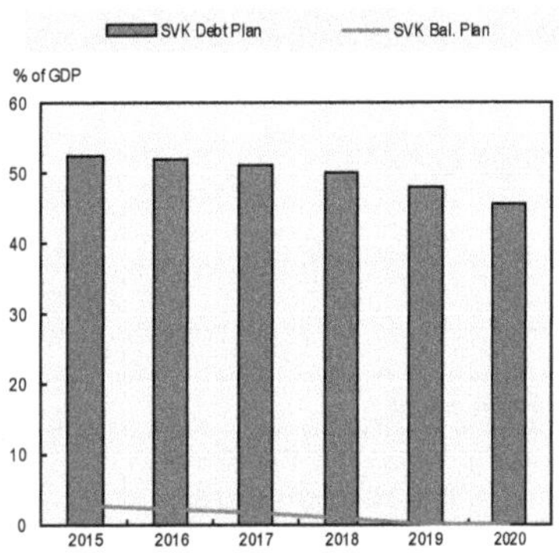


*Note:* The graph is referring to Fiscal Policy Plans that are implemented and/or officially announced as of November 2017 and as indicated by the country. Actual results in graph A may differ as the Fiscal Policy Plans are prepared by the country beforehand and as the Debt and Balance Plan reported by the country are based on the country's own definition; Data are referring to general government.

*Source:* 2018 OECD Fiscal Plans and Budgeting Framework Survey.

**C: Public Investment**

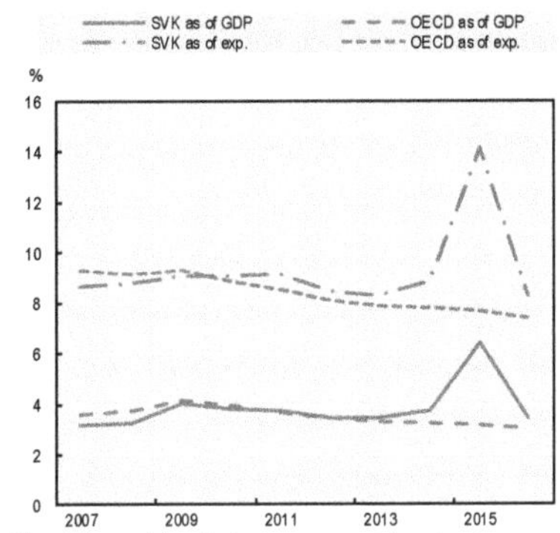


*Note:* The graph is referring to government investment as a percentage of GDP and as a share of total government expenditures.

*Source*: OECD National Accounts Statistics (database).

**D: Expenditure by function (2016)**

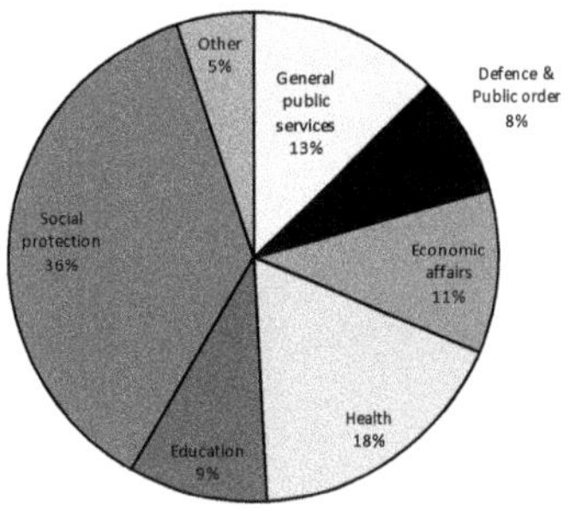


*Source:* OECD National Accounts Statistics (database); Eurostat Government finance statistics (database).

### *Developments in budgetary governance*

In 2017, the Slovak Government significantly reformed the investment assessment process. The "Value for Money Project" introduced spending reviews and a new evaluation procedure for major investment projects (above EUR 40 million, or above EUR 10 million for digitalisation projects) in accordance with value for money principles as defined in the Public Investment Project Assessment Framework. In the upcoming period, 124 transport projects amounting to EUR 32.5 billion, are expected to be assessed. The development is closely related to the Slovak Republic's current plans for developing a national infrastructure and investment plan.

The Slovak Republic has a programme budgeting framework in place, which includes budgetary allocations with information about performance, objectives and results. However, the use of the performance information is only included as background information for the purposes of accountability and information and is not significantly involved in any decision-making process on allocations. Closer reflections on how to more formally integrate SDGs in the budgeting process are underway.

There are still relatively low levels of budget transparency and parliamentary engagement in the budget process. Although most core budget reports are publically available, budget impact analyses or additional citizen's guides are usually not published, and access to open data is limited. There is also limited citizen engagement in the budget process.

| Central Budget Authority |
| --- |
| Ministry of Finance<br><br>Weblink: www.finance.gov.sk/ |

| Legal Framework |
| --- |
| The legal and constitutional grounding for the Slovak budget process is provided by the Act on the General Government Budgetary Rules, by the Constitutional Act on Fiscal Responsibility and the Act on Budgetary rules on the municipalities. The budget process is also regulated by Government resolutions on the general government budget. |

| Budget coverage |
| --- |
| The executive's budget proposal applies to central government. Only the State budget (which includes central government) is approved by Parliament as a Budget law. The Budget of other subjects of the public administration includes mainly health insurance, social security, municipalities, and state-owned companies. Regions and municipalities have limited revenue-raising power and must run balanced budgets. |

| Budget cycle | |
| --- | --- |
| Budget circular | April |
| Pre-budget fiscal policy statement[28] | April |
| Negotiations with line ministries | April-Oct. |
| Executive budget proposal | 15 October |
| Parliamentary vote on budget | December |
| *Start of financial year* | *1 Jan.* |
| In-year budget execution reports | regularly |
| Mid-year implementation report | October |
| *End of financial year* | *31 Dec.* |
| Year-end financial statement | April |
| Audited financial report | n/a[29] |
| Parliamentary accounting | November |

[28]The EU-related Stability Programme Update (SPU) currently serves as the main pre-budget fiscal report.

[29] Consolidated financial reports in public sector are audited by commercial auditors.

| Slovak Republic's application of OECD budget principles "at a glance" | | |
|---|---|---|
| 1. | Fiscal policy objectives | Fiscal rules are in compliance with SGP and Two Pack. This contains corrective mechanism in case of deviation from the trajectory of achieving the MTO. The Constitutional Act on budget responsibility (493/2011) includes automatic corrective mechanisms if the debt exceeds the set level. A balanced budget is to be achieved by 2020. |
| 2a. | Strategic alignment | The CBA takes the lead promoting the alignment between the annual budgetary allocations, and the medium-term strategic plans and priorities of the government that are set out in the stability programme. Systematic linkages of SDG targets and performance information are weak. |
| 2b. | MTEF | 3-year rolling ceilings; creation of a MTEF legally-grounded, whereby annual budgets are managed in line with indicative medium-term ceilings. The expenditure ceilings are binding for the first budgetary year of such three year budgetary framework and not for the two subsequent years. |
| 3. | Capital and infrastructure | Capital expenditures are included in the General Government Budget the same way as other expenditures. The Ministry of Finance must additionally approve infrastructure projects that involve large costs. The budget requests funding for the entire cost of multi-year projects up-front. The first national infrastructure plan is being prepared by the Deputy Prime Minister for Investments and Informatisation. |
| 4. | Transparency and accessibility | 7 of the core budget reports are publicly available; 8 of 9 ancillary reports, of which 7 are publicly available. There is a user friendly on-line budget data portal, but open data is limited. There are no budget impact analyses published, and no citizen's guides are available. |
| 5a. | Parliamentary engagement | Power to amend the State budget. A vote on the budget is however not considered a vote of confidence. Specialised staff of the Budget Committee offer advice on the budgetary issues to parliamentarians. |
| 5b. | Inclusive public / civic debate | There are no formal or informal mechanisms for citizen and stakeholder participation. |
| 6. | Budget accounting and financial reporting | Cash and accrual budgeting and reporting, initiated by the Public Finance Management Reform (Accounting Law 431, 2003). Accrual accounting was introduced 2008 and is applied for the whole public sector, including governmental institutions, municipalities as well as public organisations financed from the state budget. |
| 7. | Budget execution | Line ministers can re-allocate funds within their own budget envelope during the course of budget execution, except for binding indicators, which require the CBA's approval. Supplementary budgets are produced and publically available. |
| 8a. | Performance budgeting | The national performance budgeting framework includes information about performance, objectives and results and is compulsory for line ministries and agencies. In practice performance information is not evaluated or used. |
| **8b.** | **Evaluation and VFM** | **There are legally binding requirements for *ex ante* evaluation of all programmes over a certain estimated cost. Spending reviews are an annual exercise and are closely linked to the newly introduced "Value for Money Project".** |
| **9.** | **Fiscal risk and long-term sustainability** | **The Council for Budget Responsibility (CBR) was formed in 2012 as an independent fiscal institution of the Slovak Republic. It's main objective is to monitor and evaluate the fiscal performance of the Slovak Republic. The IFI produces long-term fiscal projections that cover a 50 years horizon and are updated every year. Contingency funds are in place.** |
| 10. | Quality assurance and audit | Supreme Audit Office of the Slovak Republic provides compliance control on public spending, but has a limited role on and financial and performance audit. Its independence is based on primary legislation. |

*Note*: Rows in **bold** represent notable international practice.

## Budgetary Governance in Practice: Slovenia

### *Economic context*

Slovenia's strong and broad-based economic expansion in 2017 is likely to moderate in 2018 and 2019, though with growth remaining above potential. Private consumption and housing investment will be supported by continued employment gains and faster real wage growth. Robust investment growth will decelerate as a new cycle of EU structural funds matures. Growth of exports, and imports of intermediary inputs, should ease as external competitiveness deteriorates due to the intensification of labour market tensions.

### *Fiscal policy plans*

Slovenia aims to reach the medium-term budgetary objective (MTO) by 2020. In accordance with the country-specific recommendations approved by the Council in July 2017, this will require making structural adjustments towards the MTO of at least 0.6% of GDP. Compensation of employees in the structure of general government expenditure will grow slower than nominal GDP in 2018 and 2019.

**A: Fiscal Balance and Public Debt**

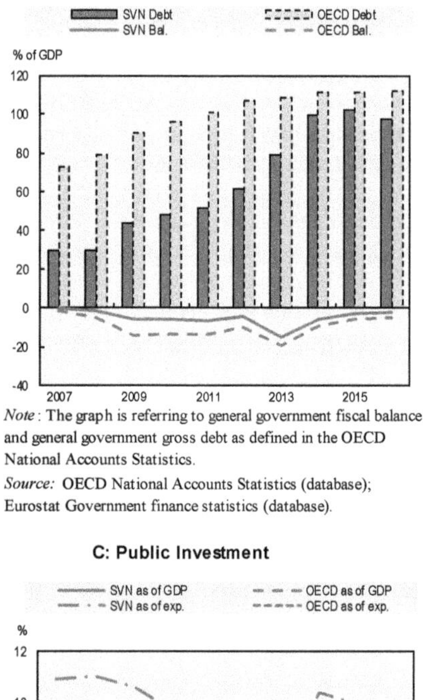


*Note*: The graph is referring to general government fiscal balance and general government gross debt as defined in the OECD National Accounts Statistics.

*Source:* OECD National Accounts Statistics (database); Eurostat Government finance statistics (database).

**C: Public Investment**

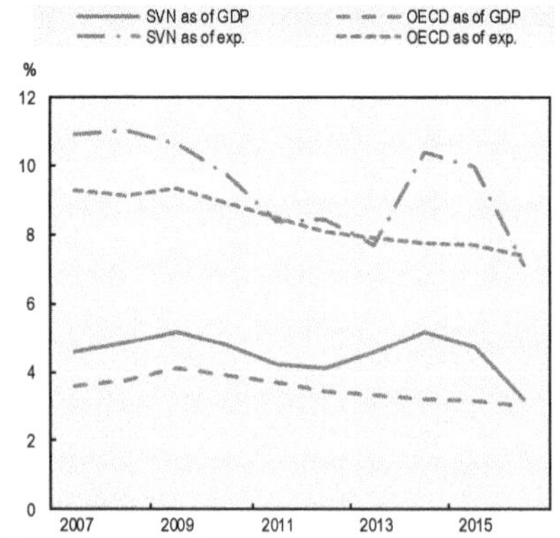


*Note:* The graph is referring to government investment as a percentage of GDP and as a share of total government expenditures.

*Source*: OECD National Accounts Statistics (database).

**D: Expenditure by function (2016)**

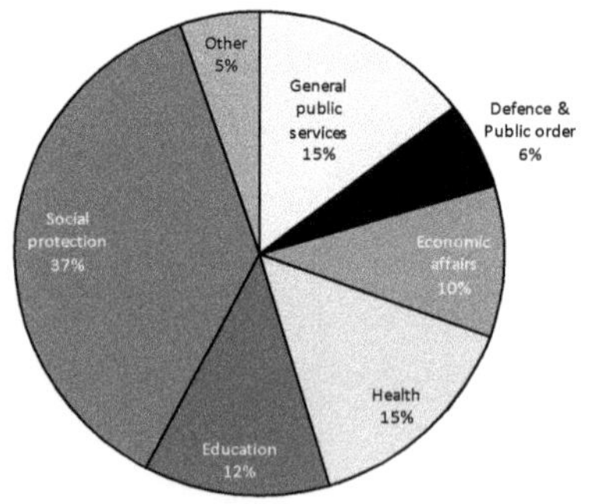


*Source:* OECD National Accounts Statistics (database); Eurostat Government finance statistics (database).

### *Developments in budgetary governance*

The Fiscal Rule Act adopted in 2015 defines the upper ceiling for General Government and four public funds as well as the medium-term budgetary framework.

The Institute of Macroeconomic Analysis and Development (IMAD), a semi-independent body[30], prepares the economic forecasts used by Slovenia's government in preparing economic policy measures and drafting the budget. In 2017 Slovenia established a new Fiscal Council which monitors the sustainability of the fiscal policy and compliance with the fiscal rules.

| Central Budget Authority |
|---|
| Ministry of Finance<br><br>Weblink: www.mf.gov.si/en/ |

| Legal Framework |
|---|
| The Constitution stipulates that "all revenues and expenditures for the financing of public spending must be included in the budgets of the state", as well as the principle of maintaining a balanced budget in the medium term, and requirements for legislative approval. The *Public Finance Act* (1999, last amended in 2018) sets out principles and requirements for preparation and adoption of the budget and these two phases are underpinned by the *Decree on Strategic Development Documents and on the Bases and Procedures for Preparation of a Proposed National Budget* and the Parliament's Rules of Procedure. |

| Budget coverage |
|---|
| The executive's budget covers central government. |

| Budget cycle | |
|---|---|
| Budget circular | April |
| Pre-budget fiscal policy statement | To date, not published annually |
| Negotiations with line ministries | April-June |
| Executive budget proposal | 1 October |
| Parliamentary vote on budget | Mid-December |
| *Start of financial year* | *1 January* |
| In-year budget execution reports | Monthly |
| Mid-year implementation report | End July |
| *End of financial year* | *31 December* |
| Year-end financial statement | 31 March |
| Audited financial report | 1 October |
| Parliamentary accounting | 1 October |

[30] Originally modelled after the Swedish Konjunkturinstitutet

| | Slovenia's application of OECD budget principles "at a glance" | |
|---|---|---|
| 1. | Fiscal policy objectives | In addition to the EU fiscal rules, Slovenia's budget rule ensures medium-term balance of revenue and expenditure of state budgets without (long-term) borrowing. |
| **2a.** | **Strategic alignment** | **Slovenia's Development Strategy defines national outcome goals and these must be linked with sectoral output/outcome objectives.** |
| 2b. | MTEF | The MTEF covers three years on a rolling basis with ceilings revised annually reflecting new independent forecast, additional requirements by Fiscal Rule Act, or exceptional circumstances. Ceiling are set for the general government and separately for the central budget, health, pension fund and municipalities (aggregated). |
| 3. | Capital and infrastructure | Capital and current expenditure requests are submitted separately by line ministries and the process for deciding upon capital and operating budget requests are distinct in the central budget (as capital expenditure is budgeted under the Development Programmes Plan (DPP)). All infrastructure projects and PPPs above a certain threshold must show value for money. |
| 4. | Transparency and accessibility | The budget and related reports are published and in some cases there are also official summaries for policymakers (budget proposal, approved budget, and long-term fiscal sustainability report), a citizens' guide for the approved budget (since 2017), and open data for most budget-related documents. |
| 5a. | Parliamentary engagement | The parliament holds a pre-budget debate and sends a report to government. During the approval process the parliament votes first on the budget totals before the annual appropriations and revenue measures are considered. It can amend the budget within the executive's aggregates. Some support is provided by an in-house unit of 5 people, and specialised staff in the Budget Committee and Party Secretariats. |
| 5b. | Inclusive public / civic debate | Limited engagement of policy stakeholders in budget cycle. |
| 6. | Budget accounting and financial reporting | Cash and/or commitment budgeting and reporting. |
| 7. | Budget execution | Single treasury fund is mandatory for all revenues and expenditures of central government. Line ministries can reallocate up to 10% of funds between programmes, subject to some additional limitations. Supplementary budgets are possible. |
| 8a. | Performance budgeting | Slovenia has over a decade of performance budgeting experience, mainly at the presentational level, and focused on increasing transparency. |
| 8b. | Evaluation and VFM | Line ministries are responsible for choosing *ex post* evaluations and the SAI carries out *ex post* evaluations. However there are no formal mechanisms to consider evaluation findings in the budget process. |
| 9. | Fiscal risk and long-term sustainability | The CBA produces projections covering up to five years. The CBA is responsible for identifying and managing fiscal risks. IMAD and the Fiscal Council also play a role identifying fiscal risks. There is a contingency reserve for unforeseen expenditure such as a natural disaster and for foreseen expenditure on policies not yet decided or announced. |
| **10.** | **Quality assurance and audit** | **IMAD provides independent input in forecasting. The Fiscal Council monitors the sustainability of the fiscal policy and compliance with the fiscal rules and evaluates forecasts and budgetary projections[31]. The Independent Court of Audit (established in the Constitution) audits government financial report and also carries out audits of performance information.** |

*Note*: Rows in **bold** represent notable international practice.

## Budgetary Governance in Practice: Spain

### *Economic context*

Economic growth in Spain is projected to remain robust in 2018 and 2019. Domestic demand will ease, as the support provided by low oil prices and lower taxes dissipates. On the other hand, political tensions in Catalonia have increased uncertainty. Competitiveness gains will continue to support exports, even as external demand growth declines slightly. Inflation is projected to fall to 1.3% in 2018, before bouncing back somewhat in 2019.

### *Fiscal policy plans*

The fiscal plan was detailed in the Stability Programme 2017-20 approved by the Government and submitted to the European institutions in April 2017. More recently it has been updated in the Draft Budgetary Plan also submitted to the European Commission in October 2017. The 2017-20 Stability Programme Update presents a prudent and realistic macroeconomic scenario based on conservative assumptions.

**A: Fiscal Balance and Public Debt**

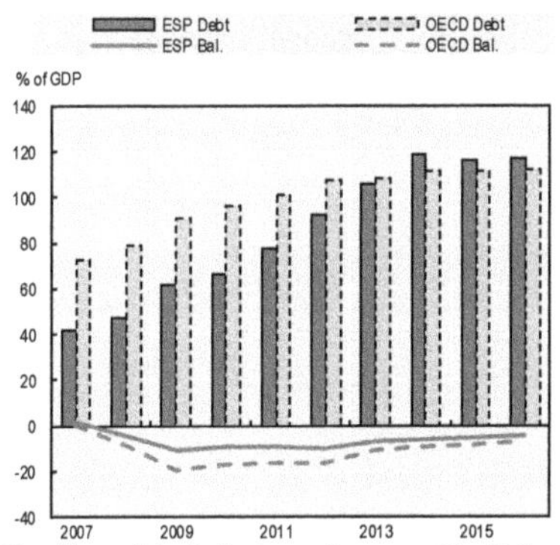


*Note*: The graph is referring to general government fiscal balance and general government gross debt as defined in the OECD National Accounts Statistics.

*Source:* OECD National Accounts Statistics (database); Eurostat Government finance statistics (database).

**B: Fiscal Policy Plans**

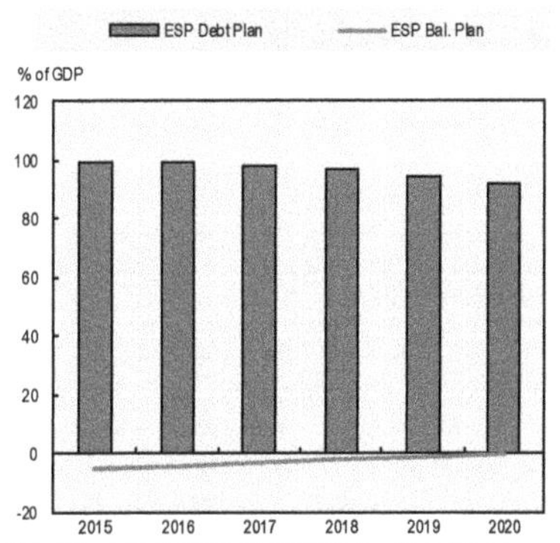


*Note*: The graph is referring to Fiscal Policy Plans that are implemented and/or officially announced as of November 2017 and as indicated by the country. Actual results in graph A may differ as the Fiscal Policy Plans are prepared by the country beforehand and as the Debt and Balance Plan reported by the country are based on the country's own definition; Data are referring to general government.

*Source:* 2018 OECD Fiscal Plans and Budgeting Framework Survey.

**C: Public Investment**

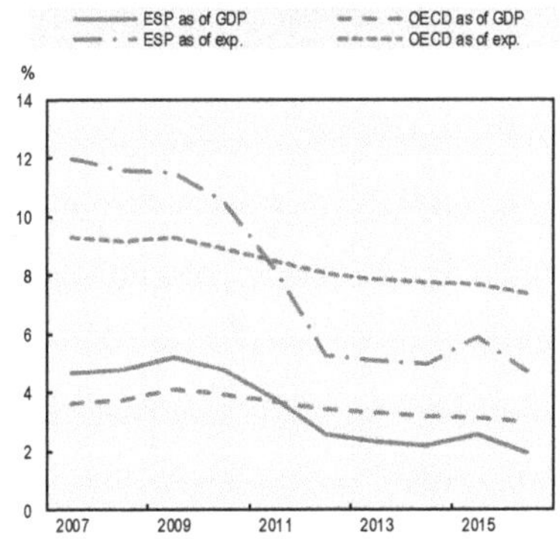


*Note:* The graph is referring to government investment as a percentage of GDP and as a share of total government expenditures.

*Source*: OECD National Accounts Statistics (database).

**D: Expenditure by function (2016)**

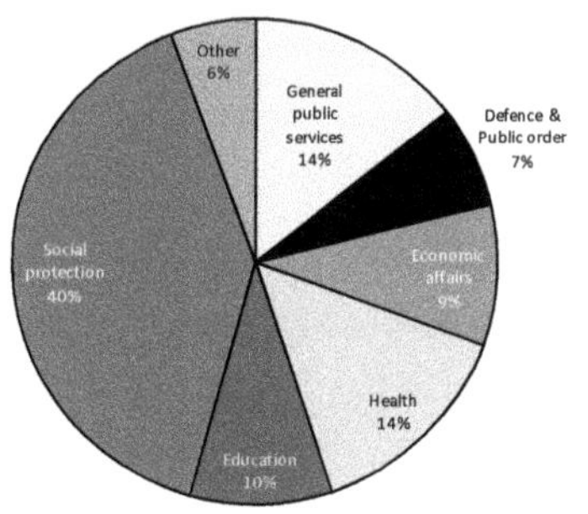


*Source:* OECD National Accounts Statistics (database); Eurostat Government finance statistics (database).

*Developments in budgetary governance*

In 2011 Spain implemented a national reform process to reinforce the fiscal framework and put in place strict new budgetary rules across all levels of government with the goal of meeting European commitments, restoring sound public finances and setting them on a sustainable path. The draft budget submitted by the government must take into account the three-year budgetary stability targets previously agreed upon by the parliament.

Gender budgeting has been implemented for a number of years in Spain. The legal framework requires that each ministerial department sends the Secretary of State for Budget and Expenditure a report analysing the gender impact of its spending programmes. These reports constitute the basis of an overall Gender Impact Report accompanying the budget proposal.

Performance information does not play a significant role in decision making on budget allocations. Different forms of spending reviews have been introduced to improve flexibility and responsiveness in the budget system.

**Central Budget Authority**

Ministry of Finance/Economy

Weblink: www.sepg.pap.minhafp.gob.es/sitios/sepg/es-ES/ClnSEPG/Paginas/dgpresupuestos.aspx

**Legal Framework**

The Constitution includes foundational principles for public financial management, including the form and structure of the annual budget, the roles and responsibilities of the Legislature and the Executive, as well as requirements for legislative authorisation of spending and taxation.

The general Budget Law (2003) and the Organic Law for Budget Stability and Financial Sustainability (2012) further specify the comprehensive budgeting framework.

**Budget coverage**

The state budget document applies to the central government, including ministries, public agencies, and social security funds.

| Budget cycle | |
|---|---|
| Budget circular | July |
| Pre-budget fiscal policy statement | 30 April |
| Negotiations with line ministries | July/August |
| Executive budget proposal | September |
| Parliamentary vote on budget | December |
| *Start of financial year* | *1 Jan.* |
| In-year budget execution reports | Monthly |
| Mid-year implementation report | July |
| *End of financial year* | *31 Dec.* |
| Year-end financial statement | October *(year+1)* |
| Audited financial report | June *(year+2)* |
| Parliamentary accounting | June *(year+2)* |

| Spain's application of OECD budget principles "at a glance" | | |
|---|---|---|
| 1. | Fiscal policy objectives | Structural budget balance and debt ceilings defined in the Constitution; supplemented by EU fiscal rules. |
| **2a.** | **Strategic alignment** | **Medium-term strategic plans and priorities are set in the National Development Plan and the MTEF. The CBA has a leadership role in promoting alignment between annual budgets and medium-term priorities. There are other formal and informal mechanisms to ensure alignment (e.g. discussions at Cabinet, strategic plan milestones and coordination subcommittees).** |
| 2b. | MTEF | Medium-term budgetary plan covering three years. Any amendment or deviation must be explained. |
| 3. | Capital and infrastructure | Capital and current expenditure requests are submitted separately by line ministries and the process for deciding upon capital and operating budget requests are distinct. There is an overall long-term strategic infrastructure plan as well as sectoral infrastructure plans. There are formal processes for ensuring absolute and relative value for money. |
| 4. | Transparency and accessibility | All core budget reports and most ancillary reports are produced and made public; some impact assessments showing incidence of budget measures (e.g. gender and regional); budget data is available in downloadable form; Citizen's guide only available for budget proposal. |
| 5a. | Parliamentary engagement | Parliamentary amendments are restricted in so far as they cannot change the total deficit/surplus proposed by the Executive. The budget committees typically adopt a decision to hold quarterly hearings to monitor budget implementation and budget trends<br>Comprehensive technical support for parliamentary scrutiny: secretaries of the budget committees, Public Finances and Economic research sections, the *Cortes Generales* Budget Office. |
| 5b. | Inclusive public / civic debate | Limited engagement of policy stakeholders in budget cycle; no participatory budgeting and no engagement from minority & marginalised groups from decision-making process. |
| 6. | Budget accounting and financial reporting | Cash budgeting; comprehensive coverage;<br>The Central Government maintains coverage of all main reports on public finances. |
| 7. | Budget execution | Use of a single treasury fund is mandatory for all revenues and expenditures of central government; except for major public-service funds (e.g. social security, healthcare).<br>Line ministers receive detailed operating expenditure. They can re-allocate funds within their own budget up to a certain limit; above that limit they need approval from the CBA. Limited budget carry-over from year to year; approval required. All supplementary budgets require advance parliamentary approval |
| 8a. | Performance budgeting | Performance information is presented with budgeting documents or other government documents but is included as background information. Performance information does not play a significant role in decision making on allocations nor is it intended to do so. |
| 8b. | Evaluation and VFM | Monitoring and evaluation within line ministries;<br>Comprehensive cross-cutting, sectoral and sub-sectoral reviews have been performed. However, they are not carried out every year.<br>AIReF (Spain IFI) was asked by the government to take on a role in spending review over 2017 and 2018. To date, it is the only OECD IFI to take on a spending review task. |
| **9.** | **Fiscal risk and long-term sustainability** | **Long-term fiscal risk projections are produced every three years; public long-term sustainability report prepared by IFI; specific linkages to budgetary policy of the government (e.g. projections regarding age-related public expenditure).The Ministry of Finance and Civil Service manages and identifies fiscal risks. There are centrally defined criteria to decide which fiscal risk needs to be measured and monitored. There is a contingency reserve for unforeseen expenditure (e.g. natural disasters)** |
| 10. | Quality assurance and audit | Constitutionally-independent SAI (*Tribunal de Cuentas*) provides financial audit; limited role in performance audit or governance systems audit. The IFI (AIReF) was established in 2013, helping generate improvements in economic forecast methods, the monitoring of budget implementation and early detection of non-compliance with fiscal rules. |

## Budgetary Governance in Practice: Sweden

### *Economic context*

After several years of high GDP growth and rapidly increasing employment, Sweden has entered a phase of more subdued GDP growth. Housing construction has increased rapidly in recent years, but housing investment has started to fall and are expected to continue to fall somewhat in the coming years. Although growth is more subdued, economic activity is still strong and labour demand is high. Despite this, the unemployment rate is levelling off as difficult-to-hire low-skilled workers made up a rising share of jobbseekers.

### *Fiscal policy plans*

Prudent fiscal policy has helped turn a deficit into a surplus, and the surplus target will be met in 2018 (a net lending of 1% over a cycle, i.e structural balance). Combining fully financed proposals and automatic budget consolidation has led to strengthened public finances. In the Budget Bill for 2018 there was room for unfinanced discretionary fiscal policy and the Government proposed new policy measures that increase net lending by 0.9, 1.2 and 1.5% of GDP in 2018-20.

**A: Fiscal Balance and Public Debt**

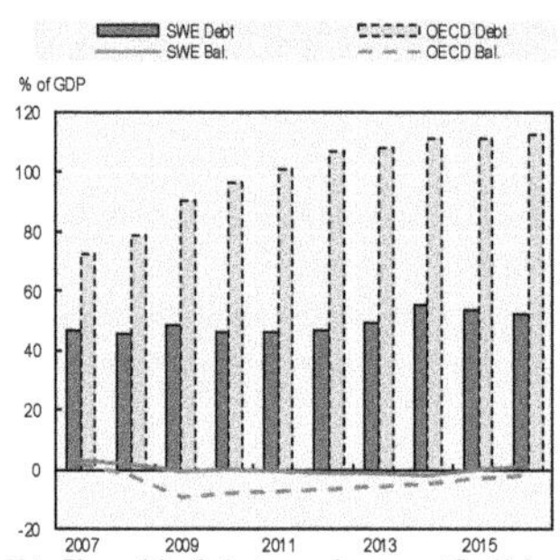


Note: The graph is referring to general government fiscal balance and general government gross debt as defined in the OECD National Accounts Statistics.

*Source:* OECD National Accounts Statistics (database); Eurostat Government finance statistics (database).

**B: Fiscal Policy Plans**

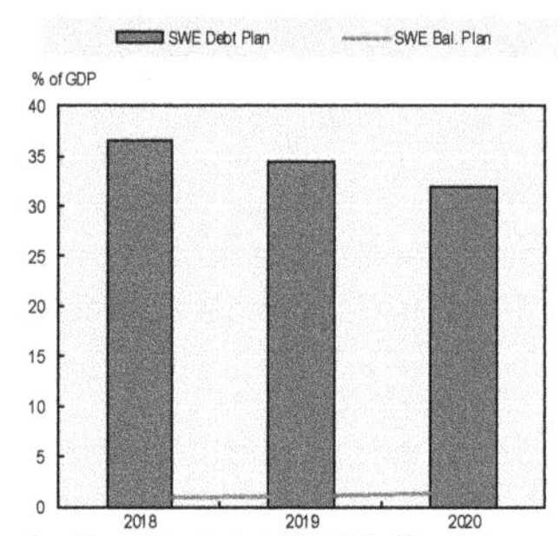


*Note*: The graph is referring to Fiscal Policy Plans that are implemented and/or officially announced as of November 2017 and as indicated by the country. Actual results in graph A may differ as the Fiscal Policy Plans are prepared by the country beforehand and as the Debt and Balance Plan reported by the country are based on the country's own definition; Data are referring to general government; No data available from 2015 to 2017.

*Source:* 2018 OECD Fiscal Plans and Budgeting Framework Survey.

**C: Public Investment**

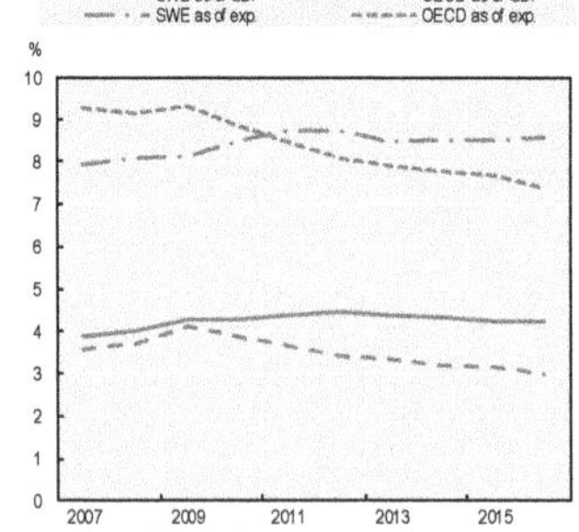


*Note:* The graph is referring to government investment as a percentage of GDP and as a share of total government expenditures.

*Source*: OECD National Accounts Statistics (database).

**D: Expenditure by function (2016)**

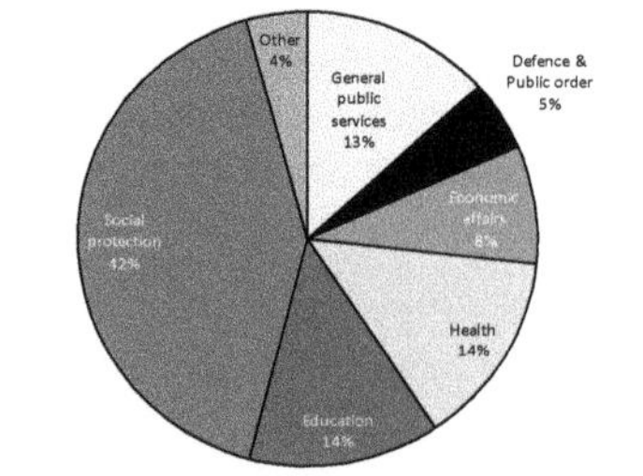


*Source:* OECD National Accounts Statistics (database); Eurostat Government finance statistics (database).

### *Developments in budgetary governance*

Sweden's budgetary and broader fiscal framework is characterised since the mid-1990s by 1) a 1% surplus target for the entire general government sector; 2) a central government expenditure ceiling; 3) the requirement for the local government sector to maintain balanced budgets; and 4) a disciplined budget process.

The fiscal policy and budget frameworks have remained largely in place but, in June 2016, a cross-party agreement was concluded on improvements to the fiscal policy and budgetary frameworks and presented to Parliament by a cross-party committee of inquiry in autumn 2016. As a result of the agreement, the surplus target will be changed beginning with the budget work for 2019 from 1% to one third of a per cent of GDP on average over a business cycle and a debt anchor of 35% of GDP for the Maastricht debt was also introduced.

Other important recent developments include the adoption of gender budgeting in 2016 to bring a clearer gender-responsive perspective to bear upon the budget and resource-allocation processes.

| Central Budget Authority |
|---|
| Budget Department in Ministry of Finance<br><br>Weblink: www.regeringen.se/sveriges-regering/finansdepartementet/budgetavdelningen/ |

| Legal Framework |
|---|
| Constitution includes role of legislature and executive in a defined budget process; Budget Act includes additional principles for public financial management, including fiscal rules (surplus target and expenditure ceiling). |

| Budget coverage |
|---|
| Budget includes *all* central government financial transactions that affect central government borrowing. The expenditure ceiling covers central government expenditures, including expenditures in the pension system, but excluding interest payments on national debt. Municipal governments are further subject to balanced budget rules, but not included in central budget. |

| Budget cycle | |
|---|---|
| Pre-budget fiscal policy statement | April |
| Ministry of Finance negotiations with line ministries | Spring |
| Parliament approves aggregates | June |
| Budget document prepared | Summer |
| Executive budget proposal | September |
| Parliamentary vote on budget | November |
| Parliamentary vote on budget | December |
| *Start of financial year* | *1 Jan.* |
| In-year budget execution reports | Monthly |
| Mid-year implementation report | Spring |
| *End of financial year* | *31 Dec.* |
| Year-end financial statement | April |
| Audit of financial statement | May |
| Parliamentary scrutiny of audited financial statement | 15 June (final date) |

| | | Sweden's application of OECD budget principles "at a glance" |
|---|---|---|
| 1. | Fiscal policy objectives | Sweden's 1% surplus rule provides a very clear fiscal anchor and is well-understood as a core element in the top-down budgeting system. |
| 2a. | Strategic alignment | Government priorities are discussed in December of Budget Year-2. |
| **2b.** | **MTEF** | **A sound and particularly stable MTEF allows visibility of resources in line ministries. Characteristics are: 3-year rolling ceilings legally-grounded in Budget Act; 'budget margin' for built in flexibility. Average of 2.5 supplementary budgets approved since FY2014.** |
| 3. | Capital and infrastructure | Sweden's planning and budgeting framework is well codified and financially integrated with general budget and MTEF. The Budget Department is required to approve all projects above a certain threshold. |
| 4. | Transparency and accessibility | Budgets, financial reports and statements available publicly. Information is designed to be easily understood by citizens |
| 5a. | Parliamentary engagement | Strong engagement with Parliament through sectoral committees. The budget proposal must be approved as a whole. Parliament can approve an alternative whole budget if it collects more votes than the government's proposal. The budget proposal includes budget ceilings and allocations to 27 expenditure areas. |
| **5b.** | **Inclusive public / civic debate** | **Sweden's policy-making system is highly collaborative and includes opportunities for public consultation in particular sectors. Transport infrastructure planning involves consultation with local authorities. The budget process, however, is not designed to allow for *ex ante* engagement with parliament or with civil society.** |
| 6. | Budget accounting and financial reporting | Sweden has advanced financial reporting standards within agencies, and regular high-quality reports throughout the accountability cycle. Comprehensive cash and accrual reporting. |
| 7. | Budget execution | A single fund covers all central government spending. Up to 3% of operational spending can be carried-over from year to year without approval; all other carry-over requires approval from the CBA. |
| 8a. | Performance budgeting | Non-financial performance targets included in Budget Bill. Budget arranged around 27 'expenditure areas' as the structural basis for setting and reporting on results |
| 8b. | Evaluation and VFM | Fragmented systems lead by sector-specific 'inspectorates'. Not specifically used to promote public or parliamentary discourse |
| 9. | Fiscal risk and long-term sustainability | Long-term sustainability plan is updated annually with the Spring Fiscal Policy Bill, per the Budget Act. Strong focus on monitoring fiscal risks, with overall fiscal risk is monitored by the Ministry of Finance, with sector-specific risk assessments delegated to relevant government body |
| 10. | Quality assurance and audit | A constitutionally-independent SAI provides financial audit; limited resources for performance audits or governance systems audits. Strong network of independent fiscal institutions and professional agencies to underpin quality of budgetary forecasts. Fiscal council assesses compliance with fiscal rules, fiscal sustainability and fiscal policy stance. |

*Note*: Rows in **bold** represent notable international practice.

## Budgetary Governance in Practice: Switzerland

### *Economic context*

Economic activity in Switzerland is picking up after a weak 2017 outturn. An improving external environment and competitiveness gains will revive activity, raising export growth and invigorating investment. Domestic demand should provide additional stimulus as unemployment decreases and incomes rise. Inflation is projected to remain low given excess capacity. The large current account surplus will persist.

**A: Fiscal Balance and Public Debt**

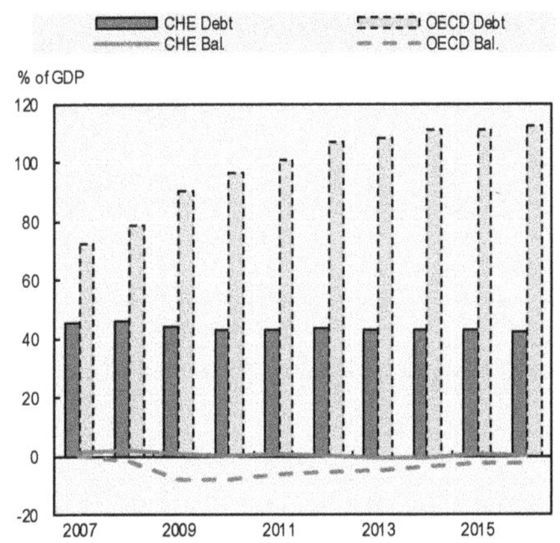


*Note*: The graph is referring to general government fiscal balance and general government gross debt as defined in the OECD National Accounts Statistics.

*Source:* OECD National Accounts Statistics (database); Eurostat Government finance statistics (database).

**C: Public Investment**

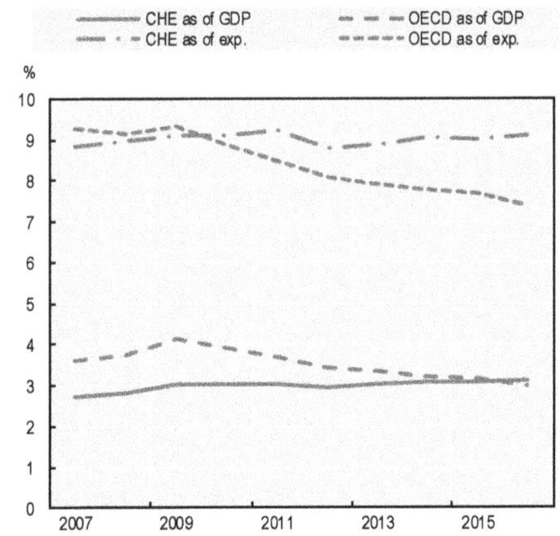


*Note:* The graph is referring to government investment as a percentage of GDP and as a share of total government expenditures.

*Source*: OECD National Accounts Statistics (database).

**D: Expenditure by function (2016)**

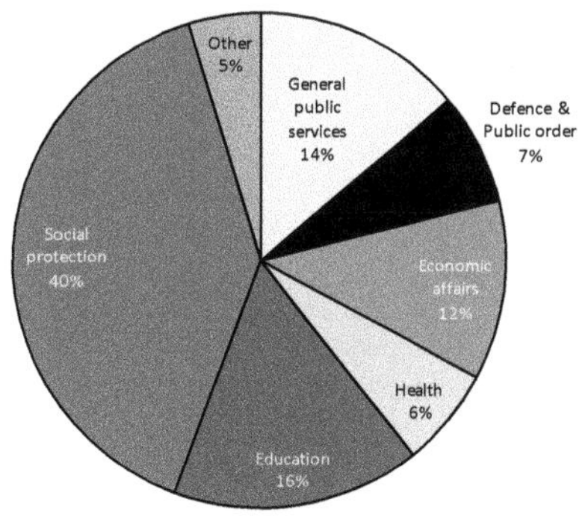


*Source:* OECD National Accounts Statistics (database); Eurostat Government finance statistics (database).

### *Developments in budgetary governance*

The debt level in Switzerland has been reduced since the "debt brake" expenditure rule was first applied in 2003. The general government debt has progressively declined from around 60% of GDP to 42% of GDP in 2017. As a result of the reduction in debt in recent years, important amounts can be saved on interest payments each year, which creates the scope for investments and other important tasks (e.g. social welfare due to ageing population). Switzerland's public finances rank amongst the best in terms of solidity.

The country has also made progress in terms of budget consolidation, implementing the task evaluation project, defining target growth rates for total expenditure and for expenditure by task area, and putting in place a structural reform package. If a deficit emerges despite the medium-term planning and structural evaluation of federal tasks, the Federal Council can deploy short-term austerity measures to ensure a balanced budget and compliance with the debt brake.

| **Central Budget Authority** |
|---|
| Ministry of Finance/Economy<br><br>Weblink: www.efv.admin.ch |

| **Legal Framework** |
|---|
| The General Budget Law includes an exhaustive budgeting framework, legislative authorisation of spending, requirements for internal audit, and public employment provisions. The household law does not foresee a formal procedure in case of budget refusal by parliament. |

| **Budget coverage** |
|---|
| The executive's budget covers central government. |

| **Budget cycle** | |
|---|---|
| Budget circular | February |
| Pre-budget fiscal policy statement | n/a |
| Negotiations with line ministries | April |
| Executive budget proposal | Mid Aug. |
| Parliamentary vote on budget | December |
| *Start of financial year* | *1 Jan.* |
| In-year budget execution reports | Monthly |
| Mid-year implementation report | End of Aug. |
| *End of financial year* | *31 Dec.* |
| Year-end financial statement | April |
| Audited financial report | End of Apr. |
| Parliamentary accounting | Mid June |

**Switzerland 's application of OECD budget principles "at a glance"**

| | | |
|---|---|---|
| **1.** | **Fiscal policy objectives** | **Switzerland employs a countercyclical fiscal policy "debt-brake" rule, allowing limited cyclical deficits during downturn phases of the economic cycle and requiring surpluses when the economy is booming. The debt brake therefore addresses two classical objectives of fiscal policy: ensuring the sustainability of public finances and smoothing economic cycle and growth fluctuations.** |
| 2a. | Strategic alignment | Co-ordination and alignment between the annual budgetary allocations and the medium-term strategic plans and priorities of the government is handled via discussions at Cabinet / Council of ministers |
| 2b. | MTEF | The MTEF operates as an extension of the budget over three more years. The planning comprises all budget items and is rolled over every year. |
| 3. | Capital and infrastructure | Capital and current expenditure are submitted and considered in an integrated way. There is no integrated infrastructure strategy, but there are two long-term strategic development plans for road and rail infrastructure. |
| 4. | Transparency and accessibility | Except for the pre-budget fiscal policy report, for which there is only a press release, all core budget reports are produced and publicly available. Budget data is available in downloadable form. A citizen's budget guide is available on the internet. Budget data can also be examined with a special internet tool ("data center"). |
| 5a. | Parliamentary engagement | Congress has unrestricted powers to amend the budget. A vote on the Executive's budget proposal is not considered a vote of confidence in the government. Both chambers of parliament have co-equal budgetary powers. In case the two chambers do not agree about a certain position of the budget, the lower amount is accepted.<br>The parliament has different forms of support for specialised information/advice on budgetary issues, including specialised staff of Budget/Finance Committee , specialised staff in political party Secretariats, and individual member's staff |
| 5b. | Inclusive public / civic debate | No participatory budgeting and no specific mechanisms in place to seek the views of people from minority communities and/or marginalised groups. |
| 6 | Budget accounting and financial reporting | The budget is prepared on accrual and cash basis. Most of the reports on public finances cover the Central Government; except the long-term sustainability report that covers the General Public Sector. |
| 7. | Budget execution | A single treasury covers all central government revenues and expenditures, with no exceptions. Agencies are allowed to re-allocate funds within their global budget (consisting mainly of personnel, IT and consulting services) up to a limit of 3% of the corresponding credit. Other expenditure adjustments require a supplementary budget. |
| 8a. | Performance budgeting | Performance information plays a role in spending decisions; however, resources are related either to proposed future performance or to performance results in an indirect manner. There is no automatic linkage between performance and funding levels. The weight given to performance information depends on particular circumstances. |
| 8b. | Evaluation and VFM | Line ministries are in charge of monitoring project execution and *ex ante* evaluation, while Supreme Audit Institution (SAI) is in charge of *ex post* evaluation. |
| **9.** | **Fiscal risk and long-term sustainability** | **Fiscal risk are managed in the overall risk management system of the Swiss Confederation, run by the Federal Council and carried out by the line ministries according to their competence. Several specific earmarked contingency reserves are in place (e.g. health care insurances, pension funds etc.). Independently, the Ministry of Finance provides every 4 years a report assessing fiscal risks and the long-term sustainability of public finances.** |
| 10. | Quality assurance and audit | The Swiss Federal Audit Office provide financial audit according to international auditing standards. |

*Note*: Rows in **bold** represent notable international practice.

## Budgetary Governance in Practice: Turkey

### *Economic context*

After a strong performance in 2017, Turkey's economic growth is projected to edge down but to stay between 5% and 5.5 in 2018 and 2019. Consumer price inflation remains far above the target and disinflation is projected to be slow.

### *Fiscal policy plans*

The fiscal policy strategy, which covers the time frame of 2018-20, is to contribute to maintaining economic stability, increasing growth potential, keeping current account deficit at a sustainable level, increasing domestic savings and promoting investments. The fiscal policy targets of public sector borrowing are 2.1% of GDP in 2018, 1.9% in 2019, 1.3% in 2020.

**A: Fiscal Balance and Public Debt**

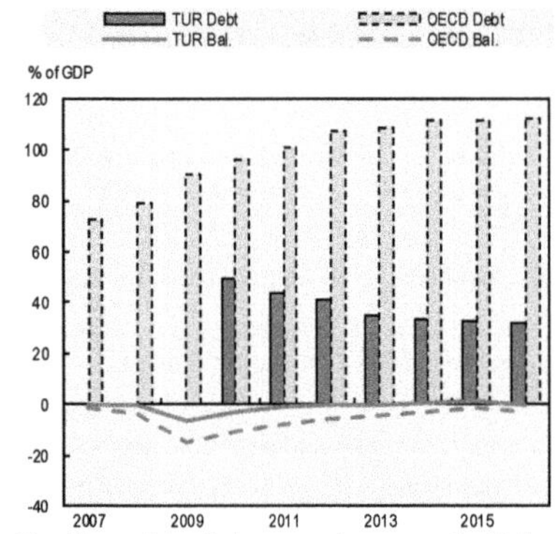


*Note*: The graph is referring to general government fiscal balance and general government gross debt as defined in the OECD National Accounts Statistics.

*Source:* OECD National Accounts Statistics (database); Eurostat Government finance statistics (database).

**B: Fiscal Policy Plans**

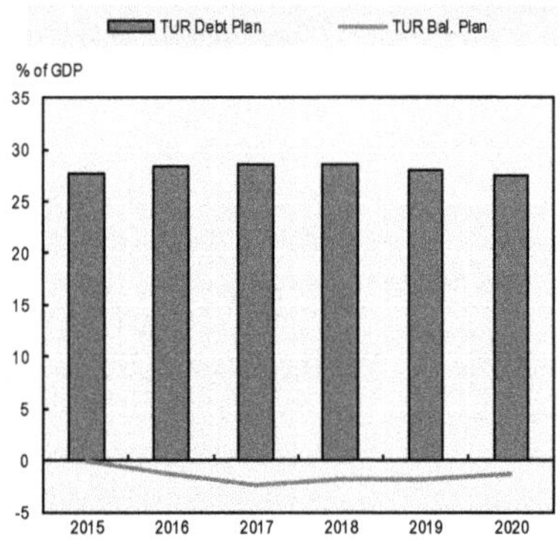


*Note*: The graph is referring to Fiscal Policy Plans that are implemented and/or officially announced as of November 2017 and as indicated by the country. Actual results in graph A may differ as the Fiscal Policy Plans are prepared by the country beforehand and as the Debt and Balance Plan reported by the country are based on the country's own definition; Data are referring to general government.

*Source:* 2018 OECD Fiscal Plans and Budgeting Framework Survey.

**C: Public Investment**

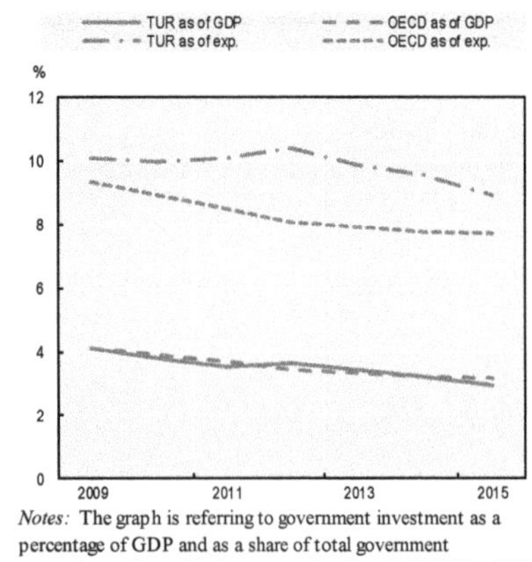


*Notes:* The graph is referring to government investment as a percentage of GDP and as a share of total government expenditures; No public investment data for 2007, 2008 and 2016 available for Turkey.

*Source*: OECD National Accounts Statistics (database).

### *Developments in budgetary governance*

After the financial crisis of 2001, Turkey modernised the legislation concerning the budget process. The main change was the introduction of the Public Financial Management and Control Law (PFMC), adopted by the Turkish parliament in December 2003. The PFMC Law is being implemented step by step, covering public financial management and control at all levels of government.

Turkey started to publish citizens' version of the budget as of 2017 in order to enhance budget transparency. In addition, the tables that are prepared in line with the IMF's GFS manual that are sent to the IMF since 2008 have been extended to the national legislation as of 2015. Therefore, together with the regulation entered into force in 2015, financial statistics, that are prepared and published at the national level, have been harmonised with international financial statistics.

| Central Budget Authority |
|---|
| Republic of Turkey Ministry of Finance<br><br>Weblink: www.maliye.gov.tr |

| Legal Framework |
|---|
| Constitution (Basic Law) includes foundational principles for public financial management; the Public Financial Management and Control Law No.5018 and its corresponding Budget Preparation Manual further specify the comprehensive budgeting framework. |

| Budget coverage |
|---|
| The executive's budget covers central government. |

| Budget cycle | |
|---|---|
| Budget circular | n/a |
| Pre-budget statement | 15 September |
| Negotiations with line ministries | June-October |
| Executive budget proposal | 17 October |
| Parliamentary vote on budget | By 31 December |
| *Start of financial year* | *1 Jan.* |
| In-year budget execution reports | monthly |
| Mid-year implementation report | End of July |
| *End of financial year* | *31 Dec.* |
| Year-end financial statement | End of June |
| Audited financial report | Mid Sep. |
| Parliamentary accounting | 17 Oct. |

| | Turkey's application of OECD budget principles "at a glance" | |
|---|---|---|
| 1. | Fiscal policy objectives | The Medium Term Programme - prepared by the Ministry of Development and the Medium Term Fiscal Plan –prepared by the MoF put in forth the fiscal policy objectives for the next three years. |
| **2a.** | **Strategic alignment** | **The five-year Development Plan, the three-year Medium Term Programme and the three-year Medium Term Expenditure Programme determine the strategic plans and priorities of the government. CBA has a leadership role in promoting alignment between annual budgets and medium-term plans.** |
| 2b. | MTEF | The three-year Medium Term Programme (MTP) which includes macro policies, principles and economic figures as targets and indicators is approved by the Council of Ministers. The three-year Medium Term Expenditure Plan (deficit and borrowing positions targeted) is approved by the High Planning Committee. The ceilings are set at economic classification level. |
| 3. | Capital and infrastructure | Five-year National Development Plan is the overall long-term strategic plan including infrastructure. Capital and current expenditure requests are submitted separately by line ministries and the budget requests funding incrementally each year until the project is completed. |
| 4. | Transparency and accessibility | Budget data is available in downloadable form. Turkey started to publish citizens' version of the budget as of 2017 in order to enhance budget transparency. All core budget reports are open data. |
| 5a. | Parliamentary engagement | In the Budget and Plan Committee, any change in the budget is possible, however in plenary session the legislature has no right to increase expenditures or decrease revenues. |
| 5b. | Inclusive public / civic debate | Citizens do not have a formal voice in budget deliberations. A participative approach to budgeting has not yet been integrated into the budget procedures. |
| 6. | Financial reporting and accounting | Financial statements are prepared on an accrual basis and the budget is prepared on cash and/or commitment basis. |
| 7. | Budget execution | The single treasury fund is mandatory for all revenues and expenditures of central government except for special budget institutions, special accounts of the general budget institutions, extra budgetary funds and revolving funds. |
| 8a. | Performance budgeting | Within the scope of the Public Financial Management Reform carried out in Turkey, performance-based budgeting system has been introduced in public administrations since 2006. In this context, annual performance plans are prepared by public administrations including performance objectives and indicators. Since 2012, work is ongoing to include the programme structure in the budget classification system in order to strengthen the link between government priorities, annual performance plans and budgets. |
| 8b. | Evaluation and VFM | Line ministries are in charge of ex *ante* and *ex post* evaluation, while CBA and SAI are in charge of *ex post* evaluation. |
| 9. | Fiscal risk and long-term sustainability | Economic Co-ordination Board is responsible for identification and management of overall fiscal risks. Internal co-ordination of fiscal management is conducted by main councils/boards composed of ministers and high position level.<br>The long-term fiscal projections cover up to five years and every year it is revised. |
| 10. | Quality assurance and audit | Turkish Court of Accounts is responsible for the year-end financial reporting including quality control over performance information and compliance control on public spending. |

*Note*: Rows in **bold** represent notable international practice.

# Budgetary Governance in Practice: United Kingdom

## *Economic context*

Economic growth in the UK is forecast to weaken in 2018 and 2019. Private consumption is projected to remain subdued as higher inflation, pushed up by the past depreciation of sterling, holds back household purchasing power. The unemployment rate is at a record low, but with slower growth this is unlikely to persist. Exchange rate depreciation should support exports, while import growth is projected to fall owing to weaker private consumption. An agreement about a transition period linked to the EU exit after March 2019 is assumed and should support growth in 2018 and in 2019, reducing the extent to which uncertainty weighs on domestic spending. Prospects of maintaining the closest possible economic relationship between the United Kingdom and the European Union would further support economic growth.

## *Fiscal policy plans*

The fiscal policy strategy is to return the public finances to balance by the middle of the next decade. Interim targets are the reduction of the cyclically adjusted deficit to below 2% of GDP by 2020-21, and Public sector net debt as a share of GDP falling in 2020-21.

**A: Fiscal Balance and Public Debt**

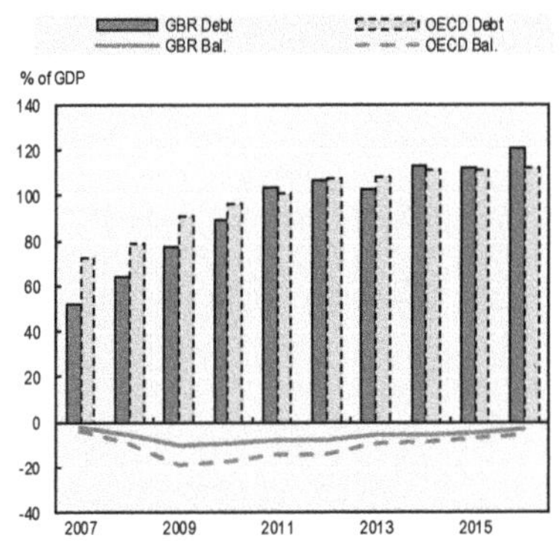


*Note*: The graph is referring to general government fiscal balance and general government gross debt as defined in the OECD National Accounts Statistics.

*Source:* OECD National Accounts Statistics (database); Eurostat Government finance statistics (database).

**C: Public Investment**

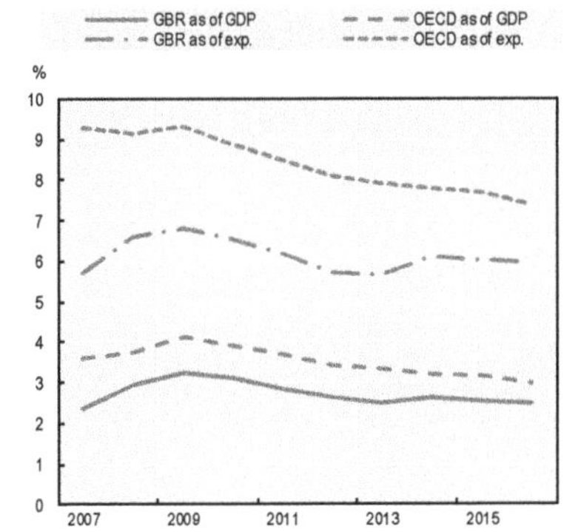


*Note:* The graph is referring to government investment as a percentage of GDP and as a share of total government expenditures.

*Source*: OECD National Accounts Statistics (database).

**D: Expenditure by function (2016)**

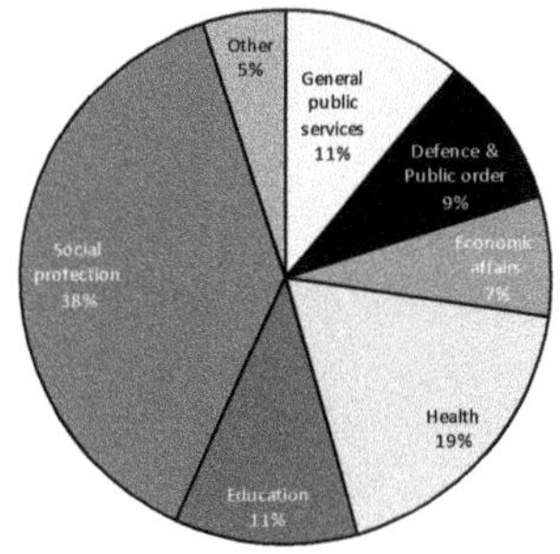


*Source:* OECD National Accounts Statistics (database); Eurostat Government finance statistics (database).

### *Developments in budgetary governance*

In 2015 a revised Charter for Budget Responsibility was approved by Parliament. Key changes introduced under the charter included; two new fiscal rules (a forward-looking target to achieve cyclically-adjusted current balance by the end of the rolling, five-year forecast period; and a target for public sector net debt as a percentage of GDP to be falling at a fixed date of 2015-16) and a "Welfare Cap" intended to ensure that expenditure on welfare remains sustainable during five-year forecast period and is contained within a predetermined ceiling.

The Office for Budget Responsibility was created in 2010 to provide an independent and authoritative analysis of the UK's public finances. In December 2013, the Office for Budget Responsibility was given additional responsibilities in relation to the 'Welfare Cap', to assess the Government's performance against the cap and to prepare, and to publish information on the trends in and drivers of welfare spending within the cap.

Budget transparency is generally high although limited distributional analysis is produced. Gender budgeting is not yet a feature of budgeting in the UK.

**Central Budget Authority**

Her Majesty's Treasury is the central budget authority, covering both economic and financial policy functions. In preparing and communicating budget proposals the Treasury co-ordinates closely with Cabinet Ministers who have ultimate responsibility for determining overall budget parameters and ceilings for line ministries.

Website: www.gov.uk/government/organisations/hm-treasury

**Legal Framework**

The Exchequer and Audit Department Acts of 1866 and 1921 govern the processes of budget preparation and approval by Parliament. The 1998 Finance Act (Code for Fiscal Sustainability) and the 2015 Charter for Budget Responsibility set out requirements in respect of fiscal sustainability. The 2000 Government Resources and Accounts Act introduced the requirement to prepare budget and accounts on the accruals basis.

**Budget coverage**

The United Kingdom is a unitary state, but significant spending powers are devolved to the governments of N. Ireland and Scotland. The Scottish government also has limited revenue raising powers. The national budget is comprehensive in coverage. Financial disclosure rules do not permit any off budget expenditures.

**Budget cycle**

The UK does not have a published budget calendar. The annual budget cycle is in transition, with a single fiscal event replacing the traditional Autumn Statement and Spring Budget. The old and new processes are outlined in the figure below.

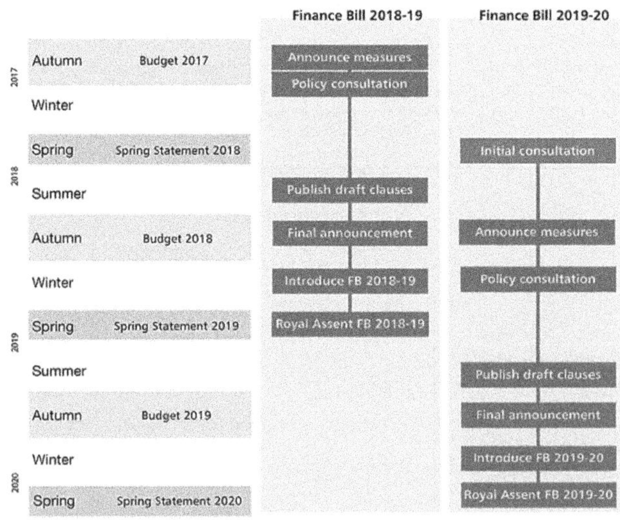

| The United Kingdom's application of OECD budget principles "at a glance" | | |
|---|---|---|
| 1. | Fiscal policy objectives | Government has traditionally set out its fiscal policy and strategy in the annual Autumn Statement. This has presented the macro-economic context, the medium-term outlook for public finances and government's priorities and goals in respect of revenue, expenditure and debt. From 2018 these will be incorporated into a single spring budget statement. |
| 2a. | Strategic alignment | Budget closely linked to the policy programme of the government. Periodic spending reviews identify efficiency saving and redirect spending towards policy priorities. Performance budgeting requires spending departments to set their strategic priorities and spending proposal in a "Single Departmental Plan". |
| 2b. | MTEF | The UK budget statement incorporates a five-year forward perspective. |
| **3.** | **Capital and Infrastructure** | **Five-yearly spending reviews provide annual capital budget allocations by department. All capital spending proposals are appraised following standard rules (Green Book).**<br>**Capital and current expenditure requests are submitted together by line ministries, but the process for deciding upon capital and operating budget requests are distinct.** |
| 4. | Transparency and accessibility | Major budget reports are publicly available, although the budget information provided is highly aggregated and lacks detail especially on the executed budget. The practice of providing a citizens' budget was recently discontinued. |
| 5a. | Parliamentary engagement | Members of parliament have limited engagement in the process of budget preparation, but the Office of Budget Responsibility provides parliament with an independent analysis of fiscal policy and spending proposals. The public accounts committee plays a strong role in monitoring budget results supported by the National Audit office<br>Parliament has very limited power to amend executive budget proposals.<br>The UK Office of Budget Responsibility is an independent fiscal institution. |
| 5b. | Inclusive public / civic debate | The UK has limited public participation in the process of budget preparation. |
| **6.** | **Budget accounting and financial reporting** | **Both budgeting and financial reporting in the UK are accruals based, prepared on a whole of government basis and conform to international financial reporting standards.** |
| 7. | Budget execution | All budget expenditures are made through the Consolidated Fund which is a single treasury account. There are subsidiary consolidated funds for Scotland, Wales and N. Ireland.<br>Departments may reallocate resources freely, subject to expenditure limits approved by parliament, and funds cannot be moved between capital and recurrent spending which are subject to separate limits.<br>Departments are allowed to surrender an underspend in advance of the end of the financial year, in return for a corresponding increase in their budget in the following year, subject to a prudent limit. |
| 8a. | Performance budgeting | Managerial performance budgeting, i.e. using performance information primarily as a tool of performance management and accountability at an organisational and management level<br>Annual performance reporting includes reporting on progress towards achievement of strategic objectives and performance targets. |
| 8b. | Evaluation and VFM | Legal requirement to evaluate all expenditure programmes; both *ex ante* and *ex post*, *ex post* evaluation is also carried out by the SAI.<br>The UK has a history of periodic, comprehensive spending reviews focused on deficit reduction and re-alignment of spending to match the priorities of new administrations. |
| 9. | Fiscal risk and long-term sustainability | The budget statement includes discussion of the government's fiscal strategy, including short-term risks and measures to ensure long-term fiscal sustainability. Independently, the Office of Budget Responsibility provides a report to Parliament assessing fiscal risks and the long-term sustainability of public finances. |
| **10.** | **Quality assurance and audit** | **The National Audit Office, a constitutionally independent SAI, audits all public entities either directly or using private sector audit firms. The NAO audits government's financial statements and carries out value for money audits on a more limited number of areas of spending. The independent Office of Budget responsibility also exercises a range of functions to promote objective, informed budgetary policy-making and accountability.** |

*Note*: Rows in **bold** represent notable international practice.

# Annex A. General Government country data overview

### Table A A.1. General government fiscal balance as a percentage of GDP

| | General government fiscal balance as a percentage of GDP | | | | | | | | | |
|---|---|---|---|---|---|---|---|---|---|---|
| | 2007 | 2008 | 2009 | 2010 | 2011 | 2012 | 2013 | 2014 | 2015 | 2016 |
| Australia | 0.71 | -3.75 | -5.5 | -4.38 | -4.56 | -2.86 | -2.83 | -2.36 | -2.24 | -1.44 |
| Austria | -1.35 | -1.5 | -5.33 | -4.44 | -2.55 | -2.19 | -1.95 | -2.73 | -1.05 | -1.59 |
| Belgium | 0.07 | -1.1 | -5.38 | -4 | -4.13 | -4.23 | -3.14 | -3.08 | -2.48 | -2.48 |
| Canada | 1.82 | 0.18 | -3.89 | -4.75 | -3.32 | -2.53 | -1.87 | 0.18 | -0.13 | -1.1 |
| Chile | 7.74 | 4.67 | -4.04 | -0.17 | 1.29 | 0.54 | -0.52 | -1.51 | -2.07 | -2.68 |
| Czech Republic | -0.65 | -1.98 | -5.45 | -4.19 | -2.72 | -3.93 | -1.25 | -2.1 | -0.61 | 0.73 |
| Denmark | 5.02 | 3.17 | -2.8 | -2.71 | -2.06 | -3.49 | -1.24 | 1.14 | -1.47 | -0.41 |
| Estonia | 2.72 | -2.67 | -2.18 | 0.19 | 1.16 | -0.26 | -0.17 | 0.68 | 0.07 | -0.29 |
| Finland | 5.13 | 4.18 | -2.53 | -2.61 | -1.04 | -2.18 | -2.61 | -3.21 | -2.76 | -1.79 |
| France | -2.64 | -3.26 | -7.17 | -6.89 | -5.15 | -4.98 | -4.08 | -3.9 | -3.63 | -3.41 |
| Germany | 0.19 | -0.18 | -3.23 | -4.22 | -0.96 | -0.03 | -0.14 | 0.53 | 0.84 | 1.01 |
| Greece | -6.71 | -10.18 | -15.14 | -11.2 | -10.28 | -8.87 | -13.15 | -3.62 | -5.67 | 0.63 |
| Hungary | -5.02 | -3.68 | -4.54 | -4.47 | -5.41 | -2.4 | -2.62 | -2.6 | -1.91 | -1.66 |
| Iceland | 4.91 | -13.03 | -9.64 | -9.72 | -5.56 | -3.72 | -1.83 | -0.07 | -0.81 | 12.57 |
| Ireland | 0.32 | -6.96 | -13.8 | -32.05 | -12.72 | -8.03 | -6.1 | -3.63 | -1.89 | -0.52 |
| Israel | -0.68 | -2.77 | -5.66 | -3.68 | -2.93 | -4.79 | -4.14 | -3.35 | -2.11 | -2.11 |
| Italy | -1.46 | -2.63 | -5.25 | -4.21 | -3.68 | -2.92 | -2.92 | -2.99 | -2.58 | -2.48 |
| Japan | -2.76 | -4.12 | -9.78 | -9.15 | -9.09 | -8.3 | -7.64 | -5.38 | -3.55 | -3.42 |
| Korea | 4.24 | 2.34 | -1.32 | 0.97 | 0.98 | 1.01 | 1.34 | 1.27 | 1.28 | 2.37 |
| Latvia | -0.51 | -4.2 | -9.13 | -8.69 | -4.31 | -1.21 | -1.16 | -1.49 | -1.36 | 0.06 |
| Lithuania | -0.82 | -3.08 | -9.11 | -6.9 | -8.94 | -3.15 | -2.61 | -0.62 | -0.24 | 0.27 |
| Luxembourg | 4.15 | 3.32 | -0.67 | -0.66 | 0.51 | 0.34 | 0.98 | 1.33 | 1.36 | 1.61 |
| Mexico | -0.71 | -0.93 | -3.08 | -2.97 | -5.3 | -4.72 | -4.55 | -4.21 | -5.16 | -2.7 |
| Netherlands | 0.21 | 0.22 | -5.43 | -4.99 | -4.29 | -3.88 | -2.37 | -2.27 | -2.05 | 0.37 |
| New Zealand | 4.27 | 0.47 | -2.84 | -7.22 | -4.08 | -2.2 | -0.37 | 0.19 | 0.21 | 1.18 |
| Norway | 17.11 | 18.67 | 10.33 | 10.99 | 13.43 | 13.83 | 10.77 | 8.75 | 6.06 | 3.99 |
| Poland | -1.85 | -3.6 | -7.25 | -7.34 | -4.83 | -3.71 | -4.11 | -3.62 | -2.65 | -2.35 |
| Portugal | -3.01 | -3.77 | -9.81 | -11.17 | -7.38 | -5.66 | -4.84 | -7.17 | -4.4 | -1.98 |
| Slovak Republic | -1.95 | -2.43 | -7.8 | -7.48 | -4.28 | -4.34 | -2.72 | -2.7 | -2.73 | -2.21 |
| Slovenia | -0.08 | -1.41 | -5.84 | -5.63 | -6.67 | -4.04 | -14.68 | -5.52 | -2.86 | -1.93 |
| Spain | 1.92 | -4.42 | -10.95 | -9.38 | -9.64 | -10.47 | -6.99 | -5.97 | -5.28 | -4.51 |
| Sweden | 3.35 | 1.9 | -0.72 | -0.03 | -0.21 | -0.98 | -1.36 | -1.56 | 0.18 | 1.19 |
| Switzerland | 1.61 | 1.93 | 0.5 | 0.36 | 0.74 | 0.38 | -0.43 | -0.21 | 0.65 | 0.33 |
| Turkey | .. | .. | -6.17 | -2.68 | -0.74 | -0.19 | 0.21 | 0.24 | 1.31 | .. |
| United Kingdom | -2.64 | -5.17 | -10.12 | -9.42 | -7.47 | -8.15 | -5.4 | -5.45 | -4.26 | -2.97 |
| United States | -3.55 | -7.02 | -12.67 | -12.01 | -10.61 | -8.86 | -5.36 | -4.78 | -4.22 | -4.94 |
| OECD | -1.58 | -3.82 | -8.5 | -8.02 | -6.79 | -5.9 | -4.22 | -3.52 | -2.97 | -2.83 |

*Note*: Data for Chile and Turkey are not included in the OECD average because of missing time series or main non-financial government aggregates; Information on data for Israel: http://dx.doi.org/10.1787/888932315602.
*Source*: OECD National Accounts Statistics (database).

**Table A A.2. General government gross debt as a percentage of GDP**

| | General government gross debt as a percentage of GDP | | | | | | | | | |
|---|---|---|---|---|---|---|---|---|---|---|
| | 2007 | 2008 | 2009 | 2010 | 2011 | 2012 | 2013 | 2014 | 2015 | 2016 |
| Australia | 13.39 | 15.66 | 21.23 | 23.97 | 29.05 | 33.56 | 34.75 | 38.99 | 40.04 | 40.83 |
| Austria | 68.96 | 74.19 | 86.33 | 90.54 | 91.47 | 99.37 | 96.53 | 104.13 | 102.64 | 103.71 |
| Belgium | 93.85 | 101.14 | 109.49 | 107.76 | 110.38 | 120.36 | 118.32 | 130.55 | 127.34 | 128.37 |
| Canada | 70.63 | 71.52 | 83.9 | 86.33 | 89.14 | 92.91 | 90.07 | 91.89 | 97.48 | 97.77 |
| Chile | 11.26 | 12.43 | 13.31 | 15.27 | 17.85 | 18.37 | 18.99 | 22.39 | 24.41 | 28.08 |
| Czech Republic | 30.54 | 34.31 | 41.08 | 45.58 | 48.35 | 57.88 | 57.96 | 55.25 | 52.01 | 47.64 |
| Denmark | 34.59 | 41.94 | 49.27 | 53.44 | 60.11 | 60.62 | 56.73 | 59.14 | 53.79 | 52.45 |
| Estonia | 7.25 | 8.41 | 12.74 | 11.93 | 9.54 | 13.15 | 13.62 | 14.06 | 12.95 | 13.08 |
| Finland | 39.09 | 38.28 | 49.23 | 55.06 | 57.52 | 64.34 | 64.77 | 71.67 | 75.15 | 75.44 |
| France | 75.73 | 81.65 | 93.28 | 96.98 | 100.74 | 110.32 | 110.89 | 119.81 | 120.27 | 123.38 |
| Germany | 64.18 | 68.08 | 75.47 | 84.45 | 84.18 | 88.11 | 83.27 | 83.52 | 79.1 | 76.39 |
| Greece | 112.78 | 117.45 | 134.68 | 128.97 | 110.89 | 163.76 | 178.98 | 180.47 | 183.56 | 187.89 |
| Hungary | 70.93 | 74.51 | 83.44 | 85.27 | 94.22 | 97.31 | 95.31 | 98.56 | 97.43 | 97.28 |
| Iceland | 30.17 | 70.41 | 84.99 | 90.43 | 97.1 | 94.85 | 86.85 | 79.51 | 72.49 | 66.39 |
| Ireland | 27.46 | 47.47 | 67.54 | 83.57 | 110.94 | 129.1 | 131.42 | 121.65 | 88.66 | 83.45 |
| Israel | 80.08 | 80.62 | 83.87 | 80.06 | 78.21 | 78.99 | 76.59 | 77.88 | 77.94 | 75.63 |
| Italy | 110.7 | 112.99 | 125.98 | 124.88 | 117.94 | 136.24 | 143.72 | 156.1 | 157.01 | 155.74 |
| Japan | 156.68 | 162.17 | 182.59 | 186.22 | 203.05 | 211.17 | 213.32 | 221.22 | 223.38 | 221.49 |
| Korea | 27.65 | 28.63 | 31.36 | 33.33 | 35.95 | 38.39 | 40.38 | 43.63 | 45.64 | 45.12 |
| Latvia | 12.51 | 22.65 | 41.02 | 52.68 | 48.56 | 47.58 | 44.37 | 49.82 | 45.36 | 49.35 |
| Lithuania | 19.38 | 17.12 | 34.13 | 45.47 | 45.73 | 51.26 | 48 | 52.57 | 53.82 | 51.73 |
| Luxembourg | 15.84 | 24.43 | 21.98 | 27.02 | 26.54 | 28.32 | 28.83 | 29.1 | 28.74 | 27.4 |
| Mexico | 32.44 | 34.32 | 30.56 | 31.15 | 37.14 | 41.13 | 47.11 | 49.52 | 53.47 | 52.97 |
| Netherlands | 48.46 | 61.26 | 64.07 | 67.97 | 71.93 | 77.67 | 76.62 | 81.22 | 77.47 | 75.32 |
| New Zealand | 33.47 | 35.55 | 39.14 | 43.26 | 55.25 | 60.53 | 62.18 | 55.82 | 54.38 | 50.84 |
| Norway | 55.53 | 54.15 | 48.04 | 48.35 | 33.76 | 34.88 | 35.21 | 32.97 | 38.57 | 42.5 |
| Poland | 51.06 | 53.36 | 56.73 | 61.05 | 61.21 | 64.39 | 64.99 | 70.11 | 69.46 | 72.11 |
| Portugal | 78.1 | 82.76 | 96.11 | 104.07 | 107.85 | 137.1 | 141.43 | 151.4 | 149.15 | 146.07 |
| Slovak Republic | 34.79 | 33.79 | 42.46 | 47.39 | 49.95 | 58.3 | 61.16 | 60.43 | 59.98 | 59.98 |
| Slovenia | 30.06 | 29.69 | 43.73 | 47.84 | 51.41 | 61.69 | 78.84 | 99.28 | 102.37 | 97.17 |
| Spain | 41.73 | 47.21 | 61.81 | 66.56 | 77.69 | 92.53 | 105.73 | 118.41 | 116.44 | 116.56 |
| Sweden | 46.45 | 45.08 | 48.24 | 45.91 | 46.08 | 46.72 | 49.03 | 55.28 | 53.52 | 51.93 |
| Switzerland | 45.61 | 45.94 | 44.21 | 42.62 | 43.03 | 43.81 | 43.08 | 43.14 | 43.18 | 42.46 |
| Turkey | .. | .. | .. | 49.22 | 43.93 | 41.25 | 34.54 | 33.4 | 32.77 | 32.06 |
| United Kingdom | 51.65 | 63.58 | 77.06 | 89.22 | 103.36 | 106.87 | 102.48 | 112.83 | 112.15 | 121.02 |
| United States | 64.59 | 73.69 | 86.95 | 95.64 | 99.95 | 103.52 | 105.39 | 105.06 | 105.28 | 107.23 |
| OECD | 72.75 | 78.93 | 90.47 | 96.28 | 100.86 | 107.1 | 108.26 | 111.55 | 111.49 | 112.45 |

*Note*: Data for Australia, Canada, Iceland, Sweden and the United States are reported on an adjusted basis (i.e. excluding unfunded pension liabilities); Data for Turkey and Mexico are not included in the OECD average due to missing time-series or statistical discrepancies in the recording of financial instruments; Information on data for Israel: http://dx.doi.org/10.1787/888932315602.

*Source*: OECD National Accounts Statistics (database); Eurostat Government finance statistics (database).

**Table A A.3. Government investment as a share of total government expenditures**

| | Government investment as a share of total government expenditures | | | | | | | | | |
|---|---|---|---|---|---|---|---|---|---|---|
| | 2007 | 2008 | 2009 | 2010 | 2011 | 2012 | 2013 | 2014 | 2015 | 2016 |
| Australia | 9.15 | 9.26 | 11.38 | 10.34 | 10.11 | 8.45 | 8.71 | 8.31 | 8.82 | 9.78 |
| Austria | 6.38 | 6.73 | 6.26 | 6.28 | 5.95 | 5.7 | 5.86 | 5.58 | 5.81 | 5.95 |
| Belgium | 4.2 | 4.33 | 4.52 | 4.43 | 4.76 | 4.75 | 4.43 | 4.23 | 4.28 | 4.15 |
| Canada | 9.52 | 9.38 | 10.35 | 11.06 | 10.22 | 10.13 | 9.46 | 8.55 | 8.84 | 9.46 |
| Czech Republic | 11.23 | 12.95 | 12.9 | 11.25 | 10.41 | 9.23 | 8.61 | 9.5 | 12.22 | 8.19 |
| Denmark | 5.73 | 5.75 | 5.4 | 5.54 | 5.69 | 6.37 | 6.36 | 6.84 | 6.3 | 6.92 |
| Estonia | 17.41 | 16.26 | 13.68 | 8.37 | 9.39 | 16.04 | 13.64 | 13.44 | 12.93 | 11.64 |
| Finland | 7.25 | 7.37 | 7.24 | 6.72 | 6.99 | 7.18 | 7.19 | 7.25 | 6.68 | 6.87 |
| France | 7.79 | 7.69 | 7.78 | 7.57 | 7.27 | 7.43 | 7.24 | 6.71 | 6.19 | 6.16 |
| Germany | 4.34 | 4.59 | 4.86 | 4.4 | 4.95 | 4.91 | 4.64 | 4.51 | 4.73 | 4.74 |
| Greece | 10.8 | 11.29 | 9.76 | 7.13 | 4.63 | 4.65 | 7.67 | 7.96 | 8.78 | 6.99 |
| Hungary | 8.56 | 6.34 | 6.76 | 7.42 | 6.73 | 7.72 | 8.93 | 10.96 | 13.18 | 6.03 |
| Iceland | 11.52 | 8.78 | 8.35 | 6.96 | 5.97 | 5.91 | 6.61 | 6.79 | 6.74 | 6.11 |
| Ireland | 12.84 | 12.73 | 7.8 | 5.03 | 5.37 | 4.83 | 4.98 | 5.88 | 6.12 | 6.89 |
| Israel | 3.91 | 4.25 | 3.8 | 3.36 | 3.39 | 4.33 | 4.6 | 4.62 | 3.68 | 4.29 |
| Italy | 6.15 | 6.17 | 6.75 | 5.86 | 5.61 | 5.09 | 4.77 | 4.55 | 4.57 | 4.39 |
| Japan | 11.23 | 10.79 | 10.64 | 10.26 | 9.57 | 9.58 | 10.16 | 10.46 | 10.03 | 9.79 |
| Korea | 20.05 | 19.32 | 22.53 | 19.67 | 17.42 | 16.98 | 17.2 | 15.67 | 15.48 | 15.28 |
| Latvia | 18.79 | 13.31 | 9.48 | 9.89 | 11.84 | 12.57 | 11.79 | 11.81 | 12.65 | 10.08 |
| Lithuania | 15.31 | 14.37 | 9.93 | 11.59 | 10.42 | 10.44 | 9.68 | 9.61 | 10.5 | 8.81 |
| Luxembourg | 9.19 | 9.18 | 9.81 | 10.76 | 9.83 | 9.02 | 8.32 | 8.94 | 9.03 | 9.74 |
| Mexico | 9.39 | 10.47 | 11.97 | 11.27 | 9.48 | 8.38 | 7.92 | 7.09 | 6.48 | 2.06 |
| Netherlands | 8.31 | 8.5 | 8.9 | 8.36 | 8 | 7.64 | 6.29 | 7.16 | 7.32 | 7.3 |
| New Zealand | 10.7 | 10.81 | 11.02 | 9.11 | 9.43 | 10.01 | 10.47 | 10.13 | 10.55 | 10.38 |
| Norway | 8.89 | 9.35 | 9.76 | 9.05 | 9.08 | 8.86 | 9.51 | 9.96 | 9.83 | 10.29 |
| Poland | 10.56 | 10.73 | 11.32 | 12.31 | 12.95 | 10.48 | 9.01 | 9.94 | 10.12 | 7.77 |
| Portugal | 7.15 | 6.26 | 8.46 | 10.31 | 6.94 | 4.7 | 4.53 | 3.94 | 4.88 | 3.36 |
| Slovak Republic | 8.67 | 8.82 | 9.1 | 9.05 | 9.12 | 8.43 | 8.31 | 8.88 | 14.17 | 8.33 |
| Slovenia | 10.91 | 11.02 | 10.68 | 9.76 | 8.38 | 8.45 | 7.72 | 10.38 | 9.96 | 7.13 |
| Spain | 12.03 | 11.58 | 11.48 | 10.54 | 8.27 | 5.31 | 5.08 | 4.96 | 5.9 | 4.72 |
| Sweden | 7.94 | 8.08 | 8.14 | 8.5 | 8.73 | 8.73 | 8.48 | 8.51 | 8.54 | 8.58 |
| Switzerland | 8.83 | 8.95 | 9.1 | 9.12 | 9.24 | 8.81 | 8.86 | 9.06 | 9.02 | 9.08 |
| Turkey | .. | .. | 10.08 | 9.98 | 10.1 | 10.38 | 9.87 | 9.53 | 8.9 | .. |
| United Kingdom | 5.72 | 6.59 | 6.83 | 6.54 | 6.19 | 5.71 | 5.66 | 6.11 | 6.03 | 5.97 |
| United States | 10.54 | 10.12 | 9.84 | 9.65 | 9.39 | 9.07 | 8.7 | 8.49 | 8.07 | 8.19 |
| OECD | 9.26 | 9.15 | 9.31 | 8.89 | 8.5 | 8.08 | 7.89 | 7.77 | 7.68 | 7.4 |

*Note*: Data for Chile are not available. Data for Turkey are not included in the OECD average because of missing time series; Information on data for Israel: http://dx.doi.org/10.1787/888932315602.
*Source*: OECD National Accounts Statistics (database).

**Table A A.4. Government investment as a percentage of GDP**

| | Government investment as a percentage of GDP | | | | | | | | | |
|---|---|---|---|---|---|---|---|---|---|---|
| | 2007 | 2008 | 2009 | 2010 | 2011 | 2012 | 2013 | 2014 | 2015 | 2016 |
| Australia | 3.23 | 3.48 | 4.47 | 3.93 | 3.85 | 3.14 | 3.25 | 3.1 | 3.33 | 3.59 |
| Austria | 3.14 | 3.36 | 3.39 | 3.32 | 3.03 | 2.92 | 3.03 | 2.92 | 2.96 | 3.01 |
| Belgium | 2.03 | 2.18 | 2.45 | 2.36 | 2.59 | 2.65 | 2.48 | 2.34 | 2.31 | 2.21 |
| Canada | 3.76 | 3.72 | 4.6 | 4.87 | 4.34 | 4.23 | 3.88 | 3.36 | 3.6 | 3.92 |
| Czech Republic | 4.53 | 5.26 | 5.7 | 4.9 | 4.48 | 4.11 | 3.67 | 4.03 | 5.1 | 3.23 |
| Denmark | 2.84 | 2.9 | 3.05 | 3.14 | 3.21 | 3.69 | 3.55 | 3.77 | 3.45 | 3.71 |
| Estonia | 5.93 | 6.46 | 6.3 | 3.39 | 3.51 | 6.31 | 5.25 | 5.17 | 5.2 | 4.73 |
| Finland | 3.39 | 3.56 | 3.96 | 3.68 | 3.8 | 4.04 | 4.13 | 4.21 | 3.81 | 3.85 |
| France | 4.09 | 4.1 | 4.45 | 4.31 | 4.09 | 4.24 | 4.15 | 3.84 | 3.52 | 3.48 |
| Germany | 1.86 | 2 | 2.31 | 2.08 | 2.21 | 2.18 | 2.07 | 1.99 | 2.06 | 2.08 |
| Greece | 5.09 | 5.74 | 5.28 | 3.74 | 2.51 | 2.59 | 4.78 | 4 | 4.73 | 3.46 |
| Hungary | 4.27 | 3.08 | 3.4 | 3.65 | 3.33 | 3.74 | 4.4 | 5.41 | 6.61 | 2.8 |
| Iceland | 4.72 | 4.85 | 4.03 | 3.42 | 2.72 | 2.67 | 2.89 | 3.05 | 2.86 | 2.76 |
| Ireland | 4.61 | 5.32 | 3.67 | 3.27 | 2.49 | 2.02 | 2 | 2.21 | 1.77 | 1.87 |
| Israel | 1.67 | 1.8 | 1.61 | 1.39 | 1.38 | 1.8 | 1.9 | 1.89 | 1.46 | 1.7 |
| Italy | 2.88 | 2.95 | 3.45 | 2.92 | 2.77 | 2.58 | 2.43 | 2.31 | 2.3 | 2.17 |
| Japan | 3.93 | 3.89 | 4.33 | 4.08 | 3.89 | 3.89 | 4.14 | 4.21 | 3.94 | 3.83 |
| Korea | 5.95 | 6.18 | 7.86 | 6.1 | 5.64 | 5.56 | 5.46 | 5.01 | 5 | 4.93 |
| Latvia | 6.39 | 5.01 | 4.19 | 4.5 | 4.79 | 4.77 | 4.45 | 4.5 | 4.84 | 3.74 |
| Lithuania | 5.4 | 5.47 | 4.46 | 4.9 | 4.43 | 3.77 | 3.44 | 3.33 | 3.66 | 3.01 |
| Luxembourg | 3.48 | 3.65 | 4.43 | 4.75 | 4.16 | 3.98 | 3.6 | 3.74 | 3.75 | 4.11 |
| Mexico | 2.03 | 2.62 | 3.05 | 2.87 | 2.73 | 2.39 | 2.25 | 1.99 | 1.83 | 0.56 |
| Netherlands | 3.53 | 3.7 | 4.29 | 4.02 | 3.76 | 3.6 | 2.91 | 3.31 | 3.29 | 3.17 |
| New Zealand | 4.12 | 4.47 | 4.63 | 4.37 | 4.13 | 4.24 | 4.2 | 4.04 | 4.12 | 4.02 |
| Norway | 3.68 | 3.76 | 4.5 | 4.07 | 3.97 | 3.8 | 4.18 | 4.56 | 4.8 | 5.23 |
| Poland | 4.56 | 4.75 | 5.1 | 5.64 | 5.68 | 4.49 | 3.84 | 4.2 | 4.21 | 3.19 |
| Portugal | 3.18 | 2.84 | 4.25 | 5.34 | 3.47 | 2.28 | 2.26 | 2.04 | 2.35 | 1.51 |
| Slovak Republic | 3.15 | 3.26 | 4.01 | 3.81 | 3.72 | 3.42 | 3.44 | 3.73 | 6.41 | 3.46 |
| Slovenia | 4.6 | 4.84 | 5.15 | 4.81 | 4.19 | 4.1 | 4.59 | 5.18 | 4.75 | 3.23 |
| Spain | 4.69 | 4.77 | 5.25 | 4.81 | 3.79 | 2.55 | 2.31 | 2.22 | 2.58 | 1.99 |
| Sweden | 3.92 | 4.04 | 4.29 | 4.32 | 4.39 | 4.48 | 4.41 | 4.35 | 4.24 | 4.24 |
| Switzerland | 2.71 | 2.8 | 3.02 | 3.01 | 3.04 | 2.93 | 3.03 | 3.06 | 3.07 | 3.12 |
| Turkey | .. | .. | 4.12 | 3.8 | 3.55 | 3.64 | 3.4 | 3.21 | 2.95 | .. |
| United Kingdom | 2.35 | 2.94 | 3.25 | 3.13 | 2.86 | 2.63 | 2.5 | 2.64 | 2.56 | 2.48 |
| United States | 3.89 | 3.99 | 4.23 | 4.14 | 3.93 | 3.63 | 3.37 | 3.23 | 3.03 | 3.1 |
| OECD | 3.6 | 3.73 | 4.13 | 3.91 | 3.67 | 3.44 | 3.32 | 3.22 | 3.14 | 3 |

*Note*: Data for Chile are not available. Data for Turkey are not included in the OECD average because of missing time series; Information on data for Israel: http://dx.doi.org/10.1787/888932315602.
*Source*: OECD National Accounts Statistics (database).

**Table A A.5. Structure of general government expenditures by function, 2016**

| | General public services | Defence & Public order and safety | Economic affairs | Health | Education | Social protection | Other |
|---|---|---|---|---|---|---|---|
| Australia | 12.5 | 9.3 | 10.1 | 19.8 | 14.6 | 27.4 | 6.2 |
| Austria | 13.0 | 3.9 | 11.2 | 15.8 | 9.8 | 42.6 | 3.9 |
| Belgium | 14.9 | 4.8 | 12.2 | 13.9 | 12.0 | 37.6 | 4.6 |
| Chile | 11.3 | 11.9 | 10.4 | 15.7 | 20.6 | 24.6 | 5.7 |
| Czech Republic | 10.6 | 6.2 | 15.0 | 18.9 | 11.3 | 31.2 | 6.7 |
| Denmark | 12.6 | 4.0 | 6.2 | 16.1 | 12.9 | 43.6 | 4.6 |
| Estonia | 10.4 | 10.8 | 10.5 | 13.1 | 14.6 | 33.3 | 7.4 |
| Finland | 14.4 | 4.5 | 8.1 | 12.9 | 10.8 | 45.8 | 3.6 |
| France | 10.9 | 6.2 | 9.9 | 14.4 | 9.6 | 43.3 | 5.8 |
| Germany | 13.2 | 5.9 | 7.0 | 16.2 | 9.5 | 43.6 | 4.5 |
| Greece | 18.5 | 8.7 | 7.6 | 9.9 | 8.6 | 41.5 | 5.2 |
| Hungary | 17.0 | 6.5 | 15.1 | 10.3 | 10.5 | 30.7 | 9.9 |
| Iceland | 15.1 | 3.1 | 10.7 | 16.6 | 15.8 | 29.8 | 9.0 |
| Ireland | 13.6 | 4.9 | 8.5 | 19.2 | 12.1 | 36.5 | 5.2 |
| Israel | 12.6 | 18.7 | 5.9 | 13.0 | 17.3 | 27.1 | 5.5 |
| Italy | 16.0 | 6.4 | 8.0 | 14.1 | 7.9 | 42.8 | 4.9 |
| Japan | 10.2 | 5.4 | 9.4 | 19.4 | 8.6 | 41.4 | 5.7 |
| Korea | 16.2 | 11.8 | 15.2 | 13.2 | 16.1 | 20.5 | 7.1 |
| Latvia | 11.9 | 10.2 | 13.2 | 10.0 | 14.7 | 32.2 | 7.7 |
| Lithuania | 11.9 | 8.9 | 8.8 | 17.1 | 15.1 | 32.8 | 5.4 |
| Luxembourg | 11.3 | 3.4 | 13.2 | 11.3 | 11.5 | 43.0 | 6.4 |
| Netherlands | 9.9 | 7.0 | 9.0 | 17.7 | 12.2 | 37.3 | 7.0 |
| Norway | 9.2 | 5.4 | 10.6 | 17.1 | 11.1 | 40.0 | 6.6 |
| Poland | 11.3 | 9.2 | 9.9 | 11.3 | 12.1 | 41.2 | 5.1 |
| Portugal | 18.4 | 6.1 | 7.1 | 13.2 | 10.8 | 40.0 | 4.3 |
| Slovak Republic | 12.7 | 8.0 | 10.8 | 17.7 | 9.3 | 36.5 | 5.1 |
| Slovenia | 14.6 | 5.8 | 10.1 | 14.9 | 12.4 | 37.0 | 5.3 |
| Spain | 14.4 | 6.8 | 9.3 | 14.3 | 9.5 | 39.9 | 5.7 |
| Sweden | 13.4 | 5.0 | 8.4 | 13.9 | 13.4 | 41.7 | 4.3 |
| Switzerland | 13.9 | 7.3 | 11.7 | 6.5 | 16.3 | 39.6 | 4.7 |
| United Kingdom | 11.0 | 9.1 | 7.3 | 18.3 | 11.2 | 38.1 | 5.1 |
| United States | 14.2 | 13.9 | 8.8 | 24.4 | 16.1 | 20.6 | 2.0 |
| OECD | 13.2 | 9.4 | 9.1 | 18.9 | 12.5 | 32.8 | 4.2 |

*Note*: "Other" includes environment protection, recreation, culture and religion and housing and community amenities.

Data for Australia are based on Government finance statistics provided by the Australian Bureau of Statistics; Data are not available for Canada, Mexico, New Zealand and Turkey; Data for Iceland are not included in the OECD average due to missing time-series; Information on data for Israel: http://dx.doi.org/10.1787/888932315602.

*Source*: OECD National Accounts Statistics (database); Eurostat Government finance statistics (database).

**Table A A.6. General government revenues as a percentage of GDP**

| | General government revenues as a percentage of GDP | | | | | | | | | |
|---|---|---|---|---|---|---|---|---|---|---|
| | 2007 | 2008 | 2009 | 2010 | 2011 | 2012 | 2013 | 2014 | 2015 | 2016 |
| Australia | 36.05 | 33.9 | 33.8 | 33.66 | 33.46 | 34.34 | 34.53 | 34.94 | 35.57 | 35.3 |
| Austria | 47.89 | 48.38 | 48.82 | 48.4 | 48.34 | 49.02 | 49.7 | 49.61 | 49.95 | 49.04 |
| Belgium | 48.31 | 49.18 | 48.77 | 49.34 | 50.32 | 51.63 | 52.7 | 52.18 | 51.36 | 50.81 |
| Canada | 41.27 | 39.87 | 40.51 | 39.26 | 39.17 | 39.29 | 39.14 | 39.43 | 40.55 | 40.37 |
| Czech Republic | 39.72 | 38.66 | 38.75 | 39.32 | 40.31 | 40.55 | 41.35 | 40.33 | 41.09 | 40.16 |
| Denmark | 54.61 | 53.58 | 53.74 | 53.96 | 54.37 | 54.46 | 54.58 | 56.36 | 53.31 | 53.19 |
| Estonia | 36.81 | 37.08 | 43.87 | 40.7 | 38.58 | 39.05 | 38.28 | 39.11 | 40.3 | 40.33 |
| Finland | 51.93 | 52.44 | 52.23 | 52.14 | 53.34 | 54.02 | 54.89 | 54.9 | 54.38 | 54.19 |
| France | 49.93 | 50.03 | 49.98 | 50 | 51.14 | 52.13 | 53.14 | 53.31 | 53.17 | 53.17 |
| Germany | 43 | 43.4 | 44.34 | 43.03 | 43.75 | 44.26 | 44.55 | 44.62 | 44.49 | 44.98 |
| Greece | 40.36 | 40.67 | 38.94 | 41.28 | 43.81 | 46.87 | 49.14 | 46.63 | 48.15 | 50.15 |
| Hungary | 44.8 | 44.9 | 45.82 | 44.76 | 44.03 | 46.07 | 46.68 | 46.78 | 48.2 | 44.87 |
| Iceland | 45.87 | 42.23 | 38.56 | 39.4 | 39.94 | 41.44 | 41.89 | 44.89 | 41.65 | 57.82 |
| Ireland | 36.23 | 34.86 | 33.21 | 33.04 | 33.59 | 33.89 | 34.12 | 33.94 | 27.04 | 26.63 |
| Israel | 41.99 | 39.58 | 36.65 | 37.75 | 37.71 | 36.82 | 37.17 | 37.53 | 37.66 | 37.44 |
| Italy | 45.33 | 45.2 | 45.91 | 45.68 | 45.7 | 47.87 | 48.14 | 47.92 | 47.72 | 46.87 |
| Japan | 32.24 | 31.95 | 30.92 | 30.59 | 31.55 | 32.31 | 33.12 | 34.82 | 35.73 | 35.67 |
| Korea | 33.91 | 34.34 | 33.57 | 31.97 | 33.32 | 33.74 | 33.1 | 33.25 | 33.58 | 34.64 |
| Latvia | 33.48 | 33.44 | 35.05 | 36.82 | 36.16 | 36.76 | 36.57 | 36.62 | 36.86 | 37.2 |
| Lithuania | 34.44 | 35.01 | 35.78 | 35.4 | 33.53 | 32.96 | 32.88 | 34.02 | 34.64 | 34.47 |
| Luxembourg | 41.96 | 43.02 | 44.47 | 43.47 | 42.88 | 44.41 | 44.3 | 43.14 | 42.9 | 43.74 |
| Mexico | 20.88 | 24.09 | 22.39 | 22.47 | 23.5 | 23.8 | 23.89 | 23.84 | 23.08 | 24.25 |
| Netherlands | 42.66 | 43.78 | 42.74 | 43.16 | 42.69 | 43.21 | 43.9 | 43.92 | 42.83 | 43.81 |
| New Zealand | 42.74 | 41.8 | 39.13 | 40.69 | 39.73 | 40.12 | 39.73 | 40.04 | 39.23 | 39.88 |
| Norway | 58.54 | 58.86 | 56.39 | 55.94 | 57.19 | 56.72 | 54.74 | 54.54 | 54.86 | 54.82 |
| Poland | 41.36 | 40.7 | 37.79 | 38.47 | 39.05 | 39.15 | 38.48 | 38.64 | 38.92 | 38.78 |
| Portugal | 41.48 | 41.57 | 40.42 | 40.65 | 42.63 | 42.87 | 45.1 | 44.6 | 43.8 | 42.97 |
| Slovak Republic | 34.39 | 34.51 | 36.28 | 34.66 | 36.54 | 36.29 | 38.72 | 39.33 | 42.5 | 39.3 |
| Slovenia | 42.11 | 42.46 | 42.38 | 43.62 | 43.33 | 44.47 | 44.84 | 44.34 | 44.89 | 43.34 |
| Spain | 40.95 | 36.74 | 34.83 | 36.25 | 36.19 | 37.63 | 38.57 | 38.88 | 38.49 | 37.7 |
| Sweden | 52.69 | 51.97 | 52.03 | 50.78 | 50.11 | 50.38 | 50.64 | 49.57 | 49.81 | 50.62 |
| Switzerland | 32.33 | 33.21 | 33.71 | 33.34 | 33.63 | 33.61 | 33.8 | 33.56 | 34.68 | 34.66 |
| Turkey | .. | .. | 34.69 | 35.43 | 34.45 | 34.87 | 34.67 | 33.95 | 34.42 | .. |
| United Kingdom | 38.39 | 39.43 | 37.4 | 38.38 | 38.72 | 37.83 | 38.77 | 37.74 | 38.13 | 38.56 |
| United States | 33.4 | 32.45 | 30.3 | 30.92 | 31.22 | 31.17 | 33.38 | 33.28 | 33.38 | 32.88 |
| OECD | 37.28 | 36.95 | 35.81 | 35.9 | 36.41 | 36.71 | 37.8 | 37.85 | 37.91 | 37.76 |

*Note*: Data are not available for Chile; Data for Turkey are not included in the OECD average due to missing time-series; Information on data for Israel: http://dx.doi.org/10.1787/888932315602.
*Source*: OECD National Accounts Statistics (database).

**Table A A.7. General government expenditures as a percentage of GDP**

| | General government expenditures as a percentage of GDP | | | | | | | | | |
|---|---|---|---|---|---|---|---|---|---|---|
| | 2007 | 2008 | 2009 | 2010 | 2011 | 2012 | 2013 | 2014 | 2015 | 2016 |
| Australia | 35.34 | 37.65 | 39.3 | 38.05 | 38.03 | 37.2 | 37.36 | 37.31 | 37.81 | 36.74 |
| Austria | 49.24 | 49.87 | 54.14 | 52.84 | 50.9 | 51.21 | 51.65 | 52.34 | 50.99 | 50.64 |
| Belgium | 48.25 | 50.28 | 54.15 | 53.34 | 54.45 | 55.87 | 55.83 | 55.26 | 53.85 | 53.29 |
| Canada | 39.45 | 39.68 | 44.4 | 44.01 | 42.48 | 41.82 | 41.01 | 39.25 | 40.68 | 41.46 |
| Czech Republic | 40.37 | 40.64 | 44.2 | 43.51 | 43.03 | 44.48 | 42.6 | 42.43 | 41.7 | 39.44 |
| Denmark | 49.59 | 50.41 | 56.54 | 56.67 | 56.43 | 57.95 | 55.82 | 55.22 | 54.78 | 53.6 |
| Estonia | 34.09 | 39.75 | 46.05 | 40.51 | 37.43 | 39.3 | 38.45 | 38.43 | 40.23 | 40.62 |
| Finland | 46.8 | 48.26 | 54.76 | 54.75 | 54.38 | 56.2 | 57.5 | 58.11 | 57.14 | 55.99 |
| France | 52.57 | 53.3 | 57.15 | 56.88 | 56.29 | 57.11 | 57.23 | 57.21 | 56.8 | 56.57 |
| Germany | 42.82 | 43.57 | 47.58 | 47.26 | 44.71 | 44.3 | 44.69 | 44.09 | 43.66 | 43.97 |
| Greece | 47.07 | 50.85 | 54.08 | 52.48 | 54.09 | 55.73 | 62.3 | 50.25 | 53.82 | 49.52 |
| Hungary | 49.83 | 48.58 | 50.36 | 49.24 | 49.45 | 48.47 | 49.3 | 49.37 | 50.11 | 46.53 |
| Iceland | 40.96 | 55.26 | 48.2 | 49.12 | 45.5 | 45.16 | 43.72 | 44.96 | 42.47 | 45.25 |
| Ireland | 35.91 | 41.81 | 47.01 | 65.1 | 46.31 | 41.92 | 40.22 | 37.57 | 28.93 | 27.14 |
| Israel | 42.67 | 42.35 | 42.31 | 41.43 | 40.65 | 41.61 | 41.3 | 40.88 | 39.77 | 39.55 |
| Italy | 46.79 | 47.83 | 51.16 | 49.89 | 49.38 | 50.79 | 51.06 | 50.9 | 50.29 | 49.34 |
| Japan | 35 | 36.07 | 40.69 | 39.74 | 40.64 | 40.61 | 40.76 | 40.2 | 39.28 | 39.1 |
| Korea | 29.67 | 32.01 | 34.88 | 31 | 32.35 | 32.73 | 31.76 | 31.98 | 32.3 | 32.26 |
| Latvia | 33.99 | 37.65 | 44.17 | 45.5 | 40.47 | 37.97 | 37.73 | 38.11 | 38.22 | 37.14 |
| Lithuania | 35.26 | 38.09 | 44.89 | 42.3 | 42.47 | 36.1 | 35.49 | 34.64 | 34.89 | 34.21 |
| Luxembourg | 37.81 | 39.7 | 45.14 | 44.13 | 42.37 | 44.07 | 43.32 | 41.81 | 41.54 | 42.13 |
| Mexico | 21.59 | 25.03 | 25.47 | 25.44 | 28.79 | 28.52 | 28.44 | 28.06 | 28.24 | 26.95 |
| Netherlands | 42.45 | 43.56 | 48.17 | 48.16 | 46.97 | 47.1 | 46.27 | 46.18 | 44.88 | 43.44 |
| New Zealand | 38.47 | 41.34 | 41.97 | 47.9 | 43.81 | 42.32 | 40.1 | 39.85 | 39.02 | 38.69 |
| Norway | 41.42 | 40.19 | 46.06 | 44.94 | 43.76 | 42.89 | 43.97 | 45.79 | 48.8 | 50.82 |
| Poland | 43.21 | 44.3 | 45.04 | 45.81 | 43.88 | 42.86 | 42.59 | 42.26 | 41.57 | 41.13 |
| Portugal | 44.49 | 45.34 | 50.22 | 51.82 | 50.02 | 48.53 | 49.94 | 51.77 | 48.2 | 44.95 |
| Slovak Republic | 36.34 | 36.94 | 44.08 | 42.15 | 40.82 | 40.63 | 41.44 | 42.03 | 45.23 | 41.51 |
| Slovenia | 42.19 | 43.87 | 48.22 | 49.26 | 50 | 48.52 | 59.52 | 49.86 | 47.75 | 45.28 |
| Spain | 39.03 | 41.16 | 45.78 | 45.63 | 45.83 | 48.1 | 45.56 | 44.85 | 43.77 | 42.2 |
| Sweden | 49.34 | 50.07 | 52.75 | 50.81 | 50.31 | 51.36 | 52.01 | 51.13 | 49.63 | 49.44 |
| Switzerland | 30.73 | 31.28 | 33.2 | 32.98 | 32.9 | 33.23 | 34.23 | 33.77 | 34.03 | 34.33 |
| Turkey | .. | .. | 40.86 | 38.11 | 35.19 | 35.06 | 34.46 | 33.7 | 33.11 | .. |
| United Kingdom | 41.03 | 44.61 | 47.53 | 47.79 | 46.19 | 45.98 | 44.18 | 43.19 | 42.39 | 41.53 |
| United States | 36.95 | 39.47 | 42.98 | 42.94 | 41.84 | 40.02 | 38.74 | 38.06 | 37.61 | 37.82 |
| OECD | 38.86 | 40.77 | 44.31 | 43.92 | 43.2 | 42.61 | 42.02 | 41.38 | 40.88 | 40.59 |

*Note*: Data are not available for Chile; Data for Turkey are not included in the OECD average due to missing time-series; Information on data for Israel: http://dx.doi.org/10.1787/888932315602.
*Source*: OECD National Accounts Statistics (database).

# Annex B. First pass at a composite index on gender budgeting

This publication includes a first pass at a composite index related to gender budgeting. Data used for the construction of the composites are derived from the 2018 OECD Budget Practices and Procedures Survey. Survey respondents were predominantly senior officials in the Ministry of Finance.

The composite index presented represents the best way of summarising discrete, qualitative information on key aspects of gender budgeting. "Composite indexes are much easier to interpret than trying to find a common trend in many separate indicators" (Nardo et al., 2004). However, their development and use can be controversial. These indexes are easily and often misinterpreted by users due to a lack of transparency as to how they are generated and the resulting difficulty to truly unpack what they are actually measuring.

The OECD has taken several steps to avoid or address common problems associated with composite indexes.The composite index is based on a theoretical framework set out in the OECD Publication "Towards Good Governance Guidelines for Gender Budgeting" (forthcoming). The variables comprising the index were selected based on their relevance to the concept by a group of experts within the OECD and in consultation with country delegates to the SBO Experts Group on Gender Budgeting. Sensitivity analysis was carried out to establish the robustness of the indicators to different weighting options.

The index does not purport to measure the overall quality of gender budgeting in each country. To do so would require a much stronger conceptual foundation and normative assumptions. Rather, the composite index presented is descriptive in nature. The survey questions used to create the index are the same across countries.

While the composite index was developed in co-operation with member countries and is based on best practices and/or theory, both the variables comprising the composite and their weights are offered for debate. The OECD's composite indicator on gender budgeting will be further refined over time in order to ensure it captures the elements that underpin a comprehensive gender budgeting framework.

The composite was built according to the following methodology: each of the topics was divided into broad categories comprising the theoretically relevant aspects for the subject ares. A weight was assigned to each of these broad categories. Within each of the broad categories, the relevant questions were identified, a sub-weight was assigned to each question and a score was given to each of the answers within these questions. The country scoring for each question is the product of the weight of the broad category and the sub-weight of the question multiplied by the answer provided by each country (1, 0.5 or 0). The composite is the result of adding together these scores for each country. Both composites vary from 0 to 1; a score of 1 implies the use of sound practices on a given topic.

**Figure B.1. First pass at a composite indicator on gender budgeting: variables and weights used**

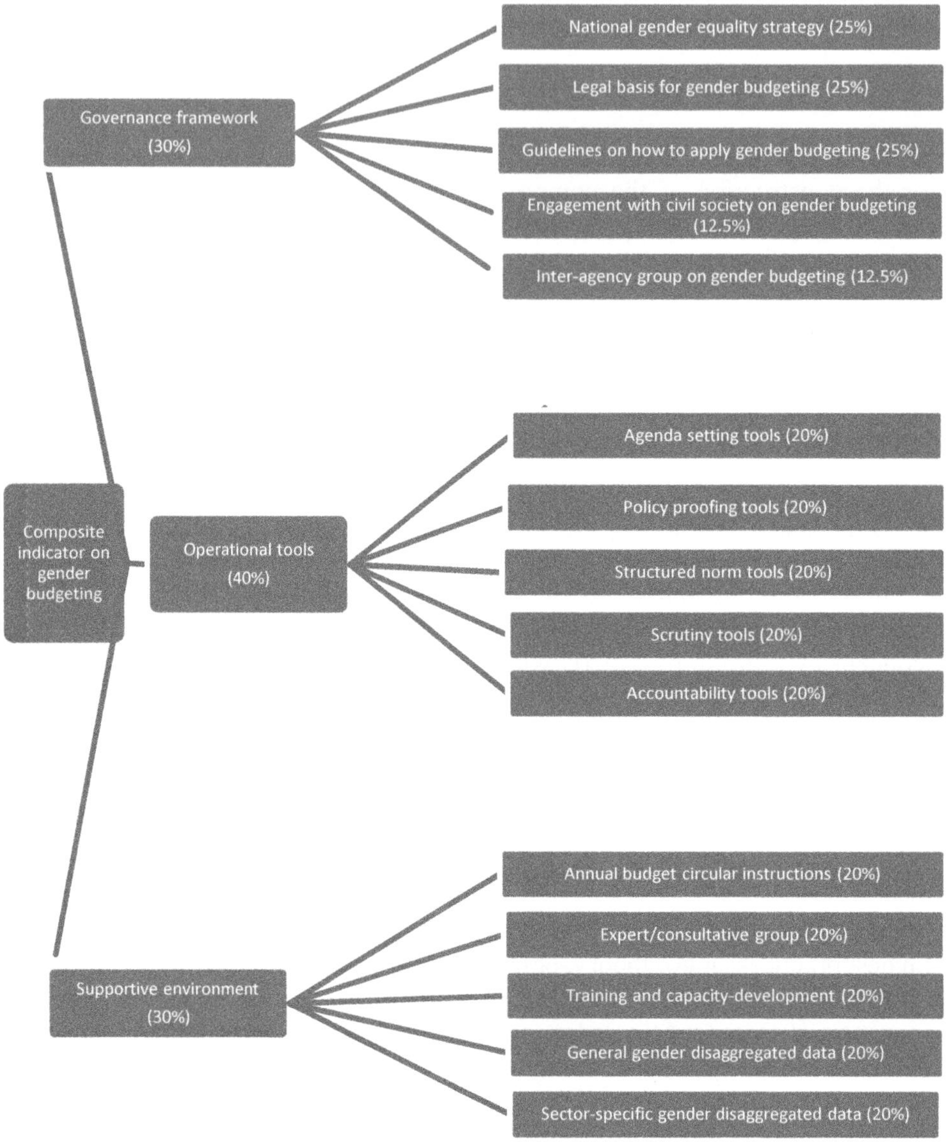

# ORGANISATION FOR ECONOMIC CO-OPERATION AND DEVELOPMENT

The OECD is a unique forum where governments work together to address the economic, social and environmental challenges of globalisation. The OECD is also at the forefront of efforts to understand and to help governments respond to new developments and concerns, such as corporate governance, the information economy and the challenges of an ageing population. The Organisation provides a setting where governments can compare policy experiences, seek answers to common problems, identify good practice and work to co-ordinate domestic and international policies.

The OECD member countries are: Australia, Austria, Belgium, Canada, Chile, the Czech Republic, Denmark, Estonia, Finland, France, Germany, Greece, Hungary, Iceland, Ireland, Israel, Italy, Japan, Korea, Latvia, Lithuania, Luxembourg, Mexico, the Netherlands, New Zealand, Norway, Poland, Portugal, the Slovak Republic, Slovenia, Spain, Sweden, Switzerland, Turkey, the United Kingdom and the United States. The European Union takes part in the work of the OECD.

OECD Publishing disseminates widely the results of the Organisation's statistics gathering and research on economic, social and environmental issues, as well as the conventions, guidelines and standards agreed by its members.

OECD PUBLISHING, 2, rue André-Pascal, 75775 PARIS CEDEX 16
(42 2018 52 1 P) ISBN 978-92-64-30794-0 – 2019

www.ingramcontent.com/pod-product-compliance
Ingram Content Group UK Ltd.
Pitfield, Milton Keynes, MK11 3LW, UK
UKHW051459290926
15471UKWH00008B/1295

9 789264 307940